Portraits of the Righteous
in the Psalms

Portraits of the Righteous in the Psalms

An Exploration of the Ethics of Book I

DANIEL C. OWENS

☙PICKWICK *Publications* · Eugene, Oregon

PORTRAITS OF THE RIGHTEOUS IN THE PSALMS
An Exploration of the Ethics of Book I

Copyright © 2013 Daniel C. Owens. All rights reserved. Except for brief quotations in critical publications or reviews, no part of this book may be reproduced in any manner without prior written permission from the publisher. Write: Permissions. Wipf and Stock Publishers, 199 W. 8th Ave., Suite 3, Eugene, OR 97401.

Pickwick Publications
An Imprint of Wipf and Stock Publishers
199 W. 8th Ave., Suite 3
Eugene, OR 97401

www.wipfandstock.com

ISBN 13: 978-1-62032-968-9

Cataloguing-in-Publication Data

Owens, Daniel C.

　　Portraits of the righteous in the Psalms : an exploration of the ethics of book I / Daniel C. Owens.

　　xiv + 240 p. ; 23 cm. Includes bibliographical references.

　　ISBN 13: 978-1-62032-968-9

　　1. Bible. Psalms—Criticism, interpretations, etc. 2. Ethics in the Bible. 3. I.

BS1430.6.E8 O934 2013

Manufactured in the U.S.A.

To Duane Linsenbardt,
teacher, mentor, friend

Contents

List of Tables • viii
Acknowledgments • ix
List of Abbreviations • xi

1 Introduction • 1
2 Psalm 15 • 21
3 Psalm 24 • 59
4 Psalm 34 • 95
5 Psalm 37 • 130
6 Ethical Ideals and Reality in Dialogic Tension in Book I • 172
7 Conclusion and Prospects for Further Research • 207

Bibliography • 223

Tables

Psalm 15:2–3 as Two Tricola • 27

A Comparison of the Syntactical Structures of Deut 10:14 and Ps 24:1 • 93

Psalm 34 as the Answer to Psalm 25 according to Benun • 109

The Concentric Structure of Psalm 34:9–15[8–14] according to Auffret • 111

A Comparison of Psalm 34:5[4] and 7[6] • 115

A Comparison of Double Questions in Psalms 15, 24, and 34 • 120

Character Traits and Behaviors in the Portraits of the Righteous • 177

Acknowledgments

How do I begin to acknowledge my debt of thanks to so many who have inspired, guided, and helped me through my doctoral studies and dissertation writing? I would like to begin by acknowledging several professors who have had an enduring influence on my life and scholarship. Dr. Scott J. Hafemann introduced me to Greek, but more importantly he modeled for me careful and passionate exegesis and teaching in a global context. Dr. C. Hassell Bullock introduced me to Hebrew, and more recently he has inspired and guided me through his own writing and our conversations from the beginning of my proposal writing down to the last missing *dāgēš* in my dissertation. His probing questions revealed one or two embarrassing oversights on my part and pushed me to think more carefully about my arguments. Dr. Willem A. VanGemeren taught me to love Hebrew poetry and interpret it holistically, but his course on the Psalms in S.E. Asia fueled my desire to pursue further studies and research in the Psalms.

More recently several of my professors have played key roles in shaping my research interests and the dissertation itself. Dr. Daniel J. Treier helped me solidify my thinking on certain methodological issues and posed important questions about the dissertation in its final stages. Dr. Richard Schultz provided helpful and substantial feedback on several papers that became chapters, as well as the defense draft. His probing inquiries have helped me think more clearly about the field of Old Testament studies and my own interaction with it. I admire his commitment to invest in young scholars. Dr. M. Daniel Carroll R. is the best external reader a student could hope for. He set me at ease with his sense of humor yet held me accountable to address the blind spots in my work. Pride of place goes to my mentor, Dr. Daniel I. Block. He is a model to me of gracious, pastoral, and careful teaching and scholarship. He invested untold hours not only in teaching me but in providing painstaking and penetrating feedback on dissertation chapters as they rolled out of the printer and took shape as a complete dissertation.

Acknowledgments

He asked me to see new connections, challenged me to be courageous in exploring new ideas, and guided me away from pitfalls of argumentation and infelicities of style. I know his clear writing style has rubbed off on me, but I hope that by God's power his ever-generous character may also make its mark. It goes without saying that I assume responsibility for any errors that remain in the dissertation, but the scholars above have helped me avoid many and have taken me beyond where I could have gone by myself.

In addition to my professors, I have enjoyed the material support of many. Space does not permit me to name them all, but Christ Community Church of Milpitas, California, College Church in Wheaton, Illinois, Christ the King Church in Batavia, Illinois, and South Church in Lansing, Michigan, have stood with me and encouraged me through my studies. Special thanks are due to Mrs. Margaret Taylor, Mr. and Mrs. Mark Taylor, and Mr. and Mrs. Knoedler, who provided for my fellowship while a student at Wheaton College.

Finally, I would like to thank my family. My parents, Robert and Jennifer Owens, have been an unfailing source of support and encouragement over the years and no less during this season. My wife's parents, David and Teresa Schepperley have shown keen interest in my progress and have generously helped us in ways too many to recount. My boys, Caleb and Nathan, have borne their share, sacrificing valuable Lego building time to allow me to work on the dissertation. Most important of all, my wife Heather deserves special mention. She not only has continued to embrace our wedding vows and taken more of her share of responsibility to keep our home going, she has also been a ready conversation partner and editor for all things related to my studies and dissertation writing. No ministry partner or friend could exceed her, and no dissertation would have appeared without her. Thanks be to God for this undeserved blessing!

Abbreviations

AB	Anchor Bible
ABD	*Anchor Bible Dictionary.* Edited by D. N. Freedman. 6 vols. New York, 1992
ANET	James B. Pritchard, editor, *Ancient Near Eastern Texts: Relating to the Old Testament,* 3rd ed., Princeton, NJ: 1969
AOAT	Alter Orient und Altes Testament
ATSAT	*Arbeiten zu Text und Sprache im Alten Testament*
Aug	*Augustinianum*
BCOT	Baker Commentary on the Old Testament
BDAG	Bauer, W., F. W. Danker, W. F. Arndt, and F. W. Gingrich. *Greek-English Lexicon of the New Testament and Other Early Christian Literature.* 3rd ed. Chicago, 1999
BDB	Brown, F., S. R. Driver, and C. A. Briggs. *A Hebrew and English Lexicon of the Old Testament.* Oxford, 1907
BHK	*Biblia Hebraica.* Edited by R. Kittel. Stuttgart, 1905–6, 1925, 1937, 1951, 1973
BHRG	*A Biblical Hebrew Reference Grammar.* Christo H. J. van der Merwe, Jackie A. Naudé, and Jan H. Kroeze. Biblical Languages: Hebrew 3. Sheffield, 1999
BHS	*Biblia Hebraica Stuttgartensia.* Edited by K. Elliger and W. Rudolph. Stuttgart, 1983
BibInt	*Biblical Interpretation*
BSac	*Bibliotheca sacra*
BZAW	Beihefte zur Zeitschrift für die alttestamentliche Wissenschaft
CBQ	*Catholic Biblical Quarterly*
CBQMS	Catholic Biblical Quarterly Monograph Series

Abbreviations

ConBOT	Coniectanea biblica: Old Testament Series
COS	*The Context of Scripture.* Edited by W. W. Hallo. 3 vols. Leiden, 1997–2002
CurBR	*Currents in Biblical Research*
CurBS	*Currents in Research: Biblical Studies*
DV	Didactic Voice
EBC	Expositor's Biblical Commentary
ECC	*Eerdmans Critical Commentary*
EJT	*European Journal of Theology*
FOTL	Forms of the Old Testament Literature
GKC	*Gesenius' Hebrew Grammar.* Edited by E. Kautzsch. Translated by A. E. Cowley. 2nd ed. Oxford, 1910
HALOT	Koehler, L., W. Baumgartner, and J. J. Stamm, *The Hebrew and Aramaic Lexicon of the Old Testament.* Translated and edited under the supervision of M. E. J. Richardson. 4 vols. Leiden, 1994–99
HBT	*Horizons in Biblical Theology*
Holladay	Holladay, William L. *A Concise Hebrew and Aramaic Lexicon of the Old Testament.* Grand Rapids, 1971
HTR	*Harvard Theological Review*
HUCA	*Hebrew Union College Annual*
IBHS	*An Introduction to Biblical Hebrew Syntax.* B. K. Waltke and M. O'Connor. Winona Lake, Indiana, 1990
ICC	International Critical Commentary
Int	*Interpretation*
IRT	Issues in Religion and Theology
JBL	*Journal of Biblical Literature*
JHS	*Journal of Hellenic Studies*
Joüon	Joüon, P. *A Grammar of Biblical Hebrew.* Translated and revised by T. Muraoka. 2 vols. Subsidia biblica 14/1–2. Rome, 1991
JSem	*Journal for Semitics*
JSOT	*Journal for the Study of the Old Testament*
JSOTSup	Journal for the Study of the Old Testament: Supplement Series
JSS	*Journal of Semitic Studies*
LW	*Luther's Works.* Edited by J. Pelikan and H. T. Lehmann. 55 vols. St. Louis, MO, 1955–86

LXX	Septuagint
MAJT	Mid-America Journal of Theology
MT	Masoretic Text
NASB	New American Standard Bible
NCBC	New Century Bible Commentary
NIBC	New International Biblical Commentary
NICOT	New International Commentary on the Old Testament
NIDOTTE	New International Dictionary of Old Testament Theology and Exegesis. Edited by Willem A. VanGemeren. 5 vols. Grand Rapids, 1997
NIVAC	NIV Application Commentary
OTE	Old Testament Essays
OtSt	Oudtestamentische Studiën
RB	Revue biblique
ResQ	Restoration Quarterly
RSR	Recherches de science religieuse
SBLDS	Society of Biblical Literature Dissertation Series
ScrHier	Scripta hierosolymitana
SJOT	Scandinavian Journal of the Old Testament
TB	Theologische Bücherei: Neudrucke und Berichte aus dem 20 Jahrhundert
TDOT	Theological Dictionary of the Old Testament. Edited by G. J. Botterweck and H. Ringgren. Translated by J. T. Willis, G. W. Bromiley, and D. E. Green. 8 vols. Grand Rapids, 1974–
TynBul	Tyndale Bulletin
UF	Ugarit-Forschungen
VT	Vetus Testamentum
VTSup	Vetus Testamentum Supplements
WBC	Word Biblical Commentary
Williams	Williams, Ronald J. *Hebrew Syntax: An Outline.* 2nd ed. Toronto, 1976
WTJ	Westminster Theological Journal
ZAW	Zeitschrift für die alttestamentliche Wissenschaft
ZTK	Zeitschrift für Theologie und Kirche

1

Introduction

BACKGROUND OF THE STUDY

What have the Psalms to do with ethics? Scholars are asking this question in the context of a flowering of new approaches to Psalms study and ethics. In Psalms study form criticism has made room for exploration of the shape and shaping of the Psalter. In ethics the moral act is now considered alongside the moral agent, due to the influence of virtue theories. In light of these two trends, this project seeks to answer the following question: What resources do we find in the Psalter for addressing moral formation from a biblical and theological perspective? This broad question cannot be answered exhaustively by a single book. Thankfully, scholarly discussion on the Psalter and on Old Testament ethics provides a context in which such a question may be focused and narrowed.

The Psalter in Old Testament Ethics

Work on the ethical dimension of the Psalter is scarce in comparison to other portions of the Hebrew canon, particularly the Pentateuch[1] and the

---

1. For examples of works with a strong focus on the Pentateuch, see Kaiser, *Toward Old Testament Ethics*; Otto, *Theologische Ethik des Alten Testaments*.

prophets.² Narrative has recently gained attention.³ Although the topical monographs of Cyril Rodd and Christopher Wright bridge various genres in biblical literature,⁴ they do not attempt systematically to explore the ethical discourse of the Psalter. Until recently the Psalms most often surfaced in studies on isolated issues or particular psalms rather than as thoroughgoing sources for ethical reflection.⁵ Only in the last ten years have scholars such as Gordon Wenham systematically explored the ethics of the Psalms.⁶

Gordon Wenham attempts to address the absence of the Psalms in Old Testament ethics, taking the Decalogue as his "departure point" and building on that with a number of additional topics.⁷ He notes that ethical study of the Psalter has largely been confined to Psalms 15 and 24, imprecatory psalms, and Psalm 72.⁸ We see the focus on Psalms 15 and 24 in the works of John T. Willis and Ronald Clements,⁹ though their work is primarily form-critical. In 2005 Wenham characterized the ethics of the Psalms as "virgin scholarly territory."¹⁰ As I note above, this state of affairs is changing, but much more can be done to clarify the ethical discourse of the Psalter.

This study seeks to advance this inquiry by considering one portion of the Psalter, namely, Book I. By surveying the ethical landscape in that collection we may be able to see more clearly how it contributes to the broader discipline of Old Testament ethics and what resources it offers for character formation. This research agenda flows naturally from recent developments in two related fields, the study of the Psalter and biblical ethics.

---

2. See especially Barton, *Ethics and the Old Testament*; Barton, *Understanding Old Testament Ethics*.

3. Janzen, *Old Testament Ethics*; Wenham, *Story as Torah*.

4. Rodd, *Glimpses of a Strange Land*; Wright, *Old Testament Ethics*.

5. See, e.g., Day, "The Imprecatory Psalms and Christian Ethics," 166–86; Houston, "The King's Preferential Option for the Poor," 341–67; Waltke, "Responding to an Unethical Society," 13–18.

6. See Wenham, "Ethics of the Psalms," 175–94; Wenham, "Prayer and Practice in the Psalms," 279–94; Wenham, *Psalms as Torah*. But see also Jinkins, "The Virtues of the Righteous in Psalm 37," 164–201; McCann, "The Way of the Righteous," 135–49; Otto, "Myth and Hebrew Ethics in the Psalms," 26–37; Groenewald, "Ethics of the Psalms," 421–33; Durant, "Imitation of God."

7. Wenham, "Ethics of the Psalms."

8. Ibid., 178.

9. Willis, "Ethics in a Cultic Setting," 145–69; Clements, "Worship and Ethics," 78–94.

10. Wenham, "Ethics of the Psalms," 178. See also Wenham, *Psalms as Torah*, 5–6.

Introduction

Developments in Psalms Study and Ethics as the Impetus for This Study

Psalms study underwent a transformation in the wake of Gerald Wilson's dissertation.[11] For most of the twentieth century, the form-critical work of Gunkel and Mowinckel dominated the field.[12] While form criticism remains a viable scholarly method for many,[13] it has lost its dominant position in Psalms study. Wilson's ground-breaking work has stimulated numerous studies attempting to describe the editorial agendas affecting the final shape of the Psalter.

This flowering of research into the canonical shape of the Psalter has produced fruitful discussion about the theological issues raised by the Psalter as a whole. In relationship to Book I, three important observations have been made. First, Pierre Auffret identified a sub-collection in Psalms 15–24 that has a concentric structure, with a torah psalm in the center (Psalm 19) and the two so-called entrance liturgies (Psalms 15 and 24) at the outer edges.[14] Second, J. Clinton McCann notes that the first and last two psalms in Book I (Psalms 1, 2, 40, and 41) all contain beatitudes (that begin with אַשְׁרֵי), and he argues that this detail functions as a "framing device" inviting us to read Book I as a "guide to a 'happy' life."[15] Third, Jerome Creach notes the unusual number of "general descriptions of those who are righteous," including Psalms 15, 24, 34, and 37.[16] Creach labels these psalms "portraits of the righteous."[17] Although Psalms 15 and 24 are most readily associated with the temple and Psalms 34 and 37 are associated with the wisdom tradition, they exhibit formal and material similarities. At a formal level Psalms 15, 24, and 34 involve a question-answer-benefit structure. Furthermore, all four psalms describe the righteous person in the third person. At a material

---

11. Wilson, *The Editing of the Hebrew Psalter*. For helpful summaries of this transformation, see Howard, Jr., "Editorial Activity in the Psalter," 52–70; Howard, Jr., "Recent Trends in Psalms Study," 329–68.

12. While many works could be mentioned, the following have proven most influential: Gunkel and Begrich, *Introduction to Psalms*; Gunkel, *Psalms*; Mowinckel, *The Psalms in Israel's Worship*; Muilenburg, "Form Criticism and Beyond," 1–18; Westermann, *Praise and Lament in the Psalms*.

13. Sweeney and Ben Zvi, *The Changing Face of Form Criticism*.

14. Auffret, *La sagesse a bâti sa maison*, 407–38. See also Miller, "Kingship, Torah Obedience, and Prayer," 127–42; Hossfeld and Zenger, "Wer darf hinaufziehn zum Berg JHWHs?" 166–82.

15. McCann, "The Shape of Book I of the Psalter," 341–42.

16. Creach, *Yahweh as Refuge*, 79.

17. Ibid., 77. This term is also employed in Maloney, "A Portrait of the Righteous Person," 151–64.

level, several of the ethical concerns occur across several of the portraits without respect to the hypothetical social contexts of temple and wisdom. All four situate ethics in relationship to a *telos*, sharing the metaphor of refuge, though the metaphors and concepts for this *telos* vary from psalm to psalm. Finally, the concise form of these descriptions may support calling them "character sketches."[18] However, given scholarly familiarity with the phrase "portraits of the righteous," I employ this phrase and occasionally shorten it to "the portraits" for the sake of brevity.

Nonetheless, the three observations about Book I above provide an impetus for this study, suggesting the following question: How do the four portraits of the righteous function in their canonical context?

In addition to developments in psalms study, developments in ethics provide an impetus for this project. In recent years many moral philosophers and theologians have sought to revive Aristotelian virtue ethics.[19] Although the methods and concerns of "defenders of virtue" are diverse, Martha Nussbaum suggests that they share three common interests: the moral agent, the inner moral life (such as intention, motive, emotion, and reasoning), and the overall course of the moral agent's life.[20] Aside from the specifics of Aristotle's *Nicomachean Ethics*, which post-dates the Hebrew Bible and arises from an entirely different cultural milieu, the revival of interest in the moral agent is a welcome development.

Modern interest in virtue or character ethics[21] has only recently begun to gain traction in biblical studies. The Character Ethics and Biblical Interpretation group in the Society of Biblical Literature has produced three volumes on character ethics in the Bible.[22] These volumes contain only one chapter on the Psalms. In this chapter J. Clinton McCann attempts to abstract a portrait of the generic "psalmist" as embodying "the way of the righteous."[23] The article suggests that a combination of virtue ethics and a synchronic reading of the Psalter is possible and perhaps even suggested

---

18. Leland Ryken applies this label to Psalm 15 (*Words of Delight*, 294–95).

19. Seminal works in this field include MacIntyre, *After Virtue*; Hauerwas, *A Community of Character*.

20. Nussbaum, "Virtue Ethics," 170.

21. I treat "virtue ethics" and "character ethics" here as basically synonymous even though their associations are not entirely identical.

22. Brown, *Character and Scripture*; Carroll R. and Lapsley, *Character Ethics and the Old Testament*; Brawley, *Character Ethics and the New Testament*. Unfortunately, as Richard Briggs notes, few of the articles explicitly engage the concerns of virtue ethics (*The Virtuous Reader*, 28).

23. McCann, "The Way of the Righteous."

Introduction

by the Psalter itself.[24] Several papers were read in the Book of Psalms section at the 2010 SBL annual meeting that took up the connection between the Psalms and the formation of virtuous people.[25] The Hebrew Bible has proven to be a fruitful field in which to explore the nature of the formation of moral agents. For this reason, the revival of virtue ethics provides another impetus for this book.

DEFINITION AND THESIS OF THE STUDY

Building on the scholarly trends noted above, this study seeks to answer two questions: (1) What place do the portraits of the righteous occupy on the ethical landscape of Book I of the Psalter? (2) What resources do Book I generally and the portraits specifically offer for the formation of character today? The study begins by examining the ethical concerns and theological context of the portraits in four successive chapters (2–5). With that foundation, chapter 6 explores the place of the portraits in Book I as a whole in order to answer question 1 above. Chapter 7 then addresses question 2 above, exploring the ways in which readers of Book I may find their character formed through the act of reading and praying the psalms.

This study will demonstrate that the portraits of righteous character (Psalms 15, 24, 34, and 37) provide an ethic of community within a theological framework of hope in YHWH's life-giving presence. In the metaphorical terms of the Psalter, the way of YHWH reaches its destination in refuge and life with YHWH. However, the collection as a whole enacts a dialogue about the connection between ethical behavior (pathway) and its *telos* (refuge and life with YHWH), challenging the notion that there is a simple connection between doing good and enjoying the good life.[26] However, in spite of the disorientation expressed in lament psalms about the delay of YHWH's deliverance, the psalmists do not abandon hope but remain steadfast in their affirmation of the ethical content of the portraits and in the worth of the God whose presence on Mount Zion means life for his people. Therefore Book I offers a paradigm of other-oriented love motivated by

---

24. Jinkins self-consciously works with the Aristotelian account of virtue, with guidance from Alasdair MacIntyre, to translate Psalm 37 for our time ("The Virtues of the Righteous in Psalm 37").

25. The papers read at the annual meeting included the following: Reed, "Virtue Ethics and Psalms 111–112"; Foster, "Led in Paths of Justice"; Rine, "Singing the Psalms to Profit the Soul"; James, "Let The Redeemed of the Lord Say So."

26. The phrase "the good life" is familiar to modern readers, but it corresponds in many respects to the Hebrew words טוֹב, "good," and חַיִּים, "life" (Whybray, *The Good Life in the Old Testament*, 3).

5

hope in YHWH, tested by the pain of experience, and formed in the context of worship. This dialogic ethic offers a diversity of expressions of faith that helps shape the character of the people of God to "entrust themselves to a faithful Creator, while continuing to do good" (1 Pet 4:19, NRSV).

SUMMARY OF INFORMING APPROACHES OF THE STUDY

The aims and approaches to reading are fundamental to the task of biblical theology and ethics. With regard to aims, I take the main task of reading to be discovering the intended meaning of the authors of Scripture as expressed in the text, recognizing this involves limitations due to the historical and cultural distance between the text and modern readers. Authors and readers of written texts essentially participate in a communicative transaction.[27] Good readers are good "listeners," having a high regard for the message of the author and seeking to understand it by every appropriate means. Editors also have a role in collecting, organizing, and shaping texts, so their intentions matter as well.[28]

However, these claims about reading involve basic assumptions about the communicative process that not all scholars share. Can we really know authorial intentions, even if we restrict ourselves to what we can know through the text? Hans-Georg Gadamer argues that our historical distance from the authors of Scripture affects the act of reading.[29] His critique of modern hermeneutics reminds us of our limitations and our tendency to distort the intentions of authors. However, it does not logically exclude trying to understand the communicative intent of authors. Rather, it should engender interpretive humility.[30] We cannot know exhaustively and with absolute certainty what an author intended to communicate through a text.

---

27. Vanhoozer, *Is There a Meaning in This Text?* 207.

28. For interpreters who believe in divine inspiration of the Bible, the role of editors vis-à-vis the divine author has implications for the authority of Scripture and the aims of reading. Vanhoozer rightly employs E. D. Hirsch's distinction between meaning and significance, arguing that the canon as a context produces a "unified communicative act" (ibid., 264–65). Divine intention does not contradict the intentions of the human author but supervenes on them, and we see this at the editorial level. Thus understanding the communicative intentions of authors embodied in a text remains the aim of reading, but our concept of authorship and communicative intention must include multiple levels of intention (including editorial intention) in order to account for the complexity of the Bible's content.

29. Thiselton, *New Horizons in Hermeneutics*, 315.

30. Richard Briggs observes that interpretive humility is the most well-established maxim of recent hermeneutics (Briggs, *The Virtuous Reader*, 45).

However, we can gain true understanding. Kevin Vanhoozer rightly suggests that "our knowledge must be tempered by humility, and . . . our skepticism must be countered by conviction."[31] However, to interpret with conviction, we must be clear about the approaches that inform reading.

Methods help us become competent readers.[32] Rather than "scientific" procedures one may follow to discover the meaning of a text, John Barton argues they are theories of reading.[33] Critical methods are not techniques that will on their own lead to correct understanding. Reading is a complex process and requires multiple methods. No doubt a myriad of methodological influences and judgments contribute to this study. In what follows I shall mention the most significant methodological influences on reading at three levels: that of the individual psalm, of the Psalter as a collection, and of application to ethics.

Approaches to Individual Psalms

Canonical context has become a common level of investigation in psalms scholarship. However, Roland Murphy offers a word of caution: canonical context may not prove any more helpful than historical, theological, or emotional context.[34] The contextual approach should not replace study of individual psalms but complement it, with the literal historical meaning serving as a control on interpretation.[35] Therefore this book begins by studying the portraits as individual compositions.

Form Criticism

Form criticism takes pride of place in the study of individual psalms. Hermann Gunkel brought two fresh insights to the study of the Psalms. He explored the generic features of various forms or *Gattungen* within the Psalter, and he attempted to reconstruct the oral pre-history of these forms in order to shed light on their meaning and purpose. Gunkel sought to delineate the various genres based on their origin in a specific worship service,

---

31. Vanhoozer, *Is There a Meaning in This Text?* 462.
32. Barton, *Reading the Old Testament*, 10–11.
33. Ibid., 244–45.
34. Murphy, "Reflections on Contextual Interpretation of the Psalms," 23, 25.
35. Ibid., 26–28.

possession of common thoughts and moods arising from the *Sitz im Leben* of that service, as well as common language, and to identify motifs within genres.[36]

Claiming that Gunkel had proved the cultic origin of the psalms, Sigmund Mowinckel sought to set "each one of them in relation to the definite cultic act—or the cultic acts—to which it belonged" in order to classify psalms for the purpose of mutual illumination.[37] Claus Westermann rightly argues that Mowinckel radicalized Gunkel's method, forcing nearly all psalms to fit within a particular mold.[38] For that reason many scholars reject Mowinckel's reconstructions of *Sitz im Leben*.

Still, Klaus Koch insists the exploration of such a life setting is essential for adequate understanding of *any* biblical text. Although the details of the setting may not be accessible to us, such study remains necessary.[39] To identify this setting, one must ask who is speaking, who is the audience, what is the prevailing mood, and what effect is sought in the speech.[40]

According to Antony Campbell, the essential insight of form criticism is that it considers each individual text as a whole and seeks to understand the typical elements that contribute to the meaning of the whole.[41] Earlier form critics aimed at the oral prehistory of texts.[42] This occasionally resulted in speculation about the *Sitz im Leben* of texts that appears at best imaginative (Gunkel's own term[43]) and at worst hopelessly subjective.[44] Yet their excesses need not negate the insights they offer about what is typical of various psalm genres.

As form criticism has developed, the more speculative reconstructions of original oral settings have ceased to be as convincing as they once were, and the notion of only one *Sitz im Leben* for each form appeared reductionist. A form may actually have many social settings, including both intellectual settings and social/liturgical ones.[45] Nevertheless, psalms study continues under the shadow of Gunkel and Mowinckel. Yet their analysis of the psalms needs to be seen in light of its limitations. If carried out with-

---

36. Gunkel and Begrich, *Introduction to Psalms*, 15–16.
37. Mowinckel, *The Psalms in Israel's Worship*, 23.
38. Westermann, *Praise and Lament in the Psalms*, 20–21, 165.
39. Koch, *The Growth of the Biblical Tradition*, 33.
40. Ibid.
41. Campbell, "Form Criticism's Future," 23–24.
42. Ibid., 18.
43. Gunkel, "Jesaia 33," 193.
44. So argues Wendland, "Genre Criticism and the Psalms," 383.
45. Longman, "Form Criticism," 63–64.

out wholesale speculation, the reconstructions of *oral* prehistory depends upon extant *written* texts, often the very texts such reconstructions seek to illumine. For modern readers who have access only to written texts, the direction of illumination is more clearly from written to presumptive oral texts. And as a basic aim, biblical theology and ethics seek to account for the text, not its original oral setting.

Campbell rightly suggests form criticism should be more concerned to name the nature of a text and examine its structure.[46] The genius of Gunkel's work may lie in helping us see literary relationships between psalms. On the basis of those literary relationships we can perform comparative analysis and illuminate the one in relationship to the many. The work of Gunkel and his successors offers insight into those literary relationships.

Genre Analysis

However, as Tremper Longman argues, Gunkel's approach to genre requires modification in light of modern literary theory. Gunkel's concept of pure oral genres that were tied to a single social setting and degraded when reduced to writing must be modified.[47] Drawing on E. D. Hirsch's account of genre,[48] Longman seeks to define genre in terms of the expectations that readers bring to reading.[49] According to Longman, genres enable communication between author and reader—readers come to texts with expectations of a genre, and genres shape the way authors write.[50] This provides for a more fluid concept of genre in which classification can exist at many levels of generality.[51] I will argue that the portraits of the righteous all involve didactic texts, by which I mean texts aimed to instruct a human audience. Didactic discourse differs from prayer in that the latter is addressed directly to God rather than a human audience. At this broad level of generality, it is helpful to compare the individual portraits.

Walter Brueggemann also expresses concern over the influence of Gunkel's genre categories, categories with which the psalmists themselves might not have agreed. This rightly leads him to recommend that focus on the individual psalm itself should override genre analysis.[52] Genre study

---

46. Campbell, "Form Criticism's Future," 16.
47. Longman, "Form Criticism," 49.
48. Hirsch, *Validity in Interpretation*.
49. Longman, "Form Criticism," 51.
50. Ibid., 53.
51. Ibid., 57.
52. Brueggemann, "Response to James L. Mays," 34–35.

must involve a symbiotic relationship between the specific expression of individual psalms and the general features of a genre.

Rhetorical Criticism and Discourse Analysis

James Muilenberg identifies a danger in emphasizing what is typical to the exclusion of the unique manifestation in an individual poem: it may obscure the ideas of the original author.[53] For that purpose Muilenberg commends rhetorical criticism, the work of exploring the structural patterns and rhetorical devices that contribute to a unified whole in a literary composition.[54] His call to study the particularities of texts reveals that form criticism and genre analysis, while necessary, are not sufficient by themselves.

If genre study identifies the parameters of expectation and a broad perspective on what is typical for a given kind of poem,[55] discourse analysis examines the structure and argument of a particular literary unit. The focus of discourse analysis is on units of language beyond the sentence.[56] It has an interdisciplinary character, drawing together concepts and tools from philosophy, literary theory, and linguistics.[57] Terrance Wardlaw sees discourse analysis exploring discourse structure, pragmatics (of language use), speech acts, intertextuality, genre analysis, and rhetorical analysis.[58] In short, discourse analysis seeks to integrate the various tools useful for understanding what and how an author is trying to communicate through a text. Such an integrative approach encourages holistic interpretation and allows for form criticism to play a complementary role alongside other valid approaches.

Poetic Analysis

The Psalter is composed of poems. Scholars often recognize that parallelism is a fundamental feature of biblical poetry.[59] James Kugel notes that parallelism usually involves a development of thought between parallel poetic lines, often expressing a development from one line to the next akin to "A is so,

---

53. Muilenburg, "Form Criticism and Beyond," 5.
54. Ibid., 8.
55. While genre study *should* be a broader perspective, Walter Bodine argues that form criticism in particular has not been able to make a complete move to literary study and suffers the same analytic tendency as source criticism ("Introduction," 6).
56. Ibid., 1.
57. Wardlaw, Jr., "Discourse Analysis," 267.
58. Ibid., 271–74.
59. Kugel, *The Idea of Biblical Poetry*, 1–2.

Introduction

and *what's more*, B is so."[60] Similarly, Robert Alter contends that parallelism in Hebrew poetry evidences two basic operations within the parallel line: intensification and specification.[61] In addition to parallelism, Adele Berlin suggests that terseness is a defining trait of poetry.[62]

Terse parallel lines often use imagery that enriches the theological enterprise. Some scholars suggest that images are the fundamental unit of poetry.[63] Daniel Estes asserts, "As imaginative literature, poetry endeavors to re-create the poet's experience in the reader, rather than merely reporting what the poet experienced."[64] Leland Ryken suggests that poets construct reality using images and pictures.[65] This is certainly true of the Psalter—the collection is full of images—but form criticism has not always treated this feature of poetry as an operative interpretive principle. According to William Brown, the lack of attention to imagery comes "at great theological cost."[66] To be fair, Gunkel's form criticism involved imagining *Sitz im Leben*,[67] but the imagination was aimed at the world behind the text, precisely the pillar of form criticism that has been called into question in recent years. Gunkel was right to involve his faculty of imagination when reading the Psalter, but his imagination was focused on the blurry background of the images he was studying. This book seeks to follow Luis Alonso Schökel's advice and employ the imagination in the interpretive task with a focus on the images that occur in the psalms themselves.[68] To interpret psalms well we must become students of the psalmists' way of thinking, to enter their metaphorical world.

But how do we get into the psalmists' way of thinking? Often images are placed before us without cues to fill in the gaps of our metaphorical understanding. William Brown's work on the Psalter provides an important start to recovering the images of the Psalter. He explores what he takes to be central metaphors chosen because of "the organizing power they wield

---

60. Ibid., 8.

61. Alter, *The Art of Biblical Poetry*, 62–63. Certainly more operations can be discerned within the varied uses of parallelism in Hebrew poetry, but intensification and specification are two common operations.

62. Berlin, *The Dynamics of Biblical Parallelism*, 5–6.

63. Schökel, *A Manual of Hebrew Poetics*, 95; Ryken, *Words of Delight*, 159; Brown, *Seeing the Psalms*, 3.

64. Estes, "The Hermeneutics of Biblical Lyric Poetry," 419.

65. Ryken, *Words of Delight*, 160.

66. Brown, *Seeing the Psalms*, ix.

67. Gunkel, "Jesaia 33," 193.

68. Schökel, *A Manual of Hebrew Poetics*, 104.

both within particular psalms and throughout the Psalter as a whole."[69] The psalter employs related metaphors in multiple psalms. Two such metaphors are refuge and pathway.[70] Brown's work shows us that the best place to become immersed in the experiential world of the psalmists is to see how they use images.

Approaches to the Study of the Psalter

Interpretation of psalms as individual compositions is the foundation for all psalms study, involving genre identification as well as the exploration of the specific structure and rhetorical/poetic devices that express the meaning of the poet. However, psalms study today is also concerned with how individual psalms are situated within their canonical context.

Treating the Psalter at the level of the book involves all the methods outlined above that are traditionally applied to individual psalms, but the scale is much larger and the issues more complex. I shall explore two main methods for interpreting the Psalter, namely, the contextual approach and dialogic criticism.[71]

Contextual Approach

Outlining the interpretive concerns of the contextual approach, Jerome Creach suggests that there is a difference between the "form" and the "formation" of the Psalter. The latter involves the history of the Psalter's editorial shaping. In contrast, the former concerns the Psalter's literary structure.[72] Both are theologically sensitive, but studies in the formation of the Psalter seek to reconstruct the concerns of historical editors, to the extent that they are recoverable. Studies in the form of the final shape of the Psalter are also theological, but they are less concerned with tying that theological shape to

---

69. Brown, *Seeing the Psalms*, 14.

70. Ibid., 16.

71. I will refer to the approach spawned by Gerald Wilson's work as the contextual approach to the Psalter. Both the label "canonical" and "contextual" are applied to this approach. However, there is a risk that the term "canonical" may evoke Brevard Childs' canonical approach. While there is a relationship, the concern of the canonical/contextual approach to the Psalter is more limited. Therefore, to avoid confusion, I adopt the label "contextual approach" or "contextual interpretation" following Murphy ("Reflections on Contextual Interpretation of the Psalms," 21).

72. Creach, *Yahweh as Refuge*, 11.

historical and sociological circumstances.⁷³ Having made this distinction of interpretive interests, there is a great deal of overlap in method.

Most agree that Gerald Wilson's monograph, *The Editing of the Hebrew Psalter*, represents a watershed in psalms study. In it he claims that the book of Psalms exhibits signs of a broad editorial movement to unify the Hebrew Psalter.⁷⁴ This editorial activity was a response to "the agony of loss in the exilic community."⁷⁵ Wilson looks at psalms at the "seams" of the five books of the Psalter, arguing that in Books I–III the transitional psalms (Pss 2, 72, and 89) show a concern for the Davidic monarchy that is replaced in Books IV and V by a focus on wisdom (Pss 90, 107, and 145).⁷⁶ The later emphasis on Torah in Psalms 1 and 119 constitutes a response to the exile that shifts attention away from wrestling with the failure of the Davidic covenant.⁷⁷

Subsequent to Wilson, theories accounting for the final editorial arrangement of the Psalter largely build upon Wilson's work,⁷⁸ amend his proposals,⁷⁹ or consider smaller units within books.⁸⁰ Following Erich Zenger, Jamie Grant argues that contextual interpretation ought to give attention to psalms that are located at central junctures within books in addition to material at the beginning and ending of books.⁸¹ One of the psalms he considers, Psalm 19, lies within what Auffret argues is an earlier collection consisting of Psalms 15-24.⁸² Contextual interpretation of the Psalter thus involves the identification of editorial agendas at the level of the entire Psalter and lower-level interpretation of psalms within the context of smaller collections.

This study is concerned with the latter level of investigation, with a particular focus on Book I. What does "contextual interpretation" at a low level involve? A number of scholars have debated how we should assess claims about individual psalms in relation to their place in the Psalter. The dreaded

---

73. See, e.g., Brown, *Seeing the Psalms*; Collins, "Decoding the Psalms," 41–60. Creach also appears to pursue this interest, though in his thesis he consciously tries to tie this to editorial interest (*Yahweh as Refuge*, 17). More literary and theological is Creach, *Destiny of the Righteous*.
74. Wilson, *The Editing of the Hebrew Psalter*, 11.
75. Wilson, "The Structure of the Psalter," 235.
76. Wilson, *The Editing of the Hebrew Psalter*, 209.
77. Wilson, "The Structure of the Psalter," 235–36.
78. McCann, "Books I–III and the Editorial Purpose of the Hebrew Psalter," 93.
79. Brueggemann, "Response to James L. Mays," 39–40.
80. Howard, Jr., *The Structure of Psalms 93–100*.
81. Grant, *The King as Exemplar*, 16–17.
82. Auffret, *La sagesse a bâti sa maison*, 407–38.

label of subjectivism seems to haunt those who employ the approach.[83] Both Roland E. Murphy and R. N. Whybray argue that the contextual approach does not necessarily avoid the kind of speculation that many have associated with form criticism.[84] After comparing various theories about how the final form of the Psalter was shaped, Whybray concludes that such theories can only be speculative and that we can only say with certainty that the process by which the Psalter reached its final form was complex and involved multiple editorial agendas.[85] His critique casts doubt on the ability to assert with certainty that a single theory accounts for how all the psalms came to be in their current position and came to have their current shape, but it does not negate the general consensus that the Psalter has undergone editorial shaping. Murphy is less skeptical than Whybray and seeks a middle road between rejection of the approach and uncritical acceptance of it. He advocates criteria to guard against unhelpful or incorrect contextual readings and argues that one should pursue continuity with the multiple levels of context in which the Bible is read.[86] My aim is to explore the continuity between individual psalms and their place in larger collections or even the broader structure of the Psalter. The starting point must be the "historical literal meaning,"[87] provided that it is construed on the basis of literary and theological sensitivity. Yet the well-established fact of editorial shaping suggests that inter-psalm relationships may offer possibilities for theological reflection that supervene on the conscious intent of the original psalmists.[88]

How do we distinguish between good contextual readings, that is, credible claims of inter-psalm relationships, and speculative or subjective readings? Wilson warns against beginning with a working hypothesis because of the danger of creating self-fulfilling prophecies or engaging in circular reasoning.[89] For him the only valid hypothesis is a cautious one, that purposeful editorial arrangement is evident in the Psalter, the purpose of which should be discerned by detailed analysis.[90] In what does this detailed analysis consist? Wilson explains that it is examination of "linguistic, the-

---

83. See, for example, Grant, *The King as Exemplar*, 14.

84. Murphy, "Reflections on Contextual Interpretation of the Psalms," 21.

85. Whybray, *Reading the Psalms as a Book*, 119.

86. Murphy, "Reflections on Contextual Interpretation of the Psalms," 26–27.

87. Ibid., 28.

88. So also Mays, "The Question of Context in Psalm Interpretation," 19. Brueggemann likewise sees the promise of the approach in being relating the parts to the whole ("Response to James L. Mays," 36).

89. Wilson, "Understanding the Purposeful Arrangement of Psalms in the Psalter," 44–45.

90. Ibid., 48.

matic, literary and theological links and relationships" between the psalms concerned.[91] On that basis we can discern larger patterns of inter-psalm relationships, such as the collection in Psalms 15–24 mentioned above. This includes verbal links, semantically related terms, and broader conceptual parallels.

Dialogic Criticism

In addition to contextual interpretation of the Psalter, Book I may also be interpreted as a social dialogue. Carleen Mandolfo explores the dialogic character of the lament psalms. She demonstrates that in these psalms the voice of the supplicant speaks in dialogue with a Didactic Voice (hereafter DV).[92] She employs the dialogic criticism of the Russian literary critic and philosopher Mikhail Bakhtin, who argues that language is fundamentally dialogic:

> The living utterance, having taken meaning and shape at a particular historical moment in a socially specific environment, cannot fail to brush up against thousands of living dialogic threads, woven by socio-ideological consciousness around the given object of an utterance; it cannot fail to become an active participant in social dialogue.[93]

Bakhtin writes primarily about the modern novel, but he argues that a dialogic orientation can be found in *any* discourse. Words are always uttered as part of a larger conversation.[94]

Applying Bakhtin's insight to the lament psalms, Mandolfo interprets the DV with help from Walter Brueggemann. His Old Testament theology describes the diversity of the Hebrew Bible using the language of the courtroom and identifies various kinds of testimony. Among others, this includes Israel's core testimony to YHWH and a countertestimony best exemplified in lament and wisdom, especially Job and Ecclesiastes.[95] His literary-theological reconstruction of ideological conflict inspires Mandolfo's interpretation of the significance of the DV in the lament psalms. She asserts that

---

91. Ibid.

92. Mandolfo's seminal work on this is *God in the Dock*. However see also Mandolfo, "Finding Their Voices," 27–52; Mandolfo, "Dialogic Form Criticism," 69–90; Mandolfo, "A Generic Renegade," 45–63.

93. Bakhtin, "Discourse in the Novel," 276.

94. Ibid., 279.

95. Brueggemann, *Theology of the Old Testament*.

the tension between the DV and the voice of the supplicant illustrates the tension between Brueggemann's core testimony and its countertestimony.[96] In one place she suggests that this tension may not be a matter of outright countertestimony but rather a venue in which Israel resolved its ideological conflicts.[97] She admits that the DV and the supplicant may not be distinct voices at all.[98] However, overall she holds a dim view of the DV's relationship to the supplicant: "The DV only knows one language through which to speak its comfort, and that language is unbending and tends to stifle the full meaning of the supplicant's experience."[99] Furthermore, this voice has certain political implications:

> The Deuteronomistic theology of retribution that became dominant and exercises such sway over much of biblical literature, and apparently the worldview of Israelites, sets people up for disappointment, while at the same time, so long as it can maintain leverage, is a useful tool for controlling social chaos.[100]

The reader's role is to "wrest the DV's power away, by means of imposing on the psalm a dialogic reading."[101] This last comment notwithstanding, Mandolfo helpfully applies Bakhtin's insight about the dialogic nature of language to the Psalter.

Although Mandolfo is not the first to study the Psalms with inspiration from Bakhtin,[102] her work has inspired further examination of the dialogic character of psalms.[103] Thus far this work has focused on the dialogic qualities of *individual* psalms, but Bakhtin's insight about language can be applied to the Psalter *as a whole*. The DV found in the lament psalms appears on its own in the portraits of the righteous considered in this study. Seen

---

96. Mandolfo, *God in the Dock*, 121–22.

97. Ibid., 192.

98. Ibid., 204.

99. Ibid., 182. This is consistent with Brueggemann's own skepticism about the psalms of orientation. He regards them as lacking any tension to resolve, describing Psalm 37 as promoting an "undisturbed, uncritical equilibrium," with Psalm 145 celebrating the status quo (Brueggemann, "Psalms and the Life of Faith," 10).

100. Mandolfo, *God in the Dock*, 142.

101. Ibid., 195.

102. For a study of quotations in the Psalms given in conscious dependence on Bakhtin, see Levine, "The Dialogic Discourse of Psalms," 145–61; Levine, *Sing unto God a New Song: A Contemporary Reading of the Psalms*. Cf. Olson, "Biblical Theology as Provisional Monologization," 162–80.

103. See Tull, "Bakhtin's Confessional Self-accounting and Psalms of Lament," 41–55; Brueggemann, "Psalms as Subversive Practice of Dialogue," 3–25; Brown, "The Psalms and 'I,'" 27–44; Suderman and Grebel, "Deaf Communities."

Introduction

in this light, Book I participates in a dialogue about the nature of Israel's covenant faith.

In addition to Mandolfo, an article by Terrence Collins is relevant to our study.[104] Although he operates in conscious dependence on structuralism rather than Bakhtinian dialogic criticism, Collins identifies a dialectic movement in the Psalter between various spiritual stances. The first begins with an unflinching affirmation that "all is right with the world, that God is in control," and that walking in his ways leads to happiness (see Psalm 1). Next comes a moment of crisis that calls this situation into question by the experience of violence and oppression, pressuring the psalmist to give up confidence (see Psalm 14). Finally, other psalms affirm confidence in the face of danger (see Psalm 23).[105] Collins qualifies this: "No matter how strong the reaffirmation of faith, there is still a desire and need to see its realization, to see God's help translated from the theoretical plane to that of lived experience."[106] Collins' work parallels Brueggemann's functional typology of psalms in terms of orientation, disorientation, and reorientation,[107] but he offers a somewhat different narrative from Brueggemann. Collins argues that the whole Psalter addresses the complexity of theodicy, not with philosophical argumentation, but with an ethical response that ends with praise:

> One effect of this development is that we are led to revise our view of all the other psalms of praise in the book. They must all be taken in conjunction with the psalms of pain and questioning with which they combine as two halves of a whole. Therefore, the stance of naïve praise, although a useful theoretical category, is not in fact an existential reality in the book of Psalms.[108]

This challenges the notion that Mandolfo's DV necessarily exercises power over the voice of the supplicant and invites a revised reading of the social dialogue in the Psalter.

---

104. Collins, "Decoding the Psalms." As part of his structuralist method, Collins sees the Psalter as a whole comprising a complex didactic message that transcends the intentions of the original authors.

105. Ibid., 46–47.

106. Ibid., 47.

107. Collins acknowledges this (ibid., 58 n. 8). See Brueggemann, "Psalms and the Life of Faith," 3–32.

108. Collins, "Decoding the Psalms," 47.

Approaches to Biblical Ethics

Interpreting the Psalter as a collection involves identifying its structural and theological contours using linguistic and thematic links between psalms. The goal of attending to the Psalter at an editorial level is to discern the broader ethical and theological issues that are at stake, so I shall briefly examine the question of method in ethics.

Few works on Old Testament ethics define what they mean by "ethics."[109] To avoid confusion, I shall define what I mean by "ethics" and outline how I seek to pursue the study of ethics in the Psalter.

The term "ethics" may refer variously to systems of values and customs, concrete principles of morality, or the discourse about such systems and principles.[110] I understand the task of Old Testament ethics to be primarily aimed at describing the values and moral traditions of the Old Testament. As such Old Testament ethics is first a descriptive exercise.[111]

At the very least, this descriptive task involves values and moral traditions concerning the character and behavior of human beings. Arthur Holmes suggests that "ethics is about the good (that is, what values and virtues we should cultivate) and about the right (that is, what our moral duties may be)."[112] However, ethics involves more than defining right and wrong action or even good character and behavior. It also involves an understanding of the good life (or human flourishing, or *eudaimonia*).[113]

Not all ethical systems account equally for concepts of the good life for human beings. Alasdair MacIntyre correctly observes that the work of Immanuel Kant has shaped ethical discourse in the western philosophical tradition to such an extent that even those who oppose his ethics are influenced by the way he defines the conversation.[114] To understand this influence, we may note MacIntyre's summary of the difference between the ancient Greek conception of ethics and the modern conception of ethics: "In general, Greek ethics asks, What am I to do if I am to fare well? Modern ethics asks, What ought I to do if I am to do right? and it asks this ques-

---

109. Notable exceptions include Rodd, *Glimpses of a Strange Land*, 1; Durant, "Imitation of God," 1.

110. Crisp, "Ethics," 435.

111. This is in accord with the common assumption that biblical theology is first a descriptive enterprise. For a helpful summary of the relationship between the descriptive and normative in biblical theology, see Hasel, *Old Testament Theology*, 28–38. I shall return to the question of normativity below.

112. Holmes, *Ethics*, 12.

113. Slote, "Moral Philosophy, Problems of," 629.

114. MacIntyre, *A Short History of Ethics*, 190.

tion in such a way that doing right is made something quite independent of faring well."[115] In Kant's ethics, questions of *eudaimonia* are not helpful.[116] This perspective is foreign to the world of the Bible. As we shall see in the portraits, the Old Testament conception of what we call "ethics" is much closer to that of the ancient Greeks than our own.[117] This is not to say that Old Testament ethics follows Aristotle's conception of the virtues as lying on a mean, and it certainly does not mean that the Old Testament advocates Aristotle's magnanimous man. Instead, the structures of both Old Testament ethics and Aristotle's Nicomachean *Ethics* are teleological. In Old Testament terms, having life and seeing good is wrapped up in turning from evil and doing good (Ps 34:13-15[12-14]). I shall define what this means in the chapters that follow.

Old Testament ethics is fundamentally theological. The distinction between theology and ethics is a useful heuristic tool for analyzing texts and constructing curricula for theological schools, but the distinction is foreign to the Bible. Childs rightly emphasizes that in the Hebrew Bible ethics and theology are inseparably intertwined.[118] In this project I seek to clarify the ethical concerns in the portraits and place them in their theological context. Ethical concerns include the character traits and behaviors that the psalmist identifies, and the theological context includes the way the psalmist describes the good life.[119]

I use the term "character" as a shorthand for the ethical characteristics of a person, though the term is closely related to the term "virtue."[120] Birch and Rasmussen define their relationship as follows:

---

115. Ibid., 84.

116. Ibid., 195.

117. Rodd likewise suggests that the Old Testament ethical world was more like Greek virtues than Kantian deontology or the utilitarianism of Bentham and Mill (*Glimpses of a Strange Land*, 276-77).

118. Childs, *Biblical Theology of the Old and New Testaments*, 676. So also Wright, *Old Testament Ethics*, 17.

119. For a study on concepts of the good life in the Hebrew Bible, see Whybray, *The Good Life in the Old Testament*.

120. In this study I have chosen to use the term "character" rather than "virtue." The latter term is associated with a particular philosophical tradition and often involves discussion of the four cardinal and three theological virtues. This can be applied to OT ethics with profit. See Carroll R., "Seeking the Virtues among the Prophets," 77-96. Carroll's discussion centers on the virtue of justice (ibid., 83). My own discussion does not seek specifically to relate these texts to the seven virtues, so a term with a broader reference is needed. The term "character" serves this purpose. Cf. Carroll's definition of character as "habitual behavior, attitudes, and intentions" (ibid., 82), which fits my texts perfectly.

> The cultivation of virtue has traditionally been the aim of character formation. Virtue is a disposition, which denotes the pattern of choices an individual makes. Dispositions comprise persistent attitudes or "habits" of the heart and mind that dispose one to a consistency of certain action and expression.[121]

The portraits, as well as much of the rest of the Psalter, describe the moral characteristics of persons by recounting their actions. But actions reflect the character of a person, and the label "the righteous" or "the wicked" is applied to persons, not actions alone. Therefore, I use the term "character" to refer in a summary way to the actions, dispositions, and traits that typify persons.

Finally, I must declare an assumption to which some readers are likely to object, namely, that Old Testament ethics involves a normative dimension. Rodd rejects this possibility because he is skeptical about the value of ancient custom for today.[122] With Rodd, it is important to recognize the historical and cultural distance between the world in which the text of the Hebrew Bible was written and the diverse cultural contexts in which we now live.[123] However, we need not be constrained by Rodd's skepticism to the extent that we only see the Bible as valuable for the alternative perspective that it offers. Christopher Wright offers a solution to the problem of cultural (and theological) distance. He suggests that Israel's ethics are paradigmatic for our own, that is, we do not imitate them in every respect.[124] Furthermore, historical and cultural distance does not preclude the basic common ground that human beings share. Therefore, I proceed under the assumption that the ethical concerns and theological context we shall explore in the portraits of the righteous and Book I are relevant to readers today.

With these methodological aims, approaches, and assumptions declared, I shall examine the first portrait to clarify its ethical concerns and theological context.

---

121. Birch and Rasmussen, *Bible and Ethics in the Christian Life*, 79–80; quoted in Brown, *Character in Crisis*, 9.

122. Rodd, *Glimpses of a Strange Land*, 17.

123. One obvious point of discontinuity for many moderns is the imprecatory psalms. For a study of these psalms, see Zenger, *A God of Vengeance?*

124. For a more complete discussion of moving from Old Testament ethics to contemporary ethics, see Wright, *Old Testament Ethics*, 62–74.

2

Psalm 15

INTRODUCTION

Interpretation of Psalm 15 over the past century has been mired in form-critical debate about the original *Sitz im Leben* of this psalm. This debate has meant that the ethical and theological resources the psalm contains have been largely overlooked, especially in its relationship to the rest of the Psalter. Instead of engaging that debate in detail, I shall pursue a literary approach that is aware of the insights of the form-critical discussion but focuses on the use of imagery in Psalm 15. This imagery clarifies the theological framework in which the ethical concerns of Psalm 15 are expressed.

I shall argue that Psalm 15 presents a character sketch of the righteous person with a didactic purpose. This psalm provides something of a pencil sketch of those who may be with YHWH in worship and thus enjoy the benefit of a secure dwelling in his presence. It is intended to shape the character of those who desire to be with YHWH in order to build a secure and righteous community before YHWH. Thus the linguistically foregrounded concern of temple worship is ultimately aimed to address the core ethical concern of worshippers' relationships to YHWH and his people. The psalm is both social and theological in its focus. Communion with and protection from YHWH is wrapped up with community with the people of YHWH.

In addition to text-critical analysis and translation of the psalm, this chapter offers an analysis of its literary structure and genre, a construal of the metaphorical frame of the psalm in verses 1bc and 5cd that constitutes its theology, a detailed account of the individual ethical concerns in the psalm, and a consideration of three prophetic parallels to Psalm 15.

TRANSLATION AND TEXT-CRITICAL ANALYSIS OF PSALM 15

What follows is my English translation of Psalm 15, which reflects a number of text-critical decisions, one of which is outlined following the translation:

מִזְמוֹר לְדָוִד	1a	A psalm of David.
יְהוָה מִי־יָגוּר בְּאָהֳלֶךָ	1b	O YHWH, who may sojourn in your tent?
מִי־יִשְׁכֹּן בְּהַר קָדְשֶׁךָ	1c	Who may dwell on your holy hill?
הוֹלֵךְ תָּמִים	2a	He who walks blamelessly,
וּפֹעֵל צֶדֶק	2b	And does righteousness,
וְדֹבֵר אֱמֶת בִּלְבָבוֹ׃	2c	And speaks truth in his heart.
לֹא־רָגַל עַל־לְשֹׁנוֹ	3a	He has not slandered with his tongue,
לֹא־עָשָׂה לְרֵעֵהוּ רָעָה	3b	He has done no evil to his friend,
וְחֶרְפָּה לֹא־נָשָׂא עַל־קְרֹבוֹ׃	3c	And he has not raised a taunt against his neighbor.
נִבְזֶה בְּעֵינָיו נִמְאָס	4a	Despised in his eyes is a rejected person,
וְאֶת־יִרְאֵי יְהוָה יְכַבֵּד	4b	But those who fear YHWH he honors.
נִשְׁבַּע לְהָרַע וְלֹא יָמִר	4c	He has sworn to his harm and does not change.
כַּסְפּוֹ לֹא־נָתַן בְּנֶשֶׁךְ	5a	He has not given his silver with interest,
וְשֹׁחַד עַל־נָקִי לֹא לָקָח	5b	And a bribe against the innocent he has not taken.
עֹשֵׂה־אֵלֶּה	5c	He who does these things,
לֹא יִמּוֹט לְעוֹלָם	5d	He will not be shaken forever.

In verse 1b instead of בְּאָהֳלֶךָ, "in your tent," fragments from Cairo Geniza and a number of medieval manuscripts have the plural form, בְּאָהֳלֶיךָ, "in your tents." Kraus suggests the plural "tents" belong to pilgrims pitched near the sanctuary,[1] but this interpretation is unlikely. Elsewhere in the Psalter the plural form is used of the tents of the wicked or enemies (69:26[25]; 84:11[10]), of the righteous (118:15), of foreign nations (78:51; 83:7[6]; 120:5), or of Israel (78:55; 106:25), and it is *always* identified by

---

1. Kraus, *Psalms 1–59*, 225.

Psalm 15

the collective owner, not YHWH. Therefore, one would expect the tents of pilgrims to be similarly identified by their owners if they belonged to the pilgrims.

The textual issue remains, however. The plural would certainly be a more difficult reading for two reasons. First, the second line of the double question has the "holy mountain" as singular. Second, elsewhere in the Psalter when YHWH is connected to tents, the tent is always singular (27:5, 6; 61:5[4]; 78:60). Therefore, the singular reading is the more likely and easier reading (cf. verbal parallel in Psalm 120:5). However, commentators do not take the plural reading seriously, perhaps in part because of the form-critical emphasis on entrance into the *one* temple in Jerusalem. Further, in view of the usage of אֹהֶל in the Psalter, the *lectio dificilior* would be anomalous, and this suggests that such a reading is *too* difficult to be original. Perhaps the extra *yôd* may have been inadvertently added at some point in copying. We cannot be certain, but in the end the singular reading of the MT is preferred.

A variant in verse 4c concerning לְהָרַע requires extensive treatment. LXX (as well as Syriac) has τῷ πλησίον αὐτοῦ, "to his neighbor." Dahood's translation of MT, "he swore to do wrong and he did not retract,"[2] suggests that the MT reading would create a contradiction with the previous verse where the righteous person does *not* do wrong. Scholars suggest six different solutions.

First, English translations almost universally prefer the MT reading, with a translation such as "who stand by their oath even to their hurt."[3] Suggesting MT is the *lectio brevior,* Hossfeld prefers it to the LXX reading outlined below.[4] However, the principle does not seem to apply since the LXX reading is nearly as brief. Also, the word lacks a pronominal suffix identifying the object of harm, though that does not rule out the interpretation, particularly since this is poetry where terseness is important.[5]

Second, Goldingay retains the reading of the MT but rejects the first solution as requiring "a considerable inference."[6] Instead, he sees it applying to someone in the role of a judge, so the harm done is a just punishment.[7] This would dovetail with the moral judgment presented in verse 4ab and with the financial issues that follow, namely lending and bribe taking. How-

---

2. Dahood, "Note on Psalm 15," 302.
3. NRSV; similarly KJV, RSV, NIV, NJPS, NLT, ESV. Commentators include, e.g., Rashi, *Rashi's Commentary on Psalms*, 225; Weiser, *The Psalms*, 167; Terrien, *The Psalms*, 172; VanGemeren, *Psalms*, 184–85.
4. Hossfeld and Zenger, *Die Psalmen I*, 106.
5. So Ibid.
6. Goldingay, *Psalms*, 218.
7. Ibid., 1:222.

ever, Goldingay's solution may in fact require a more considerable inference than the first solution. It presupposes a particular judicial setting behind a rather general statement.

Third, Steingrimsson defends the MT and treats it as an abbreviated version of Lev 5:4, which offers instruction about a case in which someone makes a rash oath "to do evil or to do good" (לְהָרַע אוֹ לְהֵיטִיב).[8] The verbal and conceptual parallel to another oath text seems to support this. However, it introduces more interpretive problems than it solves. Lev 5:4 is addressing a matter requiring confession and atonement (Lev 5:5–6), not a virtuous act of keeping one's word.

Dahood suggests a fourth solution for retaining the MT reading. By analogy to Ugaritic he interprets the *lāmed* preposition in a separative sense, translating it, "he swore off doing wrong." He points to a semantically identical case in Isa 54:9 involving נִשְׁבַּעְתִּי מִקְּצֹף ("I swore off anger"). He suggests that the verb נִשְׁבַּע plus לְ has a similar separative force to the *lāmed* prepositions in Ps 40:11 ("I do not hide your steadfast love and your faithfulness *from the great assembly*," לְקָהָל רָב) and Ps 84:12 ("he does not withhold good from *those who walk in integrity*," לַהֹלְכִים בְּתָמִים).[9] However, the verbs כחד and מנע indicate a separative sense (hiding or withholding always entail a separative relationship). This does not apply to שׁבע.

The fifth solution is to follow the LXX,[10] which has τῷ πλησίον αὐτοῦ "to his neighbor." Thus Robert Alter translates, "When he vows to his fellow man he does not revoke it." He argues that several consonants seem to have been misplaced. Instead of להרע, the text originally read לרעהו.[11] Although Alter does not note it, the next letter after this word is the *waw* conjunction. It is thus plausible that a scribe inadvertently transposed the *hê* to before the *rêš* and dropped the *waw*. However, this does not fit the context well,[12] though that is the argument Briggs uses in support of the LXX.[13]

Kraus suggests the sixth and most radical solution, namely that the corruption of the verse noted in *BHS* consists of the deletion of portions of

---

8. Steingrimsson, *Tor der Gerechtigkeit*, 1–2.

9. Dahood, "Note on Psalm 15," 302; Dahood, *Psalms I, 1–50*, 84. So also Craigie, *Psalms 1–50*, 150.

10. Which is followed by Syriac. Symmachus Greek version has a related though different reading: ἑταῖρος εἶναι, "to be a companion." This may be explained as a paraphrase of a similar manuscript tradition to that of the LXX, or perhaps even as evidence of influence by the LXX.

11. Alter, *Psalms*, 44.

12. Goldingay, *Psalms*, 1:218.

13. Briggs, *Psalms*, 114. Commentators following this reading also include Broyles, *Psalms*, 95.

the second half-verse. He argues that, by analogy to the sentence structure of Ps 24:4bc, a series of clauses introduced by negative particles (לֹא ... וְלֹא) is missing, so we should insert לֹא before נִשְׁבַּע and then presuppose an additional word after יָמֵר. Kraus suggests that the LXX reading is meant to remedy this corruption. On the basis of that emendation, Kraus translates the verse: "Who does 'not' swear to an evil deed and does not change '. . . .'"[14] This is possible but unlikely. The so-called "entrance liturgies" do not have identical sentence structure in the answer portion of the form. Psalm 15:2, for example, has participial phrases, while Ps 24:4 has nominal phrases. Furthermore the negated perfects in Ps 15:3 are not picked up in 15:4ab, where a participle and an imperfect are employed without negation. Therefore the parallel in Psalm 24 is of limited or no value for reconstructing sentence structure in Psalm 15.

What is the best reading? Anderson rightly notes that oath-keeping is the central concern here, regardless of the reading preferred.[15] His caution is well taken, but caution does not preclude evaluating the evidence as best as we can. I prefer the MT for two reasons. First, the MT is the *lectio difficilior*, as the preceding history of interpretation shows. Goldingay's interpretation is enticing but novel, and it is easier to explain the difficult phrase by presupposing an unexpressed third-person pronominal suffix than to propose a more elaborate sociological background. Second, the MT offers the best explanation for the presence of the LXX reading. While the LXX translators *may* have been working with a different manuscript tradition, it is also conceivable that they sought to clarify and soften the verse in their translation. While certainty over this word eludes us, the ethical concern identified in verse 4c, a commitment to keep one's vows, remains clear.

With the text and translation above, I shall now proceed to the complex web of generic and structural issues in Psalm 15.

LITERARY STRUCTURE AND GENRE OF PSALM 15

At the highest level of abstraction Psalm 15 may be classified as a poem. It is structured as a series of parallel lines, uses terse language, and is framed by two images. However, at a lower level of abstraction, we may be able to identify its literary type with greater specificity.

Hermann Gunkel suggested that originally Psalm 15 was an "entrance liturgy," performed antiphonally by pilgrims and priests at the temple gate in Jerusalem in order to determine who was permitted to enter the holy

---

14. Kraus, *Psalms 1–59*, 225–26.
15. Anderson, *The Book of Psalms*, 139.

precincts.[16] Gunkel argues that this "entrance liturgy" form includes a question, an answer, and a blessing/benefit.[17] On this last point there is widespread agreement among scholars, since this literary structure is also found in Ps 24:3–5 and Isa 33:14–16. The fact that three texts display such a similar macro structure offers strong evidence for a standardized pattern.[18] However, when it comes to Gunkel's construal of the *Sitz im Leben* of the psalm, opinions divide. Although the "entrance liturgy" label seems to roll off the page comfortably for many commentators, others use the term with the qualifier "so-called" prefixed, reflecting an ambivalence among interpreters about construing the psalm with such sociological specificity. Therefore it will be helpful to take a step back and consider structural and generic issues from a broader frame of reference.

Literary Structure

No one has improved upon Gunkel's description of the basic elements of the psalm. We may represent this structure as follows:

Title (v. 1a)

1. Question (v. 1bc)

2. Answer (vv. 2a–5b)

3. Benefit (vv. 5cd)

The overall structure of Psalm 15 is beyond doubt and debate among scholars.

Most of the debate about its structure deals with the central answer section (vv. 2–5b). Several articles addressing this micro-structural level have recognized the interplay between various ethical concepts in the answer section, but no single scheme has generated a consensus. However, it is clear that Psalm 15 is an integrated composition that includes general and specific elements, speech and conduct, and interior attitudes and external behavior.

This study is focused on the final form of Psalm 15. This excludes a line of inquiry initiated by Klaus Koch in which scholars seek layers of tradition.[19] While it *may* be beneficial for identifying strands of tradition, it does

---

16. Gunkel and Begrich, *Introduction to Psalms*, 72.

17. Ibid., 313.

18. I shall argue in chapter 4 that Ps 34:13–15[12–14] likewise follows this structure, and there the stated aim is instruction (v. 12[11]).

19. Koch proposes that the portions with negated perfects are later insertions reflecting the influence of the Decalogue ("Tempeleinlassliturgien und Dekaloge," 50–51).

not significantly clarify the ethical concerns in the final form of the text and is of limited value for this inquiry.[20]

Studies in the literary structure of the final form abound. Patrick Miller argues that ambiguity *within the text* of Psalm 15 allows for multiple structural options.[21] He focuses on verses 2–3, where the layouts of *BHK* and *BHS* reveal two distinct interpretations.[22] *BHK* (cf. RSV) presents the lines as a bicolon, a monocolon, and a bicolon:

הוֹלֵךְ תָּמִים וּפֹעֵל צֶדֶק // וְדֹבֵר אֱמֶת בִּלְבָבוֹ
לֹא־רָגַל עַל־לְשֹׁנוֹ
לֹא־עָשָׂה לְרֵעֵהוּ רָעָה // וְחֶרְפָּה לֹא־נָשָׂא עַל־קְרֹבוֹ

However, *BHS* presents the parallel lines as three bicola:

הוֹלֵךְ תָּמִים // וּפֹעֵל צֶדֶק
וְדֹבֵר אֱמֶת בִּלְבָבוֹ // לֹא־רָגַל עַל־לְשֹׁנוֹ
לֹא־עָשָׂה לְרֵעֵהוּ רָעָה // וְחֶרְפָּה לֹא־נָשָׂא עַל־קְרֹבוֹ

Miller argues that the second construal in three bicola shows the progression of thought from general statements of right conduct in the first bicolon to concrete explication in the second bicolon.[23] Although he affirms this interpretation, Miller suggests another way. Verses 2–3 may also involve two tricola, with corresponding general-specific correspondences between the three elements of the two verses. I represent this using vertical columns for each verse:

Table a. Psalm 15:2–3 as Two Tricola

Verse 3	//	Verse 2
לֹא־רָגַל עַל־לְשֹׁנוֹ	//	הוֹלֵךְ תָּמִים
לֹא־עָשָׂה לְרֵעֵהוּ רָעָה	//	וּפֹעֵל צֶדֶק
וְחֶרְפָּה לֹא־נָשָׂא עַל־קְרֹבוֹ	//	וְדֹבֵר אֱמֶת בִּלְבָבוֹ

Three negated perfects balance three participles. Doing צֶדֶק in verse 2b is balanced by not doing רָעָה in verse 3b, while speaking truth in verse 2c

---

20. For a helpful summary of this discussion, see Hossfeld, "Nachlese," 135–56. He summarizes several studies, including Steingrimsson, *Tor der Gerechtigkeit*; Beyerlin, *Weisheitlich-Kultische Heilsordnung*; Otto, "Kultus und Ethos in Jerusalemer Theologie," 161–79. More recent studies pursuing this method include Hertog, "Gaat tot zijn poorten in met lof," 17–33; Podella, "Transformationen kultischer Darstellungen," 95–130.
21. Miller, "Poetic Ambiguity and Balance in Psalm 15," 418.
22. Note that Miller refers to the 3rd edition.
23. Miller, "Poetic Ambiguity and Balance in Psalm 15," 419–20.

is balanced by not raising a taunt against one's friend in verse 3c. Miller argues that these correspondences explain the use in verse 3a of the rare verb רגל, which means "to slander," but may be understood as a play. Literally, one does "not 'foot' over one's tongue." This balances the הלך of verse 2a.[24] Whatever the original compositional history, placing general participles with negated perfects yields a poetically balanced construction.[25]

Pierre Auffret has written two studies that grapple with the structure of the psalm and extend Miller's work.[26] Auffret contends that if the balance is extended into verses 4–5b a concentric structure may be discerned. Thus verse 4ab concerns the internal motivation for external behavior, namely contempt of injustice and regard for those who fear YHWH. Then just as verse 2 has two lines on conduct and one on speech, so verses 4c–5b have one line on speech (taking verse 4cd as one line) and two on conduct in verse 5ab.[27]

In contrast to the text/reader-centered approaches of Miller and Auffret, Lloyd Barré argues that the structure must be tied to authorial intention.[28] He recognizes a chiastic structure in both form and content:

יְהוָה מִי־יָגוּר בְּאָהֳלֶךָ   A
מִי־יִשְׁכֹּן בְּהַר קָדְשֶׁךָ (v. 1)

הוֹלֵךְ תָּמִים   B
וּפֹעֵל צֶדֶק
וְדֹבֵר אֱמֶת בִּלְבָבוֹ (v. 2)

לֹא־רָגַל עַל־לְשֹׁנוֹ   C
לֹא־עָשָׂה לְרֵעֵהוּ רָעָה
וְחֶרְפָּה לֹא־נָשָׂא עַל־קְרֹבוֹ (v. 3)

נִבְזֶה בְּעֵינָיו נִמְאָס   D
וְאֶת־יִרְאֵי יְהוָה יְכַבֵּד (v. 4ab)

נִשְׁבַּע לְהָרַע וְלֹא יָמִר   C'
כַּסְפּוֹ לֹא־נָתַן בְּנֶשֶׁךְ
וְשֹׁחַד עַל־נָקִי לֹא לָקָח (vv. 4c-5b)

עֹשֵׂה־אֵלֶּה (v. c5)   B'
לֹא יִמּוֹט לְעוֹלָם (v. d5)[29]   A'

24. Ibid., 422–23.

25. Ibid., 423–24.

26. Auffret, "Essai sur la structure littéraire du Psaume 15," 385-99; Auffret, "YHWH, qui séjournera en ta tente?" 143-51. His second article builds on the work of Miller and Barré and focuses particularly on the macro-structure and the relation of verses 1 and 5cd to the answer.

27. Auffret, "Essai sur la structure littéraire du Psaume 15," 439.

28. Barré, "Recovering the Literary Structure of Psalm 15," 207.

29. Ibid., 207–8.

Thus A:A' both have prefixed forms and correspond in content as the metaphorical frame outlined below. B:B' are formally parallel in the use of positive (i.e., not negated) participles and involve a general quality. C:C' are negated suffixed forms and concern more specific outward behavior that is oriented to the welfare of one's neighbor. Finally, D stands at the center with a focus on inner attitude.[30] While Barré does not explain why this structure represents the authorial viewpoint, his interpretation accounts for both form and content and incorporates Miller's contention that the two tricola of verses 2–3 show correspondences in content. The weakest link in this interpretation is B'A' (v. 5cd), which constitutes an integrated sentence and must be divided into two statements for the structure to work.[31] However, this weakness is not fatal. As noted below,[32] some have recognized that verse 5c recapitulates the entirety of the answer. This lends credibility to Barré's structural analysis. Furthermore, the overall correspondence of form and content is striking, throwing into relief the increasing specificity of the answer, pivoting on the inner attitude of the righteous in verse 4ab.

In its present form Psalm 15 is a unified composition displaying poetic artistry and semantic balance, with a movement from the general to the specific to the inner attitudes and back out again. But how should we read the psalm? What literary genre would create the appropriate expectations for readers of the psalm?

Literary Genre

The structure and typical elements of the form represented by Psalm 15 are clear. What is less clear is the second aspect of Gunkel's theory, namely Psalm 15's *Sitz im Leben* in ancient Israel, which affects how we understand the psalm's genre. My purpose here is not to rehearse in detail the debate that has unfolded over the "entrance liturgies" throughout the last several decades.[33] We know less about the historical setting of this psalm than we would like.[34] Therefore, instead of seeking an ever-elusive reconstruction for

30. Ibid., 208–10.
31. Ibid., 208 n. 7.
32. See p. 41 below.
33. For a fairly exhaustive summary of the state of discussion up to the mid 1970s, see Willis, "Ethics in a Cultic Setting." For a summary of three German-language studies focused on the tradition-historical context of the "entrance liturgies," see Hossfeld, "Nachlese." He examines Steingrimsson, *Tor der Gerechtigkeit*; Beyerlin, *Weisheitlich-Kultische Heilsordnung*; Otto, "Kultus und Ethos in Jerusalemer Theologie."
34. Willis, "Ethics in a Cultic Setting," 161; Maloney, "A Portrait of the Righteous Person," 151–52.

the original *Sitz im Leben* of Psalm 15, my intent is to explore the issues that most affect our understanding of the purpose of the psalm. The key question is that of the relationship of the psalm to the world. Was it a procedural liturgy meant to differentiate between would-be worshippers or a didactic poem meant to help would-be worshippers know what kind of persons they should be?

First, is Psalm 15 a liturgical text? Gunkel's own definition is that a liturgy is "a poem that has been performed by alternating voices."[35] For Gunkel, vocal participation of lay people separates liturgy from a word of instruction. Joachim Begrich argues that "entrance liturgies" and the whole of the priestly torah arose out of conversations between worshippers and priests like the one found in Hag 2:10ff.[36] Egyptian parallels have also been suggested as a cultural analog. Kurt Galling cites a parallel in chapter 125 of the Book of the Dead.[37] This first-person declaration of innocence set in a posthumous context of judgment contains seventy-eight individual assertions of innocence on matters of ethics and cult and instructions about its performance.[38] In addition, Eckart Otto mentions an entrance text addressed to priests from the Temple of Horus at Edfu with motifs similar to Psalms 15 and 24:

> Do not be greedy, slander not,
> Take no bribes,
> Make no distinction between rich and poor,
> Swear no oath, make no lie about the truth in speech!
> Give the lie no advantage over the truth through slander.[39]

Most notably, this text exhibits a concern for correct speech and economic justice that is found in Psalms 15 and 24.

Critics of the "entrance liturgy" theory object to the "liturgy" aspect of the label. Clements argues that even if the Egyptian parallels do exist, they do not prove the existence of antiphonal liturgies in Israel.[40] O. García de

---

35. Gunkel, "Jesaia 33," 182.

36. Begrich, "Die priesterliche Tora," 251. Hertog likewise follows this model and suggests that liturgies *in general* are formed as spontaneous conversation attains a fixed format ("Gaat tot zijn poorten in met lof," 19).

37. Galling, "Der Beichtspiegel," 174-75; also Koch, "Tempeleinlassliturgien und Dekaloge," 49.

38. *ANET* 34-36.

39. Author's translation of text quoted in Otto, *Theologische Ethik des Alten Testaments*, 95 n. 38. Otto also points to parallels dealing with temple entry from Mesopotamia and Sumeria.

40. Clements, "Worship and Ethics," 83.

Psalm 15

la Fuente goes further and questions the appropriateness of the supposed parallels from Egypt, for they are not themselves liturgies but rather publicly posted entrance requirements.[41] He further argues that the double question of Ps 15:1 was addressed to YHWH, not to a priest.[42] C. G. den Hertog points out that Psalm 15 lacks even a trace of priestly involvement,[43] though that observation could be made about most psalms. We must also note that the Egyptian parallels are distinct from Psalms 15 and 24 in their grammatical form. The Book of the Dead is cast in the first person (bearing greater similarity to the personal confession of Deut 26:12–15 identified by Galling),[44] while the text from Edfu is in the second person. We lack sufficient evidence to determine whether Psalm 15 is a liturgy, either in the form of narrative texts discussing their use or appropriate liturgical parallels in the ANE.

Critics also object to Gunkel's assertion that the "entrance liturgies" were used by priests for determining whether pilgrims/worshippers may enter the temple for worship.[45] John T. Willis questions whether this reconstruction is feasible. A priest could not tell whether or not a pilgrim met the conditions, making it difficult to exclude anyone on the basis of such conditions.[46] Even the otherwise supportive Klaus Koch questions whether priests would stand confidently at the temple gate and deny entrance to wealthy landowners. He concludes that we should not overlook the priests—they were not mere functionaries. They could struggle in the cause of holiness on behalf of YHWH.[47] This possibility suggests a purpose other than checking worshippers at the door.

A further problem with the "entrance liturgy" theory is the lack of ritual requirements, which *are* present in most Egyptian entry texts.[48] This is an important objection, especially in view of the qualifications for ritual

---

41. García de la Fuente, "Liturgias de entrada," 280.

42. Ibid.; this argument is also suggested by Clements, "Worship and Ethics," 85.

43. Hertog, "Gaat tot zijn poorten in met lof," 26.

44. Galling, "Der Beichtspiegel," 170. Galling identifies a parallel to this personal confession from Deut 26:12ff. In Ps 24:6, a matter I will consider in chapter 3.

45. Gunkel and Begrich, *Introduction to Psalms*, 72; cf. Gunkel, "Jesaia 33," 193, which construes the Isaianic parallel as a prophetic liturgy. This line of interpretation has been followed by Koch, "Tempeleinlassliturgien und Dekaloge," 46; Begrich, "Die priesterliche Tora," 249.

46. Willis, "Ethics in a Cultic Setting," 157.

47. Koch, "Tempeleinlassliturgien und Dekaloge," 59.

48. Weinfeld, "Instructions for Temple Visitors," 239; Hertog, "Gaat tot zijn poorten in met lof," 30.

participation in the Pentateuch.⁴⁹ In addition, Weinfeld notes that even the Egyptian texts were intended to inculcate virtue.⁵⁰ If the Egyptian parallels are valid, then this suggests that Psalm 15 is primarily didactic in nature.

The growing consensus in German-language scholarship is that in its present form Psalm 15 was transformed for use other than determining who may enter the temple. Although they may have been entrance liturgies at an earlier point, Koch argues that in their present forms Psalms 15 and 24 served as confessional statements for self-examination rather than entrance liturgies.⁵¹ Likewise, Gerstenberger affirms that an ancient form of the "entrance liturgy" underlies Psalm 15, but the lack of ritual elements suggests it was reinterpreted in light of the non-sacrificial context of the early Jewish community.⁵² Several follow the theory that what may have originally been an "entrance liturgy" has been transformed for a different use.⁵³ This diachronic argument seems to beg the question. If the text we have is not an entrance liturgy, then we lack unequivocal evidence for entrance liturgies. On what basis do we suppose that Israelite worship ever involved an "entrance liturgy" used in the manner imagined by Gunkel?

It should be acknowledged that liturgy can and should instruct the worshipper. Sigmund Mowinkel acknowledges the didactic power of liturgy when he calls Psalm 15 a "moral catechism"⁵⁴: "In the 'liturgy of entry' the commandments are of such a nature that the challenge must be taken up by the individual, who is put face to face with his personal responsibility, both for his own 'blessing' and for the future of the people."⁵⁵ More recently, Craig Broyles argues clearly that liturgy can educate:

> For the sake of pedagogical clarity, the temple liturgies present the congregation with two alternatives—the two "ways." Each worshiper is presented with a clear choice: with what kind of company does one identify? Either one identifies with "the righteous" and is thus regarded as "righteous" or one identifies with "the wicked" and is thus regarded as "wicked. . . ." We also see how liturgy educates: liturgy is putting words in a worshiper's

---

49. In addition to the purity laws in Leviticus, qualifications for ritual participation include circumcision (Exod 12:43–49) and an unblemished body (Lev 21:16–23). Cf. Num 16:40.

50. Weinfeld, "Instructions for Temple Visitors," 235.

51. Koch, "Tempeleinlassliturgien und Dekaloge," 60.

52. Gerstenberger, *Psalms: Part 1*, 88.

53. See Hossfeld, "Nachlese," 153; Clements, "Worship and Ethics," 87; Podella, "Transformationen kultischer Darstellungen," 107, 128–29.

54. Mowinckel, *The Psalms in Israel's Worship*, 1:179.

55. Ibid., 1:180.

mouth. Mere instructions can be cerebral, but hearing oneself make certain claims (or at least standing to be counted among those who endorse such claims) should lead to heart searching and changes in attitude and behavior.[56]

Scholars seem agreed that Psalms 15 and 24 were intended to instruct in order to inculcate virtue in worshippers. According to Patrick Miller, regardless of a possible original cultic setting, the intention of these psalms was to declare the nature and importance of righteous character for appearing before YHWH.[57] Psalm 15 is primarily descriptive. But how can description teach?

Leland Ryken offers a fresh literary perspective to the discussion. He compares Psalm 15 to the encomium: "An *encomium* is a work of literature written in praise of an abstract quality or general character type." Encomia introduce the subject, praise the ancestry of the subject, present a catalog of the subject's noteworthy acts and qualities and its indispensable nature (possibly including rewards), and urge the reader to emulate the subject.[58] Although not all of the features of encomia are present in Psalm 15, some fundamentals are. The double question of Ps 15:1 serves as an indirect introduction to the character type, while the mention of the benefit in verse 5cd has the effect of urging "the reader to emulate the subject." This urging is subtle and indirect, but the persuasive power of enlightened self-interest points to the didactic purpose of the psalm: "The effect of [the] concluding assertion is to make the reader want to be such a person, which is always the final impression left by an encomium."[59] Ryken notes further that Psalm 15 concerns a general character type, what the Psalter calls "the righteous," and therefore has affinities with the literary form pioneered in Western literature by the Greek writer Theophrastus, the character sketch.[60] This terminology is preferable to "entrance liturgy" because "character sketch" *actually describes the content of Psalm 15*. Furthermore, Ryken's analysis of this literary type helps explain how the form manifests a didactic purpose.

However, some might object that this label is etic and anachronistic, foreign to the world of the Bible and taken from a time later than that in which Psalm 15 was written. But this objection could be leveled at almost any theory, including the "entrance liturgy" theory. The "entrance liturgy" is similarly foreign as a label and rests on a shaky historical basis. Although

---

56. Broyles, "Psalms Concerning the Liturgies of Temple Entry," 286.
57. Miller, "Poetic Ambiguity and Balance in Psalm 15," 416.
58. Ryken, *Words of Delight*, 293.
59. Ibid., 295.
60. Ibid., 294.

the label "character sketch" is not found in the Bible, texts that teach in the manner of the character sketch are known from the ANE. O. García de la Fuente points to a text from Edfu with a structure similar to Psalms 15 and 24:3–6. It begins with a series of questions, the first of which is, "Do you wish a long life, without destruction inside the temple?" What follows is a litany of instructions that include both cultic and moral items. The inscription ends with the assertion: "Whoever does so will be rewarded on earth, and God will not have any complaint against him."[61] This mirrors exactly the question-answer-benefit structure of Psalms 15 and 24:3–6. The didactic nature of this text can hardly be doubted given the second-person form of address and the persuasive appeal to a motive clause in the last line.

A number of *biblical* texts exhibit a didactic purpose and employ a question-answer form. I will explore the form of Ps 34:12–15[11–14] in chapter four, but it employs a question-answer form to present a character sketch and explicitly identifies a didactic purpose (v. 12[11]).

Micah 6:6–8 is frequently mentioned in connection with the "entrance liturgies" as a prophetic imitation or transformation of this form.[62] Broyles even suggests that Micah 6:8 alludes to the "entrance liturgies" in its list of YHWH's requirements to his people.[63] However, even if it has ritual themes, the Micah text is clearly didactic, not a ritual for determining who may enter the temple. The question-answer form likely is characteristic of a didactic form.

Deuteronomy 10:12–22 is a likely model for this because it also employs a question and a character sketch. In verses 12–13 the introductory question itself constitutes a character sketch of the faithful covenant keeper in Israel:

וְעַתָּה יִשְׂרָאֵל מָה יְהוָה אֱלֹהֶיךָ שֹׁאֵל מֵעִמָּךְ כִּי אִם־לְיִרְאָה אֶת־יְהוָה אֱלֹהֶיךָ לָלֶכֶת בְּכָל־דְּרָכָיו וּלְאַהֲבָה אֹתוֹ וְלַעֲבֹד אֶת־יְהוָה אֱלֹהֶיךָ בְּכָל־לְבָבְךָ וּבְכָל־נַפְשֶׁךָ: לִשְׁמֹר אֶת־מִצְוֹת יְהוָה וְאֶת־חֻקֹּתָיו אֲשֶׁר אָנֹכִי מְצַוְּךָ הַיּוֹם לְטוֹב לָךְ:

> And now O Israel, what does YHWH your God ask of you, but to fear YHWH your God, to walk in all his ways, and to serve YHWH your God with all your heart and with all your life, to keep the commands of YHWH and the decrees which I am commanding you this day for your good?

---

61. García de la Fuente, "Liturgias de entrada," 282. Translations of his Spanish translations listed below are mine.

62. Gunkel and Begrich, *Introduction to Psalms*, 289, 318; Koch, "Tempeleinlassliturgien und Dekaloge," 54–55; Hossfeld, "Nachlese," 154.

63. Broyles, "Psalms Concerning the Liturgies of Temple Entry," 287.

Psalm 15

On the basis of YHWH's gracious election of Israel (v. 15), Moses urges the people not to be stubborn (v. 16) but to circumcise their hearts. Thus Moses introduces a character sketch of YHWH in verses 17–18 to buttress his plea:

כִּי יְהוָה אֱלֹהֵיכֶם הוּא אֱלֹהֵי הָאֱלֹהִים וַאֲדֹנֵי הָאֲדֹנִים הָאֵל הַגָּדֹל הַגִּבֹּר וְהַנּוֹרָא אֲשֶׁר לֹא־יִשָּׂא פָנִים וְלֹא יִקַּח שֹׁחַד: עֹשֶׂה מִשְׁפַּט יָתוֹם וְאַלְמָנָה וְאֹהֵב גֵּר לָתֶת לוֹ לֶחֶם וְשִׂמְלָה:

> For YHWH your God is God of gods and Lord of lords, the great God, mighty and awesome, who has not lifted faces,[64] and he has not taken a bribe. He does justice for the orphan and widow, and he loves the sojourner by giving him bread and clothing.

This character sketch balances general statements (v. 17ab) with specific cases (vv. 17cd–18) as in Psalms 15 and 24. Also, verbless clauses (v. 17ab; cf. Ps 24:4ab) and participles (v. 18; cf. Ps 15:2) stand alongside negated finite forms (v. 17cd; cf. Ps 15:3, 24:4cd). The next verse directly instructs Israel to love the sojourner in the same way that YHWH loves the sojourner. Therefore, the didactic purpose of this character sketch is beyond doubt. In contrast to Psalm 15, Deuteronomy 10 presents YHWH's character as the model for the character of his people (cf. Psalms 111 and 112).[65] Nonetheless, Psalm 34, Mic 6:8, and Deut 10:12–22 show that the question-answer form was used in diverse literary settings in the Hebrew Bible for a didactic purpose.

Thus I take Psalm 15 to be a character sketch. This psalm may have been used by priests for instruction in the temple or perhaps even village life,[66] but we lack sufficient evidence to be firm about any sociological context underlying this psalm. From a literary perspective it is designed to inculcate virtue in the reader/hearer. Its didactic content is framed by the introductory double question introducing the details of the character sketch and the statement of benefit at the end. This frame is loaded with imagery that sets the theological context of this psalm, so to this frame I now turn.

THE METAPHORICAL FRAME (VERSES 1BC AND 5CD)

One costly loss due to preoccupation with the world behind the text is that interpreters have not adequately explored the theological freight of Psalm

---

64. NRSV: "is not partial."
65. Reed, "Virtue Ethics and Psalms 111–112."
66. Gerstenberger, *Psalms: Part 1*, 88.

15. Scholars assume that the introductory double question refers to temple entry or worship, and they may be correct. But overlooking the metaphorical-conceptual dynamic of the psalm in the context of the Psalter bypasses the experiential and emotional associations this brings to the Israelite who hears, reads, or recites Psalm 15. This has perpetuated a theologically anemic interpretation of the psalm. That is *not* to say no one has considered this, as I will show below. But to date no sustained effort has been made to interpret Psalm 15 within the conceptual world of the Psalter.

The double question is addressed to YHWH in the vocative. This suggests the image of a supplicant looking upward, perhaps toward the temple itself. But it is framed as if the supplicant were looking toward the face of YHWH to ask him a question.[67] Following the vocative, the two questions exhibit an identical syntactical structure: Interrogative + Imperfect verb + Prepositional phrase:

יְהוָה	1b	O YHWH,
מִי־יָגוּר בְּאָהֳלֶךָ		who may sojourn in your tent,
מִי־יִשְׁכֹּן בְּהַר קָדְשֶׁךָ	1c	Who may dwell on your holy hill?

This parallelism may be an example of intensification. In the first line both the verb and the prepositional phrase connote a temporary residence, while the second line envisions a more permanent residence.

The verb גור in the first line has drawn the interest of interpreters.[68] Hossfeld considers whether the verb should be taken to mean "to dwell as a sojourner" or generally "to stay" (that is, as an expression of cult competence). He follows the latter because, in his view, the use of tent terminology is metaphorical.[69] Also, the same verb is used in a similar metaphorical sense in Pss 5:5[4] and 61:5[4].[70] These parallels are striking because of their conceptual connections to Ps 15:1:

כִּי לֹא אֵל־חָפֵץ רֶשַׁע	5:5a	For you are not a God who desires wickedness,
אַתָּה לֹא יְגֻרְךָ רָע	5:5b	Nor may evil sojourn with you.

67. In chapter 1 I distinguish between prayer and didactic discourse by the direction of address. Although Psalm 15 begins with address to YHWH, the bulk of the psalm is addressed to a human audience, the questioner (possibly worshippers) or an audience of a teacher who asks the questions.

68. Lienhard Delekat argues that Psalm 15 has in mind three cases in which an individual might approach the temple seeking asylum. The priest must differentiate between legitimate and illegitimate asylum seekers (*Asylie und Schutzorakel am Zionheiligtum*, 169–73). This interpretation has generally been rejected or ignored. See García de la Fuente, "Liturgias de entrada," 269–70.

69. See more on this below on p. 37.

70. Hossfeld, "Nachlese," 144–45.

אָג֣וּרָה בְ֭אָהָלְךָ עוֹלָמִ֑ים	61:5a	Let me sojourn in your tent forever!
אֶ֖חֱסֶ֥ה בְסֵ֖תֶר כְּנָפֶ֣יךָ	61:5b	Let me find refuge under the cover of your wings!

Both instances of גור are imperfects with the same modal force as in Ps 15:1. These may be what Waltke and O'Connor call either the "non-perfective of capability" or "non-perfective of permission."[71] Psalm 5:5 explicitly focuses on "being with YHWH." To be in the tent of YHWH or on his holy mountain is not merely to be in a place called the tabernacle, the temple, or the temple mount. Rather, it is being *with YHWH*.

While in Ps 5:5 the psalmist states that evil may not stay with YHWH,[72] in Ps 61:5 the psalmist is seeking permission to do so for himself because of the security that being with YHWH involves. This highlights an aspect of the conceptual world of the Psalter that enriches our reading of Psalm 15. The second line of Ps 61:5 specifies the meaning of the first. Sojourning in the tent of YHWH is about seeking refuge in YHWH's protection.[73]

This also applies to another key parallel. It is common to treat the tent in Ps 15:1 as a poetic term for the temple, a sort of archaism warranted given the similar language in Ps 27:4–5:[74]

אַחַ֤ת שָׁאַ֣לְתִּי מֵֽאֵת־יְהוָה֮	4a	One thing I ask of YHWH,
אוֹתָ֪הּ אֲבַ֫קֵּ֥שׁ	4b	That thing I seek,
שִׁבְתִּ֣י בְּבֵית־יְ֭הוָה	4c	That I dwell in the house of YHWH
כָּל־יְמֵ֣י חַיַּ֑י	4d	all the days of my life,
לַחֲז֥וֹת בְּנֹֽעַם־יְהוָ֗ה	4e	To see the kindness of YHWH
וּלְבַקֵּ֥ר בְּהֵיכָלֽוֹ׃	4f	and to investigate in his temple.
כִּ֤י יִצְפְּנֵ֨נִי ׀ בְּסֻכֹּה֮ בְּי֪וֹם רָ֫עָ֥ה	5a	For he will hide me in a shelter on the day of trouble,
יַ֭סְתִּרֵנִי בְּסֵ֣תֶר אָהֳל֑וֹ	5b	He will hide me in the secrecy of his tent,
בְּ֝צ֗וּר יְרוֹמְמֵֽנִי	5c	On the rock he will lift me.

This parallel clarifies two details. First, the tent of YHWH and the temple are directly linked. The "house of YHWH" (בְּבֵית־יְהוָה), "his temple"

---

71. *IBHS* §31.4.c, d. They prefer the latter modal use of the imperfect for Ps 15:1, but in relationship to God permission and ability are sometimes inextricably linked.

72. Evil is not hypostasized here. Instead, the deeds stand for those who perform evil deeds. The adjective רַע may refer to evil persons or evil in the abstract (*HALOT* 1250).

73. So also Avishur, "Psalm XV," 125. He remarks that the question could be rephrased: "Who is worthy of dwelling in the *protection* of the Almighty?" (italics his).

74. Goldingay, *Psalms*, 1:220; Broyles, *Psalms*, 91; Hossfeld, "Nachlese," 145; Hossfeld and Zenger, *Die Psalmen I*, 106.

(הֵיכָלוֹ), and "his tent" (אָהֳלוֹ) all seem to refer to the same place. This supports seeing the referent of the tent on YHWH's holy mountain as the temple in Jerusalem. But why speak of the temple in Jerusalem as a tent?

Anderson argues that the reference to the tent in Ps 15:1 is not an archaism but rather a reflection of the tent tradition in Israel.[75] Terrien points out that this tent tradition may have included a number of tents in which YHWH resided (1 Chr 17:5).[76] However, the tent as a location is not the focus, per se. Instead, its resident is the focus.

In light of Psalm 27, YHWH's presence in the tent makes it a place of safety. It is a place of refuge, a place of shelter on the day of trouble, and a place to hide.[77] The metaphorical association underlying the parallelism may be expressed as follows: YHWH'S TENT is A SAFE PLACE.[78] YHWH's tent is a desirable place to be, a haven from the dangerous world outside. Other references to the tent of YHWH likewise point in the direction of a place of refuge from one's enemies. Psalm 27:6 speaks of this tent as a place where the psalmist offers sacrifices and his head is lifted above his enemies. Psalm 78:60 provides the foil. There YHWH withdraws his dwelling, and therefore his protective favor, from Israel. He lets his tent at Shiloh be given over to foreign capture and his people to foreign domination. When YHWH is in his tent, it is a safe place and his people are safe, but when he withdraws his presence he withdraws his protection.[79]

The positive association with YHWH's tent undergirds the instruction of Psalm 15. The reader is motivated to righteous living by the promise of being with YHWH. However, this image is not univocal. In the Hebrew Bible the tent of YHWH refers first to the tent of meeting, the temporary structure in the Exodus narratives that is designed for worship and for YHWH to meet with Moses during Israel's wanderings in the desert (Exod 33:7–11). In Exodus, when Moses enters the tent of meeting to be with YHWH a cloud descends on the tent. This image evokes awe and wonder, if not fear. But does this tent tradition underly the text of Psalm 15? To decide that question we must complete the parallelism in Ps 15:1.

---

75. Anderson, *The Book of Psalms*, 1:137.

76. Terrien, *The Psalms*, 170.

77. Clements suggests that the tent image may involve an image of hospitality or of protection ("Worship and Ethics," 90). On construing Psalm 15 in terms of hospitality, see Manahan, "The Worshiper's Approach to God," 68.

78. I follow the convention of representing metaphors using all capital letters used in Lakoff and Johnson, *Metaphors We Live By* and Lakoff and Turner, *More than Cool Reason*.

79. YHWH's tent is not always a safe place.

As noted above, in the move from the first to the second parts of the double question we observe an intensification, particularly in the verb, since שׁכן usually connotes a more permanent settling—though it is also used of less permanent dwelling.[80] The reference to הַר קָדְשֶׁךָ ("your holy mountain") provides more firm ground. This phrase unmistakably moves the image to a permanent dwelling, for mountains do not normally move.

The metaphorical-conceptual background to the holy mountain is wrapped up in a series of phrases found in Pss 15:1c and 24:3ab: "on your holy mountain" (בְּהַר קָדְשֶׁךָ, Ps 15:1), "on the mountain of YHWH" (בְּהַר־יְהוָה, Ps 24:3), and "his holy place" (בִּמְקוֹם קָדְשׁוֹ, Ps 24:3). I will explore the latter two phrases in chapter 3.

In the MT text of the Psalter, occurrences of הַר and קֹדֶשׁ in a construct relationship clarifies the metaphorical-conceptual background of Psalm 15. Based on cases involving some modifier to describe this mountain, it is identified as:

1. Zion or Jerusalem (Pss 2:6; 48:2; 87:1),
2. a place from which Yahweh speaks or a source of knowledge of him (Ps 3:5),
3. the dwelling place of Yahweh (Ps 43:3),
4. a place of refuge (Pss 43:3; 48:2), and
5. a place of worship (Pss 43:3; 99:9).

This varied picture betrays the complex of ideas represented by Zion theology. J. J. M. Roberts states that this theology includes a notion of YHWH as the great king and his choice of Zion as the place for his dwelling.[81] All the associations above accord with the notion that YHWH has chosen Zion as his abode. The holy mountain is the focus of Yahweh's presence among his people, a feature that was central to the covenant relationship (Exod 29:45–46). Among other benefits, that presence involved security for Zion and for those who dwell there.[82]

This accords with two important studies on the metaphorical world of the Psalter. Jerome Creach argues convincingly that the metaphor of "refuge" represents an editorial interest throughout the Psalter. The effect of the Psalter's editorial arrangement is to encourage "readers to seek refuge in Yahweh, that is, to choose the eternal king as a source of protection and sustenance vis-à-vis human power."[83] He further claims that "'refuge' is central

---

80. *HALOT* 1497–98.
81. Roberts, "Zion in the Theology of the Davidic-Solomonic Empire," 94.
82. Ibid.
83. Creach, *Yahweh as Refuge*, 17–18.

to the shape of the Psalter, both in the general sense of the 'thought world' of the book and in the more specific sense of literary structure."[84] Creach notes that the comment on YHWH as refuge is linked to YHWH in his temple, and this link between refuge and the temple is made elsewhere in the Psalms (e.g., Pss 5:7, 11; 36:7-8).[85]

William Brown picks up on Creach's observations and suggests that two iconic metaphors, that of "refuge" and "pathway," are "constitutive of the Psalter's theological shape."[86] He further notes the connection between the two:

> These two motifs help define the Psalter's deep structure. The didactic dimension, connoted by "pathway," is contextualized within the sacred parameters of "refuge," concretized by Zion. At the same time, "refuge," via "pathway," constitutes the *telos* of learning and moral conduct, as well as the *locus* of divine presence and activity. Together they evoke a powerful setting for the praxis of faithful living, for righteousness and reverence, obedience and worship.[87]

Brown connects this convergence of metaphors in the so-called entrance liturgies in Pss 15:1 and 24:3; those seeking to dwell on God's "holy hill" find security in righteousness.[88]

To summarize, the holy mountain in the Psalter is often associated with refuge. The metaphor may be described as follows: YHWH'S MOUNTAIN is A SAFE PLACE. In the Hebrew Bible as a whole this metaphor is far from univocal. The mountain of Exodus 19 is YHWH's preeminent mountain, the place where he establishes a covenant with Israel. There YHWH is present with his people, but the connotations of *that* mountain are entirely different. It is a place of terror, where YHWH asks Moses to instruct the people to keep their distance out of fear of death (Exod 19:12-13; cf. Deut 5:23-27). The people observe in terror as YHWH descends like fire on the mountain (Exod 19:18).

In a transformation of the literary form found in Psalm 15, Isa 33:14-16 offers a perspective on the presence of YHWH that matches the Sinai tradition:

---

84. Ibid., 19.
85. Ibid., 30.
86. Brown, *Seeing the Psalms*, 16.
87. Ibid., 50. Italics his.
88. Ibid., 27. Creach notes that one interesting development of the metaphor of "refuge" is that *tôrâ* is pictured as a kind of refuge, most notably in Psalm 119 *(Yahweh as Refuge, 69)*.

פָּחֲדוּ בְצִיּוֹן חַטָּאִים	14a	Sinners tremble in Zion,
אָחֲזָה רְעָדָה חֲנֵפִים	14b	trembling seizes godless ones,
מִי יָגוּר לָנוּ אֵשׁ אוֹכֵלָה	14c	"Who among us may sojourn in the consuming fire?
מִי־יָגוּר לָנוּ מוֹקְדֵי עוֹלָם׃	14d	Who among us may sojourn on the everlasting hearth?"

Walter Brueggemann suggests Isaiah is representing the same question we encounter in Pss 15:1 and 24:3 but with a much harsher tone.[89] The referent is the same, namely the presence of YHWH, but the association is different. Both use the same verb, גור, but in Isaiah the "sojourning" takes place in "the consuming fire" (אֵשׁ אוֹכֵלָה) and at "the everlasting hearth" (מוֹקְדֵי עוֹלָם). Some have suggested that this fire refers to the coals on the altar.[90] However, an explanation for the fire is closer at hand. YHWH reveals his purpose to arise and be exalted in verse 10. This involves judgment.[91] Surprisingly in verses 11–12 this judgment is actually the result of the wicked person's own doing: "You conceive chaff, you give birth to straw, your breath is a fire that will consume you (אֵשׁ תֹּאכַלְכֶם). And the peoples will be the burnings of lime, thorns cut off—they are burned in the fire." The sinners speaking in verse 14 fear the fire of YHWH's judgment, and they know they cannot endure it.[92] Their question expresses despair.

Does the despair in Isaiah 33 underlie Psalm 15? The surface of the text suggests a positive association. However, the psalm asks, "Who may dwell in YHWH's place?" The question itself implies that some may and some may not. Psalm 15 does not refer to those who may not, though it is likely not far from the mind of the ancient Israelite familiar with the Sinai tradition (cf. Deut 4:33; 5:23–27).

To summarize what we have seen to this point, the metaphorical frame of Psalm 15 begins with a question, who may be in YHWH's place? The assumption is that the worshipper *wants* to be in this place, for, as our analysis of the metaphorical-conceptual world of the Psalter makes clear, YHWH'S PLACE is A SAFE PLACE.

The second half of the metaphorical frame in Ps 15:5cd shifts the image to a pathway. The one who performs righteous deeds as those presented

---

89. Brueggemann, *Isaiah 1–39*, 263.

90. Gunkel, "Jesaia 33," 193.

91. John Goldingay points out the verbal link here with Isa 29:6 and 30:27, 30, where the consuming fire is one of judgment and not the fire on the altar (*Isaiah*, 189).

92. Clements, *Isaiah 1–39*, 268; Goldingay, *Isaiah*, 189–90, construes the question in Isaiah as an acknowledgement from the people that they cannot keep the prescription of Psalm 15. We cannot escape the association with Exodus 19, where YHWH instructs Moses to set up boundaries to prevent the people from ascending the mountain (v. 12) and where fire is the visible representation of God's terrifying presence (v. 18).

in verses 2–5b[93] is rewarded with a sure foot: "he will not be made to stagger forever" (לֹא יִמּוֹט לְעוֹלָם).[94] Most occurrences of the root מוט in the MT are found in the Psalter. The verb describes a slipping foot when combined with רֶגֶל or פַּעַם (see Deut 32:35), but when negated it has an abstract connotation of security and dependability.[95] No foot is mentioned here, but it does not need to be. On a February day in Chicago when I say to my wife, "I slipped outside," I need not specify that it is actually my foot that slipped on the ice. In a time and place where people journeyed on foot over rocky ground, sure feet were needed to travel safely from one place to the next. Therefore the image of the pathway may be introduced simply by the use of this term. However, slipping in the metaphorical sense may have multiple interpretations.

According to Goldingay, the verb here commends persistence in righteous living.[96] The one who does "these things" does not slip from the pathway he is on. In this understanding, Ps 15:5cd simply affirms that such a person is not distracted from the path of life he has chosen or does not fail. However, this interpretation suggests that Ps 15:5cd is simply expressing a tautology: "he who does these things always does these things." It would add nothing to the psalm. Furthermore, the connotation of security is far more common in other occurrences of this term. In Prov 10:30 the word occurs in a comparison of the righteous who are not shaken (צַדִּיק לְעוֹלָם בַּל־יִמּוֹט) and the wicked who may not dwell in the land. In Ps 16:8 the psalmist is confident because of YHWH's presence with him: "Because he is at my right hand I will not be shaken" (כִּי מִימִינִי בַּל־אֶמּוֹט). In Ps 21:8[7] the king is secure to the extent that he trusts in YHWH: "The king trusts in YHWH, and by the steadfast love of the Most High he is not shaken" (וּבְחֶסֶד עֶלְיוֹן בַּל־יִמּוֹט). However, Ps 17:5 seems to support Goldingay's interpretation:[97]

| תָּמֹךְ אֲשֻׁרַי בְּמַעְגְּלוֹתֶיךָ | 17:5a | My steps hold fast to your tracks, |
| בַּל־נָמוֹטּוּ פְעָמָי׃ | 17:5b | My feet are not shaken. |

Broadly speaking this seems to be simple synonymous parallelism; the psalmist says he does not deviate from the pathway of YHWH. However, the second half of the parallelism may also involve a double entendre. In addition to affirming the psalmist's reliability in doing good, it explicates

---

93. So Hossfeld and Zenger, *Die Psalmen I*, 107; Auffret, "YHWH, qui séjournera en ta tente?" 150.

94. For this gloss of מוט, see *HALOT* 555.

95. Van Pelt and Kaiser, "מוט (*môṭ* I)," 865.

96. Goldingay, *Psalms*, 1:223.

97. Ibid.

the outcome of walking in the tracks of YHWH: his feet do not slip, he experiences sure-footedness. In abstract terms, he is secure. However, we must acknowledge that this abstract use of the verb poses a challenge to the security interpretation of מוט in Ps 15:5d. This parallelism in Ps 17:5 stands at the end of a sequence of declarations starting in Ps 17:3 affirming the moral dependability of the psalmist.

However, is moral dependability the intended connotation of מוט in Ps 15:5? Except for Goldingay, commentators unanimously interpret the verb מוט here to refer to some kind of security, whether it is security on Mt. Zion,[98] security in the temple,[99] security in dwelling with YHWH,[100] a secure life in general,[101] or a lack of misfortune.[102] Gross and Reinelt note that in offering such security the final line goes beyond the initial question in verse 1, which anticipates access to the temple.[103] However, once we recognize the metaphorical-conceptual background of the question as permitting access to a SAFE PLACE, then the concluding benefit restates the import of the initial question in terms of the pathway.[104] This may also imply that the security of Zion extends to the righteous person even when he is not physically present on Zion.[105] In any case, Ps 15:5d creates a thematic or conceptual inclusion with 15:1bc.

In summary, the metaphorical frame of Psalm 15 incorporates the two constitutive metaphors of the Psalter's conceptual world identified by Brown:[106]

1. YHWH is A SAFE PLACE and
2. A RIGHTEOUS LIFE is A SAFE PATH.

Refuge and pathway thus converge in Psalm 15 to create a context for the ethical life. Character involves two conceptions of the good life: being in the presence of YHWH (and therefore refuge in the presence of YHWH) and in his righteous pathway (and therefore in a secure place). What kind of character is needed to enjoy this good life? To answer those questions we must analyze the ethical concerns expressed in the answer in verses 2–5b.

---

98. Briggs, *Psalms*, 1:115.
99. Broyles, *Psalms*, 95.
100. VanGemeren, *Psalms*, 185.
101. Gerstenberger, *Psalms: Part 1*, 87; Miller, "Poetic Ambiguity and Balance in Psalm 15," 424.
102. Dahood, *Psalms I, 1–50*, 85; Anderson, *The Book of Psalms*, 1:139–40.
103. Gross and Reinelt, *Das Buch der Psalmen*, 86.
104. So Avishur, "Psalm XV," 126.
105. Zenger, "Geld als Lebensmittel?" 89.
106. See p. 40 above.

Portraits of the Righteous in the Psalms

THE ETHICAL CONCERNS OF THE ANSWER (VV. 2–5B)

Since Gunkel some interpreters have suggested that Psalm 15 includes a "decalogue" of ethical descriptors.[107] Craigie explains that ten items were chosen so that a person may tick off one for each finger as he recites the psalm, like the Decalogue.[108] However, we may identify eleven elements,[109] as we have seen in Barré's structural analysis above on p. 28.

The number of items is secondary to the question of the ethical concerns represented in the answer in Ps 15:2–5b. The concerns span general statements and specific cases, conduct and speech, inner attitudes and outward behavior. The result is a fundamentally social ethical vision: A righteous life is characterized by upright relationships with one's fellows.

General Sketch of the Righteous (v. 2)

Psalm 15:2 begins its character sketch of the righteous with a series of three participles that draw the outlines of a life of integrity:

הוֹלֵךְ תָּמִים	2a	He walks with integrity
וּפֹעֵל צֶדֶק	2b	And does righteousness
וְדֹבֵר אֱמֶת בִּלְבָבוֹ׃	2c	And speaks truth in his heart.

Three participles highlight the habitual pattern of life of the acceptable worshipper.[110] The first line introduces the image of the pathway. This is reinforced by the first term in verse 2a, הוֹלֵךְ, "he walks." The collocation הוֹלֵךְ תָּמִים occurs only here, but the adjective תָּמִים is used in association with the root הלך in several passages to express the image of the pathway. Genesis 6:9b describes Noah: "Noah was ... blameless (תָּמִים) in his generation; Noah walked (הִתְהַלֶּךְ) with God." This brief description of Noah combines the root צדק with תָּמִים and the root הלך, all of which are found in Ps 15:2. Genesis 17:1b likewise presents YHWH's demands to Abraham using the adjective תָּמִים and the root הלך: "I am El Shaddai, walk (הִתְהַלֵּךְ) before me and be blameless (תָּמִים)." Within the poetical books this connection is made even more frequently. A close parallel is found in the Psalter, in Ps 84:12[11]:

---

107. Gunkel, *Die Psalmen*, 49.

108. So Craigie, *Psalms 1–50*, 150–51.

109. Miller, "Poetic Ambiguity and Balance in Psalm 15," 417. Avishur notes a rabbinic tradition identifying eleven elements ("Psalm XV," 127).

110. *BHRG* §20.3; Joüon §121.

כִּי שֶׁמֶשׁ וּמָגֵן יְהוָה אֱלֹהִים	12a	For a sun and a shield is YHWH God
חֵן וְכָבוֹד יִתֵּן יְהוָה	12b	Favor and honor YHWH gives
לֹא יִמְנַע־טוֹב	12c	He does not withhold good
לַהֹלְכִים בְּתָמִים׃	12d	from those who walk in blamelessness.

Those who walk the pathway of תָמִים enjoy the favor and protection of YHWH. In addition to הלך, the noun דֶּרֶךְ connects תָמִים with the pathway metaphor. Psalm 101:2 and 6 include the phrase בְּדֶרֶךְ תָּמִים "in the way of blamelessness."[111] Two verses may shed light on the meaning of this collocation. First, Psalm 119:1 relates the way of the blameless to Torah:

אַשְׁרֵי תְמִימֵי־דָרֶךְ	1a	Blessed are the blameless of way
הַהֹלְכִים בְּתוֹרַת יְהוָה׃	1b	Who walk in the torah of YHWH.

Proverbs 28:18 compares the end of the blameless to the one who rejects this way:

הוֹלֵךְ תָּמִים יִוָּשֵׁעַ	18a	He who walks in blamelessness is saved
וְנֶעְקַשׁ דְּרָכַיִם יִפּוֹל בְּאֶחָת׃	18b	The one who walks in crooked paths will fall at once.

Psalm 15:2a may not explain how one walks blamelessly, but it connects Psalm 15 to a tradition of picturing the pattern of life, the pathway of the individual, as the key to experiencing refuge in the presence of YHWH.

The second line describes the righteous person doing what is right (פֹּעַל צֶדֶק). This collocation is unique in the MT, though the wicked in Ps 5:6[5] are said to do sin (פֹּעֲלֵי אָוֶן) and are therefore unable to stand before YHWH.[112] The synonymous verb עשה occurs in Isa 64:4[5] (עֹשֵׂה צֶדֶק) with the parallel line, "in your ways they remember you" (בִּדְרָכֶיךָ יִזְכְּרוּךָ), suggesting covenantal associations. Likewise in Ps 119:121 the psalmist declares that he has done justice and righteousness (עָשִׂיתִי מִשְׁפָּט וָצֶדֶק). Deuteronomy 16:20 commends the pursuit of צֶדֶק as the way to life. Although in that text justice involves a legal dimension, the broader concept of justice in the Pentateuch also includes just weights and measures (Lev 19:36; Deut 25:15) and right sacrifices (Deut 33:19). Thus the term concerns a spectrum of theological and social matters. The collocation פֹּעַל צֶדֶק appears generally to describe right conduct in the context of covenant fidelity.

The third line isolates speech. Although אֱמֶת is often paired with חֶסֶד and has a semantic range that includes notions of constancy and

---

111. The root הלך also occurs in both verses.
112. Maloney, "A Portrait of the Righteous Person," 154.

trustworthiness,[113] here it is the object of a verb for speaking. This implies that אֱמֶת refers either to the *content* of speech or the faithful *manner* of speech.[114] And yet the speaking is done בִּלְבָבוֹ. In a footnote, Miller discusses the possible ways to understand this prepositional relationship.[115] He cites four possibilities:

1. "in his heart," meaning "the innermost stirrings of thought and will, which should be true and reliable."[116] Such an interpretation is suggested by the consistent use of the root אמר with לֵב (see Gen 8:21; 17:17; 1 Sam 27:1; Isa 47:10) and the fact that Deut 8:17 and 9:4 speak of a heart that is not true to YHWH.

2. "from his heart," meaning one speaks the truth as one knows it, which Miller suggests fits the context and various uses of the Qal participle דֹּבֵר with nouns such as תָּמִים, אֱמֶת, and others, often in social situations (see Amos 5:10); he also suggests that it matches the use of the root דבר with אֱמֶת for moral instruction (Zech 8:16).[117]

3. "with his heart," that is in an instrumental sense, or

4. "(that is) in his heart," such as in 2 Chr 32:31 (referring to אֱמֶת).

Miller doubts we can have certainty on the question. However, option 4 seems inappropriate here and is hard to distinguish from option 2. It is hard to imagine how option 3 works—is the inner self a *means* of speaking? His example of option 2 in Zech 8:16 suggests a correspondence to option 1 when the context of verse 17 is taken into account:

אֵלֶּה הַדְּבָרִים אֲשֶׁר תַּעֲשׂוּ דַּבְּרוּ אֱמֶת אִישׁ אֶת־רֵעֵהוּ אֱמֶת וּמִשְׁפַּט שָׁלוֹם
שִׁפְטוּ בְּשַׁעֲרֵיכֶם: וְאִישׁ אֶת־רָעַת רֵעֵהוּ אַל־תַּחְשְׁבוּ בִּלְבַבְכֶם וּשְׁבֻעַת
שֶׁקֶר אַל־תֶּאֱהָבוּ כִּי אֶת־כָּל־אֵלֶּה אֲשֶׁר שָׂנֵאתִי נְאֻם־יְהוָה:

> These are the things that you shall do: speak faithfulness each with his friend, render faithfulness and judgment of peace in your gates. And do not let a man think up evil to his neighbor in your hearts and do not love a false oath, for all these things I hate, the declaration of YHWH.

---

113. *HALOT* 68–69.

114. I am indebted to my doctoral mentor Dr. Daniel I. Block for pointing out that אֱמֶת could be functioning as an adverbial accusative.

115. Miller, "Poetic Ambiguity and Balance in Psalm 15," 420 n. 13.

116. Cf. Kraus, *Psalms 1–59*, 229.

117. So Dahood, *Psalms I, 1–50*, 83; apparently Craigie follows this interpretation since he emphasizes the source of speech as the heart (*Psalms 1–50*, 151).

Psalm 15

The ambiguity may be resolved by noting that Ps 15:2c actually combines options 1 and 2, picturing speech proceeding from the innermost being of a person that reflects a fidelity from the inside out.[118] What he speaks in his heart he speaks with his mouth. The line describes consistency between the interior and exterior of a person. Such a person does not plot evil toward his neighbor while at the same time speaking peace (such as in Ps 41:7-8[6-7]).[119]

Kraus rightly notes generally verse 2 describes the exemplary character of a person whose life is above reproach.[120] But does this mean a sinless character? VanGemeren insists this is not the case, but rather that a life of תָּמִים is a moral way of life that seeks to please God.[121] Psalm 15:2 may not speak specifically to this question, but it emphasizes that the pathway, the course of a person's life, affects whether one can enjoy the safe place with YHWH.

Specific Cases 1 (v. 3)

The character sketch becomes more specific in verse 3. The first set of specific cases all concern matters of social concern, including speech (v. 3a and c) and conduct (v. 3b).[122]

The first specific case poses a significant interpretive challenge. Along with most English translations, VanGemeren renders this phrase, "he does not slander with his tongue," citing "to slander" as the usual meaning of רָגַל in the Qal.[123] Rashi notes the use of this verb meaning "slander" in 2 Sam 19:28[27].[124] Merrill suggests that the verb used for slandering in Ps 15:3 (רָגַל) may indicate the secretive nature of such speech.[125] In contrast, Goldingay doubts that the verb ever means this and points rather to its use in regard to spying, thus associating the phrase with plotting with one's tongue,

---

118. Cf. the concentric structure of fidelity to YHWH described in Deut 6:5. See Block, "How Many is God?" 87.

119. So also Goldingay, *Psalms*, 1:221; VanGemeren, Psalms, 183. Akin to this is the suggestion of Hossfeld and Zenger that Prov 15:28 provides a parallel in which the righteous ponders his words before speaking in contrast to the wicked who gush evil (*Die Psalmen I*, 107).

120. Kraus, *Psalms 1–59*, 229.

121. VanGemeren, *Psalms*, 182–83.

122. Kraus, *Psalms 1–59*, 230.

123. VanGemeren, *Psalms*, 183. So also *HALOT* 1184.

124. Rashi, *Rashi's Commentary on Psalms*, 225.

125. Merrill, "רָגַל (*rāgal*)," 1046–47.

Portraits of the Righteous in the Psalms

or "he has not gone about talking."[126] Dahood suggests the verb רָגַל derives from the noun רֶגֶל, thus rendering the phrase "trip over his tongue."[127] The LXX renders this clause ὃς οὐκ ἐδόλωσεν ἐν γλώσσῃ αὐτοῦ, "Who has not falsified with his tongue." Such a rendering construes this as speaking falsehood, which may be a translation influenced by verse 2c. Hossfeld notes that this rare phrase also occurs in Sirach 5:14,[128] where the first line reads: אל תקרא בעל שתים ובלשונך אל תרגל רע.[129] This verse exhibits several verbal parallels to Ps 15:3, including negated finite forms,[130] the same verb root, רגל, and a prepositional phrase with לָשׁוֹן with a pronominal suffix.[131] The verbal link between the two texts is strong. However, the parallel may not offer a decisive solution. Against Dahood, Anderson argues that this means "who does not go about (with slander) on his lips," citing the Sirach parallel as well as Ps 101:5, where the verb form לשׁן is used of slander offered in secret.[132] The LXX renders Sirach 5:14, Μὴ κληθῇς ψίθυρος καὶ τῇ γλώσσῃ σου μὴ ἐνέδρευε, "Do not call out the slanderous and do not plot/lie in wait with your tongue." The NRSV renders the verse, "Do not be called double-tongued and do not lay traps with your tongue." This parallel affirms what we already know from the mention of the tongue in Ps 15:3a, that this concerns a verbal sin. However, does it describe someone who is clumsy with his words or who is double-tongued? The exact connotation of this phrase may remain obscure to us. I have tentatively translated it with the traditional "slander" because the imagery and parallels noted by interpreters[133] may suggest the careless nature of such words. The only certain conclusion is that it concerns speech, and speech involves social relationships.

The second specific case clarifies the social focus of this series. Fortunately this case involves less obscure language—a righteous person does no evil to his friend (לֹא־עָשָׂה לְרֵעֵהוּ רָעָה). This clearly parallels verse 2b, where

---

126. Goldingay, *Psalms*, 1:221.

127. Dahood, *Psalms I, 1–50*, 84. He notes the penchant for this in both Ugaritic and Hebrew, citing Ps 39:2, which speaks of stumbling over the tongue. So also Miller, "Poetic Ambiguity and Balance in Psalm 15," 423.

128. Hossfeld and Zenger, *Die Psalmen I*, 107.

129. Beentjes, *The Book of Ben Sira in Hebrew*, 27.

130. The two differ in aspect and person. However, this can be explained as the differing generic context. Psalm 15:3a is part of a third-person character sketch while Sirach 5:14 is part of a series of second-person exhortations using אל plus the jussive form.

131. Note the difference in preposition.

132. Anderson, *The Book of Psalms*, 1:138.

133. Hossfeld and Zenger suggest that the rash tongue of the wicked in Prov 15:28 is the foil here, echoed in the confidence of the wicked in the power of their tongues in Ps 12:3–5 (*Die Psalmen I*, 107).

the righteous do what is right, but the "beneficiary" here is the friend. Goldingay rightly notes that the scandalous nature of doing evil to one's friend is highlighted by the similar morphology of the words for evil and friend (both containing רעה).[134] Hossfeld points out that this line serves as a counterpoint to Ps 14:1, 3, for there no one does good.[135]

The character sketch returns to a verbal sin in verse 3c; the righteous person does not "raise a taunt against his neighbor" (וְחֶרְפָּה לֹא־נָשָׂא עַל־קְרֹבוֹ). Again the issue is social, concerning the well-being of one near to the righteous. Although the play on words of verse 3b is not repeated in verse 3c, we cannot escape the irony. If רגל refers to slander uttered in private, a taunt or "reviling" (חֶרְפָּה) is a direct public affront.[136] Terrien interprets this verse differently from most commentators. Instead of identifying the חֶרְפָּה as something one levels against another, Terrien sees this as shame brought upon one's kinship unit, translating "brings no opprobium to his family." Misdeeds reflect on the family, and righteousness entails responsibility to "collective solidarity."[137] The root נשא and the noun חֶרְפָּה may signify "to bear shame" based on Jer 15:15, 31:19, Ezek 36:15, and Ps 69:8. This may even be the usual connotation of the collocation. However, because Ps 15:3c is parallel to Ps 15:3b, where the righteous do not do evil to another, it seems best to take this verse as referring to a taunt or disgrace that one person heaps on another. To be sure, such behavior could bring shame to one's family, as Terrien notes, but this does not seem to be the point of Ps 15:3c.

So far the character sketch of Psalm 15 has focused mostly on issues of outward behavior, particularly in reference to social relationships. But social relationships proceed from interior dispositions, as we see in the next verse.

Inner Attitudes (v. 4ab)

In Ps 15:4ab the righteous are depicted as maintaining a proper orientation toward the righteous and the wicked.[138] This verse gains clarity in the second line. In the first line two Niphal participles occur with an intervening prepositional phrase. Commentators and modern translations tend to

---

134. Goldingay, *Psalms*, 1:221.
135. Hossfeld and Zenger, *Die Psalmen I*, 107.
136. *HALOT* 356.
137. Terrien, *The Psalms*, 168.
138. In order to maintain the number 10 as the number of conditions, commentators such as Craigie must treat Ps 15:4ab as one condition even though it is a bicolon (*Psalms 1–50*, 152).

assume that the second participle functions as the subject of the first,[139] as I have translated it. However, either participle may function as the subject because the two terms are virtually synonymous and grammatically identical. Kraus plausibly suggests that נִמְאָס refers to the person hated/rejected by YHWH.[140] Jeremiah 6:20 applies the same Niphal participle to the "silver" rejected by YHWH in the refining judgment of his people (cf. v. 27). While this cannot be determinative, it suggests that the first participle functions as the predicate of the clause. In any case, here the righteous make moral judgments distinguishing between the righteous and the wicked. Terrien sees the potentially scandalous nature of this bicolon,[141] but two things should be borne in mind. First, this bicolon emphasizes loyalty to YHWH, not to one's own social preferences.[142] Second, the response to the wicked is an inner attitude, while the righteous actively honor those who fear YHWH. It is surely significant that the otherwise mainly horizontal conditions of the answer incorporate a pair of conditions that concern a vertical relationship, namely that one's social relationships are shaped by the attitude of YHWH himself.

Specific Cases 2 (vv. 4c–5b)

The counterpart to the general social orientation in verse 3 is a series of cases set in a particular social setting in verses 4c–5b, namely the legal and economic concerns of the community. As noted above,[143] Ps 15:4c declares that the righteous person exhibits an unswerving commitment to keeping oaths.[144] Although we cannot be certain of the intended force of this text, it likely means the righteous keep oaths even if it results in their own harm. However, clearly the core ethical concern is for truthful speech, specifically giving oaths and fulfilling those oaths.[145] What matters is not strictly the truth value of the locution of the oath but rather its enactment by the one who swears. The oft-cited background for this condition is Lev 5:4, where a

---

139. So Lunn, *Word-Order Variation*, 297. This is consistent with the judgment that Hebrew canonical word order is Verb-Subject-Object (ibid., 4–5).

140. Kraus, *Psalms 1–59*, 230.

141. Terrien, *The Psalms*, 171.

142. Broyles, *Psalms*, 94.

143. See p. 25.

144. *HALOT* 1397.

145. Craigie, *Psalms 1–50*, 213. Yael Ziegler notes that this psalm does not mention the name in which the oath is given, thus applying to all oaths (*Promises to Keep*, 42 n. 81).

rash oath may bring guilt.¹⁴⁶ However, as mentioned above, the value of this parallel is questionable. In Lev 5:4 *giving* a rash oath brings guilt, but in Ps 15:4c *keeping* an uncomfortable oath is worthy of praise.

Economic issues surface in verse 5ab. First, the righteous do not give out their money at interest. This condition distinguishes Psalm 15 from non-Israelite character sketches because the prohibition of interest was unique to the Israelite legal code.¹⁴⁷ Kraus notes the high rate of interest charged in Babylonia (33.3%) and Assyria (up to 50%),¹⁴⁸ and Goldingay notes that these kinds of high interest rates may have been in the background.¹⁴⁹ However, it is doubtful that the concern was high interest rates. In fact, the Pentateuch prohibits lending at interest at *any* interest rate in Exod 22:25, Lev 25:35–38, and Deut 23:19–20, and likewise no interest rate is mentioned in Psalm 15. While the provisions in Exodus and Leviticus single out the poverty of the borrower as the main concern, the Deuteronomic teaching isolates national solidarity within Israel, therefore permitting commercial loans to foreigners. The overriding concern seems to have been to protect the poor within Israel.¹⁵⁰ Israelites were instructed to protect fellow-Israelites who became poor, and that included lending at no interest (see Lev 25:35–36). Commentators often note the similarity of language here to the provision in Lev 25:37a:¹⁵¹ "Your silver you shall not give to him [i.e., the poor man] at interest" (אֶת־כַּסְפְּךָ לֹא־תִתֵּן לוֹ בְּנֶשֶׁךְ). The verbal link from Ps 15:5a to Lev 25:37a is quite strong considering the similarity of vocabulary and the word order: כַּסְפּוֹ לֹא־נָתַן בְּנֶשֶׁךְ. Slightly less strong, though still significant, is the verbal link to Ezek 18:8, which employs two terms for interest: בְּנֶשֶׁךְ לֹא־יִתֵּן וְתַרְבִּית. While Lev 25:37 involves a second-person command and Psalm 15 and Ezekiel 18 uses the third-person description, that is a change required by the genre of the character sketch.¹⁵² Although Ps 15:5a makes no mention of the poor, the second half of the bicolon clarifies that poverty is at the heart of the concern.

Psalm 15:5b concerns economic disparity, but this time the context is legal. The righteous person accepts no bribe to the disadvantage of the

---

146. Hossfeld and Zenger, *Die Psalmen I*, 107.

147. Neufeld, "The Prohibitions against Loans at Interest in Ancient Hebrew Laws," 359; Zenger, "Geld als Lebensmittel?" 77; Baker, *Tight Fists or Open Hands?* 254.

148. Kraus, *Psalms 1–59*, 230. See also Baker, *Tight Fists or Open Hands?* 73–74.

149. Goldingay, *Psalms*, 1:223.

150. Ibid. So also Baker, *Tight Fists or Open Hands?* 265.

151. Hossfeld and Zenger, *Die Psalmen I*, 107.

152. Hossfeld notes that another parallel can be found in Ezek 18:8, 13 ("Nachlese," 151). Ezekiel also exhibits the transformation to the third person that is appropriate to the character sketch, where the righteous person does not lend at interest (בְּנֶשֶׁךְ לֹא־יִתֵּן).

innocent. The implication is that the bribe is offered by the wealthy to pervert justice in his favor. A number of passages in the Pentateuch offer verbal parallels based on their use of the verb לקח and the noun שֹׁחַד (Exod 23:8; Deut 16:19; 27:25). Of these Deut 27:25a provides the most substantial verbal parallel: "Cursed be the one who takes a bribe to strike the life of innocent blood" (אָרוּר לֹקֵחַ שֹׁחַד לְהַכּוֹת נֶפֶשׁ דָּם נָקִי). The verb לקח in combination with שֹׁחַד is not itself noteworthy, but this is the only other occurrence of that phrase with נָקִי, "innocent," in the Hebrew Bible. Therefore Deuteronomy seems to be the background for this line.[153]

Why are lending at interest and taking bribes paired in Ps 15:5ab? The obvious answer is that the two share an economic dimension. However, since parallel texts in Isaiah and Ezekiel show that protection of the poor is a hallmark of the righteous in other character sketches, we must consider these parallels.

A CONSIDERATION OF THREE KEY PROPHETIC PARALLELS TO PSALM 15

I have argued that Psalm 15 is best seen as a character sketch, a third-person summary of characteristics of a righteous person, and that this sketch is intended to inculcate such characteristics in those who hear and recite this psalm. Form-critical studies from the time of Gunkel and Begrich and Galling have recognized important parallels in the prophets, particularly Isaiah 33:14–16, but also Ezek 18:5–8 and 22:12.[154] These parallels shed light on three aspects of Psalm 15: its literary context, the selection of ethical content, and the implied audience.

The prophetic parallels are often viewed as later transformations of the "entrance liturgy."[155] However, in light of the tenuous historical basis

---

153. So also Zenger, "Geld als Lebensmittel?" 89.

154. Gunkel and Begrich, *Introduction to Psalms*, 289; Galling, "Der Beichtspiegel," 168.

155. Koch, "Tempeleinlassliturgien und Dekaloge," 55, 58. Not all agree that Isa 33:14–16 post-dates Psalm 15. Gunkel resolves this by arguing that we simply have two instances of the same form (Gunkel, *Die Psalmen*, 47–48; Gunkel, "Jesaia 33," 192–93; so also Gerstenberger, *Psalms: Part 1*, 117), but no one seriously questions the antiquity of the form represented in the two. Interestingly, Gunkel and Begrich elsewhere recognize prophetic influence on the Psalter in the focus on ethical, rather than cultic concerns (*Introduction to Psalms*, 289) and elsewhere that the prophetic parallels show an influence of the Psalter on the prophets (ibid., 313). This last view has appeared to rule the day, with J. J. M. Roberts arguing for Isaianic dependence on Psalm 15 ("The Divine King and the Human Community," 135). Even if one rejects the Davidic superscription as late and therefore unreliable, one additional verbal echo offers a reason to

of the "entrance liturgy" theory we may question whether either Isaiah or Ezekiel should be interpreted as a didactic transformation of the "entrance liturgy" or a later manifestation of didactic discourse. Since all three passages isolate a list of qualities and behaviors that characterize the righteous or the wicked, from a purely literary perspective the label "character sketch" captures their similarities in literary form. But a more detailed comparison of these texts from a literary perspective shows that they exhibit a common metaphorical-conceptual context. All turn on questions of the people's relationship to YHWH and thus touch on life and death issues.

I have acknowledged above that we know less than we would like about the original setting of Psalm 15, which complicates comparisons to the prophetic parallels. Nonetheless, these parallels appear to have a similar didactic purpose and metaphorical-conceptual context to Psalm 15. Blenkinsopp describes Isa 33:14–16 as an "ethical catechism," which in Isaiah has been adapted to an eschatological context of final judgment.[156] As we mentioned on p. 41 above, that context is couched in more stark terms, but clearly the question is who may be with YHWH:

פָּחֲדוּ בְצִיּוֹן חַטָּאִים	14a	Sinners tremble in Zion,
אָחֲזָה רְעָדָה חֲנֵפִים	14b	trembling seizes godless ones,
מִי יָגוּר לָנוּ אֵשׁ אוֹכֵלָה	14c	"Who among us may sojourn in the consuming fire?
מִי־יָגוּר לָנוּ מוֹקְדֵי עוֹלָם׃	14d	Who among us may sojourn on the everlasting hearth?"

Isaiah 33:14 frames the question in a transformed metaphorical context, namely that YHWH is A DANGEROUS PLACE. However, the ideal of the righteous life in verse 15 is then framed by a more positive statement in verse 16. This verse serves as the counterpart to Ps 15:5cd and clearly makes the point that THE RIGHTEOUS LIFE is A SAFE PLACE:

הוּא מְרוֹמִים יִשְׁכֹּן	16a	He will dwell on the heights,
מְצָדוֹת סְלָעִים מִשְׂגַּבּוֹ	16b	Strongholds of rocks will be his refuge;
לַחְמוֹ נִתָּן	16c	His bread is given,
מֵימָיו נֶאֱמָנִים׃	16d	His water is reliable.

Therefore, Isa 33:14–16 motivates one to a righteous life not only out of fear of being consumed by fire but also with the promise of security, the carrot and the stick.

---

believe that Isaiah is adapting Psalm 15. In the question Isaiah twice employs a phrase, מִי־יָגוּר ("who may sojourn . . . ?"), that Psalm 15 employs once. Isaiah may be tying into Psalm 15:1 in a purposeful way, forgoing the punch of poetic variation in order to make an explicit link with a familiar "text."

156. Blenkinsopp, *Isaiah*, 442.

The literary context of Ezekiel 18 is different from Psalm 15, but it nonetheless employs character sketches for a didactic purpose. Gordon Matties argues that Ezekiel 18 should be understood *rhetorically* as a sermon given at the temple gates.[157] His placement of Ezekiel 18 at the temple gates is no doubt influenced by the form-critical tradition surrounding the "entrance liturgies," though, as I have shown above, this tradition does not rest on as firm a foundation as many assume.[158] Most importantly, Matties recognizes the didactic nature of Ezekiel 18, a perspective shared in general by Daniel Block. He classifies it as a disputation speech, which is evident given the quotation of a contemporary proverb in verse 2, a counter-thesis in verses 3-4, and a systematic exposition of the counter-thesis in verses 5-18.[159] This systematic exposition includes three "hypothetical case studies" illustrating the administration of justice.[160] These case studies can then be understood as analogous to the instruction of priests in Egypt identified by Weinfeld.[161] The disputation has a practical purpose, namely, to challenge each successive generation to choose righteousness and life instead of wickedness and death. This is analogous to the metaphorical-conceptual context of Psalm 15, for it assumes that A RIGHTEOUS LIFE is A SAFE PLACE.

Weinfeld also discusses the status of Psalm 15 in relationship to other character sketches. He pictures the Decalogue as a foundational expectation of all in Israel, with Psalms 15 and 24:3-6 representing the utopian ethical ideal for the especially pious who want to be near to God. Ezekiel stands between these two poles, offering both ethical and cultic definitions for the righteous.[162] We may question whether such a differentiation of levels of piety is warranted, but Weinfeld's perspective is helpful in pointing to the covenantal character of the character sketches. The Decalogue occurs within the context of a covenant ceremony in Exodus 19-20, a covenant relationship that appears to be assumed in Psalm 15. Also, the promise in Exod 20:12 // Deut 5:16 of long life in the land is analogous to the promise of security in Ps 15:5cd.

In contrast to Ezekiel 18, the literary genre of Ezekiel 22:1-12 is very different from Psalm 15. Block notes that it comes in the context of

---

157. Matties, *Ezekiel 18 and the Rhetoric of Moral Discourse*, 185.

158. I admit this may be the best explanation of the original social setting of Psalm 15, but no one can be certain.

159. Block, *Ezekiel 1-24*, 554-55.

160. Ibid., 564.

161. Ibid., 567; cf. Weinfeld, "Instructions for Temple Visitors," 232-35.

162. Weinfeld, "Instructions for Temple Visitors," 240-41.

judgment—hope for averting disaster is essentially gone.[163] It is a litany of charges, not a character sketch meant to inculcate virtue. Nonetheless, if there is hope for successive generations (as Ezekiel 18 argues), then we may infer that the next generation may learn from the indictment of their fathers. More to the point, Ezek 22:2 is full of irony when read in relationship to Psalm 15. In the Psalter Jerusalem is a place of refuge under the protection of YHWH, but in Ezek 22:2 Jerusalem is a "city of blood" (עִיר הַדָּמִים). This city, once considered a safe place, is not safe because of the wickedness of its rulers; therefore the city has lost its God-given status as a safe place vis-à-vis foreign powers and remains under threat of judgment and exile (vv. 13–16).

Blessing from YHWH is at stake in Isaiah 33 as well as Ezekiel 18 and 22. Therefore these prophetic traditions present a theological context for ethics that is continuous with Psalm 15.

These parallels also shed light on the selection of topics in Psalm 15, both in their overlap and in their departures from Psalm 15. Isaiah 33:15 mentions a similar set of ethical concerns. Although the verbal parallels are more distant, the conceptual parallels are numerous:

הֹלֵךְ צְדָקוֹת	15a	He walks in righteousness,
וְדֹבֵר מֵישָׁרִים	15b	And he speaks uprightly;
מֹאֵס בְּבֶצַע מַעֲשַׁקּוֹת	15c	He rejects the profit of extortion,
נֹעֵר כַּפָּיו מִתְּמֹךְ בַּשֹּׁחַד	15d	He shakes his hands lest they hold on to a bribe;
אֹטֵם אָזְנוֹ מִשְּׁמֹעַ דָּמִים	15e	He stops his ears from hearing of bloodshed,
וְעֹצֵם עֵינָיו מֵרְאוֹת בְּרָע׃	15f	And he closes his eyes from seeing evil.

Isaiah 33 employs participles throughout, much like Ps 15:2. Isaiah 33:15ab also expresses the same twin concern for righteous conduct and speech. Its use of the root הלך parallels Ps 15:2a, invoking the metaphor of the pathway. The inner attitudes of Ps 15:4ab are reflected in the attitude in Isa 33:15c toward extortion (both use the root מאס). Although lending at interest is not mentioned, economic concerns surface in the mention of illicit profit (v. 15c) and bribery (v. 15d).

Isaiah 33:15edf sets itself apart from Psalm 15 by using body parts to structure its description. The hands, ears, and eyes all turn from evil. Koch asserts that Ps 15:3b, "He does no evil to his friend," refers to acts of violence,[164] but the general nature of the language precludes such a specific interpretation. It probably includes violence, but it may also include other evils. On the other hand, Isa 33:15e mentions bloodshed and thus provides

---

163. Block, *Ezekiel 1–24*, 702.
164. Koch, "Tempeleinlassliturgien und Dekaloge," 47.

a more specific description of the general expression in Psalm 15. Isaiah's mention of faculties of perception (ears and eyes) is another new feature, but they likely indicate a set of ethical dispositions similar to those of Psalm 15.

In Ezekiel the most significant overlap involves the dual concern for judicial and economic justice. Lending at interest and bribery are explicit concerns in Ezek 22:12,[165] which contains three verbal parallels to Ps 15:5ab:

שֹׁחַד לָקְחוּ־בָךְ לְמַעַן שְׁפָךְ־דָּם נֶשֶׁךְ וְתַרְבִּית לָקַחַתְּ וַתְּבַצְּעִי רֵעַיִךְ בַּעֹשֶׁק וְאֹתִי שָׁכַחַתְּ נְאֻם אֲדֹנָי יְהוִה:

A bribe they have taken among you to shed blood; interest and profit you take, and you injure your friend with oppression, and me you have forgotten, the declaration of the Lord YHWH.

Although Ezek 18:8 does not mention bribery, clearly a concern for injustice is paired with a concern about lending at interest:[166]

בַּנֶּשֶׁךְ לֹא־יִתֵּן וְתַרְבִּית לֹא יִקָּח מֵעָוֶל יָשִׁיב יָדוֹ מִשְׁפַּט אֱמֶת יַעֲשֶׂה בֵּין אִישׁ לְאִישׁ:

He does not lend at interest and profit he does not take; from iniquity he turns his hand; true justice he does between man and man.

In short, Ezekiel's concern for both economic and legal justice mirrors that of Psalm 15.

Nonetheless, the differences between Psalm 15 and Ezekiel 18 and 22 are of equal interest. Ezekiel 18 is more specific about treatment of the poor (vv. 7–8, 12, 13, 16, 17) and violence (v. 10). Also, it mentions several ethical issues not mentioned in Psalm 15, namely, idolatry (vv. 5, 11, 12, 15), sexual sin (vv. 5, 11, 15), and torah obedience: "In my statutes (בְּחֻקּוֹתַי) he walks (יְהַלֵּךְ) and my judgments (וּמִשְׁפָּטַי) he keeps by doing faithfulness," שָׁמַר לַעֲשׂוֹת אֱמֶת (v. 9; cf. v. 17).[167] Ezekiel 22:1–12 likewise expresses concern about violence (vv. 2–4, 6, 9), idolatry (vv. 2–4, 9), disrespect for parents (v. 7), sabbath-breaking (v. 8), sexual sin (v. 9–11), and speaks more

---

165. Hossfeld, "Nachlese," 152; Matties, *Ezekiel 18 and the Rhetoric of Moral Discourse*, 171.

166. Weinfeld, "Instructions for Temple Visitors," 227, notes that the similarities to Ezek 18:5ff. were noted by rabbis, so this link is long-standing in the history of interpretation.

167. Note that this verse presents torah obedience in terms of the pathway metaphor.

specifically about treatment of the poor (i.e., resident aliens, orphans, and widows; v. 7).

The similarities in content between Psalm 15, Isaiah 33, and Ezekiel 18 and 22 suggest such character sketches often isolated a common set of ethical concerns. In spite of his theory of influence from the Decalogue on Psalm 15, Koch notes that the selection in Psalm 15 does not reflect the Decalogue as a whole but rather a characteristic selection.[168] Gerhard von Rad makes the same claim about Ezekiel 18.[169] However, as we have seen, the lists of what is characteristic are not identical in Psalm 15 and Ezekiel 18. Ezekiel 18 and 22 mention four items found in the Decalogue but absent from Psalm 15: idolatry, sabbath-keeping, respect for parents, and coveting the wife of one's neighbor. Weinfeld also notes that Psalms 15 and 24:3–6 lack ritual or purity requirements, something characteristic of Ezekiel 18 and 22 as well as Haggai 2 and the Egyptian inscriptions at Edfu.[170] What determined the selection of material for Psalm 15? Were social factors affecting selection, such as a prevalence of certain sins in certain time periods?[171] Or are literary factors at work? I will argue in chapter 6 that a broader literary context in the Psalter may indicate editorial factors for the selection of ethical concerns. At this stage, though, we may confidently state that while Psalm 15 bears numerous similarities with other similar character sketches in Israel's corpus of sacred texts as well as Egyptian texts, it also is characteristically non-cultic. The vertical relationship between YHWH and the worshipper depends on the horizontal relationships between the worshipper and his fellows.

One final observation on the prophetic parallels should be noted. Because of the economic ramifications of the last two conditions in Psalm 15:5ab, we may infer that the implied audience of Psalm 15 at the very least includes the social elite—anyone with sufficient means or authority within the community to lend money or to decide on judicial matters.[172] This address to the elite is explicit in Ezekiel 22, in which Ezekiel indicts the "princes of Israel" (נְשִׂיאֵי יִשְׂרָאֵל) for a failure to live up to the same ideals of justice found in Psalm 15.[173] Block notes that the juxtaposition of pericopes concerning Davidic kings in Ezekiel 17 and 19 suggests that the disputation

---

168. Koch, "Tempeleinlassliturgien und Dekaloge," 51.

169. Von Rad, "'Gerechtigkeit' und 'Leben' in der Kultsprache der Psalmen," 420.

170. Weinfeld, "Instructions for Temple Visitors," 231.

171. Answering this question is virtually impossible because of the lack of consensus on the date of Psalm 15. As is often the case, the psalm is generalized to the extent that precise dating is tenuous at best.

172. Terrien, *The Psalms*, 172.

173. Weinfeld, "Instructions for Temple Visitors," 229.

in chapter 18 concerns the trans-generational succession of Davidic kings, likewise framing the ethical discourse in terms of the social elite.[174] Is Psalm 15 similarly addressed to a royal audience? We can say confidently that the social elite are at least included in the implied audience of the psalm, but a special focus on kings is not on the surface of the text.

CONCLUSION

Psalm 15 places ethics within a relational framework. First there is the relationship between the worshipper and YHWH. The metaphorical frame of Psalm 15 assumes that people *desire* relationship with YHWH. Being with YHWH is the *telos* of the ethical life. He is the supreme ethical good, for in the presence of YHWH one finds refuge. This is because the metaphorical-conceptual assumption of verse 1bc is that YHWH is A SAFE PLACE. In addition, in verse 5cd we find that A RIGHTEOUS LIFE is A SAFE PATH. However, the YHWH-to-worshipper relationship is reinforced in the central element of the ethical answer in relationship to others, namely that the inner attitude of the righteous person shows a loyalty to YHWH (v. 4ab). But the relational framework is not only God-ward.

The answer in verses 2–5b introduces another dimension of this relational framework, namely, the relationship between the righteous person and others, particularly those in his immediate community. For the righteous person to enjoy the ethical good of relationship with YHWH he must live in a just relationship to others.[175] His general conduct, his speech, and his economic dealings are to be carried out in the interest of the other. When self-interest conflicts with the interest of the other, the interest of the other must win. However, it happens that giving priority to the interest of the other reverberates with benefit for the worshipper. Self-interest is not excluded, but it is subordinate to loving one's neighbor as a means of loving YHWH (cf. Lev 19:18; Deut 6:5).

---

174. Block, *Ezekiel 1–24*, 555.

175. Creach describes this as a "symbiotic relationship" in which the righteous seek refuge in YHWH while at the same time making that refuge real for others by their own actions (*Destiny of the Righteous*, 37).

3

Psalm 24

INTRODUCTION

Psalm 24 shares some important features with Psalm 15, but it is distinct in two respects. First, Psalm 15 stands on its own as a character sketch, but the ethical content in Ps 24:3–6 is framed by two sections focused on YHWH the Divine King (vv. 1–2 and 7–10). Second, Psalm 15 offers an extended character sketch including eleven lines of description, but Psalm 24 sketches character in only four lines (v. 4). These differences combine to give Psalm 24 its own focus and mood. What is the ethic that we find in it?

Psalm 24 presents a theocentric ethic framed by a vision of the glorious Divine King. This vision of YHWH undergirds the call for righteousness in the central section and places it in the context of entering the presence and protection of the Sovereign King. The coherence of the whole is found not in a *Sitz im Leben* but in the union of theology and ethics. As in Deut 10:12–22, YHWH's role in creation and his unparalleled might give rise to the call for moral transformation. But the link between YHWH and his worshippers in this case is not *imitatio dei*. Rather, the description of YHWH provides the theological context furnishing the ethical authority of the instruction in section two and creating a sphere in which worshippers may flourish in the presence of the Divine King, the covenant suzerain. This union of theology and ethics is the union of the metaphors of pathway and refuge. Those who are righteous (in deed and in disposition) and seek YHWH (the journey) enjoy a relationship (the destination) with the one who has the power as Sovereign Creator and Divine Warrior to provide the security that the psalmist seeks in covenant relationship.

As in the previous chapter, the goal here is to clarify the ethical concerns of Psalm 24. Therefore, my focus is on section two where the ethical content is situated. However, in the history of interpretation of this psalm, scholars have wrestled with the relationship between section two and sections one and three.[1] Yet when the connections between each of these sections are clarified, a holistic theological ethic emerges. After establishing and translating the text and identifying key issues related to literary genre and structure, the goal of this chapter is to identify the ethical concerns in section two and then clarify the theological framework in which they are situated.

TRANSLATION AND TEXT-CRITICAL ANALYSIS OF PSALM 24

The following text and translation serve as the basis for further interpretation of Psalm 24:

לְדָוִד מִזְמוֹר	1a	A psalm of David
לַיהוָה הָאָרֶץ וּמְלוֹאָהּ	1b	To YHWH belong the earth and its fullness,
תֵּבֵל וְיֹשְׁבֵי בָהּ׃	1c	the world and those who dwell in it.
כִּי־הוּא עַל־יַמִּים יְסָדָהּ	2a	For on the seas he founded it
וְעַל־נְהָרוֹת יְכוֹנְנֶהָ׃	2b	And on the rivers he established it.
מִי־יַעֲלֶה בְהַר־יְהוָה	3a	Who may ascend the mountain of the YHWH?
וּמִי־יָקוּם בִּמְקוֹם קָדְשׁוֹ׃	3b	And who may stand in his holy place?
נְקִי כַפַּיִם	4a	The one who is innocent of hands
וּבַר־לֵבָב	4b	And pure of heart,
אֲשֶׁר לֹא־נָשָׂא לַשָּׁוְא נַפְשִׁי	4c	Who has not lifted up his soul to what is false
וְלֹא נִשְׁבַּע לְמִרְמָה׃	4d	And has not sworn deceitfully.
יִשָּׂא בְרָכָה מֵאֵת יְהוָה	5a	He will take up blessing from YHWH
וּצְדָקָה מֵאֱלֹהֵי יִשְׁעוֹ׃	5b	And righteousness from the God of his salvation.

1. For simplicity I refer to the three sections of the psalm as section one (vv. 1–2), section two (vv. 3–6), and section 3 (vv. 7–10).

זֶה דּוֹר דֹּרְשָׁו	6a	This is the generation that seeks him
מְבַקְשֵׁי פָנֶיךָ אֱלֹהֵי יַעֲקֹב	6b	Who seek your face, O God of Jacob.
סֶלָה:		Selah
שְׂאוּ שְׁעָרִים רָאשֵׁיכֶם	7a	Lift up your heads, O gates
וְהִנָּשְׂאוּ פִּתְחֵי עוֹלָם	7b	And be lifted up, O ancient doors
וְיָבוֹא מֶלֶךְ הַכָּבוֹד:	7c	And the King of Glory will come in.
מִי זֶה מֶלֶךְ הַכָּבוֹד	8a	Who is this King of Glory?
יְהוָה עִזּוּז וְגִבּוֹר	8b	YHWH, powerful and mighty
יְהוָה גִּבּוֹר מִלְחָמָה:	8c	YHWH, mighty in battle
שְׂאוּ שְׁעָרִים רָאשֵׁיכֶם	9a	Lift up your heads, O gates
וּשְׂאוּ פִּתְחֵי עוֹלָם	9b	And lift them up, O ancient doors,
וְיָבֹא מֶלֶךְ הַכָּבוֹד:	9c	And the King of Glory will come in.
מִי הוּא זֶה מֶלֶךְ הַכָּבוֹד	10a	Who is this King of Glory?
יְהוָה צְבָאוֹת	10b	YHWH of Hosts,
הוּא מֶלֶךְ הַכָּבוֹד	10c	he is the King of Glory.
סֶלָה:		Selah

Note that LXX adds τῆς μιᾶς σαββάτων, "of the first of the week." This is likely an addition reflecting the liturgical use of this psalm in Jewish worship.[2]

Several Greek versions drop the כִּי that begins verse 2. While this may reflect a different manuscript tradition, the logic of the move from verse 1 to verse 2 is not altered by its absence. Therefore, I follow the MT in preserving it.

The translation of נֶפֶשׁ in verse 4 into the English "soul" is problematic. It may invoke Greek psychology in which the soul is distinct from the body. I do not intend to communicate this.[3] In the OT the word נֶפֶשׁ may be translated in various contexts as "throat," "neck," "breath," "living being," "people," "personality," "life," "soul," or "dead soul," i.e., "corpse."[4] In this context the word seems to represent the whole person or "the praying self."

---

2. See Kraus, *Psalms 1–59*, 312; Goldingay, *Psalms*, 1:356. Cf. Koch, who suggests there is no evidence of post-exilic use of this psalm as a liturgy ("Tempeleinlassliturgien und Dekaloge," 59).

3. Cf. Fredericks, "נֶפֶשׁ [nepeš]," 133.

4. *HALOT* 712–13.

In its context it may involve a notion of desire,[5] but this involves the orientation of the whole person.[6]

In verse 4 ancient witnesses vary in the form of the the pronominal suffix attached to נֶפֶשׁ. The MT has נַפְשִׁי, "my soul," while the *BHS* suggests reading נַפְשׁוֹ, "his soul," with fragments from Cairo Geniza, some Hebrew manuscripts, and other versions (Codex Alexandrinus, the Peshitta, the Vulgate).[7] To understand the MT reading, commentators often cite a parallel in Exod 20:7a (// Deut 5:11a): "You shall not lift up the name of YHWH your God to falsehood" (לֹא תִשָּׂא אֶת־שֵׁם־יְהוָה אֱלֹהֶיךָ לַשָּׁוְא).[8] This apparent parallel shares three terms and an identical clause structure with Ps 24:4: לֹא + נשׂא + לַשָּׁוְא. In this reading "my soul" supposedly substitutes for "my name," corresponding to the "name of YHWH."[9] This reading provides a way to preserve the MT as the *lectio difficilior*.[10] However, this requires understanding verse 4 to be YHWH's voice. However, as Alter points out, the question-response structure of this section does not allow for a shift from third-person description to a first person address from YHWH.[11] Also, if "my name" were intended, we may wonder why this was not written. Seremak notes that the י and ו can easily be confused, offering an explanation for the MT reading. However, he concludes that the text cannot be established on text-critical grounds alone, so he favors the MT.[12] Goldingay points to Ps 25:1, where the psalmist lifts his own soul to YHWH (אֵלֶיךָ יְהוָה נַפְשִׁי אֶשָּׂא).[13] That could hardly be referring to YHWH's name. In addition, the language of lifting one's soul to God in Ps 25:1 finds verbal echoes in Ps 86:4 (אֵלֶיךָ אֲדֹנָי נַפְשִׁי אֶשָּׂא) and 143:8 (אֵלֶיךָ נָשָׂאתִי נַפְשִׁי). The repeated use of this vocabulary suggests the collocation is a stereotyped phrase for worship, which raises the possibility that a pious scribe could have inadvertently harmonized Ps 24:4c with that language. This would account for the presence of the MT reading and make it the *lectio facilior*. The parallel language from the Decalogue introduces problems that are not easily solved. It is preferably understood

---

5. So Seebass, "נֶפֶשׁ *nepeš*," 507.

6. Cf. Block, "How Many is God?" 85–86.

7. Seremak, *Psalm 24 als Text zwischen den Texten*, 41.

8. See Anderson, *The Book of Psalms*, 1:203; Broyles, "Psalms Concerning the Liturgies of Temple Entry," 250; Goldingay, *Psalms*, 1:355. More recently, see Imes, "Psalm 24:4 and the Decalogue."

9. Imes, "Psalm 24:4 and the Decalogue," 6–7.

10. So Seremak, *Psalm 24 als Text zwischen den Texten*, 42; Goldingay, *Psalms*, 1:355; Imes, "Psalm 24:4 and the Decalogue," 1.

11. Alter, *Psalms*, 82.

12. Seremak, *Psalm 24 als Text zwischen den Texten*, 42.

13. Goldingay, *Psalms*, 1:355.

as a *linguistic* parallel for the idiom used there, but it does not seem to offer a valid literary parallel inviting us to read Ps 24:4c in light of the Decalogue. The simpler explanation is that the MT text reflects a scribal error, for the MT reading is too difficult to be interpreted within the context.[14]

In verse 6, the singular דֹּרְשָׁו, "that seeks him" of the MT is replaced by the plural form of the participle in a fragment from Cairo Geniza, Qere, and LXX. Kraus argues that we should read this with some Greek manuscripts as דרשׁי יהוה, "those who seek YHWH," in part for the sake of meter.[15] This preserves the *lectio facilior*. The Greek reading may attempt to smooth over meter and create a closer grammatical parallelism with מְבַקְשֵׁי, "those who seek," in the second line. The same argument applies to Goldingay's decision to follow Q and read the plural form without adding יהוה,[16] for it preserves the grammatical parallelism. Therefore the MT reading is preferred.

Also in verse 6, instead of the MT's פָּנֶיךָ, "your face," LXX omits the suffix, and two medieval Hebrew manuscripts, LXX, and Syriac add a reference to God. The LXX reads τὸ πρόσωπον τοῦ θεοῦ Ιακωβ, "the face of the God of Jacob,"[17] while the others read פניך אלהי יעקב, "your face, O God of Jacob." To complicate this picture further, the Targum has a 3rd person singular suffix, "his face." The variations in these readings suggest that the ancients struggled with this verse. The Targum reading seems to attempt to smooth over the shift of perspective to second-person address, a factor evident in the lack of a personal pronoun in the LXX version. However, the most significant question concerns the reference to God. Tromp doubts that a reference to God would have been dropped from the text.[18] The MT reading, מְבַקְשֵׁי פָנֶיךָ יַעֲקֹב, is reflected in the KJV "that seek thy face, O Jacob." However, as Kraus notes, this does not fit the context—YHWH is the expected object of the worshipper.[19] One solution is to see an ABA' pattern in the clause structure, with Jacob referring to the "generation."[20] Tromp denies that an idealized interpretation of Jacob as "the generation" is appropriate since it goes against the structure of the sentence.[21] Instead, he argues

---

14. Kraus, *Psalms 1–59*, 311; Steingrimsson, *Tor der Gerechtigkeit*, 70.
15. Kraus, *Psalms 1–59*, 311; cf. Westermann, *The Living Psalms*, 277.
16. Goldingay, *Psalms*, 1:356.
17. So Kraus, *Psalms 1–59*, 311; Westermann, *The Living Psalms*, 277; Craigie, *Psalms 1–50*, 210; RSV/NRSV/ESV.
18. Tromp, "Jacob in Psalm 24," 274.
19. Kraus, *Psalms 1–59*, 311.
20. This may be reflected in the NASB: "Who seek Your face—even Jacob." NJPS reverses the order of the words, translating the second line "Jacob, who seek Your presence."
21. Tromp, "Jacob in Psalm 24," 278.

that the LXX represents the original text. However, MT reflects a universalizing trend in the Psalter that involved Israel playing an intermediary role between YHWH and the nations.[22] This cannot be proven, though it may explain the absence of a reference to God where one would expect it. In this case common sense may be the best guide.[23] The context (especially v. 3) favors YHWH as the object of the inquiry of worshippers. On the question of whether Jacob is idealized here, we should consider Galling's claim that verse 6 represents a *Beichtspiegel*, a self-report or confession on the model of Deut 26:12–15.[24] This does not seem an appropriate parallel since such confessions, including that found in the Egyptian Book of the Dead, chapter 125,[25] are typically cast in the first person. Psalm 24 maintains third-person description throughout. Although it is hard to explain why a reference to deity would have been dropped from the text, it seems preferable to understand that such has taken place.

Verse 9 has the Qal imperative form, שְׂאוּ, "lift up," in both the first and second lines, while verse 7 has the Niphal imperative form, הִנָּשְׂאוּ, "be lifted up," for the second line. A number of manuscripts and versions have the Niphal form in verse 9.[26] MT is preferable because the Niphal may be understood as an attempt to harmonize with verse 7.

LITERARY GENRE AND STRUCTURE OF PSALM 24

A number of interpreters have raised questions about the unity of Psalm 24. Its three sections appear to shift in genre, and the ethical middle section is awkwardly sandwiched between the more theological outer sections. Goldingay characterizes these three sections as originally independent compositions that are "unusually unrelated to each other."[27] Not all commentators are as skeptical as Goldingay. However, none of the solutions offered account for the presence of the central ethical section in a way that fits the form and content of the whole of Psalm 24. The psalm may be seen as a unified literary whole from a number of perspectives, and this understanding may help situate the ethical concerns of the psalm in their theological context.

---

22. Ibid., 281–82.
23. Tov, *Textual Criticism of the Hebrew Bible*, 355–56.
24. Galling, "Der Beichtspiegel," 170, 174.
25. *ANET* 34–36.
26. So also Kraus, *Psalms 1–59*, 311.
27. Goldingay, *Psalms*, 1:356.

Issues that Challenge the Unity of the Psalm

The unity of the psalm is called into question for a handful of reasons. First, form critics identify shifts in *Gattung* among the three sections. Craigie calls section one a hymn and other two sections liturgies.[28] Second, Kraus notes that the meter of the psalm shifts, and is quite irregular, particularly in section two.[29] Third, the subject and literary motif vary as well. In section one YHWH is the subject. In section two those who seek YHWH are the subject. Finally, section three alternates between two voices, one demanding entry for the King of Glory and the other demanding the identity of the King of Glory. To what extent can we speak of Psalm 24 as a single literary composition with such variation in genre, meter, and theme?

At first glance the shift in genre is a significant piece of evidence for composite origin. Briggs states without qualification that we have two originally independent compositions: Psalm 24A (vv. 1–6) and Psalm 24B (vv. 7–10). He suggests they were written at two different times and combined "in the late Greek or the Maccabean period." The current text constitutes a single psalm unified under the theme of entry into temple (24A) and city (24B).[30] But even Briggs' Psalm 24A has been split up by form critics into two distinct *Gattungen*. Hossfeld further separates verse 6 as a later addition, resulting in four distinct compositional layers in Psalm 24.[31]

However, form critics consider the psalm a unity based on historical and liturgical considerations. Kraus rejects Briggs' division of the psalm and locates its unity in a shared cultic *Sitz im Leben*.[32] Unlike Psalm 15, which may or may not be liturgical, Psalm 24 exhibits definite liturgical features. To recall Gunkel's definition of a liturgy, it is a poem performed

---

28. Craigie, *Psalms 1–50*, 211. Hossfeld and Zenger set verse 6 apart as a later comment on the liturgy in verses 3–5 (*Die Psalmen I*, 156). However, even if the comment is of later origin than the liturgy, it is a response at some level to the ethical portrait of verse 4, applying it to Israel. Thus verse 6 is intimately connected to verses 3–5 as opposed to verses 7–10. Both of the liturgies have been associated with entry to Zion, but the first concerns the entry of those who seek YHWH and the second YHWH's own entrance.

29. Kraus, *Psalms 1–59*, 311.

30. Briggs, *Psalms*, 1:212–13.

31. Hossfeld and Zenger, *Die Psalmen I*, 157.

32. Kraus, *Psalms 1–59*, 311. Other commentators following the judgment that the unity of the psalm is to be located in its cultic setting include Weiser, *The Psalms*, 232; Dahood, *Psalms I, 1–50*, 151; Anderson, *The Book of Psalms*, 1:200; Gerstenberger, *Psalms: Part 1*, 118; Westermann, *The Living Psalms*, 277; Broyles, *Psalms*, 127; Goldingay, *Psalms*, 1:356–57.

by alternating voices.[33] Gunkel himself imagines the psalm as a whole performed by alternating choirs,[34] with the dialogue in section three best understood with reference to multiple voices.[35] The question-answer form of section two appears to fulfill a didactic purpose, but its presence alongside section three suggests a liturgical use. Therefore numerous commentators affirm the liturgical nature of sections two and three.[36] Although there is broad agreement about the liturgical nature of the text, there is equally broad disagreement about its original setting.[37] Proposed settings include:

1. Some ark procession,[38] including possibly when David moved the ark to Jerusalem,[39] when Solomon dedicated the temple,[40] as a recurring event following a victory in battle,[41] or even during the dedication of the temple during the Maccabean period,[42]

2. A component of an annual festival, such as an autumn festival[43] or Mowinckel's Enthronement Festival of YHWH,[44]

3. As part of exilic worship reasserting YHWH's kingship,[45] or

4. As a drama, introduced with a prologue (section one) and then performed in two acts (sections two and three).[46]

---

33. Gunkel, "Jesaia 33," 182.
34. Gunkel, "Psalm 24," 367.
35. Watson, *Classical Hebrew Poetry*, 78.
36. See, e.g., Dahood, *Psalms I, 1–50*, 151; Alter, *Psalms*, 81–83; Goldingay, *Psalms*, 1:356.
37. VanGemeren, Psalms, 257.
38. Westermann, *The Living Psalms*, 277; Mays, *Psalms*, 122; Anderson, *The Book of Psalms*, 1:200; Broyles, "Psalms concerning the Liturgies of Temple Entry," 249.
39. Goldingay, *Psalms*, 1:356–57; Craigie, *Psalms 1–50*, 214.
40. Slotki notes a tradition in the Babylonian Talmud (*t. Sanhedrin*, fol. 107b, *t. Mo'ed Qatan*, fol. 9a) that Psalm 24 was used at the dedication of Solomon's temple ("The Text and the Ancient Form," 220). Marcel Poorthuis shows that this Jewish tradition turned into a criticism of Solomon in response to Christian Christological claims, accusing Solomon of usurping divine authority ("King Solomon and Psalms 72 and 24 in the Debate between Jews and Christians," 272–73).
41. Goldingay, *Psalms*, 1:362.
42. Treves, "Date of Psalm 24," 428–34.
43. Weiser, *The Psalms*, 232.
44. Mowinckel, *The Psalms in Israel's Worship*, 1:177.
45. Goldingay, *Psalms*, 1:362.
46. Seremak, *Psalm 24 als Text zwischen den Texten*, 60. Cf. Goldingay, *Psalms*, 1:362.

I find the last proposal the most interesting and useful for construing the content of the current form of the psalm. Section three exhibits a dramatic mood as YHWH is challenged at the gates and receives a rousing introduction as the "King of Glory." It is not difficult to imagine the psalm being used in a liturgical setting that involved a touch of the dramatic. However, VanGemeren wisely cautions that we simply do not know the original setting of this psalm.[47] Determining an original oral setting in the absence of textual evidence for its use necessarily involves imaginative speculation, which does not provide a solid basis for interpretation.

A number of commentators have raised questions about the data upon which such reconstructions have been based. Craigie notes that the psalm itself displays such a variety of themes that identifying a particular setting is difficult. Furthermore, there is no evidence that the ark was used in liturgical processions during and after Solomon's reign.[48] Hossfeld likewise notes that, although יהוה צְבָאוֹת is associated with the ark, Psalm 24 does not mention the ark.[49] To associate this procession with the ark we must assume that the ark represents YHWH and that we can infer the presence of the ark based on the reference to YHWH, which begins to sound circular. To complicate matters further, it is not certain that only temple entrance is in view. Briggs argues that section two was used at the temple gates while the military associations of section three (a psalm in its own right) suggest it is set at the gates of the city.[50]

The discussion of the *Sitz im Leben* of this psalm is at an impasse,[51] most likely because of the scarcity of evidence. The language of the psalm is generalized, and we lack texts identifying the role of the psalm in the cult or the role of priests in Israel's festivals.[52] In addition, recourse to a presumed liturgical setting does not resolve the questions regarding variations in meter and theme, nor show a "unifying bond which would account for this particular collocation."[53]

In spite of this lack of consensus, the form-critical discussion reveals that the collocation of the three sections of the psalm *can* be understood together. Furthermore, if we consider the function of the various genres represented, they exhibit continuity. Much of the discussion of the genre

---

47. VanGemeren, Psalms, 362.
48. Craigie, *Psalms 1–50*, 211–12.
49. Hossfeld and Zenger, *Die Psalmen I*, 157.
50. Briggs, *Psalms*, 1:212.
51. Hossfeld and Zenger, *Die Psalmen I*, 156.
52. Gunkel, "Psalm 24," 370.
53. Smart, "The Eschatological Interpretation of Psalm 24," 175.

and purpose of Ps 24:3–6 was taken up in the previous chapter with reference to Psalm 15 and need not be repeated in detail here. To summarize, the "entrance liturgy" theory surrounding Psalms 15 and 24 is fraught with problems. Based on their content and parallels in Egyptian and biblical sources, it is more likely that these texts were intended to instruct those who heard or recited them than to determine who would be permitted to enter the temple. In view of that discussion, the label "character sketch" is appropriate for Ps 24:3–6 because it describes the literary shape and function of the section.[54] Moving outward to sections one and three we also find character description. Sections one and three describe YHWH, first as the Sovereign Creator and then as the King of Glory, who is mighty in battle. Deuteronomy 10:12–22 also juxtaposes description of the character YHWH expects of his people (vv. 12–13) with description of YHWH's own character (vv. 17–18). In light of that parallel, the same juxtaposition in Psalm 24 is not a literary novelty,[55] and genre shifts should not deter us from reading the psalm as a unified composition.[56]

Nor should meter preclude interpreting Psalm 24 as a unified composition. Along with other data, the irregular meter contributes to the literary structure of the psalm. In their study of the psalm, Hirsch and Aschkenasy conclude that the three sections of Psalm 24 "form a meaningful symmetrical pattern that is notably balanced and harmonious." They compare this pattern to the movement of an accordion as it is compressed and extended: "The psalmist starts by presenting the broad panorama of the earth and all it holds; he then narrows his vision to focus on a particular individual—the righteous man—and finally, he broadens his scope once again as he

---

54. Mays remarks that these verses "sketch a paradigm of the 'righteous'" (*Psalms*, 121).

55. I will return to specific points of correspondence between Deut 10:12–22 and Psalm 24 below.

56. Smart suggests that the psalm's unity is to be found in reading it eschatologically, pointing to parallels in Isaiah, particularly Isa 2:3 ("The Eschatological Interpretation of Psalm 24," 176–78). God the Creator is introduced in section one, section two looks forward to a "perfect age" in which the nation is purified, and section three mirrors the coming of YHWH to his city in Isaiah 40 (ibid., 180). Terrien offers a similar eschatological interpretation of the psalm (*The Psalms*, 249–50). Admittedly the content of Psalm 24 does not preclude an eschatological interpretation, but there is no indication that it concerns hope for a new eschatological age. Marc Girard offers a variant of this interpretation. He suggests that in the three sections we have a movement from the terrestrial to the celestial. The temple on the summit of a mountain serves as the place where humans approach the heavens with their feet still on the ground (*Les Psaumes*, 206, 208). This tantalizing suggestion likewise requires evidence that an eschatological context is intended, but evidence for this is slim.

addresses "the gates of eternity."[57] They note the alternation between the large and small, the whole world and a specific place.[58] The compression begins thematically within verses 1–2. The focus shifts from the whole earth to the inhabited world and from the vast seas to orderly rivers.[59] This alternation is visible not just thematically but also metrically, as in verse 4 the meter shifts from the 3-stress half lines to the more compact 2-stress half lines, wherein we find the "compact center of energy" in the character of the individual. From there expansion begins with the community starting in verse 6.[60] Further, the psalm constitutes a God-human dialogic interplay. The focus shifts from God in section one to humanity in the first verse of section two with the question, "Who may ascend to the hill of YHWH, who may stand in his holy place?" (v. 3).[61] The shift to the community in verse 6 accords well with the liturgy at the gates in section three, in which the focus has shifted again to YHWH, who is now the King of Glory approaching the city. Undoubtedly the scene in section three is a matter of community concern.

To summarize what we have uncovered thus far about the literary shape of Psalm 24, both the literary genre and meter shift between its three sections. However, in spite of these shifts, we can identify a continuity of function, that they each describe a character. Also, the psalm's vision alternates from broad to narrow to broad, and the focus shifts from God to humans to God. However, this interpretation does not entirely resolve the discontinuity of theme between the three sections, an essential step for determining the theological context of Psalm 24:3–6.

Thematic Proposals for the Unity of the Psalm

Several commentators have sought to relate the three sections by identifying a common theological motif, namely the divine warrior or divine kingship. In the following analysis I do not distinguish sharply between the two, for the kingship motif is a root metaphor for many others, especially for YHWH as the divine warrior.[62] Although this motif links the first and third sections, the connection to the second section remains tenuous.

57. Hirsch and Aschkenasy, "Translatable Structure, Untranslatable Poem," 22.
58. Ibid., 23.
59. Ibid., 24. In view of the Canaanite creation myth, the construal of rivers as orderly might be doubted, but the overall movement remains intact.
60. Ibid., 26, 29.
61. Ibid., 26.
62. Mettinger, *In Search of God*, 92–93.

Commentators often draw on a seminal essay on the divine warrior motif by Frank Moore Cross, Jr., who suggests that the Canaanite myth and ritual "pattern" in the Ba'al myth lies behind this psalm. In this myth, Ba'al's reign over the gods is challenged by Yam, who is deified sea.[63] Cross points to the link between creation and seas in Ps 24:1–2[64] and suggests that this "creation-kingship" motif of Canaanite origins appears in the command to the gate towers in Ps 24:7, 9. There the gates are personified as elders of the city waiting to see if YHWH is victorious. This corresponds to the scene in the Ba'al myth when Ba'al must rouse the gods against Yam: "Lift, O gods, your heads."[65]

Mays develops the divine warrior motif to explain the relationship between the first and third sections of Psalm 24. YHWH asserted his sovereignty over the chaos of the waters in creation in section one, by which his glorious kingship is revealed.[66] This sovereignty is then assumed in section three, which is "the dramatic version of the confession of verses 1–2."[67] This resolution makes a close thematic link between the first and third sections but leaves unresolved the connection to the second section.

To account for section two, Mays notes the description of YHWH in Ps 89:5–14 in terms of righteousness, justice, and faithfulness. Those who enter "his royal presence" must have a righteous life that "reflects the character of the sovereign to which it belongs" and be ordered by YHWH like creation "in the midst of the chaos of evil."[68] This perspective captures an important trajectory of OT ethics, namely, *imitatio Dei*.[69] However, two factors raise doubts about this aspect of Mays' solution. First, Psalm 89 does not link the character of the sovereign with the one who enters his presence. As I argue below, it is more likely that the character of YHWH described in Psalm 89 undergirds confidence in his fidelity to his covenant and his commitment to save Israel and David. It does not strictly comment on YHWH's general

---

63. Cross, Jr., "The Divine Warrior in Israel's Early Cult," 21. He also notes the parallel to the Babylonian *Enūma Elish*, in which creation is a battle between Marduk and Tiāmat, the primordial ocean. Mettinger notes that Yammu is also called "Judge Nahar," further strengthening the allusion in Ps 24:2 to the Canaanite myth (*In Search of God*, 75).

64. Cross, Jr., "The Divine Warrior in Israel's Early Cult," 22.

65. Ibid., 23–24. For the text of Ba'al myth, see COS, 1.86:246. Patrick D. Miller Jr. notes that "the Old Testament version has been demythologized only insofar as 'the gods' are replaced by 'the gates'" (*The Divine Warrior in Early Israel*, 30).

66. Mays, *Psalms*, 122.

67. Ibid., 122–23.

68. Ibid., 123–24.

69. Reed, "Virtue Ethics and Psalms 111–112"; Durant, "Imitation of God."

moral traits for the purpose of engendering virtue in his people. Second, Psalm 24 does not speak of YHWH's character, except perhaps indirectly in regard to his sovereignty over creation and his might in battle, neither of which is applied to his worshippers.[70] Mays' assertion may be a true description of one aspect of the theological-ethical dynamic of the Psalter, but Psalm 24 does not make this point. Instead, it simply juxtaposes description of YHWH the mighty sovereign with description of those who worship him.

Another solution emphasizes the polar opposites of chaos and order. In addition to arguing that the character of the worshipper should reflect the character of the one worshiped, Broyles suggests that the divine warrior motif unites the first and third sections in the realm of the entire cosmic order, and the second brings everyday social behavior within the realm of worship alongside the cosmic order.[71] There is no bifurcation between the cosmic realm and the everyday life. Again, although Broyles may assert something that is theologically accurate, does the divine warrior motif in Psalm 24 speak to a cosmic order that is supposed to be reflected in the life of faith? And more seriously, is chaos a strong element in section one? Canaanite mythology probably influenced the pairing of "seas" (יַמִּים) and "rivers" (נְהָרוֹת).[72] In the Baʻal cycle Baʻal must defeat his opponents Prince Sea (*zbl.ym*) and Judge River (*ṇpṭ.nhr*) in order to become king.[73] However, the connection to the Baʻal cycle is muted in Psalm 24. The seas and rivers are plural, not the deified singular of the Baʻal cycle. As a number of interpreters note, the seas and rivers are "demythologized and depersonified" in Ps 24:1.[74] Furthermore, if present, the notion of a cosmic battle with chaos is domesticated (cf. Psalms 74 and 89). Instead of doing battle with them, YHWH builds creation on top of the seas and rivers.[75] The divine warrior motif is muted in Ps 24:1–2 and does not unify the three sections, nor does the associated concept of establishing order out of chaos.

---

70. Just the opposite is likely the case. David J. A. Clines argues that "[i]n subscribing to Psalm 24, we are writing a blank cheque for war" ("A World Established on Water," 83). However, Goldingay rightly notes that war in Psalm 24 is something left to YHWH (*Psalms*, 1:364).

71. Broyles, *Psalms*, 132.

72. Cf. VanGemeren, who is skeptical that the Israelites were aware of Canaanite cosmogony (*Psalms*, 258).

73. Broyles, *Psalms*, 128.

74. Craigie, *Psalms 1–50*, 212; so also Konkel, "The Exaltation of the Eternal King," 17; Watson, *Chaos Uncreated*, 128.

75. Clines finds this cosmological construct rather ridiculous in view of modern science ("A World Established on Water," 79). Genre is an important consideration. The language of Psalm 24 should be understood as poetry that both taps into the Canaanite cosmogony and subverts it in order to urge people to seek refuge in YHWH not Baʻal.

Craigie offers a solution that involves the divine king motif. He notes that the order established in creation in the first section is challenged by historical experience of chaos and war, but in that YHWH stands victorious. In both he stands as king. Within this framework Craigie relates the second section to the other two:

> [J]ust as the order of creation is a moral order, symbolized by God's "holy place" (v. 3), so too the peace and victory achieved by the Warrior King belonged to Israel only so long as they possessed "innocent hands and a pure heart" (v. 4). *The recognition of the kingship of God must result in the worship of God by those who recognize his royal authority; to worship presupposes moral integrity—and that, in a sense, is the central point in the psalm.* There could be no separation between the Creation, deliverance in historical experience, and moral integrity; if there were, chaos would triumph again.[76]

Craigie helpfully relates sections one and three to each other under the rubric of YHWH's kingship. Regarding section two, he rightly notes the link between moral integrity and peace and victory, but the substance of the link depends upon the idea that the psalm is unified by a notion of a moral order. However, it is doubtful the psalmist is making the point that creation is about order. On the surface of the text it is more about ownership, about YHWH's sovereignty over creation and his victory over his foes. And the portrait of the righteous makes no mention of order per se but speaks in terms of characteristics of a person.

Thus far Mays, Broyles, and Craigie have offered the best thematic solutions to the question of Psalm 24's unity, but none seems to account for the presence of section two. The psalm offers few clues about the relationship between the three sections. It simply juxtaposes them, leaving the connections to the reader. Presumably the logic of the juxtaposition needed no further explanation when the psalm was first composed. How can we identify a thematic coherence to the psalm?

An Outline of the Way Forward

Thus far I have shown that the three sections of Psalm 24 are diverse literarily and thematically, but they are unified in function to describe. In the analysis of the psalm that follows, I shall show that the psalm's use of imagery is the literary bedrock for understanding the psalm. The rest of the

---

76. Craigie, *Psalms 1–50*, 214–15. Emphasis mine.

psalter (and the rest of the Hebrew Bible) offers a wealth of data to clarify the meaning of the imagery in this psalm. To summarize the way forward, the psalm may be understood as a creative union of theology and ethics, of the metaphors of refuge and pathway, that reflects the integrated piety of the Psalter. The broader literary context fills out our understanding of the *telos* of the pathway of the ethical life, YHWH himself. YHWH and refuge in his presence is the destination of those who are on the pathway seeking him. Even more so than Psalm 15, the ethic of Psalm 24 is theocentric. To show this I begin by clarifying the ethical concerns and thematic contours of section two and then consider sections one and three to clarify the theological context in which these concerns are situated. Finally, I consider the parallel in Deut 10:12–22, which combines description of YHWH with description of the kind of people he desires in Israel.

THE ETHICAL CONCERNS AND THEMATIC CONTOURS OF PSALM 24:3-6

Section two consists of four verses, with a shifting focus between the *telos* of the ethical life and its embodiment:

> A Who may enter the presence of the Divine King (v. 3)?
> B The person who is righteous in deed and disposition (v. 4)
> A' He who enters receives blessing and righteousness from the Divine King (v. 5)
> B' Such are those who seek the Divine King (v. 6)

This alternating focus suggests the presence of the two constitutive metaphors of the Psalter's conceptual structure identified by William Brown.[77] Refuge is the *telos* of the pathway of righteousness.

The Telos of the Ethical Life (Ps 24:3, 5)

I argued in chapter 2 that the metaphorical framework of Psalm 15 is couched in terms of the metaphor of refuge. Thus Ps 15:1 assumes that one would want to be in the presence of YHWH because, as we see elsewhere in the Psalter, YHWH'S TENT is A SAFE PLACE and YHWH'S MOUNTAIN is A SAFE PLACE. In addition, Ps 15:5 states in effect that A RIGHTEOUS LIFE is A SAFE PATH. The way of YHWH is the way of life. The *telos* of the ethical life is to be with YHWH, and in the presence of YHWH one finds life and security. That is the motivation for the ethical life.

77. Brown, *Seeing the Psalms*, 50.

Portraits of the Righteous in the Psalms

The same is true in Psalm 24, albeit with different terminology. But is it legitimate to speak in terms of the metaphor of refuge since Psalm 24 lacks terminology for "refuge"?[78] Although the terminology of refuge is not found in Psalm 24, the associated concept occurs in the double question of verse 3 and the mention of blessing and righteousness in verse 5.

Psalm 24:3 refers to the same holy mountain as Ps 15:1, though in different terms. Psalm 24:3 envisions a process. In the first line a person ascends (יַעֲלֶה) the mountain of YHWH, but in the second line he arrives and stands (יָקוּם) in the holy place. He has reached his destination and found acceptance with YHWH.

Hossfeld asserts that עלה is a technical term for pilgrimage.[79] However, the verb is often used in a fairly literal way to speak of the act of ascending, so it does not necessarily refer to pilgrimage here. Merrill notes that the verb is often used of people such as Moses (Exod 19:24), Hannah (1 Sam 1:7), Samuel (1 Sam 9:13), and Hezekiah (2 Kgs 19:14) going up to meet with God or going to a place of worship.[80] This reflects the physical reality that places of worship in the ANE were situated on mountains, so one must go up to reach them.[81] The verb is not restricted to the context of a pilgrimage.

Nonetheless, the psalms associated with pilgrimage offer insight into what pilgrims thought it meant to "go up" to the temple. We see the root עלה reflected in the titles for the Psalms of Ascent (שִׁיר הַמַּעֲלוֹת, Psalms 120–34), where the psalmists seek the presence of YHWH and his help (e.g., Pss 120:1; 121:1–2; 123:1–3; 124:8). These pilgrim psalms contain direct and indirect references to Zion as the place of security. Psalm 122:6–7 urges such pilgrims to pray for the peace and security of Jerusalem, which is the place to which the tribes of Israel "go up" (v. 4). On the other hand, that security in Zion is due to the help of YHWH is evident in Ps 125:1–2 (cf. 127:1; 128:5). Indeed it is YHWH's choice of Zion as his dwelling place that secures its peace (Ps 132:13–18). This cultic place is sought because of its resident, namely YHWH, for in YHWH one finds refuge, vindication, and peace.

---

78. Creach, *Yahweh as Refuge*, 75.

79. Hossfeld and Zenger, *Die Psalmen I*, 159. Weinfeld notes also that the affirmation in verse 6 also suggests a context of pilgrimage ("Instructions for Temple Visitors," 225). On the other hand, Broyles notes the suitability of the verb עלה for an ark procession ("Psalms Concerning the Liturgies of Temple Entry," 249).

80. Merrill, "עָלָה ('ālâ)," 403–4.

81. This is reflected in occurrences of הַר is in a construct relationship with יְהוָה. Occurrences of this collocation outside Psalm 24 include the mountain Abraham ascended to sacrifice Isaac (Gen 22:14); the mountain, Zion, to which the nations stream to obtain the knowledge of Yahweh (Isa 2:3 // Micah 4:2); the place to which one travels to the sound of a flute, presumably on a pilgrimage (Isa 30:29); and the place to which Yahweh's presence returns, to Zion (Zech 8:3).

Psalm 24

Rather than referring to the journey up the mountain, the second line in Ps 24:3 has the verb קוּם and envisions the point at which the worshipper enters the holy place and the presence of the Divine King. This verb often denotes the motion of rising or standing up (e.g., Pss 18:39; 127:2; 139:2).[82] A similar connotation is found in Ps 1:5. There the wicked are not able to stand in court in the presence of the righteous. Such judgment is closely linked to the activity of YHWH (Ps 1:6). The person permitted to stand before YHWH in Psalm 24 is therefore privileged, the exception in a world of sinners (cf. Ps 14:2–3; Isa 33:14; see also Gen 17:1; Jer 23:18–22; Ezek 1:28).

In what kind of place does one rise or stand? The collocation of מָקוֹם and קֹדֶשׁ in Ps 24:3b has strong cultic associations.[83] This collocation frequently refers to a generalized holy place in which certain aspects of the sacrificial system were to be carried out (Exod 29:31; Lev 6:9, 19, 20; 7:6; 10:13; 24:9) but also to "the Holy Place" in the tabernacle (Lev 16:24).[84] This accords with the use of קֹדֶשׁ in Exod 26:33 and elsewhere to refer to a particular place within the structure of the tabernacle. This structure was preserved in Solomon's temple (1 Kgs 6:16). Doubtless this holy place is in the temple itself. However, to reduce the significance of being in this holy place to being inside the temple precincts is to deny the theological power of the double question. With the development of the Zion tradition, as in the Psalms of Ascent, the holy place becomes not only the place of YHWH's presence but also a safe place. The "mountain of YHWH" is Mount Zion, and the "holy place" is a metonymy for Zion. As Brown notes, Zion is "the *locus* of divine presence and activity."[85] Therefore the *telos* of the ethical life in Ps 24:3 is linked conceptually to the metaphor of refuge. YHWH'S PLACE is A SAFE PLACE.

---

82. *HALOT* 1086. Many occurrences of the term involve conflict. Enemies rise up (e.g., 3:2; 17:7; 18:40, 49; 27:12). YHWH rises up in defense of the psalmists and the poor (e.g., 3:8; 7:7; 9:20; 10:12; 12:6; 17:13; 35:2; 68:2; 82:8). The psalmists look to YHWH to raise them up to prevail over their enemies (e.g., 40:3; 41:11). The verb is also used in ways that are not associated with conflict, such as in the swearing of an oath (e.g., 119:106).

83. In the analysis that follows I include occurrences of the adjectival form קָדוֹשׁ in place of the noun form קֹדֶשׁ.

84. Two other texts also use this terminology. Ecclesiastes 8:10 is likely referring to a cultic context, specifically hypocritical temple attendance by the wicked (so also Murphy, *Ecclesiastes*, 85). Ezra 9:8 is part of a prayer offered in the context of sacrifices and the corporate repentance of the returned exiles who fear YHWH. These texts reinforce the cultic association in Ps 24:3b. Deuteronomy 12:5 also employs the noun מָקוֹם, though without the modifier קֹדֶשׁ.

85. Brown, *Seeing the Psalms*, 50.

Portraits of the Righteous in the Psalms

In Psalm 15 the character sketch is completed with a statement of the benefit in verse 5. This element is also present in Ps 24:5, though in the latter the benefit concerns relationship. The character sketched in verse 4 receives the positive affirmation from his God, and this affirmation involves the protection of the divine sovereign. Much like 15:5, 24:5 indirectly invokes the concept of security, thus linking it to the refuge metaphor.

Throughout this psalm, and in particular in verse 5, we encounter common abstract terms without much clarifying context. Therefore words like "blessing" (בְּרָכָה) and "righteousness" (צְדָקָה) must be clarified in light of a broader linguistic context. Unfortunately, Ps 24:5 is the only verse in MT in which these two words occur together. Our one hint in the immediate context about the connotation of these terms is the epithet "God of his salvation" (אֱלֹהֵי יִשְׁעוֹ) in the second line. What kind of blessing and righteousness does one receive as the result of an ethical life?

First we must clarify the connotation of the verb נשׂא. Hossfeld identifies it as a *Leitwort* that originated in the liturgy in verses 7–10.[86] It appears to invoke a play on an ascent motif with verses 4, 7, and 9, all of which speak of items being lifted up.[87] Botha further suggests that the use of the verbs נשׂא (vv. 4, 5, 7, 9), בוא (vv. 7, 9), עלה (v. 3a), and קום (v. 3b) create "a feeling of vertical traffic."[88] It is doubtful that the root בוא entails a *vertical* motion, but that does not negate the sense of vertical motion created by the other three verbs. The worshipper lifts up his soul not to what is false but to YHWH, and he then lifts up blessing and righteousness, and finally the doors lift up to receive YHWH. This explains in part why the poet might have chosen to use נשׂא. But we still must clarify the nature of the action.

The last phrase implies a source: "from the God of his salvation" (מֵאֱלֹהֵי יִשְׁעוֹ). Whatever the goods (בְּרָכָה and צְדָקָה) are, they come from YHWH to the worshipper. This use of the verb is idiomatic. It may be understood with a similar idiomatic phrase, נָשָׂא אִשָּׁה, "to take a wife" (Ruth 1:4; 2 Chr 11:21; 13:21; 24:3; Ezra 10:44).[89] The subject receives some benefit to himself, so נשׂא appears in this case to act as a synonym of לקח, "to take, receive."[90] In order to preserve the sense of upward movement, I translate the verb "take up," though the translation "receive" is more idiomatic English. We may now consider what the worshipper receives from YHWH.

---

86. Hossfeld and Zenger, *Die Psalmen I*, 157.
87. Hirsch and Aschkenasy, "Translatable Structure, Untranslatable Poem," 29.
88. Botha, "Psalm 24: Unity in Diversity," 365.
89. Freedman et al., "נָשָׂא nāśā'," 38–39.
90. KJV, RSV, NRSV, ESV, NIV, NASB, and NLT all translate the verb as "receive." Cf. NJPS, "carry away," and Alter, *Psalms*, 82, "bear."

Psalm 24

Gunkel and Begrich assert that this blessing is pronounced by the priest.[91] Indeed, the root ברך can be used for this cultic activity, most famously in the priestly blessing (Num 6:24–26),[92] though there is little in the context of Psalm 24 to support a human role in mediating this blessing.[93] The psalm lacks language invoking the blessing of God, as in the priestly blessing or Ps 129:8. Priests did have the privilege of pronouncing divine blessing on the people of Israel (Deut 10:8),[94] so one could argue that it is implied that a priest mediates this "blessing and righteousness." But if that is the case in Psalm 24, this priestly involvement is far below the surface of the text and can only be inferred. The psalm itself motivates the listener to embody the righteousness found in the previous verse by holding out the promise of a transfer of "blessing and righteousness" *from YHWH* to the worshipper. The *source* of blessing and righteousness is the focus of the verse, not a mediator. So what exactly does the worshipper receive?

Both בְּרָכָה and צְדָקָה are relational terms with exalted pedigrees. From a literary-theological perspective, the priestly blessing derives from YHWH's pronouncement of blessing upon Abraham (Gen 12:1–3). Righteousness is likewise attributed to Abraham for his trust in YHWH's promise of progeny (Gen 15:6). Obtaining blessing from deity was of paramount concern in the ANE and certainly in Israel.[95] In addition to the patriarchal narratives, Israel's covenant documents underscore the importance of blessing in Lev 26:1–13 and Deut 28:1–14, in which YHWH commits himself to relationship with Israel. Richards remarks that such covenantal contexts involve both the content of blessing and the relationship that forms the ground of that blessing.[96] Blessing (ברך) and cursing (קלל/ארר) are often paired,[97] one expressing the affirmation of a relationship and the other its denial. Therefore a verbal element is fundamental to this mention of blessing.

However, as in the Aaronic blessing, the verbal pronouncement of affirmation involves a material benefit. Simple verbal pronouncement is not an end in itself. Instead, the affirmation of relationship means that the

---

91. Gunkel and Begrich, *Introduction to Psalms*, 313. This understanding is implied by NASB, "he will receive a blessing."

92. Note that this root is also often used of praise offered by a worshipper for YHWH (e.g., Pss 16:7; 26:12; 34:2[1]; but especially Psalm 103).

93. Deuteronomy 26 presents the corresponding response to this blessing. There the priest plays a mediatorial role in presenting the offering of first fruits to YHWH.

94. Brown, "בָּרַךְ (bārak II)," 761.

95. Ibid., 758.

96. Richards, "Bless/Blessing," 754.

97. This contrast is not only in the Pentateuch but also in the Ps 109:7 where קְלָלָה, "curse," is said to be the desire of the wicked man instead of בְּרָכָה, "blessing."

worshipper experiences the content of the blessing of YHWH. We see this with reference to the covenantal contexts mentioned above. For Abraham this blessing entailed numerous progeny, for Israel it was progeny, a productive and secure land, and the presence of YHWH in their midst. In the Psalter the content of blessing (בְּרָכָה) is often related to the metaphor of refuge, but the fundamental commonality is the benefits of right relationship with YHWH. For example, in Ps 3:9, "salvation" (יְשׁוּעָה) belongs to YHWH and is the manifestation of his blessing. But this blessing can be a crown on the head of the king (21:4) or the joy of God's presence (21:7). Most striking is the celebration of a unified community of brothers in Psalm 133. This "good and pleasant" community is compared with the anointing of oil on Aaron's head but also with the blessing of God:

כְּטַל־חֶרְמוֹן	3a	Like the dew of Hermon,
שֶׁיֹּרֵד עַל־הַרְרֵי צִיּוֹן	3b	which comes down on the mountains of Zion
כִּי שָׁם צִוָּה יְהוָה אֶת־הַבְּרָכָה	3c	For there YHWH has commanded blessing
חַיִּים עַד־הָעוֹלָם׃	3d	*That is*, life forevermore.

While in Deut 28:8 Moses promises that YHWH will command his blessing on the land and the economic activity of Israel, here it is life (cf. Deut 30:15). Isaiah 33:16 corresponds to Ps 24:5, and it speaks of provision of bread and water on the heights, no doubt the elements necessary to sustain life in a siege. It is implied by this promise of blessing that YHWH is A SOURCE OF LIFE. Zion is the focus of that life-giving blessing of YHWH, and therefore the metaphor of refuge is conceptually linked to this promise. The blessing of YHWH results in life for those who receive it.

The same notion of verbal pronouncement leading to material benefits is evident in צְדָקָה. Because the term is used in multiple domains, English translations have rendered it in a number of ways. The KJV renders it "righteousness"[98] while others render the word as "vindication."[99] The NLT paraphrases the line, "[they will] have a right relationship with God their savior." Alter translates צְדָקָה in light of בְּרָכָה, rendering it "bounty,"[100] while NJPS renders it "just reward." This diversity reflects the difficulty of rendering a theologically loaded term in English. As David Reimer notes, ANE cognate terms suggest that the word may be used in an active sense for right behavior and in a stative sense for "being righteous." He suggests that the word is best understood in relation to its context rather than through a

---

98. So NKJV and ESV.
99. So RSV, NIV, NRSV, NET.
100. Alter, *Psalms*, 82.

study of morphology or the root of the term.[101] The root צדק is prominent in the Psalter, and צְדָקָה occurs thirty-four times. Our concern is to clarify what kind of צְדָקָה comes from YHWH and can be bestowed on his people.

Before considering the occurrences of צְדָקָה in the Psalter, we must consider the broader theological backdrop of the term in the OT. Although צְדָקָה connotes a quality of character in Deut 9:4–6, two key texts speak of torah obedience followed by a pronouncement of righteousness. Deuteronomy 6:25 declares that torah obedience brings a pronouncement of righteousness: "And it will be righteousness (צְדָקָה) for us if we are careful to do all this command before YHWH our God as he commanded us." This verse involves a collocation of an imperfect of היה, the *lāmed* preposition, and צְדָקָה, as does Deut 24:15.[102] In the latter it is clearly a relational term. Generosity toward the poor translates into righteousness "before YHWH your God" (לִפְנֵי יְהוָה אֱלֹהֶיךָ). Ethical living is matched by YHWH's relational affirmation. By analogy to Deut 24:15, Deut 6:25 refers to a verbal pronouncement of right relationship to YHWH. This is even clearer in Ezek 18:9, though it employs the adjective צַדִּיק rather than the noun form צְדָקָה. Following the sketch of the person who obeys torah, YHWH pronounces: "he is righteous, he will surely live" (צַדִּיק הוּא חָיֹה יִחְיֶה).[103] Given the similarities between Ezekiel 18 and Psalms 15 and 24 noted in the previous chapter, it is plausible that the pronouncement of righteousness in Ezek 18:9 is mirrored in Ps 24:5. Therefore, Ps 24:5 affirms that the ethical life is met with the affirmation from YHWH that the worshipper is accepted.

In the Psalter צְדָקָה appears frequently with a number of senses, but the protection of YHWH is often associated with צְדָקָה. First, צְדָקָה is a quality attributed to YHWH that is the ground of the faithful protection of his people (cf. Deut 32:4). In Ps 5:9[8] this sense is clearly linked to the metaphor of refuge. The psalmist prays to be led by YHWH "in your righteousness" in view of the enemies of the psalmist, and this is paralleled by the plea to "make your way straight before me." This involves YHWH's punishment of the wicked who are deceitful (vv. 10–11[9–10]). He concludes with a call for those who seek refuge in YHWH to rejoice in his protection (v. 12[11]). The effect of YHWH's righteousness is that of protection and refuge for the psalmist. It is the ground of the psalmist's plea for rescue in Ps 31:2.[104] In Psalm 36 YHWH's righteousness and his justice (מִשְׁפָּט) are linked to the

---

101. Reimer, "צָדַק (ṣādaq)," 746.
102. Block, *Deuteronomy*, 195–96.
103. Corresponding pronouncements of life are made in verses 13 and 17.
104. For other psalms grounding YHWH's saving action in his righteousness, see 51:16; 71:2; 143:1, 11. Psalm 119:40 grounds a plea for life in YHWH's צְדָקָה.

salvation of humans and animals (v. 7). It is also parallel to his חֶסֶד in verse 11, thus tying YHWH's righteousness to his faithfulness.

Second, in several psalms YHWH's צְדָקָה appears as a parallel term to his saving deeds. Psalm 40:11[10] testifies to YHWH's צְדָקָה: "Your righteousness (צִדְקָתְךָ) I have not covered within my heart, / your faithfulness (אֱמוּנָתְךָ) and your salvation (וּתְשׁוּעָתְךָ) I have spoken, / I have not hidden your steadfast love (חַסְדְּךָ) and reliability (וַאֲמִתְּךָ) to the great assembly." The psalmist associates YHWH's צְדָקָה with his אֱמוּנָה, "faithfulness," and תְּשׁוּעָה, "deliverance, salvation."[105] Are we to equate the צְדָקָה of YHWH with his saving deeds, or do YHWH's saving deeds proceed from his righteousness? It is not clear that we can equate the צְדָקָה of YHWH with his saving deeds, but we may be confident that the psalmist makes a close connection between the two. We find the same connection between YHWH's צְדָקָה and his salvation in Ps 71:15–16, 19, and 24:

פִּי יְסַפֵּר צִדְקָתֶךָ	15a	My mouth will recount your righteousness,
כָּל־הַיּוֹם תְּשׁוּעָתֶךָ	15b	All the day your salvation,
כִּי לֹא יָדַעְתִּי סְפֹרוֹת:	15c	For I have not known [their] numbers.
אָבוֹא בִּגְבֻרוֹת אֲדֹנָי יְהוִה	16a	I will come in the mighty deeds of the Lord YHWH,
אַזְכִּיר צִדְקָתְךָ לְבַדֶּךָ:	16b	I will make known your righteousness alone.
וְצִדְקָתְךָ אֱלֹהִים עַד־מָרוֹם	19a	Your righteousness, O God, is to the heights,
אֲשֶׁר־עָשִׂיתָ גְדֹלוֹת אֱלֹהִים	19b	You who have done great things,
מִי כָמוֹךָ:	19c	Who is like you?
גַּם־לְשׁוֹנִי כָּל־הַיּוֹם תֶּהְגֶּה צִדְקָתֶךָ	24a	Also my tongue will meditate on your righteousness all the day,
כִּי־בֹשׁוּ	24b	For they have been put to shame,
כִּי־חָפְרוּ מְבַקְשֵׁי רָעָתִי:	24c	For they are ashamed, who sought my harm.

The connection between righteousness and salvation is unmistakable. Given the ambiguity of parallel poetic lines, we cannot be dogmatic about whether the psalmist is equating YHWH's righteousness with his saving deeds. But in both Psalms 40 and 71, the צְדָקָה of YHWH is closely linked to YHWH's saving acts (cf. Pss 88:13; 98:2).

Third, YHWH's צְדָקָה can be given to people. Psalm 72:1 speaks of צְדָקָה and מִשְׁפָּט as goods that YHWH may give to the king, just as the

---

105. *HALOT* 1801.

mountains may "lift up" peace (שָׁלוֹם) and the hills "lift up" righteousness in verse 3. The king takes on the role of protecting the poor against their oppressors (v. 4). This role is elsewhere attributed to YHWH who performs צְדָקָה for the oppressed (Pss 99:4; 103:6, 17).

To summarize, YHWH's צְדָקָה can be the ground of his saving deeds; it can be associated with his saving deeds; and it can be bestowed upon those who defend the poor much like YHWH does. David Reimer discusses the use of צְדָקָה in Ps 24:5. He concludes that the NJPS's "just reward" is appropriate, citing the link in other psalms between the righteousness of the psalmist and his reward from God (Pss 18:21, 25[20, 24]; 58:10–11[9–10]). In a cultic context, he argues, there is a reciprocal relationship between action and reward: "[P]ious acts result in צְדָקָה; but only the צַדִּיק may 'ascend the hill of the LORD' (24:3)."[106] Those who may ascend the hill of YHWH are permitted to enter the protective presence of YHWH. Thus the person who "takes up" blessing and righteousness receives entry into a place of refuge with the God of his salvation. Therefore Ps 24:5 holds promise that THE RIGHTEOUS LIFE is A SAFE PLACE due to the presence of YHWH.

This conclusion is confirmed when we consider the epithet applied to the source of that refuge, namely the "God of his salvation" (אֱלֹהֵי יִשְׁעוֹ). Psalm 4:2[1] refers to YHWH as the "God of my righteousness" (אֱלֹהֵי צִדְקִי), the one to whom the psalmist pleads for relief in the midst of distress. This divine epithet in Ps 24:5 clarifies the nature of the benefit held out to those who have innocent hands and a pure heart, that they will find refuge in their saving God. Their relationship to the Divine King ensures their security.

The *telos* of the ethical life is being in the presence of the Divine King, and being in his presence entails security. But what does the ethical life look like? Verses 4 and 6 speak of those who embody this ethical life in a way that is consistent with the metaphor of the pathway.

The Embodiment of the Ethical Life (Psalm 24:4, 6)

Although explicit language for a "pathway" is absent in verses 4 and 6, the concept of a way of life is evident in verse 4. Also, the verbs for seeking YHWH (דרש and בקש) imply a journey, a process of movement toward YHWH. Therefore we are justified in understanding these verses to be describing the ethical life in terms of a pathway: THE ETHICAL LIFE is A JOURNEY. Psalm 15 explicitly invokes the metaphor of the pathway with language such as "walks" (v. 2) and "does not stumble" (v. 5). Likewise Psalm 1 situates the life of the righteous person within the language of the pathway, especially by

---

106. Reimer, "צדק (*ṣādaq*)," 768.

way of contrast in verses 1 and 6. But the positive alternative to the way of the wicked is delight in torah (v. 2). From a conceptual perspective, the ethical concerns in Ps 24:4 reflect the ongoing pattern of a person's life. The righteous person is oriented with reference to YHWH and his torah.

The character sketch of Psalm 24 includes three or four lines of terse description of the person who embodies the ethical life. Though many treat the two nominal phrases in verse 4ab as one line, I have treated them as two lines because they are separated by a conjunction and appear to constitute two distinct parallel phrases. Although the list is short, we may observe literary balance and artistry in these short lines in a manner similar to that of Psalm 15. Hirsch and Aschkenasy note that the verse has a rich set of parallel relationships. When we treat the verse as four lines, we see syntactical parallelism in that the first two lines are nominal phrases while the second two are negated clauses with perfect verbs (4a // 4b and 4c // 4d).[107] On the semantic level, however, the structure of the verse depends upon an understanding of the individual parts. Hirsch and Aschkenasy argue that there is a chiastic semantic structure for the whole:

> A Sin against humans (v. 4a)
> B Sin against God (v. 4b)
> B' Sin against God (v. 4c)
> A' Sin against humans (v. 4d)[108]

This assumes that lifting one's soul to falsehood is idolatry. But that is not the only possible interpretation of verse 4c.

Interpreters have noted that this short sketch covers both the internal and external dimensions of a human life. Hossfeld notes that verse 4ab covers both the outer deeds and inner dispositions characteristic of integrity.[109] John Calvin remarks that purity is seated in the heart but manifest in the hands.[110] It is possible that the internal/external interplay may be extended to the entire verse, but a better characterization would be deed and disposition. Thus it may be structured:

> A Deeds: innocent hands (v. 4a)
> B Disposition: pure heart (v. 4b)
> B' Disposition: not lifted up to what is false (v. 4c)
> A' Deeds: not deceitful (v. 4d)

107. Hirsch and Aschkenasy, "Translatable Structure, Untranslatable Poem," 29.
108. So also Goldingay, *Psalms*, 1:359.
109. Hossfeld and Zenger, *Die Psalmen I*, 160.
110. Calvin, *Commentary on the Book of Psalms*, 405. Briggs sees verse 4a as a later addition that weakens the focus on the interior element by introducing action (*Psalms*, 1:215).

However, this assumes a particular interpretation of each line, so we must examine each phrase and clause in detail.

The first two lines describe the hands and the heart. These are no doubt metonymies for the righteous person, but each highlights a different aspect of character. They also appear to be intentionally ambiguous.[111]

First, verse 4a concerns the hands. The righteous person is "innocent of hands" (נְקִי כַפַּיִם). This suggests that such a righteous person is innocent in regard to his actions. But what actions would disqualify a person's hands from being considered innocent? The difficulty is that the collocation of נְקִי and כַּף in Ps 24:4 is unique in the Hebrew Bible.[112] One interpretation can be ruled out, namely that this concerns ritual purity. While the word נְקִי here is often translated "clean," it should not be confused with terms for ceremonial cleanness such as טָהוֹר. Olivier notes that while the cognate term in Akkadian corresponding to the Hebrew נָקָה is primarily used in cultic contexts, the adjective in Hebrew is never used in that way. Instead it is used in the sense of juridical innocence, often in regard to the shedding of blood.[113] Goldingay describes the "innocent of hands" as referring to those who are innocent of bloodshed, pointing to several texts in which נְקִי ("innocent" or "guiltless") is used in reference to bloodshed (Exod 21:28; Josh 2:17–20; 2 Sam 3:28; 14:9).[114] The hands are often used with reference to violence and military might. The losers in a battle are "given into the hand" (יָד) of the victor (e.g., Gen 14:20, Deut 2:24). As Dreytza notes, the metaphorical usage of hands in the OT frequently relates to power or military control, such as in Jer 15:21 (which involves יָד and כַּף).[115] VanGemeren points to a similar pairing of יָד and כַּף in Isa 1:15, where the hands are "full of blood" (יְדֵיכֶם דָּמִים מָלֵאוּ).[116] A person with such hands will not find a hearing with YHWH in prayer. Isaiah's solution is repentance, to cease doing evil (vv. 16–17), as well as the promise of forgiveness, whereby the sin of scarlet-stained hands is washed and made white as snow (v. 18).[117] It would seem

---

111. Broyles, *Psalms*, 129.

112. Apart from Gen 20:5, which I consider below.

113. Olivier, "נָקָה (*nāqâ*)," 152–53.

114. Goldingay, *Psalms*, 1:359.

115. Dreytza, "כַּף (*kap*)," 686.

116. VanGemeren, Psalms, 360.

117. Perhaps it is in view of this text that VanGemeren notes that such a person is not sinless but rather asks forgiveness. This notion is not explicitly stated in the text, but it may be inferred from the broader covenantal context of Israel as well as from Psalm 32. G. Warmuth ("נָקָה *nāqâ*," 557) notes that uses of נְקִי include cases when harm has been done but a person is exempt from punishment (Exod 21:19, 28) and when a person is clearly innocent and not just exempt from punishment (Exod 23:7, Ps 10:8).

that this phrase refers to innocence of bloodshed. However, a related phrase is found in Gen 20:5, where Abraham protests his innocence to Abimelech when he introduces Sarah as his sister, "In the blamelessness of my heart and in the innocence of my hand I have done this" (בְּתָם־לְבָבִי וּבְנִקְיֹן כַּפַּי עָשִׂיתִי זֹאת).[118] Here propriety in social relationships is the concern, not violence. Closer to our passage, Ps 26:6 places the noun form נִקָּיֹון together with כַּף: "I wash my hands in innocence" (אֶרְחַץ בְּנִקָּיֹון כַּפָּי),[119] a clause echoed verbatim in Ps 73:13 in parallel to the clause "surely in vain I have cleansed my heart" (אַךְ־רִיק זִכִּיתִי לְבָבִי).[120] Psalm 73 contrasts the wicked and the "pure of heart" (בָּרֵי לֵבָב, v. 1) at a number of levels, including the question of violence (v. 6) but also of pride and malicious speech (v. 6, 8–9). In view of the broad usage of this related phrase, it is best to see this phrase as intentionally ambiguous and referring to innocence of wrong done to others.[121] Violence and oppression are certainly included in the list of actions that can sully the hands, but it is a broad reference to moral innocence.

The second nominal phrase also is ambiguous. The righteous person is "pure of heart" (בַר־לֵבָב). The לֵב can refer to the "vital, affective, noetic, and voluntative" dimensions of the human person, but in several texts it is paired with particular external parts of the body, reflecting an internal focus with לֵב (Job 31:7; Prov 23:16–17).[122] Hamp suggests that the reference to the "pure in heart" refers to intentions, while the hand refers to the actual ethical deed performed.[123] We have little to help us determine whether this is true. Parallel texts offer little help. The combined phrase occurs in Ugaritic parallels, but these parallels offer insufficient context to further clarify what is connoted by such a description.[124] Biblical parallels do not help much either. Hossfeld notes a link to Ps 26:2, where the heart is the object of YHWH's testing.[125] As noted above, Ps 73:1 describes the "pure of heart" (בָּרֵי לֵבָב) in parallel with those in Israel to whom YHWH is

---

118. This parallel perhaps vindicates the assertion of Alastair G. Hunter that these two terse lines are referring to the same "blamelessness" as Ps 15:2 and Gen 6:9, though Psalm 24 does not employ the word תָּמִים ("The Righteous Generation," 200).

119. Hossfeld and Zenger, *Die Psalmen I*, 158.

120. Warmuth notes that the usage of this term in Pss 26:6 and 73:13 does not refer to cultic purity but rather "ethical innocence, which in turn establishes cultic purity" ("נָקָה *nāqâ*," 562).

121. So Mays, *Psalms*, 121.

122. Fabry, "לֵב *lēḇ*," 412–13.

123. Hamp, "בָּרַר *bārar*," 311.

124. Dijkstra, "A Ugaritic Pendant of the Biblical Expression 'Pure in Heart' (Pss 24:4; 73:1)," 440.

125. Hossfeld and Zenger, *Die Psalmen I*, 158.

good. Mays' suggestion that this implies fealty to YHWH is plausible.[126] This impression is strengthened when we see that both the לֵב and the נֶפֶשׁ, which occurs in verse 4c, are mentioned in the Shemaʿ in Deut 6:4–5. Daniel Block argues that the Shemaʿ calls for singleness of devotion to YHWH, a call that proceeds from the heart (לֵב) and moves outward in concentric circles to the whole person (נֶפֶשׁ) and finally to his "substance" or "possessions" (מְאֹד).[127] In this context we can see how the modifier "pure" (בַּר) corresponds conceptually to "all" (כָל)—there is no distraction or division of thoughts or affection, and this is coupled with the innocence of hands such that pure devotion to YHWH is expressed in the deeds of one's hands.

The relative pronoun אֲשֶׁר in Ps 24:4c introduces a pair of negative clauses, the first of which has been the subject of varied discussion in the commentaries. This clause needs to be clarified—does it refer to idol worship, verbal deception, or something more general? This issue involves the sense of the word שָׁוְא and its relationship to the verb and the verb's object.

According to Jerry Shepherd, שָׁוְא has two distinct senses, that of ineffectiveness and falseness. The latter sense is most common in the OT. This sense is demonstrated in the deuteronomic version of the Decalogue, where false testimony is called עֵד שָׁוְא (Deut 5:20) rather than עֵד שֶׁקֶר (Exod 20:16). Shepherd suggests that the parallel term מִרְמָה, "deceit," in Ps 24:4d, clarifies the meaning of שָׁוְא as a verbal falsehood.[128] This sense of verbal deception is clearly found elsewhere in the Psalter (12:3; 41:7; 144:8, 11).[129] In addition, Ps 26:4 employs the word שָׁוְא in a way that *may* reflect a verbal sense. Translations are divided on how to render מְתֵי־שָׁוְא in Ps 26:4. The NRSV translates it as "the worthless,"[130] while the ESV renders it as "men of falsehood."[131] The second half of the bicolon in Ps 26:4 is not decisive. Often translated as "hypocrites" (NRSV, ESV), the Niphal participle נַעֲלָמִים may be rendered "those who conceal themselves."[132] While the referent is *people* and not the *content of speech*, it is conceivable that this refers in part to the speech habits of the wicked rather than a general character of worthlessness,

---

126. Mays, *Psalms*, 121.

127. Block, *Deuteronomy*, 183–84.

128. Shepherd, "שָׁוְא (šāw')," 53–54. So also Briggs, *Psalms*, 1:215; VanGemeren, Psalms, 360.

129. We must note that Shepherd's first sense, ineffectiveness, is also in evidence in the Psalter with regard to the help of humans (60:13 // 108:13), the brevity of human life (89:48), or the worthlessness of human effort (127:1–2).

130. Following the LXX, μετὰ συνεδρίου ματαιότητος, "with a worthless council."

131. Cf. NASB "deceitful men."

132. *HALOT* 834.

although the latter may be a conclusion reached on the basis of the former.[133] In any case, if שָׁוְא in Ps 24:4c refers to a verbal falsehood, then the second line of the parallelism specifies the meaning of the first more clearly.

However, a number of interpreters believe שָׁוְא refers to idols.[134] Hunter notes a conceptual parallel in Ps 14:1, in which those who deny God's presence in the world provide a foil to those who do not lift their souls to an idol in Ps 24:4. An idol is a deception, and in contrast to the wicked of Psalm 14, the right kind of pilgrims do not follow after such false gods. Thus a right attitude of mind is necessary in order to seek God.[135] In Hunter's understanding, שָׁוְא still concerns falseness—he merely specifies that falseness is an idol. One could also argue that idols are ineffective and worthless, and for that reason שָׁוְא could be understood with reference to idols. This may be the case in Ps 31:7, which contrasts the righteous and the wicked based on the objects of their trust. The psalmist expresses hatred for those who keep "false nothingness" (הַבְלֵי־שָׁוְא) and instead the psalmist trusts in YHWH. The referent of הַבְלֵי־שָׁוְא is ambiguous, though it is likely an idol (so NRSV) because of the contrast with YHWH in the second half of the bicolon.

So, what is the referent of שָׁוְא in Ps 24:4c? The referent seems intentionally ambiguous,[136] though a theological dimension is suggested by the idiom in which it is placed.[137] All cases in the Psalter with a clear verbal connotation to שָׁוְא include a verb for speaking (דבר), as does Deut 5:20 (ענה). Psalm 31:7 also has a clarifying term and context indicating the referent as idols. Although Ps 24:4c lacks a clarifying term as in the cases above, the second line of the parallelism suggests verbal falsehood.[138] However, since the first parallelism in the verse is not a simple synonymous parallelism,[139] we need not *necessarily* be constrained to understand this parallelism as specifying the meaning of the first line to the exclusion of non-verbal falseness. Psalm 24:4c seems to *include* a notion of verbal falseness, but we should not

---

133. What is less likely is that Ps 26:4 is referring to idols (Treves, "Date of Psalm 24," 431), for in that case, instead of a construct relationship between מְתִים, "men," and שָׁוְא, we would expect a verb for worshiping.

134. Treves notes this use in Jer 18:15 where the people make offerings לַשָּׁוְא (ibid.). See also Anderson, *The Book of Psalms*, 1:203; Dahood, *Psalms I, 1–50*, 151; Kraus, *Psalms 1–59*, 314.

135. Hunter, "The Righteous Generation," 196.

136. So Broyles, *Psalms*, 129.

137. Gunkel likewise sees a God-ward dimension. He states the converse, that "the pious man 'lifts up his heart' to God alone, and does not set his soul on evil" ("Psalm 24," 368).

138. VanGemeren, Psalms, 360.

139. Imes, "Psalm 24:4 and the Decalogue," 13.

narrow the reference of the first line on the basis of the second. The first line ties into a broader linguistic context suggesting a broader reference.

The combination of נֶפֶשׁ + נשׂא occurs in a number of other texts that may suggest a theological dimension in this clause.[140] A number of interpreters note that lifting up one's soul is an act of worship (Pss 25:1; 86:4; 143:8).[141] Psalm 25:1 immediately follows Psalm 24, suggesting the two psalms may share a theological dimension. Although the preposition is different (אֶל in Ps 25:1 and לְ in Ps 24:4c), the definite article makes שָׁוְא a substantive, thus providing a grammatical parallel to YHWH in Ps 25:1. We may understand the preposition in a directional sense so that Ps 24:4c concerns the direction of one's life, prayer, and worship. In this case, the righteous person is not oriented to what is false but rather to what is true, that is, to YHWH.[142] Therefore, "lifting one's soul" may connote a kind of loyalty, which is expressed in worship but is itself descriptive of a pattern of a person's life. This is supported by the use of שָׁוְא in Ps 119:37, which distinguishes between looking at what is שָׁוְא and finding life in the ways of YHWH. Therefore, Ps 24:4c seems an intentionally ambiguous phrase meant to capture a spectrum of false objects of attention and trust, such as those enumerated in Job 31:24–28. It is implied that the righteous person is fundamentally theocentric in contrast to one who pursues what is false.

The next line specifies a social entailment of this kind of devotion to YHWH, namely that such a person does not swear deceptively (cf. Ps 15:4cd). The meaning of this line is not debated, for the terms are fairly clear and concrete. The verb נִשְׁבַּע places the concern within the realm of oaths and testimony, and the term מִרְמָה is also associated with speech (Pss 17:1; 52:4, 6) and giving evidence (Prov 12:17).[143] Mays rightly notes that this is an other-oriented concern, for the one who swears truthfully

---

140. It is likely that the linguistic parallel in Exod 20:7a // Deut 5:11a is not very helpful in our inquiry. Block examines the use of the verb נשׂא there and argues that "bearing a name" is bearing a badge of ownership, as is seen in Exod 28:12, 29 ("Bearing the Name," 63–65). It is important to note the object of the verb in each case. In Exod 20:7a the object of the verb נשׂא is אֶת־שֵׁם־יְהוָה אֱלֹהֶיךָ, "the name of YHWH your God." Therefore the subject of the verb bears the name of another, that is YHWH. But in Ps 24:4c the subject of the verb bears or lifts up *himself* לַשָּׁוְא. This contrast means that the idiom "bearing a name" does not itself shed light on Ps 24:4c.

141. Treves, "Date of Psalm 24," 431; Craigie, *Psalms 1–50*, 213. However, the phrase may also refer more generally to a desire or intention (Hos 4:8; Prov 19:18). Cf. Seebass, "נֶפֶשׁ nepeš," 507.

142. Victor Hamilton sees this phrase meaning "direct one's desire towards, long for," and entailing trust in the protection of YHWH when he is the object of the preposition ("נָשָׂא (nāśā')," 161).

143. Carpenter and Grisanti, "רָמָה (rāmâ I)," 1123.

Portraits of the Righteous in the Psalms

is faithful to his neighbor.[144] Swearing deceitfully, on the other hand, "destroys the harmony of human relations."[145]

In contrast to the answer portion of Psalm 15, which has a clear focus on social concerns, the answer portion of the character sketch in Ps 24:4 is both theocentric and social. Although the metaphor of the pathway is not employed on the surface of the text, the conceptual link to the metaphor of the pathway is evident, especially since the literary structure of Ps 24:3-6 is so close to that of Psalm 15, where the metaphor is on the surface. The righteous are oriented to God in their dispositions so that their behavior manifests fidelity to others. This reflects the singularity of devotion called for in the Shemaʿ (Deut 6:4-5) as well as fidelity to one's neighbor (Lev 19:18). In both deeds and dispositions, the ethical life is oriented to God and neighbor.

Verse 6 also describes those who embody the ethical life. Galling interpreted this verse as a *Beichtspiegel* or confession of personal integrity by analogy to Deut 26:12-15.[146] However, as I argue above,[147] the grammatical form of Ps 24:6 does not match such a self-report. Also, we have no independent confirmation of such a self-report taking place in the terms of Ps 24:4. Instead we have further description of the worshippers who embody the ethical life. They are those who seek (דרש) YHWH. Kraus asserts that the two verbs in verse 6, דרש and בקש, are technical terms for pilgrimage (cf. Amos 5:5; 2 Sam 21:1; Hos 5:15; 2 Sam 12:16).[148] Indeed, the verb is used specifically in Deut 12:5, where Moses describes seeking the chosen place for YHWH's habitation. The root עלה that occurs in Ps 24:3 has strong associations with pilgrimage,[149] so the association with pilgrimage is plausible. But this does not limit our understanding of the verbs to the act of journeying to a place of worship. That would define the sense of the verbs too narrowly, especially since the object of the verb here is not a place but a person, namely, YHWH. "Seeking God" is language for coming before YHWH in prayer and worship. One concrete manifestation of that seeking is pilgrimage (Amos 5:5), but that is not the only way to "seek God." In 2 Sam 12:16 David did not need to go on a literal pilgrimage to seek YHWH, for the ark is depicted as having been brought to Jerusalem in 2 Samuel 6. The language of seeking a deity is so common as to be *almost* a dead metaphor. To "seek" (דרש) a deity is to "make supplication," or to "seek the face of" a deity (בקש + פְּנֵי) is to "call on" that deity.[150] How-

---

144. Mays, *Psalms*, 121.
145. Terrien, *The Psalms*, 214.
146. Galling, "Der Beichtspiegel," 170, 174.
147. See p. 64.
148. Kraus, *Psalms 1-59*, 314.
149. See p. 74.
150. *HALOT* 233.

ever, Ps 24:6 is set within a context that speaks of (upward) motion to stand in the presence of YHWH. Therefore these verbs involve not simply a dead metaphor but rather invoke a notion of journeying. Seeking YHWH involves effort to reach the locus of YHWH's presence and activity on Mount Zion. In a concrete sense this may involve pilgrimage, but in a moral sense it involves purity of life (v. 4). Worshippers must negotiate a pathway to reach the end of their journey, which is YHWH himself. Verse 6 recapitulates the character sketch of verse 4 but places it in a theocentric frame of reference. The ethical life is an act of seeking YHWH, and such people do not fail to find blessing and righteousness in his presence.

The ethic of Psalm 24 is fundamentally theocentric. The pathway of righteousness ultimately is about seeking YHWH, and the end of the journey on that pathway is to be in the presence of the Divine King where one finds refuge in his blessing and righteousness. However, to this point I have assumed that the mountain of YHWH is linked to the Divine King. This assumes an understanding of the unity of the psalm, for the Divine King motif is found in sections one and three. When we see how the whole psalm is constructed we gain a deeper understanding of the theological context of ethics in Psalm 24.

THE THEOLOGICAL CONTEXT OF ETHICS IN PSALM 24 (VV. 1-2, 7-10)

At the outset I acknowledge my indebtedness to the work of Mays, Broyles, and Craigie to clarify the thematic contours of sections one and three. They are right to emphasize the Divine Warrior-King motif in Psalm 24. However, as noted above, we must clarify the function of this motif in Psalm 24 in order to see how it might help us understand the relationship of the more theological outer sections to the ethical middle section.

To clarify this relationship, we must briefly consider three other psalms that employ the Creator-as-Divine-Warrior motif. All do so to establish the might of YHWH and seek to apply it in some way to the salvation and security of his people. The first is Psalm 29, which is widely regarded to be of Canaanite origin, now with YHWH instead of Ba'al as the subject of the hymn.[151] The function of the motif is to establish the kingship of YHWH (v. 10) and to entreat this King to apply his strength to his people (v. 11).

Second, Psalm 74 makes a more explicit link between the Creator-as-Divine-Warrior and salvation or military victory for the people. The might of the Divine Warrior (vv. 12-17) is cited as a response to the taunt of the

---

151. Craigie, *Psalms 1-50*, 243-44.

enemy (v. 10), who has destroyed the temple (vv. 3–8). The function of the motif is to provide a theological basis for the plea to YHWH to act on behalf of his sanctuary (vv. 1–2), to remember his people and his covenant with them and to overturn their shame (vv. 18–23).

Third, Psalm 89 provides the most complete literary parallel. It presents the Creator-as-Divine-Warrior ruling the sea and defeating his enemies (vv. 10–11[9–10]; cf. Ps 24:8), as well as owning the world (v. 12[11]; cf. Ps 24:1). This motif undergirds a word of praise (v. 6[5]). However, since the oracle to David begins in verse 21[20], the motif also establishes the might of YHWH, to whom belongs the shield of Israel, that is the king (v. 17[18]). YHWH commits himself to give the king victory and establish him above the kings of the earth (vv. 22–28[21–27]), much like YHWH's victory mentioned above. Verse 28[27] summarizes the relationship between David and YHWH: "He will call out to me, 'You are my father, / My God, and the rock of my salvation!'" (אֵלִי וְצוּר יְשׁוּעָתִי; cf. Ps 24:5, "the God of his salvation"). The complaint that follows centers on the question of YHWH's faithfulness to this promise. YHWH has withdrawn his favor, and the king's crown is in the dust, his strongholds crumbled, his glory brought down in defeat (vv. 40–46; 39–45). The divine warrior motif links the power that rules the raging sea to the one who is available to but then withdrawn from the human king David. As in Psalm 74, the psalmist wants YHWH to remember his covenant with David (v. 50[49]). Instead of being the one who establishes a moral order to follow or who models righteous character, the Divine Warrior in these psalms is the guarantor of the security of Zion and of David and ultimately the people of Israel.

I argued above that section two is at least related to the two metaphors identified by William Brown as capturing the deep structure of the conceptual world of the Psalter. In chapter 2 I also note that Brown connects this convergence of metaphors to the "entrance liturgies" in Psalms 15 and 24:3–6.[152] However, neither he nor Jerome Creach consider the ramifications of this convergence of metaphors for explaining the thematic coherence of the whole of Psalm 24. The convergence of the metaphors of refuge and pathway provides an important conceptual framework within which to understand the relationship between the three sections of Psalm 24. The structure of Psalm 24 is further clarified when we see that *the whole psalm* is an example of the convergence of these two metaphors.

In addition to the arguments concerning the theological context of verses 3 and 5 above, several elements within the broader psalm evoke the

---

152. Brown, *Seeing the Psalms*, 27. Creach notes that one interesting development of the metaphor of "refuge" is that *tôrâ* is pictured as a kind of refuge, most notably in Psalm 119 (*Yahweh as Refuge*, 69).

Psalm 24

metaphor of refuge and clarify the theological context for ethics in Psalm 24. First, the hymn in verses 1–2 creates a sense of security because YHWH owns the entire world and founded it on the seas and rivers *without* a fight. The vision of YHWH's creative activity exudes confidence and peace. Rebecca Watson argues that the chaotic associations with the myth of the storm god "have been replaced by an assumption of the protective benefits of [YHWH's] presence."[153] The claim of ownership in Ps 24:1 is a claim of sovereignty, the claim of the Divine King who is the source of refuge in the Psalter. Second, the Divine Warrior motif in section three presents YHWH as a victorious King of Glory, whose entry at the gates signifies the security of the city atop Mount Zion. The gates are not identified specifically as temple or city gates, but in view of the battle motif, I am inclined, with Briggs, to see them as the city gates. It is possible that Psalm 24 dramatizes the arrival of the ark to the place chosen for YHWH's name to dwell (Deut 12:5), but a conversation like the one dramatized in section three makes the best sense at the city gates where the security of the city is defended. In any case, the presence of a Warrior-King who is mighty in battle is the source of great confidence for those who dwell with him.[154]

A clearer picture of the whole emerges when we see in Psalm 24 the convergence of the metaphors of refuge and pathway. In view of that convergence, the presence of the central section is not surprising. To borrow terminology from speech act theory, the locutions of the three sections are indeed disparate in form and sense, but they converge in a common perlocution: the psalm is intended to motivate the people of YHWH to seek refuge in him (theology) and to direct them in the way to do that (ethics). Therefore the three sections of description have a didactic function encouraging covenant fidelity to the Divine Suzerain. This covenantal connection is clearer when we consider a key parallel to Psalm 24 in Deuteronomy.

DEUTERONOMY 10 AS A LINGUISTIC AND THEMATIC PARALLEL TO PSALM 24

Deuteronomy 10 also pairs description of YHWH with a call to moral transformation. The linguistic and thematic parallels between Deuteronomy 10 and Psalm 24 suggest that a deuteronomic background lies behind this psalm. This background helps account for the particular collocation of themes in Psalm 24.

153. Watson, *Chaos Uncreated*, 128.
154. Cf. 1 Sam 8:20, where the people requesting a king identify his role closely with fighting battles on behalf of the people.

Portraits of the Righteous in the Psalms

First, though least in significance, the language of Moses ascending (עלה) the mountain to meet with YHWH is found in Deut 10:1, 3. In verse 10 Moses stands (עמד) on the mountain. Although the second verb is distinct from Ps 24:3, which employs קום, both passages include the progression from ascending to standing.

More significant, however, is what follows in Deut 10:12–22. In verse 12 Moses calls for wholehearted devotion to YHWH involving the לֵבָב and נֶפֶשׁ (cf. Ps 24:4bc).[155] Although the Shema' (Deut 6:4–5) also includes מְאֹד, the collocation of לֵבָב/לֵב and נֶפֶשׁ without מְאֹד is more common in Deuteronomy and is often coupled with the verbs עבד and אהב (see 4:29; 10:12; 11:13; 13:4; 30:6). In Deut 11:18 Moses employs this collocation to enjoin the people to stamp themselves with the words of YHWH, and in 26:16 to practice the word of YHWH בְּכָל־לְבָבְךָ וּבְכָל־נַפְשֶׁךָ (on obedience and this collocation, see also 30:2, 10). Many subsequent occurrences of this collocation reflect a deuteronomic influence, where deuteronomic language for fidelity, obedience, and repentance are evident (Josh 22:5; 23:14; 1 Sam 2:35; 1 Kgs 2:4; 8:48; 2 Kgs 23:3, 25; 2 Chr 22:19; 28:9; 2 Chr 6:38; 15:12; 34:31).[156] Although the language of Ps 24:4bc is not specifically deuteronomic in the same sense as the references cited above, the concept of complete fidelity to YHWH is itself deuteronomic. The use of these two terms here suggests at least a general deuteronomic background.

In addition, the language of pathway is explicit in Deut 10:12. There the people are called "to walk in all [YHWH's] ways" (לָלֶכֶת בְּכָל־דְּרָכָיו). The language of the pathway is common to a number of traditions in the Hebrew Bible (e.g., Gen 18:19; Deut 5:33; 9:12; Judg 2:22; 2 Kgs 21:22; Jer 5:4–5; Ezek ; Prov 10:29; Job 17:9; 23:11) and does not help distinguish a deuteronomic parallel from a wisdom parallel, for example. However, a number of other aspects to the parallel do function in this way.

Deuteronomy 10:12–22 and Psalm 24 describe YHWH in similar ways. First, in verse 14 the motif of YHWH as Sovereign over creation occurs:

הֵן לַיהוָה אֱלֹהֶיךָ הַשָּׁמַיִם וּשְׁמֵי הַשָּׁמָיִם הָאָרֶץ וְכָל־אֲשֶׁר־בָּהּ

See, to YHWH your God belongs the heavens and the heaven of heavens, the earth and all that is in it.

---

155. Seremak likewise sees the structural similarities between Psalm 24 and Deut 10:12–22 (*Psalm 24 als Text zwischen den Texten*, 430). In addition to the call for exclusive devotion to YHWH, he sees sections one and three of Psalm 24 providing a grounding for a promise of salvation in section two. This grounding is that YHWH owns the whole world (section one) and he enforces his dominance in the world (section three).

156. Though some are located within the wisdom tradition (Prov 2:10; 27:9).

This verse resembles Ps 24:1. YHWH's ownership of the world is declared with the *lāmed* preposition. The occurrence of הָאָרֶץ in both is not particularly noteworthy. The mention of הַשָּׁמַיִם instead of תֵּבֵל suggests that, while Deut 10:14 has a broad scope of vision to encompass all of creation, Ps 24:1 focuses on the world of human beings. However, the syntactical structure of these two verses is remarkably similar. Both are verbless clauses, both employ parallelism, both begin with the prepositional phrase attributing ownership to YHWH, and both employ a *wāw* conjunction in the middle of each line and a third feminine singular pronominal suffix for the second element (though only once in Deut 10:14). See Table a below.

Table a. A Comparison of the Syntactical Structures of Deut 10:14 and Ps 24:1

Deut 10:14	Ps 24:4bc
לַיהוָה אֱלֹהֶיךָ	לַיהוָה
הַשָּׁמַיִם וּשְׁמֵי הַשָּׁמָיִם	הָאָרֶץ וּמְלוֹאָהּ
הָאָרֶץ וְכָל־אֲשֶׁר־בָּהּ	תֵּבֵל וְיֹשְׁבֵי בָהּ

The two passages differ in their use of the theme of YHWH as Sovereign. In Deut 10:15 the election of Israel is a sign of remarkable divine grace given the breadth of YHWH's realm (cf. Exod 19:5), while in Ps 24:1 the focus is on the power of YHWH as Creator.[157]

However, the description of YHWH continues in Deuteronomy 10 with references to YHWH as the Divine Warrior, a motif prominent in Ps 24:7–10. Verse 17 describes YHWH as the "God of gods" and "Lord of lords." He is also said to be "the great, mighty, and fearsome God." The second term, הַגִּבֹּר, is applied to YHWH in Ps 24:8, who is "strong and mighty, mighty in battle" (עִזּוּז וְגִבּוֹר יְהוָה גִּבּוֹר מִלְחָמָה).[158] Similar descriptive language occurs in verse 21:

הוּא תְהִלָּתְךָ וְהוּא אֱלֹהֶיךָ אֲשֶׁר־עָשָׂה אִתְּךָ אֶת־הַגְּדֹלֹת וְאֶת־הַנּוֹרָאֹת
הָאֵלֶּה אֲשֶׁר רָאוּ עֵינֶיךָ׃

> He is your praise, and he is your God, who has done for you these great and fearful things, which your eyes have seen.

---

157. Seremak argues in addition that in contrast to Deut 10:14, the motif in Psalm 24 suggests that all people, not just Israel, should recognize YHWH wholeheartedly (v. 4) because of YHWH's universal sovereignty (v. 1; *Psalm 24 als Text zwischen den Texten*, 69–70).

158. Seremak likewise sees the connection between YHWH as גִּבּוֹר and section two in Psalm 24. The supremacy of YHWH is the guarantee of the message of salvation in verses 3–6, but it is also a warning to the enemy of YHWH who would look to idols for security instead of YHWH (ibid., 429).

What are these deeds? In Deut 1:30 it is YHWH's victory in Egypt and his act to bring them through the desert for forty years (cf. 4:34; 7:18–19). In Deut 3:21 the defeat of Sihon and Og is what Joshua's eyes have seen. Both for the previous generation and for the current generation, Moses points to YHWH's might in battle as an encouragement to be faithful to the ways of YHWH. In Deuteronomy 10 the ethical implication is moral transformation in circumcising the heart (v. 16). The basis for ethics is the character of God as Sovereign over all creation and as the Mighty Warrior who chose Israel and shepherded them out of slavery and through the desert.

In light of this parallel we see that a deuteronomic moral dynamic informs Psalm 24. The connection between the Divine King and those who seek him is not in this instance a matter of imitation but rather of hope. The people of YHWH walk in his ways because they have been chosen for relationship with the Divine Sovereign who is their security.

CONCLUSION

I have argued that in Psalm 24 the convergence of the metaphors of refuge and pathway in section two are extended in sections one and three. Theology and ethics combine in a liturgy that teaches by describing. The ethic of Psalm 24 is situated in relationship to the Divine King. Therefore the ethic is theocentric, not in the manner of *imitatio dei* but rather as an entailment of the covenant relationship between Israel and YHWH. As Creator he is the Sovereign over the whole earth, and as the victorious and mighty Warrior-King he is the guarantor of the security of the one who seeks him. This vision of the King of Glory provides a powerful context for the ethical life. Only the King of Glory can give the worshipper confidence that seeking him is of incomparable value and claim exclusive devotion. In contrast to Canaanite or Mesopotamian idolatry, in which security is found in caring for idols,[159] YHWH seeks worshippers who care for one another, the very thing that YHWH does for Israel.

---

159. Block, "The Joy of Worship," 109–10.

4

Psalm 34

INTRODUCTION

In turning to Psalm 34, we feel we have entered a different world. Instead of the focus on temple and Zion that we find in Psalms 15 and 24, Psalm 34 describes the *telos* of the righteous as life. Furthermore, the form and rhetoric match the wisdom literature in certain respects. Scholars have helpfully focused on the wisdom connections and the acrostic structure of the psalm. However, they have largely bypassed the ethical dimension of Psalm 34 and overlooked the literary and conceptual connections to the two earlier psalms as well as to Deuteronomy.

As in previous chapters, my goal is to clarify the ethical concerns of Psalm 34 and to situate those concerns within the theological context of the psalm. I will argue that the second half of the psalm (vv. 12–23[11–22]) is a structural and conceptual parallel to the character sketches in Psalms 15 and 24. It makes a close connection between doing good and enjoying the good life. Yet when compared to the earlier two psalms, Psalm 34 takes ethical instruction in a distinct direction. As in Psalms 15 and 24, the metaphor of refuge is prominent in Psalm 34 as the benefit of the pathway of the righteous, but Psalm 34 adds two important experiential dimensions. First, it moves from personal deliverance to corporate praise. Second, it confronts the problem of evil with a vision of life for the righteous sufferer. In addition to the strong wisdom resemblances, this psalm's vision of life draws on the

Portraits of the Righteous in the Psalms

Deuteronomic language of instruction to the individual to shape righteous character.

I begin by translating and clarifying the text of Psalm 34 and then discuss the literary genre and structure. With that foundation I will explore the psalm in two parts corresponding to the two strophes distinguished by the persona of the psalmist. In the first strophe the psalmist is a fellow-worshipper (vv. 2–11[1–10]), and in the second he is the wisdom teacher (vv. 12–23[11–22]).

TRANSLATION AND TEXT-CRITICAL ANALYSIS OF PSALM 34

Although I focus on the character sketch in verses 12–23[11–22], the entire psalm forms the theological context. Therefore the following translation and subsequent text-critical analysis considers the whole psalm:

לְדָוִד	1	Of David
בְּשַׁנּוֹתוֹ אֶת־טַעְמוֹ לִפְנֵי אֲבִימֶלֶךְ		when he feigned madness before Abimelech
וַיְגָרֲשֵׁהוּ וַיֵּלַךְ׃		and he drove him out, and he went.
	א	
אֲבָרֲכָה אֶת־יְהוָה בְּכָל־עֵת	2a	I will bless YHWH at all times,
תָּמִיד תְּהִלָּתוֹ בְּפִי׃	2b	His praise will continually be in my mouth.
	ב	
בַּיהוָה תִּתְהַלֵּל נַפְשִׁי	3a	In YHWH my soul boasts,
יִשְׁמְעוּ עֲנָוִים וְיִשְׂמָחוּ׃	3b	Let the poor hear and be glad.
	ג	
גַּדְּלוּ לַיהוָה אִתִּי	4a	Magnify YHWH with me,
וּנְרוֹמְמָה שְׁמוֹ יַחְדָּו׃	4b	And let us exalt his name together.
	ד	
דָּרַשְׁתִּי אֶת־יְהוָה וְעָנָנִי	5a	I sought YHWH and he answered me,
וּמִכָּל־מְגוּרוֹתַי הִצִּילָנִי׃	5b	And from all my horrors he delivered me.
	ה	
הִבִּיטוּ אֵלָיו וְנָהָרוּ	6a	They looked to him and they shone,
וּפְנֵיהֶם אַל־יֶחְפָּרוּ׃	6b	Do not let their faces be ashamed.
	ז	
זֶה עָנִי קָרָא וַיהוָה שָׁמֵעַ	7a	This poor one cried, and YHWH heard,

Psalm 34

וּמִכָּל־צָרוֹתָיו הוֹשִׁיעוֹ:	7b	And from all his distress he saved him.
ח		
חֹנֶה מַלְאַךְ־יְהוָה	8a	The angel of YHWH encamps
סָבִיב לִירֵאָיו וַיְחַלְּצֵם:	8b	around those who fear him, and he delivers them.
ט		
טַעֲמוּ וּרְאוּ כִּי־טוֹב יְהוָה	9a	Taste and see that YHWH is good,
אַשְׁרֵי הַגֶּבֶר יֶחֱסֶה־בּוֹ:	9b	Happy is the man who takes refuge in him.
י		
יְראוּ אֶת־יְהוָה קְדֹשָׁיו	10a	Fear YHWH, O his holy ones,
כִּי־אֵין מַחְסוֹר לִירֵאָיו:	10b	For there is no lack for those who fear him.
כ		
כְּפִירִים רָשׁוּ וְרָעֵבוּ	11a	Young lions are poor and hungry,
וְדֹרְשֵׁי יְהוָה לֹא־יַחְסְרוּ כָל־טוֹב:	11b	But those who seek YHWH will not lack any good thing.
ל		
לְכוּ־בָנִים שִׁמְעוּ־לִי	12a	Come, O children, listen to me,
יִרְאַת יְהוָה אֲלַמֶּדְכֶם:	12b	I will teach you the fear of YHWH.
מ		
מִי־הָאִישׁ הֶחָפֵץ חַיִּים	13a	What man is there who desires life?
אֹהֵב יָמִים לִרְאוֹת טוֹב:	13b	Who loves days to see good?
נ		
נְצֹר לְשׁוֹנְךָ מֵרָע	14a	Keep your tongue from evil,
וּשְׂפָתֶיךָ מִדַּבֵּר מִרְמָה:	14b	And your lips from speaking deceit.
ס		
סוּר מֵרָע וַעֲשֵׂה־טוֹב	15a	Turn aside from evil and do good,
בַּקֵּשׁ שָׁלוֹם וְרָדְפֵהוּ:	15b	Seek peace and pursue it.
ע		
עֵינֵי יְהוָה אֶל־צַדִּיקִים	16a	The eyes of YHWH are to the righteous ones,
וְאָזְנָיו אֶל־שַׁוְעָתָם:	16b	And his ears to their cry.
פ		
פְּנֵי יְהוָה בְּעֹשֵׂי רָע	17a	The face of YHWH is against those who do evil,
לְהַכְרִית מֵאֶרֶץ זִכְרָם:	17b	To cut off their memory from the earth.
צ		
צָעֲקוּ וַיהוָה שָׁמֵעַ	18a	They cry out, and YHWH hears,

Portraits of the Righteous in the Psalms

וּמִכָּל־צָרוֹתָם הִצִּילָם׃	18b	And from all their distress he delivers them.
ק		
קָרוֹב יְהוָה לְנִשְׁבְּרֵי־לֵב	19a	YHWH is near to the broken-hearted,
וְאֶת־דַּכְּאֵי־רוּחַ יוֹשִׁיעַ׃	19b	And the crushed of spirit he saves.
ר		
רַבּוֹת רָעוֹת צַדִּיק	20a	Many are the troubles of the righteous,
וּמִכֻּלָּם יַצִּילֶנּוּ יְהוָה׃	20b	But from them all YHWH saves him.
ש		
שֹׁמֵר כָּל־עַצְמוֹתָיו	21a	He guards all his bones,
אַחַת מֵהֵנָּה לֹא נִשְׁבָּרָה׃	21b	Not one of them will be broken.
ת		
תְּמוֹתֵת רָשָׁע רָעָה	22a	Evil slays the wicked,
וְשֹׂנְאֵי צַדִּיק יֶאְשָׁמוּ	22b	And those who hate the righteous will suffer for their guilt.
פ		
פּוֹדֶה יְהוָה נֶפֶשׁ עֲבָדָיו	23a	YHWH redeems the life of his servants,
וְלֹא יֶאְשְׁמוּ כָּל־הַחֹסִים בּוֹ׃	23b	And all those who take refuge in him will not be held guilty.

The psalm shares two unusual features with Psalm 25.[1] First, it lacks the line for *wāw*. Second, an additional line in verse 23[22] begins with *pê*. David Noel Freedman rightly contends these unusual features cannot be the result of chance.[2] He suggests the additional *pê* line compensates for the loss of the *wāw* line.[3] Another explanation is possible. Skehan suggests that the first (א, v. 2[1]), middle (ל, v. 12[11]), and last (פ, v. 23[22]) lines complete the spelling of the first letter in the alphabet (אלף, 'ālep).[4] Although the omission of the *wāw* line means that the *lāmed* line does not occur in the center, Anthony Ceresko counters that a syllable count places the middle of the poem near the middle of the *lāmed* verse.[5] Among other similarities, this unusual variation on the acrostic links Psalms 25 and 34.[6] Therefore

---

1. Anderson, *The Book of Psalms*, 1:267; Craigie, *Psalms 1–50*, 277.
2. Freedman, "Patterns in Psalms 25 and 34," 125.
3. Ibid., 126–27.
4. Skehan, "Structure of the Song of Moses," 160, n. 13.
5. Ceresko, "The ABCs of Wisdom," 100.
6. For additional correspondences between these two psalms, see Maloney, "A Word Fitly Spoken," 194, 198; Maloney, "Intertextual Links," 11–21.

it is preferable to treat verse 23[22] as an original part of the psalm.[7] On the basis of Skehan's observation,[8] Ceresko further suggests that the three letters אלף also form the verb root meaning "to learn, teach." He supports this notion by pointing to the verb למד, "to teach," in the *lāmed* verse (v. 12[11]).[9] This cannot be proven, but it provides a plausible explanation for the presence of the final line.

Interpreters have noted an additional aspect of the acrostic structure. The subject appears to shift from the wicked in verse 17[16] to the righteous in verse 18[17]. To avoid ambiguity modern translations express a subject, "the righteous," in verse 18[17].[10] BHS suggests inverting the *'ayin* (v. 16[15]) and *pê* (v. 17[16]) lines, citing the order of the alphabet attested by Lamentations 2, 3, and 4.[11] This brings together the two verses about the righteous, eliminating the problem of an unexpressed subject. However, there are two difficulties with this interpretation. First, this introduces a different order than Psalm 25, with which Psalm 34 already shares two unusual features.[12] It seems more likely that the current order is original. Second, LXX adds οἱ δίκαιοι in verse 18[17], suggesting that ancient interpreters also saw this difficulty but did not regard it as a problem of ordering. I see no compelling reason to alter the order of the MT.[13]

Several text-critical issues deserve treatment. In verse 6a BHS suggests reading הַבִּיטוּ (hiphil imperative), along with several Medieval Hebrew manuscripts (as well as Aquila, Syriac, and Jerome). LXX translates with an imperative (προσέλθατε, "come to"). BHS also suggests taking the MT's perfect form וְנָהָרוּ ("they shone") as the imperative form וּנְהָרוּ ("shine") and therefore changing וּפְנֵיהֶם ("and their faces") to וּפְנֵיכֶם ("and your faces"). While this matches the mood of the negated prefixed form in verse 6b, אַל־יֶחְפָּרוּ ("do not let them be put to shame"), it does not match the person of the verb. The subject of the verbs is the crux of the issue. Kraus argues that the change to imperative is necessary because the subject is unexpressed.[14]

---

7. Contra Briggs, *Psalms*, 1:294–95, 299; Kraus, *Psalms 1–59*, 382.

8. Skehan, "Strophic Patterns," 127.

9. Ceresko, "The ABCs of Wisdom," 101.

10. So KJV, RSV, NRSV, ESV, NET, NASB. Alter simply translates the initial verb as an imperative (*Psalms*, 119). Cf. NJPS, "they."

11. See also Briggs, *Psalms*, 1:295; Kraus, *Psalms 1–59*, 382; Weiser, *The Psalms*, 299. For a more complete discussion of the evidence for various ordering of the West-Semitic alphabet, see Brug, "Biblical Acrostics," 287–88.

12. Cheyne, *The Book of Psalms*, 143.

13. Lunn points to a parallel construction in verse 7 (*Word-Order Variation*, 239).

14. Kraus, *Psalms 1–59*, 382. Those following the suggestion of BHS include Gerstenberger, *Psalms: Part 1*, 148; Schökel, "Contemplar y gustar (Sal 34,6.9)," 12; RSV;

Briggs argues that to change the mood would be abrupt and disrupt the parallelism. The אַל in verse 6[5] may be an error of transposition of an original לֹא.[15] Goldingay comments on both readings and observes that "both apply to other worshippers the message of the testimony."[16] This keeps the variant in perspective, but still we must make some kind of decision. Both readings present difficulties, but on balance it seems best to retain the MT rather than emending a portion of the verse to follow the sense of the LXX and the other versions.

In verse 11a, LXX (and Syriac) reads πλούσιοι ("rich ones") instead of כְּפִירִים ("young lions"). Kraus suggests the text of the MT is the result of an error in transmission, and should be understood as כְּבֵדִים or כַּבִּירִים, "the mighty," in keeping with the LXX reading,[17] but such a solution appears to uphold the *lectio facilior*. The reading of the LXX seems to harmonize with the mention of עָנִי in verse 7[6]. Goldingay suggests translating the term כְּפִירִים as "apostates" based on a sense of the root in later Hebrew.[18] But this requires understanding the word כְּפִיר as כָּפַר, though the former is well-attested in the Hebrew Bible. There is no reason to lean on etymology to clarify the meaning of the word, and his proposed solution removes a potent metaphor. J. J. M. Roberts argues that lions are used as a metaphor of the impious in a number of texts. Such impious lions go hungry in Eliphaz's speech in Job 4:7–11, and given this close parallel and its abrupt presentation in Psalm 34, it is likely that this is a traditional motif requiring no further explanation.[19] A similar motif related to lions appears in the "Babylonian Theodicy"[20] and the Kutha Legend,[21] both of which speak of lions as impious.[22] Roberts summarizes, "In short, the image of the young lions in Ps 34:11, far from being the result of textual corruption, stems from an old pre-Israelite proverbial motif which, if not created by, was at least at home in the wisdom literature, and through this channel Israel inherited

---

NRSV. However, the subject need not be expressed but can be understood from the context (VanGemeren, *Psalms*, 325). Those who retain MT include Anderson, *The Book of Psalms*, 1:270; Rashi, *Rashi's Commentary on Psalms*, 303; Alter, *Psalms*, 118; NASB; NPJS; ESV; NET; NLT.

15. Briggs, *Psalms*, 1:296, 299–300.
16. Goldingay, *Psalms*, 1:480.
17. Kraus, *Psalms 1–59*, 382.
18. Goldingay, *Psalms*, 1:480.
19. Roberts, "Young Lions," 262–63.
20. *COS* 1.154.
21. Gurney and Finkelstein, *The Sultantepe Tablets*, Nr 30:80–82.
22. Roberts, "Young Lions," 263–64.

it."²³ The MT reading כְּפִירִים, "young lions," is the *lectio difficilior* and is a known motif,²⁴ so it is best to retain it.²⁵

In verse 22a, instead of a verbal clause indicating that evil brings about the death of the wicked, LXX has a verbless clause: θάνατος ἁμαρτωλῶν πονηρός ("death of sinners is evil"). This transforms the line from a statement about the cause of the death of the wicked to an evaluation of it. This seems to be a translator's gloss that obscures this causal relationship witnessed by MT. Therefore I retain the text of MT.²⁶

LITERARY GENRE AND STRUCTURE OF PSALM 34

Harry Nasuti notes that the settings of psalms mixing didactic and liturgical elements are particularly elusive for form critics.²⁷ Psalm 34 is sometimes numbered among these mixed forms since it includes both thanksgiving and instruction.²⁸ While elements of thanksgiving are present, they serve a didactic purpose (cf. Psalm 32), giving the psalm an experiential character. The psalm builds a bridge between cult and wisdom, and between temple worship and everyday life outside the temple gates.

Is Psalm 34 Wisdom?

Although form critics traditionally classify Psalm 34 as a thanksgiving psalm,²⁹ Gunkel recognizes its tendency toward wisdom,³⁰ and Mowinckel

---

23. Ibid., 265. Cf. Craigie, *Psalms 1–50*, 277; VanGemeren, Psalms, 327
24. Roberts, "Young Lions," 362.
25. See also Strawn, *What is Stronger Than a Lion?*, 51.
26. BHS notes that the Targum's *mtwt'* could be reconstructed as the polal (passive) form of מות. With a passive verb "evil" is no longer the subject of the verb but rather as a complement of the verb. Cf. BHRG §33.2.
27. Nasuti, *Defining the Sacred Songs*, 193.
28. Eriksson, *Come, Children, Listen to Me!*, 79; Kraus, Psalms 1–59, 382–83.
29. Gunkel and Begrich, *Introduction to Psalms*, 190; Mowinckel, *The Psalms in Israel's Worship*, 38; Dahood, *Psalms I, 1–50*, 205; Ridderbos, *Die Psalmen*, 245; Brown, "Come, O children," 90; Maloney, "A Word Fitly Spoken," 197. Cf. Westermann, who classifies it as a "declarative psalm of praise" (*Praise and Lament in the Psalms*, 102). Although this classification matches the vocabulary employed in the first few verses of the psalm, it has not gained wide acceptance, and it does not account for the psalm's didactic characteristics.
30. Gunkel and Begrich, *Introduction to Psalms*, 297–98, 304. So also Ridderbos, *Die Psalmen*, 245.

suggests it has many characteristics of "learned psalmography."[31] Still, this "learned psalmography" has a similar purpose to thanksgiving. Mowinckel defines the thanksgiving psalm as a "testimony by one who has experienced salvation from distress and danger by Yahweh." The testimony is often brief and can take on the general character of a hymn with the purpose of "winning" others for God.[32] Elements of thanksgiving in Psalm 34 are evident in the psalmist's praise to YHWH (vv. 2–4[1–3]) and account of deliverance (vv. 5[4], 7[6]). These are consistent with the psalm's purpose of winning others over both to praise and the fear of YHWH (vv. 12–23[11–22]).

However, not all interpreters accept that it is a thanksgiving psalm. Roland Murphy notes that the report of deliverance is minimal, making it secondary to instruction.[33] Lars Olaf Eriksson argues that it can hardly be called a thanksgiving psalm since it does not address God,[34] it lacks the thanksgiving verb ידה, and includes nothing associated with the thank offering.[35] Furthermore, the psalm explicitly declares a didactic intent in verse 12[11] with the address in the first line, "Come, my sons" (לְכוּ־בָנִים), and the root למד in the second line. In addition to the acrostic structure and certain wisdom motifs, verse 12[11] has led many to identify Psalm 34 among the "wisdom psalms."[36] Kenneth Kuntz highlights the prominence of admonition, the address to "sons," the 'ašrê formula, and the rhetorical question.[37] Although the wisdom vocabulary isolated by R. B. Y. Scott[38] is not present in large concentration in Psalm 34, he maintains that ideological elements and stylistic features, including the alphabetic acrostic, are found in abundance.[39]

However, the category "wisdom psalm" is controversial.[40] Arguing in favor for it, Murphy argues that psalms originating from a *milieu sapientel*

---

31. Mowinckel, *The Psalms in Israel's Worship*, 2:38.

32. Ibid., 2:32–33, 38.

33. Murphy, "Wisdom Psalms," 163.

34. So also Goldingay, *Psalms*, 1:477.

35. Eriksson, *Come, Children, Listen to Me!*, 64.

36. See, e.g., Murphy, "Wisdom Psalms," 167; Scott, *The Way of Wisdom in the Old Testament*, 198; Kuntz, "The Canonical Wisdom Psalms," 218; VanGemeren, Psalms, 323.

37. Kuntz, "The Canonical Wisdom Psalms," 194–98.

38. Scott, *The Way of Wisdom in the Old Testament*, 121–22. See also the discussion of wisdom vocabulary in Whybray, *The Intellectual Tradition in the Old Testament*, 74–149.

39. Kuntz, "The Canonical Wisdom Psalms," 209–10.

40. Important early contributions fueling this debate include Gunkel and Begrich, *Introduction to Psalms*, 291–305; Mowinckel, *The Psalms in Israel's Worship*, 2:104–25;

should be treated as a literary form alongside other psalm forms,[41] but scholars disagree about how to identify wisdom psalms.[42] Although a number of attempts have been made to develop criteria, none has commanded a consensus.

We may illustrate the terms of this debate using two of its most active participants. In favor of wisdom psalms, Kenneth Kuntz proposes seven features may be used to identify them:

> (1) the "better" saying, (2) the numerical saying, (3) the admonition (*Mahnspruch*) with and without motive clause, (4) the admonitory address to "sons," (5) the '*ašrê* formula, (6) the rhetorical question, and (7) the simile. Not every rhetorical element here enumerated is the sole property of wisdom discourse. Nor is each attested in the Israelite Psalter in equal measure. Indeed, no claimed wisdom psalm contains all seven. Nevertheless, concentration upon such matters should facilitate our attempts at coming to terms with the style, content, and intention of psalmic wisdom.[43]

In contrast, James Crenshaw has argued strenuously that the pursuit of "wisdom psalms" yields little. He regards Gunkel's term *Weisheitsdichtung*, or "wisdom poetry" as a cause of more confusion than clarity.[44] Four out of five of Murphy's content-related criteria for wisdom apply to Amos, so Crenshaw wonders how many wisdom features are needed to identify a wisdom text. Furthermore, features seen as typical of wisdom are all found in non-wisdom texts. This raises doubts about whether they are unique identifiers of a wisdom origin.[45] He offers a cautious conclusion:

> Perhaps we should limit ourselves to what can definitely be affirmed: some psalms resemble wisdom literature in stressing the importance of learning, struggling to ascertain life's meaning, and employing proverbial lore. Their authorship and provenance matter less than the accuracy and profundity of what they say.[46]

Murphy, "Wisdom Psalms"; Kuntz, "The Canonical Wisdom Psalms"; Perdue, *Wisdom and Cult*; Hurvitz, "Wisdom Vocabulary in the Hebrew Psalter," 41–51.

41. Murphy, "Wisdom Psalms," 157, 167.
42. Eriksson, *Come, Children, Listen to Me!*, 74.
43. Kuntz, "The Canonical Wisdom Psalms," 197. See also Kuntz, "Wisdom Psalms and the Shaping of the Hebrew Psalter," 144–60.
44. Crenshaw, "Wisdom Psalms?" 9.
45. Ibid., 11–12, 14.
46. Ibid., 15.

Portraits of the Righteous in the Psalms

Expressing similar caution, William Brown asserts that criteria for identifying wisdom psalms must attain "universal consent." Until then, "The burden of proof lies in demonstrating that the alleged wisdom material in the Psalms is uniquely sapiential, an intractably difficult, if not impossible, task."[47] I wonder whether Brown and Crenshaw have set the bar inappropriately high on this issue. It may be precarious to identify uniquely sapiential features because literature and social contexts are far less compartmentalized than form critics would lead us to believe.[48] To be fair, this is implicit in Murphy's original argument,[49] and scholars rarely reach universal agreement. My own hunch is that Psalms 34 and 37 either arose from the wisdom tradition or share such affinities to the wisdom tradition that there must have been some influence. Even so, the debate about the status of "wisdom psalms" *as a distinct form* is at an impasse.[50]

The way forward is not to deny a wisdom dimension in the Psalter, which neither Crenshaw nor Brown do, but to explore the ways that dimension takes shape in particular texts. For that purpose Brown offers a helpful model, comparing and contrasting several so-called wisdom psalms with the book of Proverbs.[51]

Brown notes that the so-called wisdom psalms share didactic aims. By didactic, Brown means "anything meant for instruction that is explicitly indicated as such by form and/or language."[52] This is helpful as long as "form" includes texts that are formally didactic even if they do not explicitly declare that aim (cf. Ps 34:12[11]). Brown notes that didactic address exhibits a slightly different character in Psalms and Proverbs. Proverbs stands largely outside the realm of temple worship, but the Psalter is closely associated with worship.[53] While Proverbs is *implicitly* theocentric (since wisdom finds its source in the creative work of YHWH [Prov 8:22–31]), Psalms is *explicitly* theocentric.

---

47. Brown, "Come, O children," 85.

48. We do well to recognize the limitations of the form-critical enterprise, especially if one tries to force psalms into well-defined categories. So also Maloney, "A Word Fitly Spoken," 197; Eriksson, *Come, Children, Listen to Me!*, 79.

49. Murphy, "Wisdom Psalms," 159. Murphy is careful to state that *milieu sapientiel* is "not precisely a life-setting" (ibid., 167), which implies that wisdom psalms should be classified along with other psalm types but not precisely in the same way.

50. A recent exchange between Crenshaw and Kuntz does not seem to have resolved the issue: Crenshaw, "Wisdom Psalms?"; Kuntz, "Reclaiming Biblical Wisdom Psalms," 145–54; Crenshaw, "Gold Dust or Nuggets?" 155–58.

51. Brown, "Come, O children."

52. Ibid., 86.

53. Ibid., 101–102.

Psalm 34

The theocentric character of psalmic wisdom raises the question whether the influence of Deuteronomy has been sufficiently recognized in the Psalter. This is not surprising in view of Moshe Weinfeld's suggestion that in Deuteronomy wisdom and law are amalgamated.[54] Patrick Miller suggests that Deuteronomy and the Psalms "are amenable to an interactive relationship."[55] Like Proverbs and some psalms, Deuteronomy is expressly didactic.[56] Miller suggests that, "When the Psalmist says, 'Come, O children, listen to me; I will teach you the fear of the Lord' (Ps 34:12[11]), one hears as well the voice of Moses in those words."[57] Weinfeld suggests that the imperative of שמע comes from the didactic vocabulary of Deuteronomy.[58] However, we also find more broad thematic connections between the Psalter and Deuteronomy, including the metaphor of the pathway (Deut 5:33; 8:6; 9:12, 16; 10:12; 11:22, 28; 13:5; 19:9; 26:17; 28:9, 29; 30:16; 31:29), the promise of life for those who embrace the righteous way (30:15, 19–20; 32:47),[59] and the contrasting end for the wicked (30:15, 19).

In Psalm 34 we see both wisdom and deuteronomic language. Resemblances to the book of Proverbs are evident in the address to sons (v. 12[11]; see Prov 4:1; 5:7; 7:24; 8:32),[60] the presentation of the choice of life (v. 13[12]; see Prov 3:2, 16, 18, 22; 4:10, 13, 22, 23; 6:23; 8:35; 9:11, etc.), and the language of the fear of YHWH (vv. 10[9], 12[11]; see Prov 1:7, 3:7, *et passim*). We can see the connection with Proverbs particularly in Prov 3:7–8:

אַל־תְּהִי חָכָם בְּעֵינֶיךָ	7a	Do not be wise in your own eyes
יְרָא אֶת־יְהוָה וְסוּר מֵרָע׃	7b	Fear YHWH and flee from evil.
רִפְאוּת תְּהִי לְשָׁרֶּךָ	8a	It will be healing for your body
וְשִׁקּוּי לְעַצְמוֹתֶיךָ׃	8b	And refreshment for your bones.

---

54. Weinfeld, *Deuteronomy and the Deuteronomic School*, 256.

55. Miller, "Deuteronomy and Psalms," 5. For one such "conversation," see Grant, *The King as Exemplar*.

56. Block, "Will the Real Moses Please Rise?" 80, n. 41. Block notes that Deuteronomy applies the Piel forms לַמֵּד, "to teach" (Deut 4:1, 5, 14; 6:1; 31:19, 22) and דִּבֶּר, "to speak" (1:1, 3, 18; 4:45; 5:1, 31; 31:30) to Moses, and it admonishes the Israelites with the Qal form לָמַד, "to learn," (4:10; 5:1; possibly 17:19; 31:12), and as well as the Piel form of למד, "to teach" (5:31; 11:19); he also notes the use of שָׁנַן, "to recite" (6:7). So also Miller, "Deuteronomy and Psalms," 15.

57. Miller, "Deuteronomy and Psalms," 15.

58. Weinfeld, *Deuteronomy and the Deuteronomic School*, 304–5.

59. Ibid., 307.

60. Gerstenberger notes that this plural address is a wisdom formula and unparalleled in the Psalter (*Psalms: Part 1*, 148).

Although Psalm 34 does not contain the epistemological element of Prov 3:7–8,[61] the admonition to fear YHWH and turn from evil closely resembles Ps 34:12[11], 15[14].

The voice of the teacher in Ps 34:12–23[11–22] resembles the words of Moses in Deut 30:15–20. Also instruction, Deut 30:15 presents a choice: "See, I have set before you this day life and good, death and evil." The terms "life" (הַחַיִּים), "the good" (הַטּוֹב), and "evil" (הָרָע) occur in Psalm 34, and the psalm also presents a choice similar to Deuteronomy 30 in the second half of the psalm.

But do the visions of the moral ideal in the two passages match? Deuteronomy 30:16 speaks of מִצְוָה, "command," a term not found in Psalm 34, but Deuteronomy closely connects מִצְוָה and walking in the ways of YHWH in 30:16 and elsewhere (11:22; 19:9). This latter metaphor is prominent in the Psalter and present in Psalm 34, as I will show below.

The "wisdom psalm" debate outlined above has distracted readers from the task of examining the similarities and differences between Psalms and Proverbs and has virtually ignored resemblances to Deuteronomy found in didactic psalms. Psalm 34 is didactic, and that is the core literary question.[62] Furthermore, this didactic character and the linguistic and thematic similarities to both Proverbs and Deuteronomy suggest that the wisdom psalm debate is in fact too narrow in its vision.

Didactic and Thanksgiving Elements in Psalm 34

The more pressing literary question for Psalm 34 is the relationship between its didactic and thanksgiving elements. Scholars answer this question in various ways. Craigie sees the first half as a thanksgiving psalm (vv. 2–11 [1–10]), and the second half as a wisdom psalm (vv. 12–23[11–22]).[63] Kraus speaks of unmistakable thanksgiving intentions being "caught up in a didactic poem which is conceived under the influence of wisdom traditions."[64] As noted above, early form critics simply posited wisdom influence, placing thanksgiving in the foreground and wisdom in the background. Some later interpreters have sought to do the opposite. Murphy speaks of the thanksgiving element as a "springboard" into wisdom teaching.[65] Although he

---

61. Brown, "Come, O children," 91.

62. Sociological questions may be helpful, but the impasse in the debate suggests that we lack sufficient information to tie psalms to wisdom circles.

63. Craigie, *Psalms 1–50*, 278.

64. Kraus, *Psalms 1–59*, 383.

65. Murphy, "Wisdom Psalms," 163. Kuntz follows Murphy in asserting that

acknowledges thanksgiving elements, Leo Perdue argues that sapiential vocabulary, the wisdom themes of retribution and the contrast between righteous and wicked, as well as an emphasis on personal experience dominate the psalm. Therefore Psalm 34 should be regarded as a didactic poem structured around a key proverb, which he locates in verse 23[22].[66] Although he suggests that strophe I (vv. 2–11[1–10]) was originally a thanksgiving psalm, "it has been taken by a wisdom teacher and used as a model thanksgiving for the instruction of young schoolboys in the 'fear of the Lord.'"[67] Is the didactic element primary or secondary?

The didactic element is primary because it is evident throughout the psalm.[68] In verses 2–11 there are admonitions of one kind or another in verses 3b[2b], 4[3], 9a[8a], and 10a[9a].[69] Gnomic or proverbial statements are scattered throughout, including verses 8[7], 9b[8b], 10b[9b], and 11 in verses 2–11. The account of deliverance is terse, suggesting that it is secondary.[70] Finally, the experience of deliverance in the first half is entirely generalized in the second half of the psalm. Deliverance and the expression of praise become the occasion for instruction.[71] Yet as Kraus points out, the "theory of retribution" in the psalm occurs in the context of experience. It is not a naïve eudaimonism; the psalmist recounts his experience before declaring the certainty of YHWH's deliverance and the suffering of the righteous.[72] Although the didactic element is primary, the element of thanksgiving cannot be overlooked without falling into a naïve interpretation.

The Acrostic Form

The acrostic form of Psalm 34 is the most conspicuous literary feature of the psalm. Since this poetic compositional style has been studied in great

---

thanksgiving is secondary to wisdom in Psalm 34 ("The Canonical Wisdom Psalms," 204).

66. Perdue, *Wisdom and Cult*, 273.

67. Ibid., 279. This intriguing possibility suffers from one methodological difficulty. As Kuntz points out, Perdue's selection of the proverb around which the psalm is supposedly structured is a rather arbitrary decision ("Wisdom Psalms and the Shaping of the Hebrew Psalter," 148). So also Gerstenberger, *Psalms: Part 1*, 148.

68. As noted above (see p. 101–2), Mowinckel defines the thanksgiving psalm in didactic terms.

69. Following the MT as I do above, verse 6[5] does not contain an imperative form.

70. Murphy, "Wisdom Psalms," 163

71. This suggests that the original *Sitz im Leben* may have been in a context of temple worship, with the wisdom tradition exerting influence in its language and form. We cannot be certain of this conclusion, however.

72. Kraus, *Psalms 1–59*, 387.

detail by others,[73] I do not need to rehearse or repeat such work. Our concern is how the acrostic form contributes to our understanding of the ethical issues in the psalm.

While earlier interpreters considered the acrostic structure to be forced at best and worthless at worst,[74] recent scholarship has emphasized the poetic artistry of the acrostics.[75] For the purpose of interpretation, we must consider the significance of the acrostic structure. Craigie summarizes three main proposals, that it serves (1) as an artistic device/framework, (2) as a mnemonic/educational device, or (3) to imply completeness. He suggests that the first is fundamental.[76] However, the significance of the structure may not be monolithic from poem to poem. Therefore I focus on the particular way in which the acrostic seems to be functioning in Psalm 34.

The similarities between Psalms 25 and 34 have drawn attention of scholars, especially the addition of the *pê* line at the end. The most obvious explanation is that initial letters of the lines at the beginning, middle, and end form אלף, or the first letter of the alphabet, thus signifying that the psalm deals with its subject in a complete manner.[77] Another explanation is that these three consonants form the verb אלף, "to learn, to teach."[78] Thus the structure of the psalm encodes its intention. Both proposals are possible. However, neither can be proved or disproved,[79] and neither sheds additional light on the psalm.

Attention to additional detail in similar acrostics seems to offer the greatest promise. Ronald Benun argues that missing letters are a part of the

---

73. For studies on meter using acrostic poems as a basis see Freedman, "Acrostics and Metrics in Hebrew Poetry," 367–92; Freedman, "Acrostic Poems," 408–31; Houk, "Acrostic Psalms and Syllables," 54–60. A number of other studies explore the acrostic structure from various angles: Bazak, "Structural Geometric Patterns," 475–502; Ceresko, "The ABCs of Wisdom"; Brug, "Biblical Acrostics"; Gaebelein, "Psalm 34 and Other Biblical Acrostics," 127–43; Freedman, "Patterns in Psalms 25 and 34"; Hurowitz, "Additional Elements," 326–33; Maloney, "A Word Fitly Spoken."

74. For a summary of earlier views on the acrostics, see Liebreich, "Psalms 34 and 145," 181–82. Commentators following the view that the acrostic is artificial include Briggs, *Psalms*, 1:295; Dahood, *Psalms I*, 1–50, 205.

75. Maloney, "A Word Fitly Spoken"; Maloney "Intertextual Links." See also Auffret, *Hymnes d'Égypte et d'Israël*, 91.

76. Craigie, *Psalms 1–50*, 129. In addition, some scholars suggest that the alphabetic structure is apparent to the eyes but not the ears, so the psalm was written to be read and not heard (Gunkel and Begrich, *Introduction to Psalms*, 211, 341; Eriksson, *Come, Children, Listen to Me!*, 43). The structure is obvious to the eye, but that does not preclude aural detection by astute listeners (personal conversation with Dr. C. Hassell Bullock).

77. Botha, "The Social Setting and Strategy of Psalm 34," 182.

78. Skehan, "Strophic Patterns," 127; also Ceresko, "The ABCs of Wisdom," 101.

79. The same can be said of the geometric argument of Bazak ("Structural Geometric Patterns").

artistry of the biblical acrostics in general and serve as signposts for the embedded meaning of each psalm.[80] First he notes that in Psalms 9/10 the acrostic structure is interrupted at key points, and the proper alphabetic order is preserved when God is present to restore order.[81] Psalm 25 lacks both the *wāw* and the *qôp* lines, two lines that restore order in Psalms 9/10. He suggests that their absence in Psalm 25 has a symbolic significance. The role of YHWH in restoring order is highlighted in both psalms, but the role of the letters is different. Psalm "9/10 is a statement about how God's presence restores order. Ps 25 is all about having hope when the situation is bleak. As noted, the word קוה, meaning hope, occurs three times in this psalm at vv 3, 5, and 21."[82] Turning to Psalm 34 he notes that there is much shared language with Psalm 25. The *mêm* verse in both has a question about what kind of person fears YHWH or desires life (25:12 // 34:13[12]), but only Psalm 34 has an answer (34:14–15[13–14]).[83] Based on a series of similarities, Benun argues that Psalm 34 is the answer to Psalm 25 (see Table a).[84]

Table a. Psalm 34 as the Answer to Psalm 25 according to Benun

Letter	Psalm 25	Psalm 34
ʿAyin	v. 15: eyes of the psalmist are toward YHWH	v. 16[15]: eyes of YHWH are toward the righteous
Pê	v. 16: פְּנֵה־אֵלַי, "Turn to me and be gracious to me"	v. 17[16]: פְּנֵי יְהוָה, "the face of YHWH is against those who do evil"
Ṣādê	v. 17: צָרוֹת לְבָבִי, "the *distress* of my heart"	v. 18[17]: צָעֲקוּ, "they [the righteous] *cry out*"
Rêš	v. 19: רְאֵה־אוֹיְבַי כִּי־רָבּוּ, "See my foes, that they are *numerous*"	v. 20[19]: רַבּוֹת רָעוֹת צַדִּיק, "*many* are the *troubles* of the righteous"
Śîn/Šîn	v. 20: שָׁמְרָה נַפְשִׁי, "*Guard* my life"	v. 21[20]: שֹׁמֵר כָּל־עַצְמוֹתָיו, "He [YHWH] *guards* all his bones"
Final Pê	v. 22: פְּדֵה אֱלֹהִים אֶת־יִשְׂרָאֵל, "*Redeem* Israel, O God"	v. 23[22]: פּוֹדֶה יהוה נֶפֶשׁ עֲבָדָיו, "YHWH *redeems* the life of his servants"

While in Psalm 25 the psalmist does not know whether his prayer is answered, Psalm 34 articulates the experience of answered prayer. This is

80. Benun, "Evil and the Disruption of Order," 2–3.
81. Ibid., 6.
82. Ibid., 12.
83. Ibid., 13.
84. Ibid., 14.

symbolically represented in the presence of the *qôp* line in Ps 34:19[18], in which YHWH is near to the broken-hearted. According to Benun,

> The missing ק verse in Ps 25, where the Psalmist must rely on simple faith alone, may poetically represent the lack of past evidence for God's intervention. Ps 34 responds to the hopeless predicament of Ps 25 with a confident announcement that God has and will again answer the prayer of the downtrodden. This is poetically represented by the return of the ק verse. . . .
>
> While the acrostic of Pss 9/10 was a meditation on the effects of evil, Pss 25 and 34 bring us into the real world where the wicked prosper, and the downtrodden have nowhere to turn. In this world, God is not yet present. Ps 25 encourages prayer, even though it seems hopeless. Ps 34 backs up that encouragement with historical instances where prayer was effective.[85]

This remarkable correspondence shows that the acrostic structure of the psalm as a whole plays a key role not just in the interpretation of Psalm 34 but also in its canonical connection to Psalm 25, a topic to which I will return in chapter 6.

The Progression of the Discourse

To return to the structure of Psalm 34, Eriksson rightly notes that multiple ways of understanding the structure of Psalm 34 are possible, and in any construal a meaningful structure is evident. However, in spite of the diversity of structural analyses, we can see that verse 12[11] is "the focal line of the psalm."[86] This verse introduces a significant shift in the discourse, though scholars debate whether verses 9–15[8–14] should be taken as a unit or as parts of two distinct strophes. At one level the discussion creates a false dilemma because the alphabetic structure of the psalm as a whole holds all the lines together as one poem. But at another level perceiving a logical division helps account for the progression of thought.

It is possible that the *pê* line was added after the *tāw* line in order to complete the root אלף using the beginning, middle, and ending letters. However, more evidence can be cited in favor of a shift in verse 12[11]. First, like some other acrostic psalms, the *lāmed* line appears to play a significant role in the structure of the poem. Will Soll notes that a similar shift takes place at the *lāmed* line in Psalm 9/10. There the shift is from thanksgiving to lament,

---

85. Ibid., 15.
86. Eriksson, *Come, Children, Listen to Me!*, 54.

but in Psalm 34 the shift is from thanksgiving to instruction. He suggests that the *lāmed* line is often pivotal in acrostics because it is the first letter in the second half of the alphabet.[87] However, as Brug points out, the absence of a *wāw* line and the presence of a second *pê* line in Psalm 34 means that the *lāmed* line is not really the middle of the poem.[88] The solution to this may be that "the writer of Psalm 34 thought it more important to retain the 22-line pattern than to get the *lamed* into the exact middle."[89] Furthermore, as noted above, the *lāmed* line is the middle of the poem based on syllable counts.[90] Therefore we have good reason to believe that the *lāmed* is meant to be understood as a significant juncture in the poem.

In addition to formal indicators, the content of the psalm supports this interpretation. Scholars debate the effect of key words on the structure of the poem, but the evidence favors both a shift in verse 12[11] and the unity of content between what precedes and what follows. Liebreich argues that verses 5–11[4–10] are marked by an inclusion involving a collocation of יהוה and דרש in verses 5a[4a] and 11b[10b]. He also shows that verses 5–11[4–10] and verses 12–15[11–14] are tied together by the occurrence of טוב (vv. 9[8], 11[10]), 13[12]; 15[14]).[91] Pierre Auffret argues that verses 9–15[8–14] need to be taken together because of the recurrence of key words. Based on the distribution of these key words Auffret identifies a concentric structure (see Table b).[92]

Table b. The Concentric Structure of Psalm 34:9–15[8–14] according to Auffret

Verse	ראה	טוב	ירא	יהוה	הַגֶּבֶר/הָאִישׁ
v. 9	ראה	טוב			הַגֶּבֶר
v. 10			ירא	יהוה	
v. 11		טוב		יהוה	
v. 12			ירא	יהוה	
v. 13	ראה	טוב			הָאִישׁ

This concentric structure clearly signals a compositional unity between verses 9–11[8–10] and verses 12–15[11–14].

---

87. Soll, *Psalm 119*, 13, 14, 30.
88. Cf. Wilson, *Psalms*, 566.
89. Brug, "Biblical Acrostics," 289.
90. Ceresko, "The ABCs of Wisdom," 100.
91. Liebreich, "Psalms 34 and 145," 183–85.
92. Auffret, *Hymnes d'Égypte et d'Israël*, 80–81.

Portraits of the Righteous in the Psalms

Marc Girard identifies a concentric structure involving three diptychs of varying length in verses 5–18[4–17], 18–21[17–20], and 22–23[21–22].[93] A diptych is a painting or other visual art with two panels mirroring each other. Girard argues that the first diptych is bounded by verses 5b[4b] and 18b[17b] since they both employ מִכָּל and the hiphil form of the verb נצל, "to deliver." As such these two verses embody the movement from an experience of deliverance to instruction of others.[94] The diptych is divided at verse 12[11]:

    A vv. 5–7
      B vv. 8–11
      B' vv. 12–15
    A' vv. 15B–18[95]

Within the center of this concentric structure he notes a correspondence of terms in an ABCA'B'C' pattern, involving fearing in verses 8[7] and 12[11], seeing good in verses 9[8] and 13[12], and seeking good in verses 10–11[9–10] and 14–15[13–14].[96] However, verse 10[9] employs the language of the fear of YHWH (parallel to verses 8[7] and 12[11]) but not seeking, while verse 14 simply resists this neat structure, lacking any linguistic counterpart in verses 8–11[7–10].

The observations above reveal the complexity of the linguistic connections within the psalm, but key words are not the only consideration in identifying the structure of a text and its progression of thought. Ridderbos notes that in verse 12[11] the psalmist takes on the persona of the wisdom teacher (*Weisheitslehrer*), though there are signs of this starting in verse 10[9].[97] The imperative address of the teacher to pupils, "Come, children, and listen to me," (לְכוּ־בָנִים שִׁמְעוּ־לִי) is a wisdom formula used repeatedly in Proverbs both in plural and singular forms (singular: 1:8, 10, 15; 2:1; 3:1; 5:1; 6:1; plural: 4:1; 5:7; 7:24; 8:32).[98] This call to hear often marks the beginning of a new discourse unit in Proverbs 1–9.[99] This suggests a new discourse unit starts in verse 12[11]. One may object that wisdom features such as the gnomic statements in verses 9–11[8–10], and the mention of the fear of YHWH in verse 10[9] tie in with verse 12[11]. This objection argues

    93. Girard, *Les Psaumes*, 1:268.
    94. Ibid., 1:270.
    95. Ibid., 1:269–70.
    96. Ibid., 1:270.
    97. Ridderbos, *Die Psalmen*, 249. So also Murphy, "Wisdom Psalms," 63; Perdue, *Wisdom and Cult*, 278; Auffret, *Hymnes d'Égypte et d'Israël*, 81.
    98. Gerstenberger, *Psalms: Part 1*, 148.
    99. Fox, *Proverbs 1–9*, 79.

for the overall unity of the psalm. Instruction begins even in the context of thanksgiving—the psalmist does not hesitate to generalize from his experience. But the psalmist does not explicitly take on the role of teacher until the wisdom formula in verse 12[11].

Therefore, based on discourse structure, Psalm 34 consists of two strophes, with the second starting in verse 12[11].[100] The psalm is an integrated whole, with the alphabet serving as the structure holding it together and shaping the form of its expression. However, this integrated whole exhibits a progression in the direction of address. In the first half the psalmist takes on the persona of the fellow-worshipper, admonishing others to join in his praise for YHWH's gracious deliverance. This praise arises from an experience of deliverance and results in instruction to others on the protective care of YHWH. Already beginning to instruct on the basis of that experiential foundation, the psalmist explicitly dons the mantle of a teacher in the second half to instruct those who desire the good life to be virtuous in speech and deed. This instruction is cast as a choice of life and death, with proverbial sayings completing the discourse. We may represent the discourse structure of Psalm 34 as follows:

I. Title (v. 1)

II. Strophe I: In the Persona of the Fellow-worshipper

   A. Declaration of Praise Leading to an Invitation to Praise (v. 2–4[1–3])

   B. Testimony Leading to Instruction (vv. 5–11[4–10])

III. Strophe II: In the Persona of the Wisdom Teacher

   A. Introduction to Instruction on the Fear of YHWH (vv. 12–13[11–12])

   B. Fear of YHWH Embodied (vv. 14–15[13–14])

   C. The End of the Fear of YHWH and its Opposite (vv. 16–23[15–22])

How does the genre and structure analysis above contribute to our analysis of the ethical concerns in Psalm 34? In what follows I seek to isolate the theological context for ethics, as well as to clarify what is characteristic of the righteous/ethical person. Psalm 34 employs the metaphor of YHWH as refuge more explicitly than either Psalms 15 and 24, but it moves beyond the metaphor of refuge to paint a picture of well-being from multiple angles of view. When we consider the broad structure of the psalm, the theological

---

100. So also Perdue, *Wisdom and Cult*, 275; Botha, "The Social Setting and Strategy of Psalm 34," 181.

context has two foci: a past orientation in the first half of the psalm and a future orientation in the second. Both affirm that the good life is to be found in fearing YHWH. However, Psalm 34 affirms the worth of fearing YHWH in the context of the suffering of the righteous, a theme that is essentially absent from Psalm 15 and 24.

INSTRUCTION FROM THE FELLOW-WORSHIPPER (VV. 2-11[1-10])

What is the theological context for ethics in Psalm 34? In the first section it is an "experiential" theology, a doxology driven by an experience of deliverance. But it is also a metaphorical theology, employing a rich mosaic of images to draw others into the experience of YHWH's deliverance and care.

In this section the psalmist is a fellow-worshipper, whose experience of deliverance motivates both praise and instruction. He assumes a connection with his audience. First, he invites the "poor" (עֲנָוִים) to rejoice with him (v. 3[2]). Then in verse 7[6] he identifies himself as one of the poor. Patrick Miller observes that the poor in Deut 15:9 (הָאֶבְיוֹן) and 24:15 (עָנִי; v. 14: אֶבְיוֹן) cry out (קרא) to YHWH when their better-situated countrymen take advantage of them for gain.[101] The poor look to YHWH to be their advocate in the case of economic oppression. However, following Martin-Achard,[102] Botha understands the עָנִי in verses 3[2] and 7[6] as poor in their spiritual state, that is, referring to a state of mind.[103] Nothing in Psalm 34 suggests economic poverty, and a mental/spiritual interpretation of the term is reasonable given the description of the righteous in verse 19[18] as broken-hearted and crushed in spirit. However, reading between the lines, the economically poor are more likely to be in such a position. Certainly the wealthy encounter hard times, but it makes more sense to see the עָנִי as at least socially oppressed, if not economically oppressed, especially in view of the fact that the language appears to echo the language of Deut 24:15. Also, the ironic proverb in verse 11[10] about young lions going hungry, as well as the general focus on YHWH's provision in verses 8–11[7–10], suggests an economic dimension. We cannot be sure about the sociological context of this psalm,[104] but by referring to himself as one of the עָנִי who addresses the עֲנָוִים, the psalmist identifies with his audience.

---

101. Miller, "Deuteronomy and Psalms," 7.
102. Martin-Achard, "ענה ʿnh II," 345–46.
103. Botha, "The Social Setting and Strategy of Psalm 34," 185.
104. Kraus, *Theology of the Psalms*, 150–51, 153, notes that the designation "poor" is applied to the psalmist, often when the psalmist is appealing for justice. So also

Psalm 34

However, the psalmist's description of YHWH and *his* relationship to the עָנִי takes precedence in the discourse and provides metaphors and concepts that shape the theological context for ethics in Psalm 34.

First, the two explicit references to past experience are confined to the first half of the psalm (vv. 5[4] and 7[6]). They share a logical structure and a theology of prayer, though the vocabulary shifts. See Table c below.

Table c. A Comparison of Psalm 34:5[4] and 7[6]

Ps 34:5[4]	Ps 34:7[6]
דָּרַשְׁתִּי אֶת־יְהוָה וְעָנָנִי	זֶה עָנִי קָרָא וַיהוָה שָׁמֵעַ
וּמִכָּל־מְגוּרוֹתַי הִצִּילָנִי:	וּמִכָּל־צָרוֹתָיו הוֹשִׁיעוֹ:
I *sought* YHWH and he *answered* me,	This poor one *cried*, and YHWH *heard*,
And from all my *fears* he *delivered* me.	And from all his *distress* he *saved* him.

The verb for seeking YHWH is דרש, "seek" on the left,[105] and קרא, "cry, call" on the right. YHWH's response is ענה on the left, and שמע on the right. In both the result is comprehensive (מִכָּל), but the psalmist seeks relief from "fears" (מְגוּרָה)[106] on the left and "distress" (צָרָה) on the right. Finally, the verbs for deliverance are נצל on the left and ישע on the right. In addition, the verbs change from first person (v. 5[4]) to third person (v. 7[6]), suggesting a movement from personal testimony to instruction (cf. Ps 51:12–13).

This movement is also evident in verses 6[5] and 8[7]. Both are cast in the third person and move away from the personal experience of the psalmist to the generalized experience of others. Thematically the latter (v. 8[7]) is closer to verses 5[4] and 7[5] because it speaks of YHWH's deliverance. The hiphil form of נצל ties in with verse 5—the psalmist's experience of deliverance happens for those who fear YHWH. Although commentators disagree over whether the "angel of YHWH" here refers to YHWH himself or a protective angel, they agree that this figure's presence brings protection.[107] The

---

Eriksson, *Come, Children, Listen to Me!*, 17. Still, the frequency of this designation need not necessarily preclude an economic dimension.

105. Cf. Ps 24:6.

106. Van Pelt and Kaiser, "גוּר (*gûr* III)," 840, seem to imply that the source of terror is YHWH himself, by analogy to Isa 66:4. However, there does not appear to be any hint that YHWH is the source of such fears here.

107. For the former view, see Briggs, *Psalms*, 1:296; Anderson, *The Book of Psalms*, 1:271. For the latter view, see Cheyne, *The Book of Psalms*, 141; Eriksson, *Come, Children, Listen to Me!*, 15, who cites Exod 14:19 as a possible parallel. So also Kraus, *Psalms 1–59*, 384. Goldingay points to 2 Kgs 6:17, in which Elisha is permitted to see a host of invisible "horses and chariots of fire" around him (*Psalms*, 1:481).

second line of the bicolon affirms that the figure camping "around those who fear him [YHWH]" (סָבִיב לִירֵאָיו) protects them.

The experiential character of Psalm 34 continues in verse 6[5] with language of sensory perception. As noted above, although a number of interpreters prefer to read the verbs as imperatives, this is unnecessary.[108] If we do not follow Briggs' suggestion that the אַל is a transposed לֹא,[109] then this is the only place in which the psalmist may address YHWH directly.[110] Since this psalm moves from the experience of the psalmist to generalized experience, the general "they" is no surprise. The psalmist describes those who looked to YHWH and shone (נָהָרוּ). This appears strange until we recognize that elsewhere the psalmist speaks of YHWH in terms of light. This verb (נהר) is only used here and in Isa 60:5 and Jer 31:12. Both prophetic occurrences speak of the joy of returning exiles, who "shall be radiant over the goodness of the Lord" (Jer 31:12, NRSV). However, the metaphor of light in the Psalter is not confined to this verb. VanGemeren points out that in looking "for the light of God's countenance" they "were blessed with the abundance of his goodness and blessing (27:1, 4)."[111] Psalm 27:1 describes YHWH as "my light and my salvation" (אוֹרִי וְיִשְׁעִי), and other psalms speak of YHWH giving light to the psalmists (4:7[6]; 36:10[9]). Psalm 37:6 describes a person's righteousness coming out "like light," while in Ps 38:11[10] the psalmist laments the loss of the "light of my eyes" (אוֹר־עֵינַי). Light therefore consistently functions as a metaphor for the goodness and joy brought by YHWH's goodness.[112]

Verse 9[8] takes the language of sensory perception to a new level, "Taste and see that YHWH is good!" This is an invitation to experience.[113] While in verse 6[5] the psalmist speaks of the experience of others, in verse 9[8] he invites others to taste and see for themselves. As John Calvin notes, this verse invokes the senses to bring the audience to a new experience.[114] Although Gerstenberger suggests this may be a spiritualized reference to a sacrificial meal,[115] the object of tasting and seeing is YHWH himself. The

---

108. See p. 99 above.

109. Briggs, *Psalms*, 1:299–300.

110. Contra Gerstenberger, *Psalms: Part 1*, 147.

111. VanGemeren, *Psalms*, 325.

112. See also the Aaronic blessing (esp. Num 6:25), in which YHWH's blessing involves his face shining (יָאֵר) on the people. I am grateful to Dr. C. Hassell Bullock for pointing this text out to me.

113. So Briggs, *Psalms*, 1:297; Kraus, *Psalms 1–59*, 384; Mays, *Psalms*, 153.

114. Calvin, *Commentary on the Book of Psalms*, 2:563.

115. Gerstenberger, *Psalms: Part 1*, 148. So also Schökel, "Contemplar y gustar (Sal 34,6.9)," 20, though he does not see this possibility detracting from the role of the

psalm seems unconcerned with cultic matters and instead uses a metaphor to make a theological statement. It says, in effect, that YHWH is both DELICIOUS FOOD and A BEAUTIFUL SIGHT.[116] The goodness of YHWH is therefore brought into the world of sense perception. This imagery is bold, given the prohibition of images in the Decalogue (Exod 20:4 // Deut 5:8), but it is especially bold in its existential entailments.[117] The psalmist claims that what he experienced is open to all.

In the second line of verse 9[8] the psalmist returns to the concept of deliverance with an explicit use of the root חסה: "Happy (אַשְׁרֵי) is the man who takes refuge (יֶחֱסֶה) in him." This explicit reference to the metaphor, YHWH is A REFUGE, provides a point of connection with the metaphorical world we have seen in Psalms 15 and 24, a matter to which I will return below. For now it is important to note the use of the 'ašrê formula. Aside from its wisdom connections,[118] this formula occurs at key points in Book I,[119] including a verbal parallel in Ps 2:12b. Psalm 2 presents the metaphor of YHWH as a refuge for the first time in the Psalter: אַשְׁרֵי כָּל־חוֹסֵי בוֹ, "Happy are all who take refuge in him [YHWH]."[120] Although the more immediate referent of "him" is the son, that is the anointed one of verses 2 and 7, the protective power of the king is directly tied to YHWH. There and in Ps 34:9[8] refuge is found in YHWH.

The next verse declares the didactic payoff. The psalmist exhorts "his [YHWH's] holy ones" (קְדֹשָׁיו) to fear YHWH (יְראוּ אֶת־יְהוָה) in verse 10[9]. Identical phrases are found in Josh 24:14 and 1 Sam 12:24. The former marks the climax of Joshua's speech to Israel at the end of the book (Josh 24:2–15), where it offers a past-orientation, reciting YHWH's faithful dealings with

---

imagination of the reader.

116. It is no wonder that later Christian tradition understood this with reference to the Eucharist (Holladay, *The Psalms through Three Thousand Years*, 168).

117. Karen H. Jobes similarly calls the use of the "taste" image in 1 Pet 2:3 a "very bold perceptual metaphor" (Jobes, "Got Milk?" 8). "Of all the sensory metaphors, tasting is the most intimate and the only one that involves ingestion. Seeing God, hearing God, even touching God, does not carry the powerful connotations that 'tasting' implies—making the experience internal to oneself" (ibid., 10).

118. Although the term אַשְׁרֵי is often connected to wisdom, it is by no means *uniquely* sapiential. It is found in Deut 33:29; 1 Kgs 10:8 (2x); Isa 30:18; 32:20; 56:2; Dan 12:12; 2 Chr 9:7 (2x), but the preponderance of occurrences is in the Psalms (1:1; 2:12; 32:1; 32:2; 33:12; 34:9; 40:5; 41:2; 65:5; 84:5; 84:6; 84:13; 89:16; 94:12; 106:3; 112:1; 119:1; 119:2; 127:5; 128:1; 128:2; 137:8; 137:9; 144:15 [2x]; 146:5) and wisdom literature (Job 5:17; Prov 3:13; 8:32, 34; 14:21; 16:20; 20:7; 28:14; Eccl 10:17).

119. McCann notes its occurrence in the first and last two psalms (Psalms 1, 2, 40, 41) as well as three consecutive Psalms in the latter half (Psalms 32, 33, 34; "The Shape of Book I of the Psalter," 341).

120. Brown, *Seeing the Psalms*, 32.

Abraham, Isaac, Jacob, and on into the exodus and conquest generations, calling for fidelity to YHWH. The latter is Samuel's "farewell" dialogic discourse with Israel (1 Sam 12:1–25), which also offers a past-orientation, recounting the exodus from Egypt by YHWH's power (vv. 6–8), the cycle of the people's infidelity, YHWH's judgment in the form of foreign domination, the people's cry for deliverance, and YHWH's gracious provision of judges to rescue them (vv. 9–11). The context is the transition to the monarchy, so Samuel proclaims his own integrity in his dealings with Israel (vv. 1–5) as well as the path to the monarchy (vv. 12–13). In addition to verse 24, in verses 14–15 Samuel presents the fear of YHWH and torah obedience on the part of the king and the people as the condition for the enjoyment of the blessings of the covenant relationship. The past-orientation, namely, YHWH's past acts of grace, provides the motivation for obedience and the fear of YHWH in the present. Remarkably, he then calls on YHWH to bring rain at a time when rain was rare, during the harvest season (vv. 16–18).[121] This strikes fear in the hearts of the people, so they ask Samuel to intercede on their behalf for their sin in asking for a king (v. 19). Samuel tells them not to fear and proceeds to instruct the people in the proper fear of YHWH (vv. 20–25). In this latter section Samuel mingles a past-orientation on the gracious acts of YHWH with a future-orientation that concerns both YHWH's fidelity to Israel (v. 22) and the vanity of seeking empty things (הַתֹּהוּ), "which will not help and will not deliver" (אֲשֶׁר לֹא־יוֹעִילוּ וְלֹא יַצִּילוּ). The use of the hiphil of נצל here parallels its use in Ps 34:5[4] and 18[17] and its synonym in verse 7[6]. However, in Psalm 34 it is YHWH who *does* deliver. The past-orientation concerns the great things YHWH has done (v. 24), which is the motive (כִּי) for the admonition to fear YHWH.

The second half of verse 10[9] offers a future-oriented motive clause, "For there is no lack for those who fear him" (כִּי־אֵין מַחְסוֹר לִירֵאָיו). In Prov 11:24 מַחְסוֹר is compared to the poverty of one who is so stingy he is impoverished himself, in contrast to the person who gives generously and grows richer. The term also occurs in Deut 15:8, where Moses urges the Israelites to lend to those who lack. The economic aspect is clearer in the proverb that follows in verse 11[10]. Although the young lion imagery has led some to follow the LXX reading and read "rich ones" here,[122] the proverb's irony is richer when the reading "young lions" is preserved. Young lions are strong and fast, so surely they lack for nothing, but the proverb asserts the opposite.

---

121. McCarter, *I Samuel*, 216. Ralph W. Klein also notes that rain during the harvest was especially ominous due to the risk of damage to the grain (*1 Samuel*, 118).

122. See p. 100.

Instead, it is those who seek YHWH (דֹּרְשֵׁי יְהוָה) who lack for nothing good (לֹא־יַחְסְרוּ כָל־טוֹב).

With these proverbs the fellow-worshipper makes a subtle transition toward the role of a teacher, a role that he explicitly assumes in verse 12[11]. Just as the prophet Samuel shifts from a past-orientation to a future-orientation and instruction, the psalmist takes on the persona of the teacher offering life to those who desire it.

INSTRUCTION FROM THE WISDOM TEACHER (VV. 12-23[11-22])

As I argue above, the discourse shifts with the phrase, "Come, children, listen to me" (לְכוּ־בָנִים שִׁמְעוּ־לִי).[123] What follows is a highly structured lesson. Botha labels verses 12-15[11-14], "the most coherent part of the whole poem, driving its message home through admonition (12a), pedagogical questions (13a and 13b), repetition (of 'evil' and 'good'), antithesis (also of 'good' and 'evil') and chiasmus (good-evil-evil-good and the elements of v. 15)."[124] What has not been adequately appreciated is that this coherence mirrors Psalms 15 and 24 (and Isa 33:14-16) with a similar three-part structure that includes an introduction (using a double question), an answer, and a statement of benefit. Psalm 34:12-23[11-22] is a structural and conceptual parallel to Psalm 15 and 24:3-6. The recognition of this parallel is not original. García notes that the rhetorical questions in Psalms 15 and 24 are mirrored in Psalm 34:13-15[12-14].[125] However, he does not develop this connection to see the extent to which the three psalms are parallel in their structure and concepts.

Why has this parallel not been explored? Because of the focus of form criticism on the original oral *Sitz im Leben* of psalms, Psalm 34 has been studied separately from Psalms 15 and 24. While the latter employ language that fits better with a temple context, Psalm 34 employs language associated with a sapiential milieu. There is value to interpreting these psalms with reference to their likely sociological settings, but that is not the only viable context for interpretation. Once we see that the introductory double-questions in the Pss 15:1 and 24:3 introduce a character sketch, then Ps 34:12-23[11-22] becomes an important literary and theological-ethical parallel. The structure of Psalm 34:12-23 mirrors the structure of the character sketches in Psalms 15 and 24, and the theological context for ethics in Psalm 34 is

123. See p. 112-13. Cf. 1 Sam 12:23.
124. Botha, "The Social Setting and Strategy of Psalm 34," 183.
125. García de la Fuente, "Liturgias de entrada," 272.

conceptually equivalent to Psalms 15 and 24. They share a perspective on the ethical life: ethical behavior leads to a good life. The language and motifs are not identical, but they offer diverse viewpoints on the same subject: the nature of human well-being. They also share a fundamental agreement about ethical behavior. In what follows I compare and contrast the question and benefit portions of Psalms 15, 24, and 34 as indicative of ethical goods or the nature of human well-being, and then I will examine the answer portion to see how Psalm 34 sketches righteous character.

The Double Question

As an introduction, the words of the teacher in Ps 34:12[11] are unparalleled in Psalms 15 and 24. It summons the audience to listen to instruction and declares the subject matter: the fear of YHWH. The root ירא may imply fear as terror, respect, or worship.[126] Its nominal form likewise corresponds to this semantic range, but Ps 34:12[11] declares an assumption about the fear of YHWH, namely, it can be taught.[127] Following the double question in verse 13[12], the answer portion (vv. 14–15[13–14]) of the character sketch defines the fear of YHWH: the fear of YHWH manifests itself in turning from evil to do good. But as the introduction to the character sketch continues, the double question in verse 13[12] brings the parallel to Psalms 15 and 24 into view.

Aside from the initial interrogative מִי, the terms of the question in Ps 34:13[12] are very different from Pss 15:1 and 24:3. See the comparison of these questions in Table d below:

Table d. A Comparison of Double Questions in Psalms 15, 24, and 34

Ps 15:1	Ps 24:3	Ps 34:13[12]
O YHWH, who may sojourn in your tent,	Who may ascend the mountain of YHWH?	What man desires life?
Who may dwell on your holy mountain	And who may stand in his holy place?	Who loves days to see good?

All three questions declare the subject matter—a description of a certain kind of person. All three assume that this person may enjoy the good life, but they do not use identical language to describe this good life. In Pss 15:1 and 24:3 this person is permitted to be in the presence of YHWH—it is assumed that being with him *is* the good life. Elsewhere in the psalter, the

126. Van Pelt and Kaiser, "יָרֵא (yārēʾ I)," 528.
127. Ibid., 533.

Psalm 34

good life is synonymous with being on the mountain of YHWH, in his holy place, for YHWH is A SAFE PLACE.¹²⁸ A safe place is a place where people find life and flourish. Psalm 34:13[12] expresses this assumption explicitly, posing a rhetorical question that draws in those who desire the good life.¹²⁹ It does not seek information, as do the questions in Psalms 15 and 24, but it draws in interested listeners to hear a description of the person who can enjoy this good life. Still, while the question in all three psalms introduces the character sketch,¹³⁰ Psalm 34 approaches the introduction from a more direct rhetorical angle. From the beginning *life* is the motivation for and *telos* of ethical living. What about the benefit section?

The Benefit

Before comparing the benefit section with the corresponding section of Psalms 15 and 24, we must acknowledge that verses 16–23[15–22] are often taken as distinct from verses 12–15[11–14].¹³¹ Brown distinguishes the explicit didactic address in verses 12–15[11–14] from the contrast between the righteous and the wicked in verses 16–23[15–22].¹³² However, Perdue identifies verses 16–22[15–21] as the conclusion of verses 12–15[11–14],¹³³ and VanGemeren sees verses 16–23[15–22] as "The Rewards of Wisdom," following a section he calls "Exhortation to Wisdom" in verses 8–14.¹³⁴ In light of the resemblances to wisdom, it is reasonable to interpret these verses as a benefit or motive section following an admonition. The introductory question holds out the promise of life, but verses 16–23[15–22] provide the theological underpinning of the admonitions in verses 14–15[13–14]. Therefore we may understand Ps 34:16–23[15–22] as the counterpart to the benefit articulated in Pss 15:5 and 24:5, as well as Isa 33:16. It departs in substance from Psalms 15 and 24 in three key ways. It speaks to the fate of the wicked in contrast to the righteous,

---

128. See chapters 2 and 3.

129. For a possible Egyptian parallel, see Couroyer, "Idéal sapientiel en Egypte et en Israël (à propos du Psaume 34:13)," 174–79. Couroyer points to a number of verbal correspondences between Ps 34:13[12] and an inscription on the tomb of Ai, the successor to Tutankhamun. He concludes that Egyptian texts had circulated and thus serve as an influence on Psalm 34.

130. So also Craigie, *Psalms 1–50*, 280.

131. So Botha, "The Social Setting and Strategy of Psalm 34," 181–82.

132. Brown, "Come, O children," 90.

133. Perdue, *Wisdom and Cult*, 278. He calls verse 23[22] the "central proverb" of the psalm (ibid., 276).

134. VanGemeren, *Psalms*, 323.

acknowledges the suffering of the righteous, and draws out the relational dimension of YHWH's care for the righteous.

First, Brown is right to call attention to the contrast between the righteous and the wicked in Ps 34:16–23[15–22]. These verses exhibit the so-called theory/principle of retribution, which Kuntz and others identify as a common feature of psalmic wisdom.[135] This motif must be seen in proper perspective. The psalmist asserts in verse 20[19], "Many are the troubles of the righteous, / But from them all YHWH saves him." Kuntz comments, "Whereas the pious may hope to be released from suffering, he cannot expect to be exempted from its sting."[136] Therefore, Craigie rightly differentiates Psalm 34 from the doctrine of retribution of Job's friends.[137]

This so-called doctrine of retribution in Psalm 34 is not an impersonal cosmic order or a deterministic principle akin to the law of gravity. It is relational. The one possible exception to this is verse 22b[21b], which asserts, "Evil slays the wicked, / And those who hate the righteous will suffer for their guilt." However, it is unlikely that this is an impersonal force that metes out punishment since the psalm focuses explicitly on the relationship between the righteous and divine blessing, and especially YHWH's opposition

---

135. Kuntz, "The Canonical Wisdom Psalms," 211. So also Murphy, "Wisdom Psalms," 160; Eriksson, *Come, Children, Listen to Me!*, 74.

136. Kuntz, "The Canonical Wisdom Psalms," 215.

137. Craigie, *Psalms 1–50*, 281. He situates Psalm 34 more broadly:

> In the context of OT theology, one of the psalm's most profound insights concerns the instruction on the fear of the Lord (v. 12). This fear is not only the foundation of the wisdom tradition, but it is also one of the biblical doctrines most easily abused or misunderstood. The fear of the Lord is indeed the foundation of life, the key to joy in life and long and happy days. But it is not a guarantee that life will be always easy, devoid of the difficulties that may seem to mar so much of human existence. The fear of the Lord establishes joy and fulfilment in all of life's experiences. It may mend the broken heart, but it does not prevent the heart from being broken; it may restore the spiritually crushed, but it does not crush the forces that may create oppression. The psalm, if fully grasped, dispels the naiveté of that faith which does not contain within it the strength to stand against the onslaught of evil (ibid., 282).

For a similarly constructive perspective on the wisdom corpus, see Schultz, "Unity or Diversity in Wisdom Theology?" 271–306.

to the wicked in verse 17[16].[138] It is more likely that verse 22[21] involves indirect language for the sake of poetic terseness.[139]

The contrast between the righteous and the wicked highlights two outcomes inherent to the two possible pathways one may take. The righteous enjoy life because of YHWH's care and nearness. The wicked, however, face death as the result of their lack of fear of YHWH. These two ends engender the fear of YHWH.

Second, the benefit section in Psalm 34 differs from Psalms 15 and 24 by engaging with the difficulties of human experience. Kraus asserts that what keeps Psalm 34 from appearing as a naïve or mechanistic retribution theory is the acknowledgement that the righteous suffer.[140] Within the context of this psalm, the experience of suffering is at least partially how the righteous are identified. In verse 20a[19a] the psalmist affirms that the righteous have many troubles. In verses 16[15] and 18[17] the righteous cry out, no doubt from distress. In verse 19[18] the righteous person is "broken-hearted" (נִשְׁבְּרֵי־לֵב) and "crushed of spirit" (דַּכְּאֵי־רוּחַ). These descriptors highlight the internal effects of suffering and underscore the urgency of their pleas to YHWH. In view of this frank acknowledgement of the suffering of the righteous, the benefit sections of Psalms 15 and 24 may seem unconnected to the realities of the suffering psalmist. For those who question the promise held out to the righteous in Psalms 15 and 24, Psalm 34 addresses the issue.[141]

---

138. Goldingay suggests that the payment of guilt could take place either in a divine or human court (*Psalms*, 1:485). In Ps 1:5–6 both the human congregation and YHWH appear to play a role in the judgment of the wicked, but we cannot be sure. It seems most likely, given the whole psalm, that divine judgment is the reason that the wicked will be punished.

139. For a more thorough defense of this interpretation with reference to Psalm 37, see chapter 5.

140. Kraus, *Psalms 1–59*, 386. Anderson remarks: "The Psalmist does not base his argument upon a doctrine of rewards and punishments, but upon his own experience. He argues from the particular to the general, because God is absolutely trustworthy" (*The Book of Psalms*, 1:272).

141. For a study engaging the question of the role of Psalm 1 in the movement from obedience to praise in the Psalter, see Brueggemann, "Bounded by Obedience and Praise," 63-92. Arguing that the Psalter begins with an expression of a deeds-consequences nexus that only the naïve would accept, his thesis is that "the way from torah obedience to self-abandoning doxology is by way of *candor about suffering* and *gratitude about hope*" (ibid., 72, emphasis his). Psalms 15 and 24 present what Brueggemann would likely classify as a psalm of orientation akin to Psalm 1, presenting a similarly reliable version of the world. He questions whether the connection between obedience and prosperity is as reliable as these psalms imply. He remarks, "God is seen to be fickle, and the confident faith of Psalm 1 is inadequate. Psalm 1 does not invite candid protest or hard, probing questions about moral coherence. Psalm 1 does not entertain or even permit the demanding question of theodicy. For that reason, the simple affirmation of

Third, although the terms for refuge in the benefit section of Psalm 34 are conceptually similar to the same sections of Psalms 15 and 24,[142] Psalm 34 engages this motif in strongly relational terms using different parts of the body as metaphors for YHWH's relationship to the righteous and the wicked. In verse 16a[15a] the eyes of YHWH communicate his fidelity to the righteous—he fixes his attentive gaze on them, which, as we have seen above, mirrors Ps 25:15. Next the ears in verse 16b[15b] are attentive to the cries of the righteous. The ears are picked up again in verse 18a[17a], where these cries turn from YHWH's hearing to his delivering them (הִצִּילָם). This echoes the testimony of the psalmist in verse 7[6], turning testimony into a proverb applied to the righteous in general. Finally, the face in verse 17a[16a] is a figure of opposition to "those who do evil" (עֹשֵׂי רָע). It is not always easy to tell whether אֶרֶץ refers to the whole earth or the land of Israel,[143] but in this case YHWH's opposition to the wicked means their legacy is wiped out from *any* living memory (whether local or global).

Verse 19a[18a] describes YHWH's support of the righteous in spatial terms—YHWH is near to them. This nearness is clarified in the second line (v. 19b[18b]) as YHWH saves (יוֹשִׁיעַ) them. YHWH's help is pictured in nearly absolute terms in verses 20–21[19–20], for YHWH saves the righteous from all troubles and preserves all his bones. Verses 22–23[21–22] again contrast the righteous and the wicked. The wicked receive their due punishment, but the righteous are redeemed. Again, verse 23[22] mirrors Psalm 25:22, answering the plea of YHWH to redeem Israel with the assertion that YHWH does redeem the righteous from all their troubles.

To summarize, when we compare Ps 34:16–23[15–22] to the benefit sections in Pss 15:5 and 24:5, two obvious differences appear: Psalm 34 engages in a much lengthier statement of the benefit of the righteous life and engages human experience. While Psalm 34 acknowledges that the righteous suffer, it encourages the righteous sufferer to persevere in righteous living in hope of YHWH's future deliverance. But what does righteous living entail? Verses 14–15[13–14] provide the answer portion of this section, and they sketch the kind of person who enjoys the good life (v. 13[12]).

Psalm 1 is not adequate to lived experience." Is this an appropriate construal of Psalm 1 and of Psalms 15 and 24? I shall return to this question in chapter 6. Suffice it to say, however, that Psalm 34 presents a similar view of the world (vv. 16–23[15–22] resemble Ps 1:6 in the contrast between the ends of the righteous and wicked), but it cannot be accused of refusing to entertain the question of theodicy.

142. Note that we identified the metaphor of Ps 15:5 as THE RIGHTEOUS LIFE is A SAFE PLACE, which is similar to Ps 24:5's affirmation that the righteous person receives "blessing and righteousness from the God of his salvation."

143. Wright, "אֶרֶץ (*ereṣ*)," 520.

The Answer

Psalms 34:14-15[13-14], 15:2-5b and 24:4 exhibit several similarities in form and content. First, all are concise: while Psalm 15 addresses eleven concerns in sequence and Psalm 24 addresses four, Psalm 34 addresses six concerns in a compact series of commands. Second, all focus on speech and action: Ps 34:14[13] concerns speech (cf. Pss 15:2c, 3a, 3c, 4bc; 24:4d),[144] but verse 15[14] concerns doing good and pursuing peace (cf. Ps 15:2ab, 3c, 5ab). Third, like Ps 15:2a and 5cd, Psalm 34 uses language that invokes the metaphor of the pathway. Negatively, the verb סור, "to turn aside," is often used as an imperative with reference to altering the course of one's journey, whether it be the course of a literal journey or of physical space (Gen 19:2; Judg 4:18; 1 Sam 15:6; 2 Sam 2:22; Isa 52:11; Ruth 4:1) or the pathway of one's life in a moral sense (Num 16:26; Isa 30:11; Prov 3:7).[145] The verb frequently occurs in other moods in Deuteronomy to describe a turning from instruction, the way of YHWH, or faithful worship of YHWH (5:32; 7:4; 9:12, 16; 11:16, 28; 17:11, 17, 20; 28:14; 31:29). Positively, verbs like בקשׁ ("to seek") and רדף ("to pursue") imply a journey, a movement toward something (cf. Ps 24:6).

Psalm 34:14-15[13-14] shares one important feature with Ps 24:4: its general statements could be read as combining the social and theological dimensions of ethics. The deception of verse 14b[13b] and the pursuit of peace in verse 15b[14b] may either be social or theological matters (i.e., a matter of one's orientation to YHWH). The text does not narrow their application. The declared subject of instruction is the fear of YHWH (v. 12[11]), so a theological orientation is assumed, but the nature of the fear of YHWH is further defined in verses 14-15[13-14]. However, there is reason to believe that a social element is also involved.

Elsewhere guarding the tongue from something (assuming that נצר and שׁמר are synonyms) concerns relationship to other human beings (Ps 39:2[1]; Prov 6:24; 21:23; cf. Prov 13:3), though guarding the lips may also refer to speech to God (Ps 141:3).[146] Anderson compares this to keeping from speech that harms one's fellows, just as we find in Ps 15:3.[147]

---

144. Broyles notes the corresponding emphasis on truthful speech in the "psalms of temple entry," such as 15:3; 24:4; 36:3; 52:2-4 (*Psalms*, 169).

145. Note that Isa 30:11 is the voice of the people who enjoin the prophet to turn aside "from the path" (מִנֵּי־דָרֶךְ), that is, from prophesying the truth. The meaning is therefore metaphorical, but it explicitly employs the term for a pathway.

146. Cf. the language of guarding knowledge (Mal 2:7; Prov 5:2).

147. Anderson, *The Book of Psalms*, 1:273.

The pursuit of peace (רדף/בקש plus שָׁלוֹם) as an expression is unique to Ps 34:15[14], and there is little in the poetic line to indicate what שָׁלוֹם involves. Philip Nel identifies three senses of שָׁלוֹם that could conceivably be relevant to this text: a material sense of well-being (Ps 38:3; Prov 3:2), a social/political sense of harmony (Gen 34:21; Ps 120:6–7), and a religious sense as part of God's plan of salvation (1 Kgs 2:33).[148] It is unlikely that the psalmist is urging pursuit of well-being because that would be tautologous. It would be like saying, "If you want life, seek life!" It is also not likely that the religious sense fits here since peace is something granted by YHWH (Num 6:26), not pursued. It seems more likely that a relational harmony is intended, or, as Briggs calls it, friendship.[149] Although the neighbor is not mentioned, the pursuit of peace here accords with the description of the righteous person in Ps 15:3, who does no evil to his neighbor.

As in Ps 24:4, both the social and theological dimensions of righteous behavior are present in this character sketch. Thus we see that the answer portion of Psalm 34's character sketch has numerous elements in common with the same portions of Psalms 15 and 24.

However, whereas Psalms 15 and 24 present the righteous ideal by means of description, the psalmist-as-teacher in Psalm 34 addresses his audience directly with imperatives. We can even detect in verse 15a[14a] an assumption about the audience that they need to repent: "turn aside from evil" (סוּר מֵרָע).[150] This is in keeping with the experiential character of Psalm 34—its instruction both arises from and addresses particular human experience.

However, we should not lean heavily on assumptions about an original audience since verses 14–15[13–14] are expressed in general terms. Looking at the structure of the answer section we see a movement from evil to good. A person who fears YHWH:

1. Keeps from evil speech (v. 14a[13a]; negative),

2. Keeps from deceit (v. 14b[13b]; negative),

3. Turns from evil (v. 15a[14a]; negative),

4. Does good (v. 15a[14a]; positive),

5. Seeks and pursues peace (v. 15b[14b]; positive, in two clauses).

---

148. Nel, "שָׁלַם (šālēm I)," 131–32.

149. Briggs, *Psalms*, 1:298.

150. The phrase, "depart from evil and do good" (סוּר מֵרָע וַעֲשֵׂה־טוֹב) is found verbatim in Ps 37:27. The phrase סוּר מֵרָע also occurs in Prov 3:7; 4:27; 13:19; 14:16; 16:6, 17.

The structure is a mirror: The first three clauses are negative in their outlook, while the last three are positive.[151] Although the internal focus evident in Psalms 15 and 24 is lacking in Psalm 34, Craigie insightfully explains that "the required integrity of speech and action presupposes integrity of mind, for words and works are rooted in a person's inner intentions."[152]

The second half of Psalm 34 presents a structural and conceptual parallel to Psalms 15 and 24, though it is distinct in several respects. This parallel demonstrates that the psalms can instruct using a number of strategies: they can pose questions to set the topic, describe the person of character, command actions in keeping with good character, and motivate with the promise of life, refuge, and other terms for well-being.

Still, what distinguishes Psalm 34 from the parallels mentioned above is the experiential foundation and orientation. The impetus for the instruction is praise for YHWH's deliverance, but that same instruction is informed by the experience of suffering. Goldingay suggests that the relationship between the goodness of God (Ps 34:9) and the goodness of the righteous (Ps 34:15[14]) is two-fold: "Yhwh's goodness lies in a generosity that gives good things. It suggests a link between the theological and the behavioral; doing the good thing is a matter of taking the right attitude to Yhwh. It also suggests a link between the behavioral and the experiential; doing good leads to enjoying good."[153]

PSALM 34 AS DEUTERONOMIC AND SAPIENTIAL INSTRUCTION

The above analysis of Psalm 34 focuses on its formal and thematic relationship to Psalms 15 and 24. Indeed, the psalm fits well within the Psalter, especially with its introductory words of testimony and praise. However, throughout this chapter a minor theme emerges, namely, its relationship to Deuteronomy and Proverbs. Psalm 34 appears to integrate the didactic spirit of both to provide an experientially sensitive covenantal and sapiential response to the problem of the suffering of the righteous.

I characterize the second half of the psalm as "instruction from the wisdom teacher." Formally, this part of Psalm 34 fits more closely with

---

151. This is flipped from the corresponding general description in Ps 15:2–3, in which the positive is stated before the negative. In Psalm 34 the mirroring effect may go beyond the formal level—peace with others is in part a function of truthful speech (so also Craigie, *Psalms 1–50*, 280).

152. Ibid.

153. Goldingay, *Psalms*, 1:480.

Proverbs 1–9 than with Deuteronomy. It begins with the call, "Come, O children" (v. 12[11]), and combines proverbial sayings that share a common theme. Furthermore, the question of the suffering of the righteous is more the province of Job and Ecclesiastes than Deuteronomy. However, Deuteronomic language occurs as well. I note above that Weinfeld hears the voice of Moses in Deuteronomy as the wisdom teacher in Ps 34:11[10] calls his audience to hear.[154] Furthermore, the didactic character is just as familiar from Deuteronomy as from Proverbs.[155]

In addition to its didactic form, Psalm 34 touches on the fear of YHWH, an important motif in both Proverbs and Deuteronomy. Proverbs 3:7 and 24:21 call for fear of YHWH (cf. Eccl 5:6; 12:13), just as Ps 34:12[11] promises to teach the fear of YHWH.[156] However, the fear of YHWH is a prominent goal of instruction in Deuteronomy as well (4:10; 5:29; 6:2, 13, 24; 8:6; 10:12, 20; 13:5; 14:23; 17:19; 25:18; 28:10, 58; 31:12, 13). Furthermore, Proverbs connects this fear with life (Prov 10:27; 14:27; 19:23; 22:4), as in Psalm 34.[157] However, Deuteronomy also connects fear of YHWH with life. Daniel Block observes a progression from instruction to fear to obedience to an experience of life, especially in Deut 5:23–29, 6:1–3, and 17:19–20.[158] Psalm 34 appears to interpret the psalmist's own experience through this grid, and on that experiential foundation to instruct others to fear YHWH. This motif is at home in both Deuteronomy and Proverbs.

The metaphor of the way is also common to both, and the occurrences of the verb סור in both help distinguish between their respective emphases. In Deuteronomy the concern is to keep Israel and its king from turning from fidelity to YHWH and his way (5:32; 7:4; 9:12, 16; 11:16, 28; 17:11, 17, 20; 28:14; 31:29). This sense also occurs in Prov 5:7; 22:6; 28:9. However, as in Ps 34:15[14], Proverbs more frequently speaks of turning from evil (3:7; 4:27; 13:19; 14:16; 16:6, 17). Deuteronomy seeks to keep Israel from turning aside from Torah, while Psalm 34 and Proverbs encourage their audience to turn from evil.

However, certain features of the Psalm are specifically Deuteronomic. Above I highlighted the similarity of language about the "good" between Ps 34:13[12] and Deut 30:15,[159] but the same motif occurs in Deut 10:12–13,

---

154. See p. 105.

155. Weinfeld, *Deuteronomy and the Deuteronomic School*, 298.

156. Also the phrase יִרְאַת יְהוָה (Prov 1:7; 1:29; 2:5; 8:13; 9:10; 10:27; 14:26, 14:27; 15:16, 33; 16:6; 19:23; 22:4; 23:17).

157. See also Prov 14:26, which connects the fear of YHWH with refuge.

158. Block, "The Burden of Leadership," 137.

159. See p. 106 above.

where the commands are said to abound to Israel's good. In Ps 34:11[10] the righteous are those who seek YHWH. The verb דרשׁ with יהוה as an object is a common phrase in the Hebrew Bible describing the righteous, but it does not occur in Proverbs.[160] Notable among its occurrences, Deut 4:29 describes repentant Israel turning from idols to seek YHWH.[161] The following verses promise YHWH's covenant fidelity to suffering but repentant Israel. God's nearness to those who seek him in Psalm 34 is a motif that is more at home in Deuteronomy than in Proverbs.

This brief comparison shows that Psalm 34 combines motifs and language that are at home in the covenantal context of Deuteronomy as well as the sapiential context of Proverbs. The similarities between those two books prompted Weinfeld to propose wisdom influence on Deuteronomy,[162] but it is also possible that the direction of influence was from Deuteronomy to Proverbs. In either case, Psalm 34 stands between the two, adding the context of worship that is at home in the Psalter.

CONCLUSION

The ethic of Psalm 34 is simple and generalized: turn from evil and do good. It combines forms and motifs from Proverbs and Deuteronomy to respond to the suffering of the righteous through the psalmist's own experience. Having experienced deliverance himself, the psalmist as fellow-worshipper invites others to praise, but he takes on the role of the wisdom teacher, instructing others in the fear of YHWH. This fear of YHWH is motivated by an experience of and confidence in the goodness of YHWH. Psalm 34 therefore complements the Zion theology of Psalms 15 and 24 with an additional perspective of well-being in relationship to YHWH.

---

160. See Gen 25:22; Deut 4:29; 1 Kgs 22:5, 8; 2 Kgs 3:11; 8:8; 22:13, 18; Isa 9:12; 31:1; 55:6; Jer 10:21; 21:2; Ezek 14:7*; 20:1; 20:3*; 20:31*; Hos 10:12; Amos 5:4*, 6; Zeph 1:6; Pss 22:27[26]*; 34:5[4], 11[10]; 105:4; Lam 3:25*; Ezra 6:21; 1 Chr 10:14; 16:11; 22:19; 28:9*; 2 Chr 12:14; 14:3, 6; 15:2*, 12, 13; 16:12; 18:7; 20:3; 22:9; 26:5; 30:19; 34:21, 26 (references marked with an asterisk indicate that the object is a pronoun but the referent of the pronoun is YHWH).

161. Cf. Deut 12:5, where the object is the place YHWH would choose for his dwelling.

162. Weinfeld, *Deuteronomy and the Deuteronomic School*, 274.

5

Psalm 37

INTRODUCTION

Instead of the concise character sketches of Psalms 15, 24, and 34, Psalm 37 offers a lengthy contrast between the character and *telos* of the righteous and the wicked. Although Psalm 37 differs in form from the previous portraits (it does not have the same question-answer-benefit structure), it shares several literary and conceptual features with them. They all have a didactic purpose, involve third-person description of the righteous person, and situate character description in relationship to its outcome. However, in Psalm 37 the psalmist dons the persona of the wisdom teacher and addresses the problem of the success of the wicked with a theologically grounded pragmatism. He urges torah obedience instead of hot-headed anger, placing his instruction in the context of hope in YHWH's rewarding the righteous and punishing the wicked in the future.

Some interpreters have dismissed the psalm as a naïve deeds-consequence theology resembling the perspective of Job's friends.[1] Walter Brueggemann asserts that the psalm is more complex, but he argues that the deeds-consequence foundation advocates a comfortable ideology for

---

1. Gunkel and Begrich, *Introduction to Psalms*, 296; Lohfink, "Die Besänftigung des Messias: Gedanken zu Psalm 37," 76; Briggs, *Psalms*, 1:324; Hossfeld and Zenger, *Die Psalmen I*, 229. For the seminal exposition of the so-called deeds-consequence relationship, see Koch, "Is There a Doctrine of Retribution in the Old Testament?"

the landed class. Only later did a second (eschatological) reading transform the psalm into a utopian hope for the landless.[2] Although Brueggemann sees the complexity of the psalm, neither he nor those who reject the psalm as simplistic interpret the psalm fairly. Read as a whole, the psalm does not simply seek to preserve a status quo by appealing to a deeds-consequence relationship. Rather Psalm 37 offers counsel for responding to the success of the wicked by applying the deuteronomic covenant ideals to the individual. Thus the wisdom teacher preserves a tension between present experience and unrealized hope.

As with the previous psalms, I begin my analysis with a translation, text-critical analysis, and examination of the literary genre and structure of the psalm. Then I clarify the ethical portrait of the righteous and the wicked painted in this psalm. Finally, I seek to understand the theological content of the psalm in light of recent scholarship.

TRANSLATION AND TEXT-CRITICAL ANALYSIS OF PSALM 37

The following translation of Psalm 37 serves as the starting point for my analysis:

לְדָוִד	1a	Of David.
א		
אַל־תִּתְחַר בַּמְּרֵעִים	1b	Do not be incensed by those who do evil,
אַל־תְּקַנֵּא בְּעֹשֵׂי עַוְלָה׃	1c	Do not be envious of those who do injustice.
כִּי כֶחָצִיר מְהֵרָה יִמָּלוּ	2a	For like grass they will dry up quickly,
וּכְיֶרֶק דֶּשֶׁא יִבּוֹלוּן׃	2b	And like fresh green plants they will wither.
ב		
בְּטַח בַּיהוָה וַעֲשֵׂה־טוֹב	3a	Trust in YHWH and do good,
שְׁכָן־אֶרֶץ וּרְעֵה אֱמוּנָה׃	3b	Inhabit the land and tend faithfulness,
וְהִתְעַנַּג עַל־יְהוָה	4a	And take pleasure in YHWH,
וְיִתֶּן־לְךָ מִשְׁאֲלֹת לִבֶּךָ׃	4b	And he will give to you the desires of your heart.
ג		
גּוֹל עַל־יְהוָה דַּרְכֶּךָ	5a	Roll your way to YHWH,
וּבְטַח עָלָיו וְהוּא יַעֲשֶׂה׃	5b	And trust in him, and he will act.
וְהוֹצִיא כָאוֹר צִדְקֶךָ	6a	He will bring out your righteousness like the light,

---

2. Brueggemann, "Psalm 37," 245–47.

Portraits of the Righteous in the Psalms

וּמִשְׁפָּטֶךָ כַּצָּהֳרָיִם:	6b	And your justice like the noon.
ד		
דּוֹם לַיהוָה	7a	Be still before YHWH,
וְהִתְחוֹלֵל לוֹ	7b	and wait for him,
אַל־תִּתְחַר בְּמַצְלִיחַ דַּרְכּוֹ	7c	Do not be incensed by the one who succeeds in his way,
בְּאִישׁ עֹשֶׂה מְזִמּוֹת:	7d	Over the man who carries out schemes.
ה		
הֶרֶף מֵאַף וַעֲזֹב חֵמָה	8a	Leave aside anger and abandon rage,
אַל־תִּתְחַר אַךְ־לְהָרֵעַ:	8b	Do not be incensed—it only leads to evil.
כִּי־מְרֵעִים יִכָּרֵתוּן	9a	For those who do evil will be cut off,
וְקֹוֵי יְהוָה הֵמָּה יִירְשׁוּ־אָרֶץ:	9b	But those who wait on YHWH, they will possess the land.
ו		
וְעוֹד מְעַט וְאֵין רָשָׁע	10a	But a little longer and the wicked will be no more,
וְהִתְבּוֹנַנְתָּ עַל־מְקוֹמוֹ וְאֵינֶנּוּ:	10b	And you will look closely at his place, but he will be no more.
וַעֲנָוִים יִירְשׁוּ־אָרֶץ	11a	And the humble ones will possess the land,
וְהִתְעַנְּגוּ עַל־רֹב שָׁלוֹם:	11b	And they will take pleasure in an abundance of peace.
ז		
זֹמֵם רָשָׁע לַצַּדִּיק	12a	The wicked plots against the righteous,
וְחֹרֵק עָלָיו שִׁנָּיו:	12b	And he gnashes his teeth at him.
אֲדֹנָי יִשְׂחַק־לוֹ	13a	The Lord laughs at him,
כִּי־רָאָה כִּי־יָבֹא יוֹמוֹ:	13b	For he sees that his day will come.
ח		
חֶרֶב פָּתְחוּ רְשָׁעִים	14a	The wicked draw a sword,
וְדָרְכוּ קַשְׁתָּם	14b	and draw their bow,
לְהַפִּיל עָנִי וְאֶבְיוֹן	14c	To make the poor and needy fall,
לִטְבוֹחַ יִשְׁרֵי־דָרֶךְ:	14d	To slaughter those whose way is upright.
חַרְבָּם תָּבוֹא בְלִבָּם	15a	Their sword will enter their own heart,
וְקַשְּׁתוֹתָם תִּשָּׁבַרְנָה:	15b	And their bows will be broken.
ט		
טוֹב־מְעַט לַצַּדִּיק	16a	Better is what little belongs to the righteous,
מֵהֲמוֹן רְשָׁעִים רַבִּים:	16b	Than the wealth (turmoil) of many wicked men.

Psalm 37

כִּי זְרוֹעוֹת רְשָׁעִים תִּשָּׁבַרְנָה	17a	For the arms of the wicked will be broken,
וְסוֹמֵךְ צַדִּיקִים יְהוָה:	17b	But YHWH supports the righteous.

י

יוֹדֵעַ יְהוָה יְמֵי תְמִימִם	18a	YHWH knows the days of the blameless,
וְנַחֲלָתָם לְעוֹלָם תִּהְיֶה:	18b	And their inheritance will be forever.
לֹא־יֵבֹשׁוּ בְּעֵת רָעָה	19a	They will not be ashamed in evil times,
וּבִימֵי רְעָבוֹן יִשְׂבָּעוּ:	19b	And in days of hunger they will eat their fill.

כ

כִּי רְשָׁעִים יֹאבֵדוּ	20a	For the wicked will perish,
וְאֹיְבֵי יְהוָה	20b	And the enemies of YHWH,
כִּיקַר כָּרִים	20c	Like the glory of pastures,
כָּלוּ בֶעָשָׁן כָּלוּ:	20d	They vanish, in smoke they vanish.

ל

לֹוֶה רָשָׁע וְלֹא יְשַׁלֵּם	21a	The wicked borrows and does not repay,
וְצַדִּיק חוֹנֵן וְנוֹתֵן:	21b	But the righteous is gracious and gives.
כִּי מְבֹרָכָיו יִירְשׁוּ אָרֶץ	22a	For his blessed ones will possess the land,
וּמְקֻלָּלָיו יִכָּרֵתוּ:	22b	And those cursed by him will be cut off.

מ

מֵיְהוָה מִצְעֲדֵי־גֶבֶר כּוֹנָנוּ	23a	By YHWH the steps of the young man are established,
וְדַרְכּוֹ יֶחְפָּץ:	23b	And in his way he delights.
כִּי־יִפֹּל לֹא־יוּטָל	24a	Though he fall he will not be hurled down,
כִּי־יְהוָה סוֹמֵךְ יָדוֹ:	24b	For YHWH supports his hand.

נ

נַעַר הָיִיתִי גַּם־זָקַנְתִּי	25a	I have been young, also I have become old,
וְלֹא־רָאִיתִי צַדִּיק נֶעֱזָב	25b	And I have not seen the righteous abandoned,
וְזַרְעוֹ מְבַקֶּשׁ־לָחֶם:	25c	And his seed seeking bread.
כָּל־הַיּוֹם חוֹנֵן וּמַלְוֶה	26a	Every day he is gracious and lending,
וְזַרְעוֹ לִבְרָכָה:	26b	And his seed becomes a blessing.

ס

סוּר מֵרָע וַעֲשֵׂה־טוֹב	27a	Turn aside from evil and do good,
וּשְׁכֹן לְעוֹלָם:	27b	And you will dwell forever.
כִּי יְהוָה אֹהֵב מִשְׁפָּט	28a	For YHWH loves justice,
וְלֹא־יַעֲזֹב אֶת־חֲסִידָיו	28b	And he will not abandon his faithful ones.

Portraits of the Righteous in the Psalms

	ע	
לְעוֹלָם נִשְׁמָרוּ	28c	They are kept forever,
וְזֶרַע רְשָׁעִים נִכְרָת׃	28d	But the seed of the wicked will be cut off.
צַדִּיקִים יִירְשׁוּ־אָרֶץ	29a	The righteous will possess the land,
וְיִשְׁכְּנוּ לָעַד עָלֶיהָ׃	29b	And they will dwell in it forever.
	פ	
פִּי־צַדִּיק יֶהְגֶּה חָכְמָה	30a	The mouth of the righteous utters wisdom,
וּלְשׁוֹנוֹ תְּדַבֵּר מִשְׁפָּט׃	30b	And his tongue speaks justice.
תּוֹרַת אֱלֹהָיו בְּלִבּוֹ	31a	The instruction of his God is in his heart,
לֹא תִמְעַד אֲשֻׁרָיו׃	31b	His steps will not stagger.
	צ	
צוֹפֶה רָשָׁע לַצַּדִּיק	32a	A wicked man lies in wait for the righteous,
וּמְבַקֵּשׁ לַהֲמִיתוֹ׃	32b	and seeks to put him to death.
יְהוָה לֹא־יַעַזְבֶנּוּ בְיָדוֹ	33a	YHWH will not abandon him into his hand,
וְלֹא יַרְשִׁיעֶנּוּ בְּהִשָּׁפְטוֹ׃	33b	And he will not cause him to be condemned in his judgment.
	ק	
קַוֵּה אֶל־יְהוָה וּשְׁמֹר דַּרְכּוֹ	34a	Wait for YHWH and keep his way,
וִירוֹמִמְךָ לָרֶשֶׁת אָרֶץ	34b	And he will raise you up to possess the land,
בְּהִכָּרֵת רְשָׁעִים תִּרְאֶה׃	34c	When the wicked are cut off you will see.
רָאִיתִי רָשָׁע עָרִיץ	35a	I have seen the wicked exultant,
וּמִתְעָרֶה כְּאֶזְרָח רַעֲנָן׃	35b	And one who raises himself like a leafy cedar tree.
וַיַּעֲבֹר וְהִנֵּה אֵינֶנּוּ	36a	And then he passes on, and look, he is not there,
וָאֲבַקְשֵׁהוּ וְלֹא נִמְצָא׃	36b	And I have sought for him but he is not found.
	שׁ	
שְׁמָר־תָּם וּרְאֵה יָשָׁר	37a	Watch the blameless and see the upright,
כִּי־אַחֲרִית לְאִישׁ שָׁלוֹם׃	37b	For there is a future for the man of peace.
וּפֹשְׁעִים נִשְׁמְדוּ יַחְדָּו	38a	But the rebellious are destroyed together,
אַחֲרִית רְשָׁעִים נִכְרָתָה׃	38b	The future of the wicked is cut off.
	ת	
וּתְשׁוּעַת צַדִּיקִים מֵיְהוָה	39a	But the deliverance of the righteous is from YHWH,
מָעוּזָּם בְּעֵת צָרָה׃	39b	Their fortress in a time of distress.
וַיַּעְזְרֵם יְהוָה וַיְפַלְּטֵם	40a	And YHWH will help them and save them,

יְפַלְּטֵם מֵרְשָׁעִים וְיוֹשִׁיעֵם	40b	He will save them from the wicked, and he will deliver them,
כִּי־חָסוּ בוֹ׃	40c	For they seek refuge in him.

In verses 1, 7, and 8 Robert Alter translates אַל־תִּתְחַר as "do not be incensed."[3] This skillfully preserves the metaphor of heat for anger, so I follow his lead in my translation above.

In verse 3b, instead of וּרְעֵה אֱמוּנָה, "and shepherd/tend to faithfulness," LXX translates ποιμανθήσῃ ἐπὶ τῷ πλούτῳ αὐτῆς, "and you will be shepherded/tended on its wealth." The verb ποιμαίνω is a straightforward choice to translate רעה, but the future passive form suggests the translator understands the Hebrew imperative as a consequence of the preceding imperatives rather than a continuation of admonition.[4] The Hebrew text may be understood this way if אֱמוּנָה is taken as an adverbial accusative, though the Qal form of the verb would not suggest the passive rendering, "you will be tended faithfully." The notion of shepherding faithfulness seems odd, as if faithfulness were conceived as an animate being requiring a shepherd. On the other hand, the LXX smooths over this language and makes it a straightforward statement of the benefit of trusting in YHWH and doing good in verse 3a. It is preferable to understand the LXX as an interpretive gloss and retain MT.

In verse 5a, instead of גֹּל, "roll" (from גלל), LXX (along with the Targum) has ἀποκάλυψον, "make known," possibly reflecting the root גלה. This changes the meaning of the admonition, though the effect is not radically different. The MT enjoins trust while the LXX enjoins transparency; in the context of prayer, transparency and trust are intimately connected. However, the imperative of גלה is גְּלֵה (found in Ezek 12:3), which requires the addition of a *hê* and the deletion of a *wāw*. It seems more likely that the LXX translation reflects a mistake on the part of the translator (and a slip of the pen by a scribe for the Targum). The MT should be retained.

In verse 7b I do not follow MT. For MT's הִתְחוֹלֵל, the hithpolel of חיל, meaning "writhe with fear,"[5] LXX (and Syriac) reads ἱκέτευσον, meaning to "supplicate" or "beseech."[6] Aquila's Greek (and Targums) read ἀποκαραδόκει "eagerly expect."[7] BHS suggests reading וְהוֹחֵל, the hiphil imperative form of

---

3. Alter, *Psalms*, 129.
4. On the imperative mood expressing a result, see GKC §110.f.
5. *HALOT* 311.
6. BDAG 473.
7. BDAG 112.

יחל, meaning "wait,"[8] though the imperfect form has also been suggested.[9] The majority of translations and commentators understand this verb to be from יחל, not חיל, and translate "wait patiently," without any comment on the textual issue.[10] The NET note suggests that the hiphil imperfect of יחל is the correct reading, corrupted by means of dittography: the initial וה from previous word is repeated, and the *lāmed* is repeated at the end. This may be the most plausible explanation since the MT reading does not seem to fit the context.

In verse 14d, instead of דַּרְכּ֗וֹ, LXX reads τῇ καρδίᾳ, "heart," along with some medieval Hebrew manuscripts that read לֵב, "heart." This changes the sense of the verse to give an internal rather than external view of a person, though either reading speaks of the upright person. It appears that the LXX tradition is defaulting to a more familiar way of speaking. Typically יָשָׁר modifies דֶּרֶךְ, such as in Jer 31:9 (בְּדֶרֶךְ יָשָׁר; cf. Hos 14:10; Ps 107:7; Prov 12:15; 14:12; 16:25; 21:2, 8, 29; 28:10; Ezra 8:21), though in Prov 29:27 יָשָׁר is the construct term as in Ps 37:14. In contrast, יִשְׁרֵי־לֵב "the upright of heart," is a common epithet in the Psalter (Pss 7:11; 11:2; 32:11; 36:11; 64:11; 94:15; 97:11; cf. 125:4, לִישָׁרִים בְּלִבּוֹתָם). Therefore I retain the MT as the *lectio difficilior*.

In verse 20c, for בִּיקַר כָּרִים, LXX translates ἅμα τῷ δοξασθῆναι αὐτοὺς καὶ ὑψωθῆναι, "together with their being glorified and exalted," from which BHS reconstructs כְּיָקָר וּכְרוּם. Also in verse 20, instead of כָּרִים "pastures," Symmachus (and Jerome) have ὡς μονοκέρωτες, which BHS uses to reconstruct כְּרֵמִים (or כְּרֵים) "as exalted." LXX may be working with a different reading tradition, but LXX may also be translating the simile abstractly, applying the glory directly to the enemies of YHWH rather than to a lush field that is consumed. It seems best to retain MT as the *lectio difficilior*.[11] Given the differences between MT, LXX, and 4QpPs 37, Craigie asserts that "any translation must remain dubious."[12]

In verse 20b, instead of בֶעָשָׁן "in smoke," BHS suggests reading with many medieval Hebrew manuscripts כֶּעָשָׁן "like smoke" (so NRSV). This construction is also found in Isa 51:6, Hos 13:3, and Prov 10:26. However, the *bêt* is found in Nah 2:14[13] and Ps 102:4[3], which is also treated as a comparative in LXX, Targums, Jerome, and medieval Hebrew manuscripts.

---

8. *HALOT* 407.

9. *HALOT* 311.

10. See, e.g., RSV; NRSV; ESV; NIV; NASB; NJPS; Alter, *Psalms*, 130; Goldingay, *Psalms*, 1:514; Kraus, *Psalms 1–59*, 405.

11. Kraus, *Psalms 1–59*, 403.

12. Craigie, *Psalms 1–50*, 296.

Nahum 2:14[13] has a verb for burning, so the *bêt* preposition fits well, but without a verb for burning it makes less sense in Pss 37:20; 102:4, so it is the *lectio difficilior*. However, in either case the metaphor changes only slightly.

In verse 22a LXX vocalizes "blessed ones" and "those cursed by him" as active participles. Goldingay simply renders both the passive and active readings.[13] I retain MT because it seems to explain the presence of the LXX reading, though there is little upon which to make this decision.

In verse 28c LXX adds ἄνομοι δὲ ἐκδιωχθήσονται, "but the lawless will be driven out." Craigie follows this reading and translates the line, "the unjust are destroyed forever." He supposes that the text originally read עוֹלִים לְעוֹלָם נִשְׁמָדוּ, suggesting that נשמדו ("are destroyed") is implied in LXX.[14] This is a plausible explanation for LXX, but I am reluctant to follow it because the MT is the *lectio brevior* and the *lectio difficilior*. The LXX is the *lectio facilior* because it resolves the problem of the missing initial *'ayin*, which we would expect at this point in the acrostic. It would match the parallel line nicely, since that line concerns the wicked.

A cluster of variants in verse 35 requires more extensive comment. Instead of MT's עָרִיץ, "acting violently,"[15] LXX reads ὑπερυψούμενον, "raised." BHS suggests עָלִיץ, "arrogant," or עָלִיז, "exultant." If LXX is correct, the *lāmed* has been replaced by a *rêš*. This same switch may have also occurred in the next line. MT's וּמִתְעָרֶה כְּאֶזְרָח רַעֲנָן, "And one who exposes himself like a native citizen full of leaves," makes little sense, as NRSV and NET acknowledge. In contrast, LXX reads καὶ ἐπαιρόμενον ὡς τὰς κέδρους τοῦ Λιβάνου, "and lifted up like the cedar trees of Lebanon." Instead of ערה, LXX presupposes עלה.[16] Fitzgerald argues that because this is the *rêš* line, several *lāmeds* are intentionally replaced by a *rêš*. He notes that l, n, and r can be interchanged in some Semitic languages, as well as in Hebrew (as in מַזָּלוֹת and מַזָּרוֹת, both of which refer to a star).[17] He also notes that the verb עלה is used of trees in Isa 55:13 and Ezek 47:12, and of vegetation in Jonah 4:6. He concludes, "The amazing lineup of r's in the lines cited makes it clear that the text must be allowed to stand with *mt'rh* understood as dialectical *mt'lh*."[18] VanGemeren rejects this proposal as "forced."[19] Indeed, MT is the

---

13. Ibid., 515.
14. Ibid., 296.
15. *HALOT* 884. So Ridderbos, *Die Psalmen*, 276.
16. So *HALOT* 882.
17. Fitzgerald, "The Interchange of L, N, and R in Biblical Hebrew," 481; cf. *HALOT* 565–66.
18. Ibid., 486.
19. VanGemeren, *Psalms*, 351.

lectio difficilior. However, Fitzgerald's linguistic explanation is possible and has manuscript support in the LXX translation, which suggests that a *lāmed* was understood where a *rêš* was written. That this is the *rêš* line also tips the argument in favor of Fitzgerald's solution. Therefore I tentatively follow the LXX reading.

The situation is different for the comparative phrase כְּאֶזְרָח רַעֲנָן. Based on LXX, BHS suggests the following reconstruction: כְּאַרְזֵי הַלְּבָנֹן. For אֶזְרָח, some have suggested reading אֶרֶז "cedar tree" based on the LXX (So *HALOT* 29). This would be the *lectio facilior*. Nonetheless, the LXX reading has merit. All but one of the seventeen occurrences of אֶזְרָח in MT refer to *native people*, often as opposed to alien residents of the land. The sense "native plant" is unattested elsewhere. Therefore, the MT is too difficult to sustain, and I follow the LXX. Gunkel likewise does so for the noun, but he proposes reading the comparative phrase כְּאֶרֶז רַעֲנָן, "like a green cedar tree."[20] The LXX reading, "Lebanon," is the *lectio facilior*, especially if one assumes that cedar trees are the image.[21] Therefore the MT reading רַעֲנָן is preferred.

In verse 36a LXX, Syriac, and Jerome read first person, "I passed by" (so RSV, NRSV). This harmonizes with the second half of the bicolon, preserving a 1st-3rd-1st-3rd person pattern. It alleviates a difficulty of translation, and therefore it is the *lectio facilior*. Preserving MT is not simple. The KJV, NIV, NASB, and ESV retain MT and take the verb עבר as a euphemism for the death of the wicked, "he passed away" (ESV). But such a use of the verb is not attested in biblical Hebrew. Allan Harman suggests that the verb עבר may be used metaphorically in Job 30:15 and Prov 22:3 to refer to passing from life to death,[22] but these two examples are not very secure. Both can be understood as movement in spatial terms rather than as a euphemism for death. Seeking to preserve MT while avoiding modern English idiom, Alter translates, "Suddenly he vanished and was gone."[23] This is something of an interpretive paraphrase, though it preserves the sense of physical movement. Perhaps NJPS offers the best translation of MT: "he passes on." This also preserves the sense of physical movement without introducing a substantial interpretive layer. In view of the NJPS translation, it is possible to preserve MT.

20. Gunkel, *Die Psalmen*, 155, 159.

21. Cf. Judg 9:15; 1 Kgs 5:13, 20; 7:2; 2 Kgs 14:9; 19:23; 2 Chr 2:7; 25:18; Ezra 3:7; Pss 29:5; 92:13; 104:16; Song 5:15; Isa 2:13; 14:8; 37:24; Jer 22:23; Ezek 17:3; 27:5; 31:3; Zech 11:1. In particular, the judgment given to Pharaoh in Ezekiel 31 stands out. Ezekiel compares Assyria to a cedar in Lebanon that is arrogant in its greatness only to be brought down.

22. Harman, "עָבַר ('ābar I)," 314.

23. Alter, *Psalms*, 133.

LITERARY GENRE AND STRUCTURE OF PSALM 37

Psalms 34 and 37 are usually numbered among the wisdom psalms, and both are alphabetic acrostics. I will not repeat the general discussion of these two issues given in chapter 4. Instead, I will focus on the issues particular to Psalm 37.

The Genre of Psalm 37

In regard to genre, scholars largely agree that Psalm 37 resembles wisdom literature, especially sections in Proverbs and Job. That the psalm is didactic is beyond dispute,[24] since no single line of prayer is addressed to God.[25] The psalmist addresses his audience as a wisdom teacher,[26] though Hossfeld and Zenger suggest that this is a fictional construct.[27]

The psalm's form is often compared to the proverbial literature. Held suggests that Ps 37:1 is a quotation of Prov 24:19.[28] According to Ricciardi, this need not imply direct literary dependence on the canonical book of Proverbs but may simply reflect the influence of the tradition of oral wisdom in Israel.[29] However, the nearly letter-for-letter correspondence between them makes a direct literary relationship likely. In any case, resemblances to the canonical wisdom books are unmistakable.[30] Brueggemann states that the psalm is the "most easily identified of the list of sapiential psalms."[31] Perdue argues that the psalm is constructed around a proverb that is repeated at key points.[32] Craigie calls Psalm 37 an anthology of proverbs, with each stanza including a complete proverb. In addition, like Prov 24:30–34, Psalm 37 contains some autobiographical information in verses 10, 25, 35, and 36.[33] In contrast, Gerstenberger argues that the mixing of admonition, instruc-

---

24. So Brug, "Biblical Acrostics," 285; Briggs, *Psalms*, 1:322; Craigie, *Psalms 1–50*, 296; Hossfeld and Zenger, *Die Psalmen I*, 234; Kraus, *Psalms 1–59*, 404.

25. Held, "Hoffen auf Gott und Entschlossenheit zum Guten," 295.

26. Anderson, *The Book of Psalms*, 1:292.

27. Hossfeld and Zenger, *Die Psalmen I*, 229.

28. Held, "Hoffen auf Gott und Entschlossenheit zum Guten," 296.

29. Ricciardi, "Los pobres y la tierra segun el Salmo 37," 225.

30. Gunkel and Begrich, *Introduction to Psalms*, 304; also Dahood, *Psalms I, 1–50*, 227; VanGemeren, Psalms, 341; Mowinckel, *The Psalms in Israel's Worship*, 1:207; Kuntz, "The Canonical Wisdom Psalms," 204, 218–19; Hurvitz, "צדיק = 'wise,'" 111–12.

31. Brueggemann, "Psalm 37," 230.

32. Perdue, *Wisdom and Cult*, 279–80. I return to this below in relationship to the structure of the psalm.

33. Craigie, *Psalms 1–50*, 296–97.

tion, and promise suggests Psalm 37 should be understood as liturgy in the sense of a homily for the synagogue.[34] Goldingay is comfortable seeing this as a homily that would have fit in the book of Proverbs itself.[35] According to Broyles, treating the psalm as wisdom literature affects interpretation in two ways: its proverbial statements should not be understood as "blanket guarantees," and one should expect educational instruction rather than philosophical engagement with the problem of evil.[36]

The didactic character of the psalm invites the question of the psalm's *Sitz im Leben*. Assuming that scribal schools existed in ancient Israel,[37] the alphabetic acrostic would have made this psalm ideal for students in a scribal school. However, the existence of scribal schools and their involvement in this psalm need to be demonstrated.

The Structure of Psalm 37

What about the structure of the psalm? Little is certain except that the psalm is an integrated whole. This poetic integrity is reinforced by the formal alphabetic acrostic structure. Unlike Psalm 34, Psalm 37 is a complete acrostic without extra letters.[38] The psalm is clearly a singular whole, so it should not be divided up, nor should one part be read in isolation from the rest. The acrostic creates a feeling of order and completeness, and apparently served a mnemonic function.[39] Beyond that we know little about the significance of this formal structure.

Many interpreters argue that the psalm exhibits no progression of thought; it merely offers variations on a single theme.[40] Craigie suggests that the alphabetic structure "is the only structure clearly established" for the

---

34. Gerstenberger, *Psalms: Part 1*, 157–58. See also Terrien, *The Psalms*, 323. He employs the term "sapiential homily" while denying that it was composed for choral use.

35. Goldingay, *Psalms*, 1:517.

36. Broyles, *Psalms*, 178–79.

37. This assumption is debated. See Hess, "Questions of Reading and Writing in Ancient Israel," 6.

38. Though Bullock notes that the ʿayin is recessed in verse 28 (*Encountering the Book of Psalms*, 43).

39. Cf. Craigie, *Psalms 1–50*, 129, 297. Jinkins suggests that the form embodies its message, that although the wicked triumph, the righteous see the moral order of the world rightly ("The Virtues of the Righteous in Psalm 37," 181–82).

40. Anderson, *The Book of Psalms*, 1:292; Kraus, *Psalms 1–59*, 404; Goldingay, *Psalms*, 1:517; VanGemeren, Psalms, 341; Kuntz, "Wisdom Psalms and the Shaping of the Hebrew Psalter," 155.

Psalm.[41] However, several scholars have recognized a structure beyond the alphabetic acrostic.[42] Two separate analyses appear the most promising.

First, Leo Perdue argues that the psalm is structured around variations on a central proverb in verses 9, 22, 28d/29a (paraphrased in verse 34bc), and 38b. He identifies four strophes:

1. *'alēp* to *wāw* (vv. 1–11)
2. *zayin* to *nûn* (vv. 12–26)
3. *sāmek* to *rêš* (vv. 27–36)
4. Conclusion: *šîn* and *tāw* (vv. 37–40)[43]

In addition to the presence of a repeated proverb, Perdue notes that the three major strophes end with "an expanded observation of the proverb which points to personal observation of the destruction of the wicked" (vv. 10–11, 25–26, 35–36).[44] While affirming Perdue's structural analysis, Maloney argues that key words also contribute to the thematic integrity of the psalm. He identifies several, including אֶרֶץ paired with ירשׁ (vv. 9, 11, 22, 29, 34; cf. v. 3) and כרת (vv. 9, 22, 28, 34, 38).[45] The analyses of Perdue and Maloney focus on one aspect of the psalm, namely, the verses the wisdom teacher offers as justification for his instruction. To the extent that this grounding pervades the psalm and provides thematic continuity throughout, it provides a helpful basis for discerning the overall theme of the psalm. However, it is not necessarily sufficient on its own to determine structural divisions. The repetition of certain admonitions, such as אַל־תִּתְחַר, "do not be incensed" (vv. 1, 7, 8), must also be taken into account in describing the structure and theme of the psalm.

Using an entirely different method, Lohfink separates the psalm into sections based on speech acts. Verses 1–11 are characterized by warning and admonition, verses 12–26 by statements on the future of the righteous and the wicked, and verses 27–40 by justification alongside two exhortations.[46] It is doubtful that speech acts alone provide the key to unlocking the struc-

---

41. Craigie, *Psalms 1–50*, 297.

42. See, e.g., Auffret, *Que seulement de tes yeux tu Regardes . . . : Etude structurelle de treize psaumes*, 294, 302.

43. Perdue, *Wisdom and Cult*, 280–82.

44. Ibid., 283.

45. Maloney, "A Word Fitly Spoken," 148, 168–69. Maloney's interest extends to the verbs that entail violent results for the wicked, including also שׁבר (vv. 15, 17) and שׁמד (v. 38). Though these are not key words in the sense that they are repeated, they extend the theme highlighted by the key words.

46. Lohfink, "Die Besänftigung des Messias: Gedanken zu Psalm 37," 79. So also Hossfeld and Zenger, *Die Psalmen I*, 230; Cortese, "Salmo 37," 31–33.

ture of the poem, since the various speech acts are scattered throughout the poem. In the first section verses 2 and 9 are both statements about the future and justifications. Verses 6, 10, and 11 likewise concern the future. In the second section the better saying of verse 16 defies Lohfink's structure. In the third section justification is complemented by statements about the future of the righteous and the wicked (vv. 28–29, 34, 37–38). Granted the exceptions in Lohfink's analysis, certain speech acts dominate each section of the poem.[47] The wisdom teacher stresses warning and admonition in the beginning but turns largely to justification and hope as the poem progresses.

The various structural analyses outlined above yield several conclusions. First, Psalm 37 is a thematically integrated whole that deals with a single theme, the problem of the prosperity of the wicked and life in the land. In its variations on this theme we gain a more complete perspective, suggesting individual strophes and proverbs should be interpreted in dialogue with the rest of the poem.[48] Second, while strictly speaking no progression of thought can be outlined in a simple structural scheme, we see a general movement from admonition to description to justification/promise. This appears to reflect an educational and rhetorical strategy that will guide the analysis that follows.

THE ETHICAL PORTRAIT OF THE RIGHTEOUS AND THE WICKED IN PSALM 37

The ethical discourse of the Psalter is inherently teleological, that is, the psalmists affirm that character yields outcomes. Having demonstrated the presence of this dynamic in Psalms 15, 24, and 34, we observe it also in Psalm 37. However, the portrait of the righteous in Psalm 37 is less concise than Psalms 15, 24, and 34 and differs markedly in its structure. Therefore, in the analysis that follows I shall examine Psalm 37 from a thematic perspective, analyzing the character traits of the righteous and the wicked first and then turning to the outcome or *telos* of each.[49]

---

47. See further analysis on this basis in Held, "Hoffen auf Gott und Entschlossenheit zum Guten," 296–97; Gerstenberger, *Psalms: Part 1*, 157.

48. Mays, *Psalms*, 159.

49. At several points character and its outcome are not easily separated, such as in verse 26. I consider ambiguous cases in both sections.

Psalm 37

Character Articulated by Admonition

The first eleven verses of the psalm are dominated by a series of admonitions. These admonitions are intended to shape the student's response to the success of the wicked, and as such they may indicate the wisdom teacher's perception that the opposite is the natural, if not actual, response of his students.

The admonitions are both negative and positive. The first admonition is repeated in verses 1b, 7c, and 8b: אַל־תִּתְחַר, "do not be incensed." The verb refers to burning in Hebrew and cognate languages, and its metaphorical use is associated with anger and the nostrils (אַף; cf. v. 8a).[50] Although English translations often render this metaphor in abstract emotional terms such as "fret" (KJV/RSV/NRSV/ESV/NIV/NASB/NET) or "worry" (NLT), or "be vexed" (NJPS), Alter's translation, "do not be incensed,"[51] preserves the metaphor of heat and communicates the emotional connotation of the verb. Each of the three occurrences of this phrase has its own context. In verse 1b, evil-doers are the potential spark. The second line specifies, "Do not be envious of those who do injustice" (אַל־תְּקַנֵּא בְּעֹשֵׂי עַוְלָה), which echoes Prov 24:19.

Why would the student envy the evildoer? In verse 7cd the teacher warns his student about envying those who prosper (בְּמַצְלִיחַ דַּרְכּוֹ) by means of injustice. The verb is the first of several terms that also occur in Psalm 1. Psalm 1:3 describes the righteous as those who prosper (יַצְלִיחַ) in all that they do. In contrast, in Ps 37:7 the one who "carries out schemes" (מְזִמּוֹת) is potentially the object of anger. Although the root זמם can simply denote plans of any kind, the nominal form often refers to evil schemes.[52] That seems to be the connotation of the term here, since verse 1c refers to their injustice. Finally, in verse 8 the phrase אַל־תִּתְחַר appears in the second line of a parallelism, the first of which counsels the student to "leave aside anger and abandon rage" (הֶרֶף מֵאַף וַעֲזֹב חֵמָה). This verse uses two terms for anger, אַף and חֵמָה. The first refers literally to the nose, which was thought to express emotion, perhaps by the flaring of nostrils.[53] The second literally means "heat,"[54] reinforcing the metaphor ANGER is HEAT. The first line counsels against such a response, and the second line offers a justification: "it only brings evil" (אַךְ־לְהָרֵעַ). This terse phrase consists of a restrictive par-

---

50. Creach, "חָרָה (ḥārâ)," 265–66.
51. Alter, *Psalms*, 129.
52. Hartley, "זָמַם (zāmam)," 1112–13.
53. Creach, "חָרָה (ḥārâ)," 266.
54. *HALOT* 326.

ticle, אַךְ,[55] and the hiphil infinitive construct of רעע. The student is warned against falling into the same trap that causes his indignation. With regard to verse 8, Craigie unconvincingly suggests the teacher warns against a kind of anger that "is almost certainly 'anger against God.'"[56] The object of anger is stated as evildoers in verses 1 and 7. Furthermore, there is no indication that the object has changed in verse 8, especially since evildoers are mentioned in the next verse. Someone who gets "heated up" over injustice may "take the law into his own hands," and that kind of a response does lead to evil or harm. The wisdom teacher may be warning against anger directed at God on account of the prosperity of the wicked, but that link is not made.[57] In fact, these negative warnings against a certain kind of emotional response to the wicked are complemented by positive admonitions that relate to YHWH.

The first cluster of these positive admonitions occurs in verses 3–4a. With language similar to Prov 3:5, verse 3 exhorts trust in YHWH (בְּטַח בַּיהוָה). Psalm 4:6[5] also enjoins trust in YHWH, but it is preceded in verse 5[4] by a strikingly similar exhortation to Ps 37:7: "Be upset and do not sin; speak in your hearts on your bed and keep still" (דֹּמּוּ; cf. דּוֹם in Ps 37:7a). However, Ps 4:6[5] commends offering right sacrifices (זִבְחֵי־צֶדֶק) instead of the general language of doing good in Ps 37:3a (וַעֲשֵׂה־טוֹב). This same general advice is found in Pss 34:15[14] and 37:27.

The second line introduces the theme of the land in an enigmatic pair of imperatives: "inhabit the land and tend to/graze on faithfulness" (שְׁכָן־אֶרֶץ וּרְעֵה אֱמוּנָה). Scholars raise several questions about this verse: Do the imperatives continue the exhortation, or do they describe the reward for trust and doing good from the first line? What does it mean to רְעֵה אֱמוּנָה? Does the subject act on the object (i.e., "shepherd it") or receive a benefit from the object (i.e., "graze on it")?

A straightforward reading of verse 3b suggests a continuation of the admonitions in verse 3a. The mood of the verbs continues to be imperative through verse 4a. Thus, the student is commanded to dwell in the land and "tend to faithfulness," that is, to do good. Apparently following this line of interpretation, Broyles notes the prevalence of pastoral language in the verb שכן ("to tent," in verses 3, 27, and 29) and the ambiguous phrase רְעֵה אֱמוּנָה. He concludes, "The strangeness of 'shepherding faithfulness

---

55. *HALOT* 45. See also *BHRG* §41.4.2. Muraoka labels this the "emphatic-restrictive" use (*Emphatic Words and Structures in Biblical Hebrew*, 130).

56. Craigie, *Psalms 1–50*, 297.

57. Kraus suggests that "[f]retting and being angry (v. 1) would be a sign of mistrust vis-à-vis the judgmental reality of Yahweh" (*Psalms 1–59*, 405). Obviously anger at YHWH is not far away if one nurses anger against the wicked, but the psalmist does not make this connection.

and uprightness,' in effect, seeks to divert one's preoccupation with material property to relational qualities that please Yahweh."[58] Similarly, Kraus preserves the admonitory sense of the imperatives, explaining the ambiguous second half as "a display of unwearied steadfastness ... in life on the land—which is thought of as the highest evidence of blessing and the epitome of the goodness of God that sustains life."[59] Thus the behavior of the righteous itself is evidence of God's blessing. But the imperative remains an exhortation and a responsibility, not a consequence. I will label this view the imperative-as-admonition view.

A number of interpreters reject the imperative-as-admonition view and see one or both of the imperatives in verse 3b as a consequence. I will call this second view the imperative-as-consequence view. This view depends on a number of considerations.

First, an imperative that logically depends on a previous imperative may express assurance or promise that some state will result from a previous action.[60] Goldingay understands the imperatives in verse 3b as "a concealed promise": "*If* you trust in Yhwh and do good, then you *will* dwell in the land and feed on truthfulness."[61] This conclusion requires that we understand the imperatives of verse 3b as logically dependent on those of verse 3a. But this kind of logical dependence is usually expressed with an intervening *wāw* conjunction, the paradigmatic example being Gen 42:18: זֹאת עֲשׂוּ וִחְיוּ, "do this and live."[62] It is possible that the parallelism in poetry also functions as the conjunction does in narrative, though the psalm contains 56 *wāw* conjunctions, making it less likely that a lack of a conjunction here is due to a poetic preference for avoiding conjunctions. However, understanding the imperative as a consequence may not be the most natural reading. LXX understands the second verb in verse 3b as a future passive, and thus a consequence, but that breaks the parallelism between the two verbs in verse 3b.[63]

If the imperatives of verse 3b are understood as a consequence of verse 3a, then the entire *bêt* strophe (vv. 3-4) would reflect an ABAB pattern of

---

58. Broyles, *Psalms*, 180.

59. Kraus, *Psalms 1-59*, 405. Cf. Vander Hart, "Possessing the Land: As Command and Promise," 139-40.

60. GKC §110.f. Cf. *IBHS* §34.4.c.

61. Goldingay, *Psalms*, 1:520. So also Miller, "The Land in the Psalms," 189-90.

62. GKC §110.f.a.

63. So Briggs, *Psalms*, 1:325-26; VanGemeren, *Psalms*, 343. The same problem confronts the interpretation of Hossfeld and Zenger, who suggest that רְעֵה אֱמוּנָה is likely a promise, pointing to similar such promises in Isa 14:30 and Ezek 34:14, 18 (*Die Psalmen I*, 234).

admonition and consequence since the imperfect in verse 4b signals a consequence. The structure could be represented as follows:

> A Trust in YHWH and do good (v. 3a),
> > B Then you will inhabit the land and graze on faithfulness (v. 3b),
> A' And take pleasure in YHWH (v. 4a),
> > B' And he will give to you the desires of your heart (v. 4b).

This structural pattern is tidy, but did the psalmist intend it to be so? An imperfect form in verse 3b would suit better if consequence were intended.

Third, understanding the imperatives in verse 3b as consequence depends upon understanding the second phrase in a particular way. The verb רעה obviously invokes a shepherding metaphor. The imperative-as-admonition view understands the subject of the verb as the shepherd, but the imperative-as-consequence view understands the subject as a sheep, as "grazing on" אֱמוּנָה, that is, enjoying the benefits of YHWH's fidelity. This aspect of the interpretation of the verse appears to be driven by theology. Anderson argues that dwelling in the land in verse 3b is the reward for fidelity. He translates the phrase רְעֵה אֱמוּנָה as "enjoy security," noting the NEB's "find safe pasture."[64] Miller translates the phrase "eat in security,"[65] which seems to force אֱמוּנָה to conform to a theological construct that is not necessarily clear from the context. Ellen Davis regards the phrase as "one of the most arresting metaphors in the Bible, when it is correctly translated." She rejects NRSV's "enjoy security" and NJPS's "remain loyal" as not compelling.[66] The word אֱמוּנָה denotes "faithfulness" or "truthfulness," which *may perhaps* have a derivative connotation of "security,"[67] but this seems to reflect more a theological assumption about the role of the land than sound linguistic argument. Dahood understands the second half as a consequence, but he follows the LXX and translates it as "feed on its riches," that is, the riches of the land.[68] However, the text-critical issue mentioned above creates a problem; LXX appears to offer an interpretive gloss. All these views depend on understanding the verb רעה in the sense "to eat" (as a sheep would graze)[69] as opposed to "to cause to eat" (as a shepherd would lead sheep to a place to graze). The former sense of the verb is attested in Isa 14:30, where

---

64. Anderson, *The Book of Psalms*, 1:293.
65. Miller, "The Land in the Psalms," 189.
66. Davis, *Scripture, Culture, and Agriculture*, 116.
67. So *HALOT* 63.
68. Dahood, *Psalms I*, 1–50, 228.
69. So Miller, "The Land in the Psalms," 189.

"the firstborn of the poor will graze" (וְרָעוּ בְכוֹרֵי דַלִּים), but both senses of the word appear in the qal stem.[70] Without further context, it is difficult to decide what sense is intended. It is preferable to preserve the subject of the previous verb, שׁכן. The shepherd pitches his tent; the sheep does not live in a tent. Therefore, the shepherd is the subject of the subsequent verb as well.

In view of these considerations, it seems preferable to understand the verse according to the imperative-as-admonition view. Although VanGemeren rejects Kraus's view that this phrase should be understood in parallel to "do good" in verse 3a, he preserves the role of the shepherd in verse 3b and translates the phrase, "tend the sheep faithfully." He points to Jeremiah's advice to the exiles in Babylon in Jer 29:5–7 as an example of a similar exhortation.[71] This series of admonitions assumes a certain theology of the land. The command implies a promise but is still a command. Daniel Block notes that the land is the place YHWH had chosen for Israel to grow and to enjoy peace and security.[72] Patrick Miller likewise sees deuteronomic theology shining through in the Psalter's approach to the land. The land is "God's covenantal gift as the place for lively and flourishing existence. . . . Again in resonance with the deuteronomic perspective, doing good is the key to continued and fruitful life in the land, the specifics of which continue to be elaborated in the psalm as they are throughout Deuteronomy."[73] To leave that place is to abandon trust in YHWH, who has provided the land as the context for the people to live faithfully with him and to flourish under his blessing. The righteous trust YHWH, do good, and continue to dwell in the land.

The positive admonitions continue in verse 4a. The wisdom teacher counsels his student to take pleasure (וְהִתְעַנַּג) in YHWH. The hithpael form of ענג is found again in verse 11, where the humble of the land "take pleasure in an abundance of peace." The act of shepherding faithfulness in verse 3b is fulfilled in the affections in verse 4a, as YHWH becomes the delight of the student.

Following a consequence in verse 4b, verse 5 reiterates the admonition of verse 3a to trust in YHWH. The verse begins with an enigmatic exhortation, "roll (גּוֹל) your way to YHWH." In Ps 22:9[8] the enemy describes the psalmist as one who "rolls to YHWH" (גֹּל אֶל־יְהוָה). Translations often render the verb as "trusts,"[74] a sense confirmed with the use of the verb בטח

---

70. *HALOT* 342.
71. VanGemeren, *Psalms*, 343.
72. Block, *The Gods of the Nations*, 101–103.
73. Miller, "The Land in the Psalms," 190.
74. ESV, NIV; NLT: "relies."

in verse 5b. This clarifies the sense of the metaphor, but the image is worth pondering. "Rolling one's way" is the act of decision, of choosing a pathway. By doing good and dwelling in the land given by YHWH, the student is "rolling his way" to YHWH and trusting that YHWH will act, as verse 5b affirms.

The final positive admonition in this first series of admonitions in verse 7 urges patience, to "be still" (דּוֹם) and wait (וְתִחֹל) for YHWH. The verb דמם connotes stillness and silence and is used elsewhere as a response to judgment or evil (Lev 10:3; Amos 5:13). The wisdom teacher counsels trust and inaction. Is it an attempt by the landowning class to preserve the *status quo*, as Brueggemann argues? I will return to that issue below, but it is important to note that the wisdom teacher does not hereby affirm the *status quo*, but rather points to a future change in the *status quo*.

The scattered admonitions in the last third of the psalm continue these themes. Verse 27a repeats verbatim Ps 34:15a[14a]: "Turn aside from evil and do good" (סוּר מֵרָע וַעֲשֵׂה־טוֹב). This admonition implies that the student is not entirely innocent. He may have fallen into the trap of responding to evil with the kind of anger that leads to evil (cf. v. 8). The second half of the parallelism also has an imperative, literally, "live forever" (וּשְׁכֹן לְעוֹלָם). This seems to involve an imperative that is logically dependent on an imperative and expresses a consequence. The second line begins with a conjunction, and a consequence or reward for faithful living is needed to set up the ground clause in the next verse. Verse 28 offers YHWH's love for justice as grounds for the promise of life in verse 27b. The next admonition in verse 34a begins the *qôp* strophe with the command to "wait for YHWH" (קַוֵּה אֶל־יְהוָה) and "keep his way" (וּשְׁמֹר דַּרְכּוֹ). This is a conceptual echo of the earlier admonitions in verse 3a, to trust in YHWH and do good, as well as the command to "roll your way to YHWH" in verse 5a, and to be silent and wait in verse 7ab. The admonitions continue to affirm for the student that YHWH will deal with evil and restore the land to those who trust in him. The final exhortation is educational, that is, to "watch the blameless and see the upright" (שְׁמָר־תָּם וּרְאֵה יָשָׁר). Were it not for the verb ראה in the second half of the line, we may understand שְׁמָר־תָּם as "guard blamelessness." But the wisdom teacher is commending learning by observation. In the previous strophe he reports that he saw (רָאִיתִי) the wicked man in his pride (v. 35), but then he was gone and could not be found (v. 36). In contrast, the student should watch the outcome of the life of the blameless and upright, further defined in verse 37b as "the man of peace." He illustrates the teacher's lesson that the righteous will live in the land—they have a future.

To summarize, the admonitions of the teacher in verses 1–8 present righteous character as cool-headed and not envious of the success gained

Psalm 37

by wickedness because of the risk of such a response. Instead the teacher counsels trust, keeping silent and waiting for YHWH to act. Later in the psalm, further admonitions reinforce this portrait, urging the student to turn from evil and to take note of the upright who enjoy the blessing of YHWH. However, in offering a portrait of righteous character, the wisdom teacher turns from admonition to description.

Character Articulated by Description

The wisdom teacher's description of character includes both the righteous and the wicked, involving both general terms and specific description.

The most common term for the first group is the "righteous" (צַדִּיקִים, verses 17b, 29a, 39a; cf. singular forms in verses 12a, 16a, 21b, 25b, 30a, 32a).[75] To a certain extent the meaning of this term is filled out by the psalm itself. The righteous are equated with "humble ones" (עֲנָוִים, v. 11a) and "the poor and needy" (עָנִי וְאֶבְיוֹן, v. 14c). This economic reference does not equate poverty with moral superiority. Otherwise the hope of the reversal of the poverty of the poor would be morally empty. Instead, the poor are poor because the wicked oppress the righteous. The righteous are those who "wait on YHWH" (קֹוֵי יְהוָה, v. 9b; cf. vv. 7b, 34a), "those whose way is upright" (יִשְׁרֵי־דָרֶךְ, v. 14d; cf. vv. 3a, 27a, 37a), and "the blameless" (תְּמִימִם, v. 18a; cf. v. 37a). In relational terms, the righteous are YHWH's "blessed ones" (מְבֹרָכָיו, v. 22a) and his "faithful ones" (חֲסִידָיו, v. 28b). Finally, the righteous person is a "man of peace" (אִישׁ שָׁלוֹם, v. 37b).

The righteous are distinct from the wicked (רָשָׁע, v. 10a, 12a, 21a, 32a, 35a; plural form, vv. 14a, 16b, 17a, 20a, 28d, 34c, 38b, 40b). In moral terms the latter are "those who do evil" (מְרֵעִים, vv. 1b, 9a), who "do injustice" (עֹשֵׂי עַוְלָה, v. 1c), and "carry out schemes" (עֹשֶׂה מְזִמּוֹת, v. 7d). In relational terms, they are "the enemies of YHWH" (אֹיְבֵי יְהוָה, v. 20b) and "the rebellious" (פֹּשְׁעִים, v. 38a).[76] The wicked are not described as wealthy, as if wealth represented an inherent moral failure. Instead, the wisdom teacher focuses on actions that reveal loyalties vis-à-vis YHWH and his people.

In addition to general terms, Psalm 37 offers a more detailed description of both the righteous and the wicked. This description begins with the

---

75. Cf. the one who "one who does righteousness" (פֹּעַל צֶדֶק) in Ps 15:2.

76. Or, perhaps, "those who are disloyal" (*HALOT* 981). English translations often render this word "transgressors" (KJV, RSV, NRSV, ESV, NET, NJPS) but the sense of "revolt, rebel" against God (Holladay, *Lexicon*, 300) makes better sense (so NLT) in light of the usage of this word elsewhere for political revolt (see, e.g., 1 Kgs 12:19; 1 Kgs 1:1).

wicked in verse 12. Picking up on the description of the man who "carries out schemes" in verse 7d, verse 12a describes the wicked as one who "plots against the righteous" (זֹמֵם רָשָׁע לַצַּדִּיק). The sense of secrecy vanishes in the next line as the wicked "gnashes his teeth at [the righteous]" (חֹרֵק עָלָיו שִׁנָּיו). The wicked display their hostility more concretely in verse 14 when they draw out sword and bow to kill the poor and needy. In verse 32 the wicked are described as lying in wait to kill the righteous. The wicked are violent, in contrast to the "man of peace" (אִישׁ שָׁלוֹם) in verse 37b, who keeps good relationships.[77]

The wisdom teacher also compares the wicked and the righteous in financial terms. In verse 21 the wicked borrow and do not repay (cf. Ps 15:4c), while the righteous "is gracious and gives" (חוֹנֵן וְנוֹתֵן; cf. Ps 15:5a, which uses the verb נתן for lending). Verse 26 returns to this theme of lending. Although the *nûn* strophe (vv. 25–26) appears to focus on the outcome of the righteous life, namely, that the righteous is supplied amply with bread (v. 25) and is able to lend (v. 26), the outcome itself reveals a disposition of character, namely, generosity. The righteous is "gracious and lending" (חוֹנֵן וּמַלְוֶה). The use of לוה echoes the provision in Exod 22:24 prohibiting lending at interest to the poor, but the same verb is found in the description of covenant blessings and curses in Deuteronomy 28. The covenant blessings for fidelity involve such agricultural productivity that Israel would be a lending nation not a borrowing nation (v. 12), but the curses for infidelity involve agricultural disaster so that the aliens living in the land will do the lending and Israel the borrowing (v. 44). Thus the wisdom teacher is thoroughly deuteronomic in his outlook, though the promise of prosperity and threat of calamity to the nation of Israel in Deuteronomy 28 is applied in Psalm 37 to the individual.

Finally, the wisdom teacher describes the righteous in terms of speech. In verse 30a his mouth "utters wisdom" (יֶהְגֶּה חָכְמָה). This is not simply secular wisdom but rather the wisdom of torah. The same verb occurs in Ps 1:2 with regard to the one who mediates on torah. At the close of Psalm 19, a torah psalm, the noun form appears in the phrase "the meditation of my heart" (הֶגְיוֹן לִבִּי, Ps 19:15[14]). This connection to torah is strengthened in the next line in which his tongue speaks justice (מִשְׁפָּט), but it is confirmed explicitly in verse 31a because the righteous has "the instruction of his God in his heart" (תּוֹרַת אֱלֹהָיו בְּלִבּוֹ).[78] The term תּוֹרָה is mentioned only four times in Book I, once in each of the two torah psalms (Pss 1:2, 19:8), here, and in

---

77. Nel, "שָׁלֵם (šālēm I)," 131.

78. Anderson suggests that this may be a connection to Jer 31:33, though he notes that a similar notion is found in Ps 40:9[8] and Isa 51:7 (*The Book of Psalms*, 1:299). Goldingay notes a similar concept in Deut 30:14 (*Psalms*, 1:531).

Ps 40:9[8]. The latter verse contains the curious statement, "your instruction is in my inner parts" (תּוֹרָתְךָ בְּתוֹךְ מֵעָי). Often translated "heart," the noun מֵעָה appears alongside לֵב to indicate the inward part of a person in Jer 4:19, Ps 22:15, and Lam 1:20. Thus we see that internalization of torah is an important category in Book I.

The character articulated by description in Psalm 37 bifurcates the righteous and the wicked. In general moral and relational terms, we encounter the righteous as people of peace, who do good, who wait on YHWH instead of grasping at power through violence. More specifically, the righteous lend generously and have the torah on their hearts and their lips. In contrast, the wicked are generally enemies of YHWH, persecute the righteous violently, and fail to meet their financial commitments. This contrast in character, however, is intricately connected to a contrast in outcomes.

Character's Outcome

Stated simply, the wisdom teacher presents two different outcomes. The righteous enjoy life and progeny in the land while the wicked are cut off from the land. This dynamic is a manifestly deuteronomic theme, as many have noted, because the outcome of the righteous life involves life in the land.

The psalm paints a grim picture of the outcome of the wicked life. In verse 2 the wisdom teacher compares the wicked to grass (כֶּחָצִיר) and "fresh green plants" (כְּיֶרֶק דֶּשֶׁא) that dries out quickly (cf. Ps 1:4; Isa 40:7–8). Grass highlights the ephemeral quality of the wicked—they will soon be gone.[79] This horticultural language is balanced in the middle (v. 20) and near the end of the psalm (vv. 35–36). Verse 20 extends the image of grass. Following the assertion that the wicked and the enemies of YHWH will perish (v. 20ab), the wisdom teacher pictures a field in its green glory that vanishes in smoke (v. 20cd). Fire can erase the glorious green grass in a field in a matter of hours. The final horticultural image is ironic. In verse 35 the wisdom teacher describes the experience of seeing the wicked prideful and standing tall like a cedar tree.[80] In contrast to the tree planted by water in Ps 1:3, this tree simply disappears. The wisdom teacher relays the experience of seeking for this "tree" in verse 36 and reports failure. The "tree" is no longer there.

The speed of the demise of the wicked is a deuteronomic theme, combining the roots אבד and מהר. Deuteronomy 4:26 threatens swift death to Israel in response to idolatry, and Deut 9:3 promises a swift death to the

---

79. Ryken et al., "Grass," 349.
80. For a defense of this reading, see p. 138 above.

nations in the land at the time of the conquest. Finally, in the covenant curses, YHWH threatens a swift death to Israel for infidelity (Deut 28:20).[81]

This future is described in non-horticultural terms as well. Earlier in the psalm the wisdom teacher predicted the student will see the outcome awaiting the wicked. In verse 10 he predicts the student will "look closely" (וְהִתְבּוֹנַנְתָּ) where the wicked once lived, and he will be gone. YHWH sees in verse 13. As in Ps 2:4, YHWH laughs (v. 13a) at the wicked who plot against the righteous (v. 12) because "he sees that his day will come" (כִּי־רָאָה כִּי־יָבֹא יוֹמוֹ). Finally, the penultimate strophe (vv. 37–38) counsels watching the blameless and seeing (רְאֵה) the upright. The man of peace has a future (אַחֲרִית, v. 37b), but the future for the wicked is grim.[82] With two niphal verbs, in verse 38 the wisdom teacher envisions a time when the wicked are destroyed (נִשְׁמָדוּ), their future "cut off" (נִכְרָתָה). The occurrence of the verb כרת links this verse with those that deal with the land (vv. 9, 22, 28, 34; cf. v. 11, which does not employ כרת).

The land is an integral category for the wisdom teacher's discourse on the future of the righteous and the wicked. The verbs ירש and כרת invoke deuteronomic associations.[83] The righteous are to possess the land but the wicked are cut off from the land. In the first reference to this motif (v. 9), evildoers "will be cut off" (יִכָּרֵתוּן), while those who wait on YHWH "will possess the land" (יִירְשׁוּ־אָרֶץ). Verse 11 focuses on the righteous, but the other verse in the strophe mentions the absence of the wicked, implying an absence from the land of promise. However, verse 11 is explicit that the humble "will possess the land" (יִירְשׁוּ־אָרֶץ). The next line specifies that this possession involves taking "pleasure in an abundance of peace" (וְהִתְעַנְּגוּ עַל־רֹב שָׁלוֹם). The verb ענג echoes verse 4, where YHWH himself is the object of the pleasure of the righteous. As a consequence of delight in YHWH, the righteous delight in שָׁלוֹם, that is, well-being.[84] In verse 22 the reference to the land is linked in the same strophe with the act of borrowing and lending. Previously I explored the description of the wicked as borrowers who do not repay in contrast to the righteous who lend generously (v. 21). The outcome of this declared in verse 22 is closely connected, namely, the blessing of the covenant (Deut 28:1–14). Those blessed by YHWH (מְבֹרָכָיו; cf. the use of ברך in Deut 28:2–6) for fidelity to the covenant possess the land (יִירְשׁוּ אָרֶץ)

---

81. I am grateful to my doctoral mentor, Dr. Daniel I. Block, for calling this motif to my attention.

82. Cf. Von Rad, *Wisdom in Israel*, 203.

83. Brueggemann, "Psalm 37," 232. The pairing of the two verbs is found only in Psalm 37 and Deut 12:29, 19:1.

84. Nel, "שָׁלֵם (šālēm I)," 131.

while those under the covenant curse (וּמְקֻלָּלָיו)[85] will be cut off (יִכָּרֵתוּ). In verses 28–29 the entire strophe is dedicated to the land. Verse 28c contrasts the "faithful ones" (identified in verse 28b) who "are kept forever" (לְעוֹלָם נִשְׁמָרוּ) with the seed of the wicked that is "cut off" (נִכְרָת). The progeny of the righteous are preserved while the progeny of the wicked come to an end.[86] The next verse ties this to the land, for the righteous possess it (יִירְשׁוּ־אָרֶץ, v. 29a) and dwell in it forever (וְיִשְׁכְּנוּ לָעַד עָלֶיהָ, v. 29b). The motif of dwelling in the land, presented as an admonition in verse 3b, is presented as an outcome in verse 29b. Finally, the land is the outcome for those who keep the way of YHWH in verse 34. The wisdom teacher adapts the concept of setting Israel high above the nations in Deut 28:1 (וּנְתָנְךָ יְהוָה אֱלֹהֶיךָ עֶלְיוֹן עַל כָּל־גּוֹיֵי הָאָרֶץ) and applies it to the individual with the verb רום: "he will raise you up to possess the land" (וִירוֹמִמְךָ לָרֶשֶׁת אָרֶץ, v. 34b). Again verse 34c contrasts the future of the wicked who are cut off (בְּהִכָּרֵת רְשָׁעִים), and the final word of the line reiterates that this is in the future (תִּרְאֶה, "you will see").

The wisdom teacher compares the outcomes of the righteous and wicked life in several more ways. In verse 4b those who take pleasure in YHWH are rewarded with the desire of their hearts. In the next verse those who trust in YHWH benefit from his action (v. 5b) to bring out their righteousness (צִדְקֶךָ; cf. Ps 24:6) and justice (וּמִשְׁפָּטֶךָ). This collocation of legal terms suggests a judicial vindication.[87] The public nature of this verbal affirmation is vividly portrayed in terms of light (כָאוֹר) and the noon (כַּצָּהֳרָיִם).

Verse 15 describes the outcome of violence against the poor and needy (v. 14). Seemingly similar to Koch's deeds-consequence construct, the violent die by their own sword (v. 15a) and have their bows broken (תִּשָּׁבַרְנָה, v. 15b).

The same form of the verb שבר is used of the arms of the wicked in the next strophe (vv. 16–17). The strophe is constructed as a "better" saying (v. 16) with a theological grounding (v. 17). The wisdom teacher prizes the meager possessions of the righteous "more than the abundance/noise of many wicked men" (מֵהֲמוֹן רְשָׁעִים רַבִּים). At first glance the comparison may not appear to stand on its own.[88] However, a hint of the reason may

---

85. Cf. the use of קלל in Deut 28:15, though ארר is used in verses 16–19.

86. For covenant blessings and curses related to progeny, see especially Lev. 26:22, 29; Deut 28:4, 11, 18, 32, 41, 46, 53, 56–57, 59. For a study of this motif in the Hebrew Bible, see Viands, "The Progeny Blessing in the Old Testament." John Walton notes that the ideal future in the ANE was to perpetuate a name, perhaps through descendants (*Ancient Near Eastern Thought and the Old Testament*, 313).

87. Enns, "מִשְׁפָּט (mišpāṭ)," 1142.

88. For most people the promise of poverty is rhetorically less persuasive than the promise of wealth. Cf. Goldingay, *Psalms*, 1:525.

be found in the term used for "abundance," הָמוֹן, as well as other better sayings in the wisdom corpus. Although KJV, NIV, and NET translate הָמוֹן as "wealth,"[89] RSV, NRSV, ESV, NJPS, and NASB render it as "abundance."[90] The latter rendering is preferable because it complements the "little" (מְעַט) of the first line. The sense of abundant wealth is attested in Ezek 29:19, 30:4, Eccl 5:9[10], and 1 Chr 29:16.[91] However, the root המה more commonly connotes "noise," particularly in the noise of human beings.[92] The notion of "abundance" or "crowds" appears to derive from the sense "noise" since noise is created by large numbers of people.

Noise is associated with gathering wealth in Ps 39:7[6], which employs the verb המה to describe the noisy activity of those heaping up stuff without knowing who will gather it. This activity is mere הֶבֶל, "breath" (cf. Qoheleth). This suggests that the poet plays with a double entendre, whereby wealth and noise (or turmoil) go hand in hand. This is consistent with a common wisdom theme of valuing wisdom over wealth. A number of the better sayings in Proverbs contrast poverty and wisdom with wealth and trouble (Prov 15:16, 15; cf. 16:8, 16). Particularly interesting is Prov 17:1, "Better is a dry morsel with quiet (שַׁלְוָה, "ease, rest")[93] / than a house full of feasting with strife" (NRSV). Returning to Psalm 37, the word הָמוֹן is intended to be understood in a negative light because the justification in the next verse forecasts that the arms of these wicked men are broken (v. 17a; cf. v. 15), while the righteous experience the support (וְסֹמֵךְ) of YHWH. While the wicked are opposed to YHWH, the righteous enjoy his sustaining help.[94]

The next strophe (vv. 18–19) develops the theme of YHWH's help. Echoing Ps 1:6, verse 18 declares that "YHWH knows the days of the blameless" (יוֹדֵעַ יְהוָה יְמֵי תְמִימִם). The second line affirms the security of their property (נַחֲלָתָם). The next verse promises that the righteous will encounter bad times without incurring shame (v. 19a), and the second line specifies that they will have plenty to eat (v. 19b). Thus the support of YHWH is material, both in preserving the family portion of the land and ensuring their physical well-being.

---

89. Cf. NLT's idiomatic paraphrase: "It is better to be godly and have little than to be evil and rich."

90. Cf. Alter's "great profusion" (*Psalms*, 131).

91. *HALOT* 250; though *HALOT* suggests another sense for the word in Ps 37:16: "multitude, crowd." Although this sense is usually negative, 1 Chr 29:16 speaks of the wealth accumulated to build the temple.

92. Domeris, "הָמָה (hāmâ)," 1041–43.

93. *HALOT* 1505.

94. *HALOT* 759; Harman, "סָמַךְ (sāmak)," 270.

The *mêm* (vv. 23–24) and *nûn* (vv. 25–26) strophes both continue to develop the idea of YHWH's support. The term סמך found in verse 17b recurs in verse 24b, but the metaphor is slightly different. In verse 24b YHWH supports the hand of the young man. The strophe as a whole is set in terms of the pathway. Verse 23a refers to "the steps of the young man" (מִצְעֲדֵי־גֶבֶר), verse 23b "his way" (דַּרְכּוֹ), and verse 24a speaks of his falling but not being "hurled down" (לֹא־יוּטָל). The delight (v. 23b) and support (v. 24b) of YHWH are decisive in ensuring that a young man's way is safe and secure (vv. 23a, 24a). The same concept appears in verse 31b. The righteous person, who speaks wisdom and justice and has torah on his heart, enjoys steps that do not stagger (לֹא תִמְעַד). The root מעד is a synonym of the root מוט, which is found in Ps 15:5. The term מעד occurs only seven times in MT, four of which associate the slipping with feet (2 Sam 22:37//Ps 18:37, Job 12:5, Prov 25:19). The usage in Ps 37:31b reflects the sense of 2 Sam 22:37//Ps 18:37, in which David credits YHWH with providing him a wide place in which to walk secure. In Ps 37:31b torah provides this protection.

The *nûn* strophe presents the most controversial of the outcomes described by the wisdom teacher, an issue to which I return below. It is important to note that the wisdom teacher speaks autobiographically, as the summation of his observations (וְלֹא־רָאִיתִי) over many years. The wisdom teacher observes that the righteous person is supported by YHWH with food, so he is never abandoned (נֶעֱזָב), "and his 'seed'" (וְזַרְעוֹ) never beg for bread. Instead, in verse 26, the wisdom teacher sees the righteous lending daily, "and his 'seed'" (וְזַרְעוֹ) becoming a blessing. Thus verses 25–26 reverse the "better" saying in verse 16, suggesting that YHWH's support results in such abundant provision that the righteous have more than enough. But this outcome spans generations so that their descendants enjoy well-being and bring good to the community.[95]

The next strophe (vv. 27–28) conceptually continues the notion of YHWH's support in connection with the land. Following the imperative to turn from evil to do good in verse 27a, verse 27b continues with a brief imperative-as-consequence, "And you will dwell forever" (וּשְׁכֹן לְעוֹלָם), meaning, "you will dwell in the land forever." Verse 28 offers the ground for this hope, namely that YHWH loves justice (מִשְׁפָּט) and will not abandon (וְלֹא־יַעֲזֹב) the faithful. This applies the experience of the previous strophe (vv. 25–26), combining admonition, outcome, and justification in a single strophe. The same two roots (שפט and עזב) appear two strophes later in verse 33. In spite

---

95. Although the language of "seed" is not in Gen 12:3, conceptually Ps 37:26 suggests that just as YHWH promised Abraham that he would be a blessing and that he would have children, the children of the righteous in Psalm 37 become a blessing. This adds to the covenantal character of this psalm.

of the violent intentions of the wicked against the righteous, YHWH "will not abandon him" or let him be condemned "in his judgment" (בְּהִשָּׁפְטוֹ). In other words, the righteous are never without a legal advocate.

Finally, the *tāw* strophe (vv. 39–40) introduces the familiar refuge metaphor. The righteous experience deliverance from YHWH, who is "their fortress" (מָעוּזָם). Following a string of statements in verse 40ab about YHWH's help (וַיַּעְזְרֵם) and his acts to save the righteous (יְפַלְּטֵם and וְיוֹשִׁיעֵם) from the wicked, verse 40c provides a justification, "for they seek refuge in him" (כִּי־חָסוּ בוֹ). As Jerome Creach argues, the root חסה and the term מָעוֹז both invoke the metaphor of refuge or a place of escape.[96] This crowning ethical description affirms that YHWH is faithful to those who are faithful to him.

To summarize, Psalm 37 compares the outcomes of the lives of the righteous and the wicked. The wicked have no future, are cut off from the land, and become victims of the violence they seek to perpetrate against the righteous. On the other hand, the righteous have a future, enjoy longevity, peace, and security in the land over multiple generations, and they have the support and help of YHWH. For many interpreters this appears to be a simplistic affirmation of a tired ideology. Is Psalm 37 a naïve affirmation of the deeds-consequence construct, or is something more subtle happening? In the following chapter I explore the relationship between Psalms 15, 24, 34, and 37 and the rest of Book I and show that the connection between righteous character and the good life is not simple. But we must consider whether taken on its own merits Psalm 37 offers a serviceable view of life.

THE THEOLOGY OF PSALM 37: IDEOLOGICALLY SIMPLISTIC OR THEOLOGICALLY COMPLEX?

In the context of current scholarship, Psalm 37 raises two key theological issues. First, interpreters often identify a deeds-consequence relationship as the theological foundation for the psalm, sometimes identifying the perspective of Job's friends as the closest analog.[97] This construct is widely accepted in OT scholarship in the terms defined by Klaus Koch, whose formulation has shaped the cool reception this psalm has received in recent scholarship.[98] Therefore we must ask if this application of Koch's thesis is appropriate. The second issue arises from Walter Brueggemann's provocative

96. Creach, *Yahweh as Refuge*, 25, 27.

97. See note 1 above.

98. Koch, "Is There a Doctrine of Retribution in the Old Testament?"; originally published in German as "Gibt es ein Vergeltungsdogma im Alten Testament?" 1–42.

essay on the psalm. He suggests that two distinct context-specific readings may arise from the psalm. In its original context, Psalm 37 affirms the *status quo* and represents a structure-legitimizing effort,[99] but in a later context an eschatological reading became possible for those who were landless.[100] On the one hand, Brueggemann helpfully identifies the complexity inherent in the psalm,[101] but neither he nor those who dismiss the psalm on account of its supposed deeds-consequence foundation have interpreted the psalm as a whole,[102] which its acrostic form invites us to do; nor have they adequately considered the covenantal and deuteronomic foundation upon which the psalm is constructed. As a whole, the psalm reflects the tension between present experience and future hope of the fulfillment of the deuteronomic covenant blessings and curses.

I begin by exploring the extent to which Psalm 37 is undergirded by a deeds-consequence construct. Koch apparently coined the phrase *Tun-Ergehen-Zusammenhang*, or "deed/consequence connection." His formulation of it has proved influential even to the extent that he has been cited in support of the very notion that he sought to deny.[103] Koch argued that a doctrine of divine retribution, that is, of divine action to bring about consequences for evil behavior, was not a significant OT category. Examining some key proverbs,[104] Koch writes: "These verses initially give one the impression that a wicked action—just like laws of nature which operate so that an action inevitably is followed by a reaction—inevitably results in disastrous consequences, whether it be unceasing flight (28:1, 17) or falling into the 'pit' (26:28; 28:10)."[105] Koch asserts that certain consequences are seen as both inevitable from certain deeds and not the judicial retribution of YHWH.[106] YHWH's role is not that of a judge, as in a Western courtroom, but "somewhat like a 'midwife who assists at a birth' by *facilitating the completion of something which previous human action has already set in motion*."[107] The human deed has built-in consequences, and YHWH is only a minor participant in the process. Although initially he focuses on Proverbs, he argues that there "is no place in the OT where the concept of actions

---

99. Brueggemann, "Psalm 37," 238–45.
100. Ibid., 246–49.
101. Ibid., 238.
102. Just as Mays suggests we ought to do (Mays, *Psalms*, 159).
103. Hatton, "A Cautionary Tale," 375–84.
104. Proverbs 25:19; 26:27, 28; 28:1, 10, 16b, 17, 18, 25b; 29:6, 23, 25.
105. Koch, "Is There a Doctrine of Retribution in the Old Testament?" 58.
106. Ibid., 59.
107. Ibid., 61. Emphasis his.

with built-in consequences is so obviously at work as is the case with the Psalms."[108] He points to Psalm 1, where the righteous are compared to a tree that bears fruit (v. 3). He argues that this plant metaphor signifies that "The manner in which one will grow and bear fruit depends on one's actions," not on divine action. He points to Ps 37:37 and a few other psalms as an example of the "Good Action-Blessings-Construct." However, he suggests that these passages are in the minority among passages mentioning "built-in consequences." The "Sin-Disaster-Relationship" is more common in the psalms. He notes that positive consequences are often related to YHWH's action to bless, but YHWH is less prominent when wicked actions are involved. He cites Ps 1:6 as an example: "Yahweh is mentioned in the first half of the verse, but the second half only mentions the action with its built-in consequences."[109] I do not intend to challenge Koch's exegesis of Ps 1:3 or his thesis in general, though some have done so.[110] However, we must examine the appropriateness of this construct with regard to Psalm 37. The psalm is often dismissed because it is assumed that the wisdom teacher posits an automatic connection between deeds and consequences.[111]

Given the similarities between Psalms 1 and 37, we would expect this construct to be found in the latter as well. However, a close reading of the entire psalm shows that divine action is the key theological grounding for its ethical instruction, and this divine action is placed within the context of the covenantal promises outlined in Deuteronomy.[112] Therefore divine action undergirds the theology of the entire psalm. For this reason Koch's deeds-consequence construct is not an appropriate model for understanding the theology of Psalm 37.

At first glance Koch's thesis seems to be affirmed by Psalm 37. Direct attributions of divine action are often linked to the rewarding of righteous action,[113] while the future of the wicked is given with passive verbs or

---

108. Ibid., 69.

109. Ibid., 71.

110. Koch's thesis has faced significant critique. See Miller, *Sin and judgment in the prophets*, 121-39; Fox, *Qohelet and His Contradictions*, 125 n. 5; Schultz, "Unity or Diversity in Wisdom Theology?"; Hatton, *Contradiction in the Book of Proverbs*.

111. Brueggemann uses the less mechanistic word "assured," but his language suggests that this is virtually automatic and certainly without exceptions ("Psalm 37," 241). Schultz demonstrates that in the wisdom corpus (Proverbs, Job, and Ecclesiastes) wisdom does not guarantee success and that "there is no God-binding mechanistic principle, as Koch claimed" ("Unity or Diversity in Wisdom Theology?" 282, 288).

112. Schultz makes a similar argument with regard to wisdom (ibid., 296-99).

113. Verses 4, 6, 17, 18-19, 23-24, 27-28, 33, 34, 39-40; less directly verse 9.

without attribution of a divine actor.[114] However, on several counts we may question whether the consequences of wicked actions are built-in to the actions themselves.

First, as Koch acknowledges with regard to Ps 37:37, at points the psalm speaks of the righteous being rewarded without mentioning divine action. Although Brueggemann acknowledges that YHWH is involved, he argues that YHWH's action in Psalm 37 is "less than direct and frontal."[115] His argument plays down the role of the divine agent and highlights the instrumentality of faithful living. However, the fact that divine action is not explicitly identified does not mean that divine action is not decisive for the outcome of the two ways.

Verse 9b mentions that "those who wait on YHWH, they will possess the land." The inclusion of the personal pronoun הֵמָּה following the divine name resumes the subject from the participial phrase at the beginning of the line. People are the subject of the verb ירשׁ, not YHWH, so one might argue that possessing the land is wrapped up in waiting for YHWH. However, it is implicit that they are waiting for YHWH to *cause* them to possess the land. The theology of the land is dependent upon the notion of the land as a gift of YHWH (e.g., Gen 12:7; 15:7; Num 14:8; Deut 3:18; 9:4–5; Josh 1:13; Ps 105:11). Koch might acknowledge this, but other examples have the righteous experiencing benefits in comparison to the disaster awaiting the wicked, without specifying an actor.

In verse 11 the humble are said to possess the land, and no divine agent is given. In verse 22 YHWH's "blessed ones" are said to possess the land, in contrast to the cursed ones who are cut off, but no divine agent is given.[116] No divine agent is listed in verses 25–26, which Brueggemann cites as a simplistic example of the deeds-consequence construct.[117] The niphal participle נֶעֱזָב (v. 25b) is pregnant with possibility about who might have done the abandoning, but no agent is given. However, an agent is necessary for the wisdom teacher's assertion to work. The community could be identified as that agent of abandonment (i.e., such a person is socially ostracized), but given the affirmation in verses 28 and 33 that YHWH does not abandon the righteous, a divine agent is more likely. Although verse 27 mentions no divine agent responsible for the enjoyment of life as a consequence of turning from evil to do good, verse 28 provides

114. Verses 9, 10, 13, 15, 17, 20, 22, 28, 34, 38; less directly in verses 2, 16, 35–36. So also Brueggemann, "Psalm 37," 234.

115. Ibid., 243.

116. No divine agent is listed, that is, unless we understand the pronominal suffix referring to divine action, which I will argue below.

117. Brueggemann, "Psalm 37," 234.

a theological justification that involves a divine agent. Verses 28c–29 likewise mention no divine agent for the protection of the righteous or their possessing the land, in contrast to the seed of the wicked that is cut off, but the divine agent is mentioned in the previous strophe (v. 28ab). In verse 31a it is possible to interpret the torah as the means by which a man does not stagger (v. 31b), but the torah is the "torah of his God."

These examples demonstrate that although the wisdom teacher does not explicitly mention a divine agent, this does not mean that he denies divine action. The rhetorical purpose of the wisdom teacher is to engender action-producing hope in his student by leading him to consider the outcomes of two ways of life. Since he does not offer a treatise on divine action in the world, we can account for the use of passive verbs by considering this rhetorical context. The passive voice may keep the question of divine action in the shadows, but it does not deny divine action.

Second, it is difficult to imagine how some deeds could contain built-in consequences without intelligent agents getting involved. For example, all the passive forms of כרת (vv. 9, 22, 28, 34, 38) imply an intelligent agent who does the "cutting off." This is especially relevant to the best candidate for the deeds-consequence construct, namely, verses 14–15. In this strophe the wicked draw the sword and bow to slay the poor and the upright (v. 14), but they die by the sword and have their bow broken (v. 15). This is rich irony,[118] not a statement about a natural inevitability built into the action of slaying the poor. Unless all who pursue the poor with the sword are assumed to be careless with their weapons, an intelligent agent is needed for verse 15 to be true, not some mechanistic/deterministic principle.[119] The consequence is not automatic from the deed.

Third, the covenantal and specifically deuteronomic backdrop of this psalm suggests that this intelligent agent is YHWH. The covenantal background is evident from the language of blessing and cursing. Psalm 37:22 speaks of "his" blessed ones (מְבֹרָכָיו) and "his" cursed ones (מְקֻלָּלָיו). The roots ברך and קלל both appear in the promises to Abraham in Gen 12:2–3.[120] The root ברך occurs frequently as a qal passive participle in Deuteronomy 28 (vv. 3–6), but in verses 8 and 12 YHWH is clearly the agent of blessing. Although Deuteronomy 28 favors the root ארר for cursing (vv. 16–19 and

118. Maloney, "A Word Fitly Spoken," 151.

119. Goldingay labors to maintain that a divine agent is uninvolved (*Psalms*, 1:524), but his repeated use of the word "mysteriously" to describe the process by which the wicked person's sword kills him stretches the imagination when a simpler explanation is closer at hand.

120. Botha, "The Relationship between Psalms 25 and 37," 556. Note that if LXX is correct and these should be active participles, there is still a covenant relationship.

Psalm 37

twelve times in ch. 27) over קלל, the two are used interchangeably in Gen 12:3, and Deut 11:27-28 employ בְּרָכָה and קְלָלָה. This is covenantal language expressing a relationship between intelligent agents, not the language of impersonal forces. They affirm that YHWH is involved with the life of Israel.

YHWH's involvement in Psalm 37 and in Deuteronomy is decisive for Israel's life in the land. As Brueggemann notes, the word pair ירש and כרת invokes Deuteronomy's conquest language and applies it to a new context. However, this language may not be applied to an entirely new argument, as Brueggemann suggests.[121] Christopher Wright correctly notes that the distribution of the term ירש suggests that it is closely connected to the deuteronomic theology of the land, often as an echo of Deuteronomy.[122] On the other hand, the verb כרת is most often used for covenant-making in Deuteronomy,[123] though physical sense of "cut" also occurs.[124] However, in two cases it is used for "cutting off" the nations from the land (12:29, 19:1), in each case in tandem with ירש. This word pair only occurs in Deuteronomy and Psalm 37, so the connection is unmistakable. There are small but important differences between the deuteronomic occurrences and their psalmic echoes. First, Israel as a nation is the subject of ירש in Deut 12:29 and 19:1, while in Psalm 37 it is "those who wait on YHWH" (v. 9), "his blessed ones" (v. 22), "the righteous" (v. 29; paired with the occurrence of כרת in the preceding line in v. 28), and those who "wait for YHWH and keep his way" (v. 34).[125] Likewise those who are "cut off" in Deuteronomy are the nations, while in Psalm 37 it is "the wicked" (vv. 9, 34) and "the ones cursed by him" (v. 22), and "the children of the wicked" (v. 28).[126] The psalmic echo of Deuteronomy appears to adapt the language

---

121. Brueggemann, "Psalm 37," 232-33. Note that Michaela Bauks denies that a deuteronomic connection is made here, insisting that the eternal possession of the land is a wisdom theme and not deuteronomic ("'Das Land erben' oder 'die Erde in Besitz nehmen' in Ps 36 (37 MT)," 517). However, the pairing of these words is undeniably deuteronomic and is unparalleled in the wisdom literature, which calls her conclusion into question.

122. Wright, "יָרַשׁ (yāraš I)," 547. Of the 232 occurrences of the verb ירש in MT, 72 occur in Deuteronomy, more than double the occurrences in the books of Joshua or Judges. After Numbers, the Psalms contain the fifth-most occurrences of the verb, and five of eleven of those occurrences appear in Psalm 37.

123. Deuteronomy 4:23; 5:2, 3; 7:2; 9:9; 28:69; 29:11, 13, 24; 31:16.

124. Deuteronomy 19:5; 20:19, 20; 23:2.

125. Note that the subject of ירש in its remaining occurrence כרת is "the humble ones" (v. 11).

126. Note that the remaining occurrence of כרת has "the future of the wicked" (v. 38) as subject.

of national conquest in more "individualistic" or familial terms for a new generation and to separate between those who will possess the land and those who will lose it based on ethical criteria.[127] The second difference to note is that in Deuteronomy YHWH explicitly does the "cutting off" and Israel does the "possessing," while in Psalm 37 the verb כרת is always passive. Given the strong connection between these passages, it stretches the imagination to argue that the psalmist does not believe that YHWH is the agent of "cutting off." YHWH is no less involved, but Psalm 37 focuses on the outcome of the life of the wicked rather than the means by which that outcome comes about.[128]

In addition, several thematic links bind Psalm 37 to the blessings and curses in Deuteronomy 28. In the latter YHWH is active in both blessing and cursing. Deuteronomy 28 and Psalm 37 both focus on life in the land. Although the pronouncement of blessing in Deut 28:3–6 is in passive voice, the remaining blessings identify YHWH as the active subject enacting the covenant blessings (vv. 1, 7–9, 11–13). Likewise the lengthy section detailing the curses begins with passive participles, but it shifts to active verbs with YHWH as the subject (vv. 20–22, 24–25, 27–28, 35–36, 48–49, 59, 63–65). While all these blessings and curses relate to life in the land, several are particularly relevant to Psalm 37. First, the curses touch on multiple generations and progeny (Deut 28:41, 53–57, 59, 62–63; cf. Ps 37:25–26, 28, 38).[129] Second, as noted above, blessing puts the faithful in a position to lend, while cursing forces them to borrow (Deut 28:12, 44; cf. Ps 37:21, 26).[130] Third, while the occurrences of the כרת/ירש word pair in Deut 12:29 and 19:1 contrast Israel and the nations, the covenant blessings and curses in Deuteronomy 28 contrast fidelity and infidelity to the covenant, as does Psalm 37. Finally, Deut 28:41 and 64 threatens exile, which is conceptually parallel to the language of "cutting off" in Psalm 37. Wicked Israel is threatened with being cut off from the land in the same manner as the nations

---

127. This is not distant from the reasons cited in Deut 9:4–5 for driving the nations out, though there the righteousness of Israel is specifically ruled out as a reason for their being given the land.

128. One additional connection between Psalm 37 and Deuteronomy is the motif of "seeing." Jeffrey Tigay notes that in Deuteronomy 4 "the argument . . . is based primarily on things that were *seen* and *not seen*" (*Deuteronomy*, 42, italics his). Admittedly the occurrence of such a common verb is not in itself noteworthy. But the argument based on experience in Psalm 37 differs from Deuteronomy 4 in the same way as the כרת/ירש word pair: what is national experience in Deuteronomy 4 is individualized experience in Psalm 37.

129. Note the occurrence of זֶרַע with the sense of "descendants" in Deut 28:46, 59 and Ps 37:25, 26, 28.

130. Cf. Weinfeld, *Deuteronomy and the Deuteronomic School*, 310.

who once dwelt in it. However, Deuteronomy 28 is not conceptually parallel to Psalm 37 at every point. Psalm 37 contains no promise of military victory (Deut 28:7) nor threat of national military defeat (Deut 28:25, 33, 36, 48–52), and the promise in Deut 28:9 that Israel would be YHWH's holy people (לוֹ לְעַם קָדוֹשׁ) is also absent. The language of torah obedience found in Deut 28:1, 13–15, 45, and 58 does not appear in Psalm 37, though the psalm profiles the person who *embodies* torah obedience and who has "the torah of his God on his heart" (v. 31). In spite of these differences, in substance both passages uphold the ideal of torah obedience—Deuteronomy 28 for the pre-conquest nation[131] and Psalm 37 for the individual in a post-conquest generation.

When read as a whole, Psalm 37 does not support Koch's account of a deeds-consequence relation in which the consequences are contained within the deeds themselves. Rather, it affirms the covenant blessings and curses from Deuteronomy and applies them to individuals. Therefore, the action of YHWH is essential to the outcomes of the two ways.[132] In spite of his own belief that the psalm speaks of in-built consequences, Goldingay rightly notes that Psalm 37 counsels trust in YHWH not in a moral order.[133] If consequences were automatic, there would be no reason for the wisdom teacher to stress the need to remain calm and not get incensed over the success of evil-doers. The results are assured, but they are not assured in any kind of mechanical or automatic way.[134] Covenant relationship is involved, and God is free to fulfill his promises in his own time.[135] The psalm's implied *Sitz im Leben* must involve a time when the consequences of wicked deeds are not apparent, thus creating the tension.

This brings us to Brueggemann's assertion that the first reading of the psalm involves a structure-legitimizing ideology.[136] Brueggemann highlights the complexity of the psalm, suggesting that it is "supple for interpretation"

---

131. Although many, if not most, scholars reject the notion that the historical Moses gave Deuteronomy as addresses to a pre-conquest Israel, the book itself represents the audience in that way.

132. Cf. Kraus, *Psalms 1–59*, 408, who maintains that the psalm is not encouraging faith in retribution but faith in YHWH. It is conceivable that the psalmist sees a moral law written into creation by YHWH (M. Daniel Carroll R., personal communication). However, the point that Koch is making is that YHWH is not conceived as the agent of retribution. In light of the argument above, this does not seem to fit with Psalm 37.

133. Goldingay, *Psalms*, 1:534.

134. Contra Brueggemann, "Psalm 37," 242.

135. Explaining the non-automatic nature of divine retribution in the Psalms, Gordon Wenham suggests that the righteous must pray for it, which explains the presence of psalms seeking an end to the activity of the wicked (*Psalms as Torah*, 143–44).

136. See note 99 above.

and "invites conflicting readings in the face of contextual requirements, interests and possibilities."[137] He notes four elements found in the psalm that give rise to this "indeterminate quality." First, he sees the כרת/ירש word pair reflecting Koch's deeds-consequence construct, with the passive form of כרת indicating a direct and possibly automatic result obtained by wickedness.[138] Second, Brueggemann highlights verses 25–26:

> These two verses lend most weight to the common judgment that this Psalm is the voice of a self-assured property-owning class which believes "the system works," and which is prepared to deny any evidence that might tell against this settled, stable, reliable, controllable view of social reality. The statement that "deeds-consequences" works is here flat and without nuance, entertaining no exception or slippage.[139]

Third, he notes the similarity between the references to the blameless in verses 18 and 27 and Joban claims of blamelessness. Although he regards Job as more courageous, the two share a struggle for moral coherence.[140] Fourth, Brueggemann notes that the psalm "concludes with a bold assertion that, in the end, matters will be sorted out according to moral distinctions (vv. 37–40). In important ways, these verses simply reiterate the teaching of the entire Psalm. The Psalm does, however, look to a resolution not yet obvious or in hand."[141] Also, he highlights the double use of אַחֲרִית, "posterity" or "future," in verses 37 and 38. "The Psalm is willing and able to look beyond a simple moral calculation to a full, climactic reckoning ultimately wrought by God."[142] In view of these four elements,

> This teaching is not a bland summary of an innocuous, optimistic prudentialism. It is, rather, alert to an important intellectual dispute that admits of no easy resolution. Moreover, it is evident that the Psalm is not one long, flat instruction marked by sameness and consistency. There is a variety of markers concerning abrupt rhetorical and substantive turns. These markers raise up

---

137. Brueggemann, "Psalm 37," 230.

138. Ibid., 234.

139. Ibid., 234. The verses he notes are admittedly hard to square with experience, an observation Brueggemann praises John Calvin for making (ibid., 235–36). For Calvin's comment, see *Commentary on the Book of Psalms*, 2:39.

140. Brueggemann, "Psalm 37," 236.

141. Ibid., 237.

142. Ibid.

issues, evidence tensions, lack of resolution and urgency in the ongoing conversation of practical faith.[143]

The intellectual dispute is between the interests of the landed and the landless. In the first reading, which he asserts fits the psalm's original social context, the interests of the land-owning class are preserved and land ownership itself is prized as both blessing and virtue.[144] Drawing on Otto Kaiser's interpretation of Psalm 37,[145] Brueggemann understands Psalm 37 as an example of an ideology that asserts the deeds-consequence construct in order to create moral coherence, without allowance for exceptions.[146] This interpretation is closely related to the first two elements outlined above, namely, the כרת/ירש word pair and verses 25–26. His second reading is based on the third and fourth elements above and is suggested by recent liberationist literature. In this second reading the psalm is "a ground for hope for the landless"[147] that rises to the level of an eschatological hope.[148] Among other considerations, he argues for this eschatological reading based on the imperfect mood of the verbs ירש and כרת, the phrase "a little longer" (עוֹד מְעַט) in v. 10, and the third and fourth elements outlined above.[149] Brueggemann places these two readings side-by-side without suggesting that the second reading is superior or dominant over the first.[150] The two readings differ in regard to their social position and their attitude toward the present: "The first reading, with self-satisfaction and self-sufficiency, celebrates a reliable present tense. The second subverts the present in its passionate embrace of a revolutionary future, a future as revolutionary as the Jubilee when the land will be given to those who have lost it."[151] Brueggemann places a question mark on any reading that seeks to adjudicate between these two readings because all readings are context-laden.[152] However, if we believe that the wisdom teacher has an idea to communicate and not simply that the text has a life of its own (a premise Brueggemann would no doubt question), then we are not permitted to play one part of the psalm off the other in an

---

143. Ibid., 238.

144. Ibid., 238–39, 244. On the social setting of this psalm, Brueggemann draws on Gordis, "The Social Background of Wisdom Literature," 160–97.

145. Kaiser, *Ideologie und Glaube*, 36–39.

146. Brueggemann, "Psalm 37," 241.

147. Ibid., 245.

148. Ibid., 246–47.

149. Ibid., 247–50.

150. Ibid., 250.

151. Ibid., 254.

152. Ibid., 255.

attempt to portray a class struggle. Since the psalm is presented as a whole in an acrostic form, a faithful and charitable reading will try to make sense of the text *as a whole*.

On two counts it is open to question whether Brueggemann has adequately accounted for the whole psalm. First, it is questionable that the psalm was originally written in order to preserve the *status quo* for a landowning class.[153] The comments of Robert Gordis on this psalm undergird Brueggemann's contention that this psalm reflects the landed class. Gordis reconstructs the social setting based on the contrast between borrowers and lenders in Ps 37:21, using it as an explanation for the confident assertion of verse 25. Based on that he asserts the class origins of the psalm.[154] Gordis appears to have missed the covenantal overtones of the psalm and instead read verse 21 as evidence of a landed class lurking behind the psalm rather than evidence of a reaffirmation of the covenant ideals. Instead of affirming the *status quo*, Psalm 37 offers comfort by holding out the promise that the *status quo* will change, that the righteous *will* possess the land. As Ellen Davis notes, Brueggemann's first reading "fails to take account of the note of keen expectation that runs throughout; the tone of the psalm is encouragement for the dispirited, not contentment with the *status quo*."[155] It also flips the equation of deeds and outcomes so that the outcome itself (land ownership) is a virtue. Such a conclusion must rule out the deuteronomic background, which highlights the ability to lend as the outcome of YHWH's blessing to Israel.

Furthermore, the language used for the righteous in Psalm 37 argues against the notion that the psalm advocates the interests of the landed class. In verse 11 the righteous are identified as the "humble ones" (עֲנָוִים) and in verse 14 as "the poor and needy" (עָנִי וְאֶבְיוֹן), which cannot be a landed class seeking to preserve a *status quo*. Instead, the righteous are those who are waiting to possess the land and be delivered from the powerful who slay them with sword and bow. On the other side of the equation, the pompous wicked are those who stand tall like a cedar tree (v. 35) or who are compared

---

153. Botha dismisses Brueggemann's first reading in the text and suggests it was written after the exile or in the Hellenistic period in response to disenchantment ("The Relationship between Psalms 25 and 37," 63). Although Botha's proposal for dating is not the only option, he rightly notes that the psalm fits best in a period of disenchantment. Earlier P. A. Munch made a similar observation about the likely historical context of the psalm, suggesting that a new class of wealthy people had gained control of the arable land ("Das Problem des Reichtums in den Psalmen 37.49.73," 37). We know little about the details of this historical context, but what is clear is that the psalm does not arise from a settled satisfaction with the *status quo*.

154. Gordis, "The Social Background of Wisdom Literature," 171.

155. Davis, *Scripture, Culture, and Agriculture*, 115.

to the glory of a grassy field (v. 20).[156] In light of these considerations, we cannot imagine that the wisdom teacher seeks to preserve a *status quo* unless he is deliberately attempting to deceive and does not believe the words he writes.[157] Given its presentation in the Psalter, such an interpretation is unlikely, so we are left with the conclusion that the wisdom teacher holds out promise of a *change* in the *status quo* in favor of those who are not among the wealthy wicked. Although the psalmist is likely representative at some level of the cultural elite, he is not deaf to the concerns of the poor. In addition, the fact that the psalm is found in a collection that has been treasured and used widely from ancient times until now and addresses common human concerns suggests that the psalm is sufficiently demoncratized to speak to and for the concerns of more than the elite.[158]

Second, the language of experience in this psalm does not affirm a faith in a "reliable present." Brueggemann rightly notes a tension in the psalm between the present and the future, but the solution is not to posit differing and contradictory testimonies.[159] Instead, a faithful reading of the psalm will try to read it as a whole.

Harry Nasuti questions Brueggemann's reconstructions of the settings of psalms, particularly with regard to socio-economic divisions in Israel.[160] He contends that part of Brueggemann's problem is that he has not adequately appreciated Mowinckel's argument regarding the world-making potential of the psalms. "For Mowinckel, the cult makes present—and helps create—an alternate world in tension with the everyday world in which we live most of our lives."[161] In the cult the worshipper experiences a present reality of the divine. It is not just "a hoped-for world that is beyond present reality."[162] It is an actual experience of the new world that is hoped for.[163]

---

156. Cf. Ezek 34:1–10.

157. Along these lines Brueggemann suggests that the perspective of these verses "might be useful as an educational ploy in a very protected environment, or in the context of the very young and the very innocent (or the very devout). Such a view might even be sound piety, the kind that pervades the most innocent sapiential teaching that has as yet experienced no failure of nerve, and has not encountered any cognitive dissonance" (Brueggemann, "Psalm 37," 235). That does not resolve the question, though, because the warning against becoming incensed suggests that cognitive dissonance is the occasion for the psalm.

158. M. Daniel Carroll R., personal communication.

159. As Brueggemann so skillfully and creatively does in *Theology of the Old Testament*.

160. Nasuti, *Defining the Sacred Songs*, 96–98.

161. Ibid., 99.

162. Brueggemann, *Israel's Praise*, 52.

163. Nasuti, *Defining the Sacred Songs*, 100–101.

Portraits of the Righteous in the Psalms

Although Psalm 37 does not share the same liturgical language that brings a present experience of divine power to the cult (such as Ps 24:7–10), Nasuti's critique of Brueggemann stands. Brueggemann is unable to account for testimony about the present and the hope for the future in a single reading.

This is clearer when we examine Brueggemann's understanding of the second reading more carefully. Following Crüsemann,[164] Brueggemann suggests that the two readings of Psalm 37 correspond to Qoheleth's two attitudes vis-à-vis the deeds-consequence relation. The first reading corresponds to Qoheleth's faith in deeds-consequences, while the second reading reflects Qoheleth's crisis of faith in deeds-consequences. However, instead of following Qoheleth's resignation to the failure of deeds-consequence, the second reading of Psalm 37 is hopeful.[165] Brueggemann helpfully summarizes:

> Restlessness and hope are grounded in the conviction that the Psalm still rings true for the very long haul, because of the undoubted promises of Yahweh. The grip of the wicked upon the land will soon (v. 3), in a little while (v. 10), in the end (vv. 37–38), be turned so that there will be "inheriting" and "cutting off," because the deeds-consequence linkage is not simply practical common sense, but a passionate conviction that Yahweh has ordained that the waiting, righteous ones will have the land that is rightly theirs, which has of late been seized from them.[166]

Brueggemann is right that the psalm makes sense only if it "still rings true for the very long haul," but that does not mean that it does not ring true at some level in the present.

Any interpretation of the psalm as a whole must take into account the psalm's claims about present experience and future change in the *status quo*. The implied social premise of the psalm corresponds to Brueggemann's theme of restlessness. The restlessness of the student in the face of the success of the wicked (in spite of the covenant promises) drives him to anger, but the wisdom teacher counsels trust in the covenant promises and holds out present experience as an indication that the righteous will one day possess the land.

The tension between present and future is evident in the verb conjugations. The majority of assertions in the psalm can be interpreted in a future or gnomic frame of reference.[167] The majority of statements about

---

164. Crüsemann, "The Unchangeable World," 57–77.
165. Brueggemann, "Psalm 37," 251–53.
166. Ibid., 253.
167. Michaela Bauks interprets the *yiqtol* form as a modal, denying a future/

the outcomes of the two ways indicate a future time using the imperfect, consecutive perfect, or an imperative indicating a result (vv. 2, 4–6, 9, 11, 13, 15, 17–20, 22, 23b, 24a, 27b, 29, 31b, 33–34, 40) or have a deictic indicator of a future time (vv. 10, 34, 37–38).[168] Brueggemann's second reading, or what Nasuti calls future eschatology, is actually the focus of the bulk of the psalm. However, a number of verses make claims about past or present experience, what Nasuti calls realized eschatology. Participles indicate YHWH's relationship to the righteous, supporting them (vv. 17, 24) and knowing their days (v. 18), as well as loving justice (v. 28). A number of perfects (or consecutive imperfects) and participles appear to indicate a past referent or a proverbial statement with gnomic force (v. 17b, 23a, 24b, 25–26, 28cd, 35–36). A verbless clause, verse 39 asserts that YHWH is the deliverance and fortress of the righteous; this is a claim with implications for the present *and* the future.

The linchpin of Brueggemann's argument for the first reading reflecting a faith in a reliable present is verses 25–26. For Brueggemann, they make grandiose claims about past experience that cannot be sustained, as if a righteous man has never begged for bread. Goldingay suggests reading the verse as hyperbole "since the preacher has just referred to the fact that the faithful do fall."[169] This may be part of the answer, but more importantly the assertion is not a gnomic statement about how things always happen. Instead, the wisdom teacher affirms one of the covenant ideals has proven true in *his* experience ("I have not seen," לֹא־רָאִיתִי). This corresponds to the

---

eschatological sense to the Hebrew text but noting that LXX translators render the *yiqtol* with the future tense ("'Das Land erben' oder 'die Erde in Besitz nehmen' in Ps 36 [37 MT], 510–12). She is not convinced that there is a strong eschatological flavor to the LXX translation, though that tendency is clear in the Pesher of Psalm 37 (QpPs37), especially in verse 11 where a cosmic battle is pictured (ibid., 521).

168. Not all interpreters agree that the verb conjugation carries a temporal meaning. Even with respect to terminology many would question the use of the terms perfect/imperfect because they may imply something about the semantics of the form that may not be accurate. However, as a matter of convention, I assume that "perfect," "suffix conjugation," and "*qatal* form" are synonymous. Likewise, "imperfect," "prefix conjugation," and "*yiqtol* form" are synonymous. I use "perfect" and "imperfect" to refer to the form of verbs and not their function or meaning (*BHRG* §15.1, 2; 19.1). However, I agree with van der Merwe, Naudé, and Kroeze that the Hebrew finite verb conjugation (perfect and imperfect) include interwoven elements of time and aspect. So the perfect usually indicates past time and/or complete action, while the imperfect usually indicates non-past time and/or non-complete action (*BHRG* §19.1). On the question of eschatological vs. proverbial reference, it is clear from the context of Psalm 37 that the experience of "possessing the land" is an experience not yet complete for the student. And certain deictic indicators clarify the future referent for those assertions and those like them.

169. Goldingay, *Psalms*, 1:528.

covenant ideal outlined in Deut 15:4, "There will not be poor among you, for YHWH will surely bless you in the land" (לֹא יִהְיֶה־בְּךָ אֶבְיוֹן כִּי־בָרֵךְ יְבָרֶכְךָ יְהוָה בָּאָרֶץ). Before we accuse the psalmist of being unrealistic, we should recall that Deut 15:7 admits that there would be poor in the land.[170] The wisdom teacher is arguing that the covenant ideals have been fulfilled in his experience, but he does not deny that the righteous can become poor. To conclude that the wisdom teacher has faith in a reliable present, we must interpret this verse in isolation from the rest of the psalm.

The wisdom teacher makes a corresponding, though less concrete, present-tense claim about the wicked in verses 35–36. Again, the wisdom teacher frames this in terms of *his own* life experience,[171] "I have seen" (רָאִיתִי, v. 35a). This verse appears less objectionable because it is so abstract, but it asserts a result that is nearly instantaneous—the wicked person disappears. Again, this mirrors the covenant ideal that the nations would be cut off completely from the land, which they were not. The wisdom teacher unflinchingly invites the student to experience the same reality in the next strophe, to watch the future of the righteous. Our postmodern skepticism about such absolute claims masks the complexity of the wisdom teacher's discourse. He makes claims about the future without the language of inaugurated eschatology that we use today. The already and the not-yet are both found in this psalm. They coexist because snatches of realized eschatology affirm the reality of a future-but-as-yet-unrealized eschatological hope for a life of שָׁלוֹם.

CONCLUSION

Psalm 37 offers a profile of the righteous in contrast to the wicked that applies the deuteronomic covenant ideals for the nation of Israel to the individual or family. The righteous refrain from wickedness and pursue the good in keeping with torah, and the outcome is life in the land. The wicked persecute the poor and are cut off from the land as the nations that preceded Israel were cut off from the land for their wickedness. However, the psalm preserves a tension between present experience and unrealized hope. The wisdom teacher points to his own experience of the covenant ideals and invites his student to experience the same, and yet the psalm awaits a future horizon in which the man of peace is rewarded with an abundance of peace.

---

170. I am grateful to my doctoral mentor, Dr. Daniel I. Block, for calling this passage to my attention.

171. Or "testimony" (Kraus, *Psalms 1–59*, 408).

This tension is not limited to Psalm 37. When we consider the canonical context of the four portraits of righteous character, we find that this tension is acute. As I show in the next chapter, Book I of the Psalter affirms the ethic of these four portraits of righteous character but engages in a complex dialogue about the *telos* of the faithful.

6

Ethical Ideals and Reality in Dialogic Tension in Book I

INTRODUCTION

What is the function of Psalms 15, 24, 34, and 37 in Book I? The portraits of the righteous provide ethical orientation in the midst of theological dissonance. The psalmist groans under suffering and wonders whether righteous character leads to a good life (i.e., refuge, security, life), but he perseveres and affirms his covenant faith by his ethical commitments and his steadfast hope in YHWH.

As an alternative perspective to the inner-Israel-ideological-conflict model of Mandolfo and Brueggemann, we may follow the contours of Book I as it presents the diverse moments in the life of *a single subject*. The book exhibits a multifaceted dialogue, involving the psalmist and his enemies, his human (didactic) audience, YHWH, or even himself. The struggle of the religious believer to make sense of his experience in view of the ideals of his faith unifies these various forms of address.

This dialogue resembles a journey through a landscape in which the psalmist rises to the heights of confidence and praise and falls to the depths of lament, all in community with others and with YHWH. On this journey the portraits serve as points of orientation and reorientation in order to encourage the reader to respond with hope in YHWH and love for neighbor. Book I consistently affirms the character commitments of the portraits, but

Ethical Ideals and Reality in Dialogic Tension in Book I

it also presents a variety of responses to their vision of the outcome of the righteous life, thus creating the contours of this varied landscape.

In support of this interpretation I will consider the ethical concerns in the portraits of the righteous and then place them within their canonical context in Book I. Finally I consider some implications of reading Book I in light of the ethico-theological dialogue that it contains. But first we must examine the presupposition that the book may be read with reference to a single subject.

READING BOOK I WITH A SINGLE SUBJECT

Carleen Mandolfo is not dogmatic about whether multiple speakers can be identified in the lament psalms. Instead, she identifies shifts in tone and voice (from first to third person). Although these shifts may represent liturgical alternation between speakers, Mandolfo prefers to call them "different consciousnesses,"[1] and she rightly regards as speculative the proposal that the voice of priests is involved.[2] She suggests the lament psalms may have been the place in which Israel "resolved ideological conflicts" rather than providing outright countertestimony.[3] Also, "The two together represent an interplay, working out in tandem of the symbolic dissonance every culture experiences."[4] However, as I have shown in chapter 1, her interpretation of the DV essentially involves social conflict. Mandolfo interprets the DV as a "rhetoric of response" to the supplicant and denies the possibility that the DV is in fact the voice of the supplicant "comforting herself in the third person."[5] In response, I would suggest that there are several reasons to read the DV with the voice of the supplicant as the words of a single subject.

First, the notion of self-comfort finds a parallel in the Psalter in Psalms 42/43 and 62. Applying Bakhtinian dialogic criticism, William Brown suggests that these two lament psalms "depict the inner deliberation of the speaking self,"[6] though the identities of the psalmist/poet and the supplicant remain obscure.[7] However, Brown suggests that in these psalms the voice of the psalmist intrudes and exerts a controlling force over the

---

1. Mandolfo, *God in the Dock*, 1–2.
2. Ibid., 197, 204.
3. Ibid., 192.
4. Ibid., 206.
5. Ibid., 139.
6. Brown, "The Psalms and 'I,'" 36.
7. Ibid., 26.

troubled voice of supplication.[8] Brown's psalmist can only "disappear" if he is distinct from the supplicant. But Brown rightly notes that the language on the surface of the psalms suggests inner deliberation. Therefore the idea that the psalmist can provide self-comfort finds a parallel within the Psalter, and inner deliberation cannot be excluded *a priori*.[9]

Second, although we may not be certain that the psalmists always identify differing voices, in many cases they do. Levine suggests that since quotations are found in all the major genres in the psalms, "quoting another's word, the concept so central to the discourse theory of Mikhail Bakhtin, is one of the stylistic hallmarks of the biblical Psalms."[10] Whether through external dialogue (quarreling with others) or internal dialogue (quarreling with oneself), "the poets struggle to reconcile what other people say with their own sense of what is real."[11] Levine identifies the conscious and explicit engagement with the wicked, whose words threaten to be internally persuasive for the psalmist (Pss 3:3[2]; 10:11; 12:5[4]; 14:1; 41:6[5]; 42:4[3], 11[10]; 71:11; 94:7).[12] All these quotations are introduced with the verb אמר. Levine rightly notes that the quoting of one's interlocutors "heightens the complexity of the psalmists' representation of their faith."[13] This not only identifies a true social conflict, it calls into question a dialogic reading that posits a fundamental conflict between the voice of the supplicant and the DV. These quotations are almost all in the voice of the supplicant,[14] so

---

8. Ibid., 38–42.

9. Craig Broyles denies that lament psalms are a "'reflection of the psalmist's soul,' as though one could read from it how the psalmist struggled to hold on to faith." He argues that reminders of God's past saving deeds are not intended to bolster the psalmist's faith but to move God to action (*The Conflict of Faith and Experience in the Psalms*, 220). But are these mutually exclusive goals? Could not the reminders of YHWH's promises and past acts of faithfulness both urge YHWH to action *and* bolster the psalmist's faith?

10. Levine, "The Dialogic Discourse of Psalms," 145.

11. Ibid., 146.

12. Ibid., 152–53.

13. Ibid., 153.

14. Of these only Psalm 12 appears in Mandolfo's study of the dialogic lament psalms. She identifies Ps 12:4–5[3–4] as the DV because it is cast in third person (*God in the Dock*, 49), but that is not the only way to understand it. Rather than an imperfective, it may be jussive in meaning, invoking the future action of YHWH and thus representing the voice of the supplicant (so Kraus, *Psalms 1–59*, 209). This is more likely given that verse 5[4] describes the speech of the enemies. In addition to the presence of the quote, the response of YHWH in verse 6[5] confirms that this is not a didactic statement but a plea to which YHWH responds. The quotes in Pss 10:11, 14:1, and 94:7 appear in third-person description of the wicked, but they are quite consistent with the attending supplication (10:1, 12; 14:7; 94:1–3). The rest are clearly part of the supplicant's complaint about the enemies and their plea to YHWH to act.

Ethical Ideals and Reality in Dialogic Tension in Book I

the supplicant's self-identified oppressor is not the DV but the enemy who denies the message of the DV.

Third, the editors clearly intended to suggest reading Book I with David. In MT's version of the Psalter, Book I stands out from the other four books in that David appears in almost every psalm.[15] Brevard Childs represents the critical consensus that psalm titles are relatively late editorial additions to the Psalter but maintains that they convey early interpretations of the Psalter.[16] This perspective has received attention of late. Mays hails the return of David as an "intra-textual reality" of the Psalter.[17] Rolf Rendtorff argues that when Psalm 2 is read as a continuation of Psalm 1, David is pictured as "the exemplary righteous king who follows the divine Torah."[18] Jamie Grant argues that the connection between torah and king in the Deuteronomic kingship law is reflected at key points in the Psalter in the pairing of royal and torah psalms, namely Psalms 1 and 2, 18/20/21 and 19, and 118 and 119.[19] Bruce Waltke suggests that the human subject of most psalms is David the king, a notion editorially enshrined in the psalm titles.[20] He suggests that associating the Psalms with David does not remove them from the grasp of average Israelites any more than modern readers, for the king represented the people.[21] VanGemeren and Stanghale suggest that there is validity to associating the Psalter with the Davidic *vox* based on traditions about David as "Israel's beloved singer" and a sage (2 Sam 23:1) and his connection to the temple.[22] There is validity, therefore, to employing

---

15. All the psalms in the book that have a title include the attribution לְדָוִד. Only Psalms 1, 2, 10, and 33 do not have titles and thus do not refer to David. Psalms 1 and 2 are widely, though not universally, regarded as introductory psalms and thus editorially distinct from the rest of Book I, so the lack of a title is no surprise. Psalm 10 lacks a title, but it was joined to Psalm 9 in the LXX and appears to be the second half of an acrostic poem. Psalm 33 has a Davidic title in the LXX and 4QPs, and there is a tradition linking Psalm 33 with Psalm 32 (Craigie, *Psalms 1–50*, 270). Book II's eighteen attributions לְדָוִד is the second highest concentration, but from there the attributions drop off dramatically. Book III has only one (Psalm 86), though in content Psalm 89 has strong Davidic associations. Book IV has two (Psalms 101 and 103), and Book V has fifteen.

16. Childs, "Psalm Titles and Midrashic Exegesis," 137.

17. Mays, "The David of the Psalms," 154.

18. Rendtorff, "The Psalms of David," 63. Note also Miller, "The Beginning of the Psalter," 89; Gillingham, "The Messiah in the Psalms," 226.

19. Grant, *The King as Exemplar*, 4. Note also Miller, "The Beginning of the Psalter," 91.

20. Waltke, "A Canonical Process Approach to the Psalms," 10–12.

21. Ibid., 13. For his "extensive royal interpretation," see also Waltke, *An Old Testament Theology*, 871–74.

22. VanGemeren and Stanghale, "A Critical-Realistic Reading of the Psalm Titles: Authenticity, Inspiration, and Evangelicals," 294–300.

a reading strategy that identifies a Davidic subject with almost all of the psalms in Book I.

Fourth, the editorial decision to attribute most of the psalms in Book I to David implies that the final editors did not consider the voice of the supplicant to be fundamentally at odds with the DV. It is possible that this voice has somehow been played down by the DV. Mandolfo suggests that the DV exercises a controlling role in the power differential between the DV and the voice of the supplicant and "never acknowledges the validity of the supplicant's articulated experience."[23] However, in light of the markedly different treatment of the voice of the enemy, this claim does not seem fair to the DV. Whether or not this speaker is distinct from the DV, the voice of the supplicant fills the Psalter and is thereby accepted and validated, not set off as a foil like the voice of the enemy, but as the voice of the faithful. Furthermore, like the ancient editors, subsequent *religious* readers must respond to the diversity of the collection in the same way that they must respond to the problem of evil.[24] Either they appropriate the entire collection as a coherent whole or decide to reject parts of it. A "dialogic reading" that rejects the DV is no less monologic than one that denies the validity of the supplicant's plea.

With the warrants listed above, I will proceed to read Book I with reference to a single subject, or at least with the assumption that the book may possess coherence as a whole, first for the editors and then for subsequent readers. I begin with a review of the ethical concerns of the four portraits of the righteous before placing them in relationship to their canonical context.

ETHICAL CONCERNS IN THE PORTRAITS OF THE RIGHTEOUS

Placing the ethical concerns of the portraits of the righteous side-by-side, we may identify a number of similarities and differences between them (see Table a).

---

23. Mandolfo, *God in the Dock*, 159.

24. For a discussion of the particular interests of religious readers in relationship to the Psalms, see Wenham, "Prayer and Practice in the Psalms." I return to this issue more fully in chapter 7.

Ethical Ideals and Reality in Dialogic Tension in Book I

Table a. Character Traits and Behaviors in the Portraits of the Righteous

Concern	Psalm 15	Psalm 24	Psalm 34	Psalm 37
General Life of Integrity	Blameless, does righteousness (v. 2)	Innocent hands, pure heart (v. 4)	Turns from evil, does good (v. 15[14])	Trusts in YHWH, does good (vv. 3, 5, 7, 9; 27, 34); blameless and upright (vv. 18, 37)
Outward Behavior to the Other	Does not slander, taunt, do evil to neighbor (v. 3)		Seeks peace (v. 15[14])	Man of peace (v. 37)
Inward Orientation to the Other	Despises the rejected, honors those who fear YHWH (v. 4)		YHWH is for the righteous, against the wicked (vv. 16–17[15–16])	Delights in YHWH (v. 4); does not get incensed over evil (vv. 1, 7–8); torah of YHWH on the heart (v. 31)
Speech	Speaks truth (v. 2); keeps oaths (v. 4)	Does not swear deceitfully (v. 4)	Keeps from deceit (v. 14[13])	Speaks wisdom and justice (v. 30)
Economic Dealings	Does not lend at interest, take bribes against the innocent (v. 5)			Gives generously (v. 21); lends generously (v. 26)

A few observations are in order. First, the portraits exhibit consistency in their ethical vision. In general, turning from evil, maintaining a blameless life, and doing what is good is highly prized, but there are more specific areas of agreement. Maintaining peace with one's neighbor, truthful speech,[25] and financial generosity appear frequently. The ethical vision of these texts is consistently social across the portraits, whether they have a temple or wisdom background.

---

25. Gordon Wenham notes that of all the commands in the Decalogue, false witness is most often condemned in the Psalter. He suggests that the Psalter's focus on speech relates to the fact that the Psalter is an anthology of prayers, thus raising the importance of speech (*Psalms as Torah*, 107–9). I shall argue below that we can understand this emphasis when we read the portraits in their canonical context.

In regard to the outcome of the righteous life, the different portraits employ different motifs. In keeping with their temple/Zion context, Psalms 15 and 24 assume the outcome of the righteous life is being with YHWH (15:1; 24:3) where one finds security, affirmation, and deliverance (15:5cd; 24:5). Turning to the two portraits with strong resemblances to wisdom, this image of refuge appears in Psalms 34 (vv. 7–9[6–8], 18–22[17–21]) and 37 (vv. 23, 28, 39–40). However, these two psalms add other motifs. Psalm 34:13[12] holds out hope for life, while Psalm 37 speaks of life in the land (vv. 3, 22, 29, 34) and long life (v. 27). This vision of life is consistent both with a deuteronomic worldview and with the wisdom tradition. The blessings of the covenant in the form of the presence of YHWH among his people and life in the land are the reward for torah obedience.

The portraits themselves acknowledge that the righteous may suffer. Psalm 15 contains little of this perspective, though verse 5cd implies that a person *may* be shaken. Psalm 24 comes closer to acknowledging sociopolitical conflict by describing the divine warrior who guarantees the security of Zion (vv. 7–10). However, Psalm 34 engages the problem of theodicy more directly. In the title (v. 1 MT) the editor identifies David as the voice of thanksgiving after his experience before the Philistine king. The thanksgiving section retells the deliverance of the psalmist (vv. 5[4], 7[6]). Finally, the didactic section affirms that the righteous do indeed suffer many troubles (v. 20[19]) but that YHWH hears them when they cry (vv. 16[15], 18[17]) and delivers them (v. 20[19]). Psalm 37 addresses the frustration of the one who sees the wicked prosper and the righteous suffer (esp. vv. 1, 7–8). The portraits of the righteous engage the problem of theodicy ever more directly as we proceed through the book. We must relate this observation to the final editorial structure of Book I.

THE PORTRAITS OF THE RIGHTEOUS IN THEIR CANONICAL CONTEXT

Book I as a whole addresses the problem of theodicy and explores the role of torah obedience in realizing the benefits of covenant relationship with YHWH. The psalmist agonizes over whether righteous character does lead to the outcome envisioned in the portraits. Although the portraits of the righteous offer hope of refuge, stability, and life in the land, the success of the wicked at the expense of the righteous seems to call this into question. The words of the wicked haunt the prayers of the righteous, so an interpretation of the portraits must be tempered by the hard experience of the psalmist in lament. Still, the psalmist remains constant in hope of being

Ethical Ideals and Reality in Dialogic Tension in Book I

with YHWH and enjoying the security he provides. Furthermore, a consistent ethic underlies the theological tension. We know the psalmist has not abandoned hope in YHWH in the face of theological dissonance because he has not abandoned torah obedience. In part this is because the wicked embody the opposite, which is the cause of the psalmist's grief. To appreciate the degree to which the portraits of the righteous interact with the book in which they are placed, we must take a journey through the complex landscape of Book I.

Before we begin this dramatic journey with the psalmist, we must introduce the players we will encounter. Claus Westermann identifies three "characters" in the lament psalms: the psalmist, God, and the others, who are often the enemies.[26] Terrence Collins suggests that these characters "implicitly . . . dominate the other psalms as well," thus providing an important basis for comparison across genres. He also helpfully divides the "others" into the enemies and the faithful.[27] Bellinger rightly notes that Book I brings together the psalmist, God, and the enemies in "a glorious and inglorious dance and wrestling match as part of the social setting of prayer."[28] This social character of the book must be recognized at the outset. It is consistent with the ethic in the portraits of the righteous. Additionally, the nagging problem of the success of the wicked explains the portraits' increasing attention to the problem of theodicy.

The structural contours of Book I are fairly clear. Psalms 1 and 2 lack titles and are tied together with an אַשְׁרֵי formula in 1:1 and 2:12.[29] This אַשְׁרֵי formula appears five additional times in the book, two of which are Psalms 40 and 41. For that reason J. Clinton McCann argues that the book is "a guide to a 'happy' life."[30] In addition to the inclusion between 1:1 and 2:12, Barbiero notes the shared motif of the two ways and the verb אבד, and he argues that the "wicked" of Psalm 1 and the "kings" of Psalm 2 relate to each other just as the "man" of Psalm 1 relates to the "messiah" of Psalm 2.[31] Psalm 3 marks a transition because it contains a title with לְדָוִד, "of David," and it begins a series of individual lament psalms. The first section is Psalms 3–14, marked by a thematic inclusion between the statement in Psalms 3:9[8] that salvation belongs to YHWH and the question in 14:7, "Who

---

26. Westermann, *Praise and Lament in the Psalms*, 169.
27. Collins, "Decoding the Psalms," 45.
28. Bellinger, "Reading from the Beginning (Again)," 124.
29. Ibid., 119.
30. McCann, "The Shape of Book I of the Psalter," 340, 342.
31. Barbiero, "Le premier livret du Psautier," 443.

Portraits of the Righteous in the Psalms

will give the salvation of Israel from Zion?"[32] Auffret identifies a concentric structure in Psalms 15–24, thus marking off the second section.[33] The third section is bounded by two acrostic poems, Psalms 25 and 34, and Psalms 35–41 conclude the book.[34]

Psalms 1 and 2

Standing at the beginning of the Psalter, Psalms 1 and 2 present two fundamental themes, torah and kingship.[35] A number of scholars have noted that these two psalms not only introduce the Psalter but also Book I.[36] What is their significance for our study?

First, torah is the foundation for the portraits of the righteous and for Book I. Psalm 1:2 prizes meditation on torah as a point of orientation for the righteous person, in contrast to the way of sinners in 1:1. In addition to the words of praise for torah in Psalm 19, both Pss 37:31 and 40:9[8] speak of the internalization of torah. Though few in number, these verbal affirmations of torah complement what I have demonstrated in the chapters above, that often Deuteronomy lurks behind the portraits of the righteous.[37] Based on Levenson's contention that the word תּוֹרָה in Psalm 119 does not refer narrowly to the Pentateuch but in a more general way to God's instruction,[38]

---

32. Hossfeld and Zenger, "Selig, wer auf die Armen achtet," 35; Barbiero, "Le premier livret du Psautier," 469.

33. Auffret, *La sagesse a bâti sa maison*, 409. See also Miller, "Kingship, Torah Obedience, and Prayer."

34. See Hossfeld and Zenger, "Selig, wer auf die Armen achtet," 23; Hossfeld and Zenger, *Die Psalmen I*, 12–16; Barbiero, "Le premier livret du Psautier," 464.

35. This is widely recognized. See Mays, "The Place of the Torah-Psalms in the Psalter," 10; Mays, "The Question of Context in Psalm Interpretation," 16; Barbiero, "Le premier livret du Psautier"; McCann, "The Shape of Book I of the Psalter and the Shape of Human Happiness." For a detailed examination of the development of these two themes in relationship to the Deuteronomic kingship law, see Grant, *The King as Exemplar*. For an exposition of these themes in terms of metaphor, see Brown, *Seeing the Psalms*. Of course there are detractors, and Patrick Miller notes that the introductory function of Psalm 2 and its relationship to Psalm 1 is a matter of debate ("The Beginning of the Psalter," 84). See also McCann, "The Shape of Book I of the Psalter," 342, who notes the debate but confidently asserts the introductory role of the psalms.

36. See Wilson, *The Editing of the Hebrew Psalter*, 173; Barbiero, "Le premier livret du Psautier," 446, 470; Bellinger, "Reading from the Beginning (Again)," 118.

37. For a literary-theological comparison of the two books, see Miller, "Deuteronomy and Psalms." See also Bullock, "The Shape of the Torah as Reflected in the Psalms, Book I."

38. Levenson, "The Source of Torah: Psalm 119 and the Modes of Revelation in Second Temple Judaism," 559–74.

Ethical Ideals and Reality in Dialogic Tension in Book I

McCann argues that this broad sense should be applied in Psalm 1:2. Therefore he argues that תּוֹרָה in Ps 1:2 refers to the five books of the Psalter itself.[39] Several arguments pose difficulties for this interpretation. Aside from the evident deuteronomic influence on the portraits of the righteous, Jamie Grant has shown a close connection between Deuteronomy and Psalm 1.[40] Daniel Block notes that the phrase תּוֹרַת יְהוָה never refers to instruction in general but always to Sinai revelation and/or Deuteronomy.[41] Whybray expresses skepticism that Psalm 1 is a guide to reading the Psalter and suggests that such an understanding of the referent of "torah" would be unique and unnatural.[42] It is most likely that the "torah" in Psalm 1 is not the Psalter itself, but perhaps the Psalter is the fruit of meditation on torah.[43] That would be consistent with what we have found in Book I.[44] Patrick Miller rightly notes that Psalm 1 sets the agenda for Psalms 3–41 by identifying a focus on the righteous and the wicked, with Psalm 37 offering the most thorough exposition of the theme.[45]

Psalm 2:6 mentions YHWH's king installed on Zion. This invokes the kingship of YHWH and of his regent David.[46] The Psalter in general and Book I in particular must be understood in a royal and national atmosphere that is explicitly picked up in Psalms 18, 20, and 21.[47] The human king may be the subject of the psalms, but the Psalter must also be understood within

---

39. McCann, "The Psalms as Instruction," 119. So also DeClaissé-Walford, *Reading from the Beginning*, 43; Wenham, *Psalms as Torah*, 7.

40. Grant, *The King as Exemplar*, 42–48.

41. Block, *How I Love Your Torah, O LORD!*, xii.

42. Whybray, *Reading the Psalms as a Book*, 39.

43. For an exploration of "the palette of colors with which the literary artist is working" in Book I, see Bullock, "The Shape of the Torah as Reflected in the Psalms, Book I." Bullock notes allusions to events, heroes, and terminology from Genesis, Exodus, Numbers, Deuteronomy, and Joshua that are reshaped for individual and corporate application in the Psalter. LeFebvre also argues "torah-meditation does not necessarily mean that the Mosaic Torah is the text being vocalized. Based on the paradigm in Deut. 31–32, it can be seen that Israel used surrogate texts for torah-contemplation, particularly songs" (LeFebvre, "Torah-Meditation and the Psalms," 225).

44. I do not deny that the Psalter is a book of instruction (McCann, "The Psalms as Instruction," 121), just not the torah to which Psalm 1 refers.

45. Miller, "The Beginning of the Psalter," 85. See also Kuntz, "Wisdom Psalms and the Shaping of the Hebrew Psalter," 155.

46. For the king as YHWH's regent, see Roberts, "Zion in the Theology of the Davidic-Solomonic Empire," 99.

47. Miller, "The Beginning of the Psalter," 87–88.

the context of the reign of YHWH.[48] In addition, Ps 2:12 invokes the refuge metaphor in relationship to Zion.

The combination of Psalms 1 and 2 also has implications for understanding Book I. Tucker rightly notes that the success and security of the faithful individual Israelite in Psalm 1 is complemented by that of the king in Psalm 2. The motif of refuge in Ps 2:12 alerts the reader to the fact that this success is ambiguous, though with an eschatological horizon one may see the reign of YHWH resolve this ambiguity.[49] Barbiero suggests that Psalm 1 concerns every person, but the coupling of Psalms 1 and 2 provides a cue that the story of Israel's king is a paradigm for humanity.[50] As I note above, Jamie Grant argues that the pairing of these two psalms suggests a connection to the deuteronomic kingship law (esp. Deut 17:18–20).[51] Psalm 1 does not explicitly narrow the subject of the psalm to the king, which affirms the spirit of the deuteronomic kingship law, namely that a king is not above his brothers (Deut 17:20).

Psalms 1 and 2 introduce Book I by providing two fundamental theological points of orientation. Torah and kingship and the security they offer are the presuppositions with which the psalmist and his readers approach the book. However, as we will see in the following section, the experience of the psalmist calls into question the security offered by torah and kingship.

Psalms 3–14

Although the first section of Book I (Psalms 3–14) does not contain any of the portraits, several lexical and conceptual connections to those portraits make it an important place to begin. The section is dominated by individual lament psalms, interrupted only by the hymn of Psalm 8 and the words of thanks and praise at the end of Psalm 7 (v. 18[17]) and the beginning of Psalm 9 (vv. 2–12).[52] These contrast sharply with the confident words in Psalms 1 and 2. Several portraits of wicked character also punctuate the section (Pss 5:5–7[4–6], 10[9]; 7:4–6[3–5], 15–17[14–16]; 10:2–11; 14:1–5).[53]

48. Mays, "The Place of the Torah-Psalms in the Psalter," 10; Barbiero, "Le premier livret du Psautier," 446–47.

49. Tucker, "Beyond the Lament," 129–30.

50. Barbiero, "Le premier livret du Psautier," 448–50.

51. Grant, *The King as Exemplar*, 41–70.

52. Barbiero notes that the predominance of lament in the first section is repeated again in the fourth section, Psalms 35–41 ("Le premier livret du Psautier," 475).

53. The phrase כָּל־פֹּעֲלֵי אָוֶן, "all workers of iniquity" (Pss 5:6[5], 6:9 and 14:4) stands in contrast to the one who "does righteousness" (פֹּעֵל צֶדֶק) in 15:2. Maloney identifies the universal wickedness described in Psalm 14 as a direct contrast with the righteous

Ethical Ideals and Reality in Dialogic Tension in Book I

This vision of the wicked person contrasts with the righteous person in Psalm 15, but this contrast highlights a consistent vision of character. On the other hand, the prominence of the wicked provokes theological dissonance about the involvement of YHWH in human affairs.

Character

Speech is the first specific indicator of character. Psalm 5:7[6] declares that YHWH loathes deception and violence. A few verses later Ps 5:10[9] describes the wicked[54]:

כִּי אֵין בְּפִיהוּ נְכוֹנָה	10a	For there is nothing firm in their mouths
קִרְבָּם הַוּוֹת	10b	Their inward part is ruin,
קֶבֶר־פָּתוּחַ גְּרוֹנָם	10c	Their throat is an open grave,
לְשׁוֹנָם יַחֲלִיקוּן׃	10d	Their tongues are slippery.

In Ps 12:3-5[2-4] the wicked speak in deceptively positive language to their neighbors in order to wield social power. This characterization of the wicked contrasts with the truthful righteous person in the portraits of the righteous (cf. Pss 15:2, 4; 24:4; 34:14[13]).

In addition to speech, the first section touches on the issue of violence against the other. In Ps 7:4-5[3-4] the psalmist invites YHWH to see "if there is injustice in my hands" (בְּכַפָּי, v. 4[3]; cf. 24:4). The next verse clarifies that this involves violence done to one's neighbor (cf. 15:3; 24:4; 34:15[14]; 37:37). Confident in his integrity, in v. 6[5] the psalmist invites violence on himself if he is guilty of it. The psalmist describes the wicked person in Ps 7:15-17[14-16] as one who plans violence for others but ends up falling into his own pit. The humor of this image is tempered by the knowledge that the psalmist seeks refuge from such a person. In Ps 10:2 and 8-9 the wicked devise schemes against the poor, lying in ambush like a lion (cf. Pss 15:3; 34:15[14]; 37:37).

Finally, we must note the economic and social issues that anticipate Psalms 15 and 24. The bribe in Ps 15:5 is taken to the disadvantage of the "innocent" (נָקִי) who are the righteous in Ps 24:4 and who are the victims of the murderous violence of the wicked in Ps 10:2 and 8. Psalm 10 offers a thesaurus of the terminology for the lowly and oppressed in Book I. The victims of the plotting of the wicked in Psalm 10 include not only the נְקִי

---

individual of Psalm 15 ("A Portrait of the Righteous Person," 161).

54. NRSV translates, "For there is no truth in their mouths." See discussion in Kraus, *Psalms 1-59*, 156.

("innocent," v. 8) but also the חֵלְכָה ("disheartened," v. 8, possibly 10)[55] and the עָנִי ("poor," v. 9).[56] In verse 12 the עָנִי seek the gracious attention of YHWH, and in verse 14 the חֵלְכָה and יָתוֹם ("fatherless") depend on YHWH for help. Finally, in verses 17 and 18, the יָתוֹם and the דָךְ ("oppressed")[57] need justice from YHWH. By far the most common term among these in Book I is עָנִי. In addition, the two terms, "the poor and needy" (עָנִי וְאֶבְיוֹן)[58] frequently occur together and exemplify the development of the theme of the lowly and oppressed in Book I. The psalmist describes the wicked as those who pursue the poor and needy (Ps 37:14; cf. 10:2–3; 14:4, 6) but finds confidence in the concern of YHWH for the poor and needy (Ps 9:19[18]; cf. 9:13[12]; 12:6[5]).

The vision of character in the first section anticipates and agrees with that of the portraits of the righteous, though the behavior of the wicked creates a problem. Therefore questions arise about character's outcome.

Character's Outcome

In some places in the first section the portraits find common cause on the question of the outcome of wickedness. In Ps 5:5–7[4–6] the psalmist affirms that YHWH does not tolerate wickedness.[59] In Ps 11:4 YHWH's holy temple is paired with his throne in the heavens where he sits watching and examining humanity. YHWH sees the psalmist and hears his prayer and in Ps 3:5[4] answers "from his holy mountain" (מֵהַר קָדְשׁוֹ). The involvement of YHWH in human affairs is focused on the holy mountain, which explains the introductory questions of Psalms 15 and 24. There the righteous may enter and find refuge, but the wicked may not. Psalm 5:5[4] asserts that "evil may not sojourn with you" (לֹא יְגֻרְךָ רָע).[60] Instead, it is the upright who may see YHWH (Ps 11:7). In view of his enemies the psalmist seeks refuge in the way of YHWH (v. 9[8]), confident that YHWH will protect the righteous (vv. 12–13[11–12]). Psalm 11:5 affirms the theological reality behind this dynamic: YHWH hates the "lover of violence" (וְאֹהֵב חָמָס), but in verse 7

55. HALOT 319.
56. HALOT 856.
57. HALOT 227.
58. Domeris, "אֶבְיוֹן (*'ebyôn*)," 228, suggests that the אֶבְיוֹן are almost destitute.
59. Maloney, "A Portrait of the Righteous Person," 154.
60. Ibid. Broyles suggests that Psalm 5 is the reverse of Psalms 15 and 24 and therefore belongs to the same rite of passage ("Psalms Concerning the Liturgies of Temple Entry," 258). He rightly notes the conceptual connection between the two, but given the dubious nature of the entrance liturgy theory his historical reconstruction is less convincing.

Ethical Ideals and Reality in Dialogic Tension in Book I

"he loves righteous deeds" (צְדָקוֹת אָהֵב).[61] Therefore the supplicant in Ps 7:9[8] confidently invites YHWH's judgment "according to my righteousness and my integrity" (כְּצִדְקִי וּכְתֻמִּי; cf. Ps 15:2).

However, toward the end of the first section the idea that righteous character leads to a simple and secure life is called into question. In Ps 10:11 the wicked oppresses the poor with impunity, and "he says in his heart (אָמַר בְּלִבּוֹ) you [that is, YHWH] will not inquire." Using the root מוט, Maloney identifies further points of contrast between the righteous person in Psalm 15 and the first section of Book I. In 10:6 the wicked person boasts that he will never be moved (בַּל־אֶמּוֹט, cf. Ps 15:5), but he persecutes the poor (עָנִי) in 10:2, murders the innocent (נָקִי) in 10:8, and is deceitful in 10:7, all of which contrast with the righteous person in Ps 15:2-5.[62] He looks at the multiple generations that have passed by and sees that no ill has come to the wicked. He thinks that God has forgotten (v. 11), so the psalmist cries out to YHWH to reverse this (v. 12). Psalm 12 confirms the need for YHWH's protection (v. 8[7]) in view of the fact that "vileness" (זֻלּוּת) is "exalted" (v. 9[8]).[63] In Ps 14:1 "The fool says in his heart, 'There is no God,'" and this leads him to oppress the poor without restraint (14:4). The wicked boast in their autonomy and act without regard for YHWH. But what of the psalmist?

The world of the psalmist is turned upside down in Psalm 13. In verses 4-5[3-4] the psalmist pleads with YHWH to act and to save him lest the enemy rejoice when the psalmist is shaken (אֶמּוֹט). In this context the ideal of security in Psalms 15 and 24 is strained by the weight of experience. In Book I as a whole מוט is a *Leitwort*, the center of a dialogue between two voices. On the one hand is the voice of confidence in the stability of the righteous and the instability of the wicked. On the other hand is the voice of horror at the psalmist's own instability in comparison to the stability of the wicked.[64]

The transition from Psalm 2 to Psalm 3 suggests a further layer to the dialogue about character's outcome. In Ps 2:1 the nations are pictured as plotting rebellion in vain, and in Ps 2:12 "happiness" is for those who find refuge in YHWH. However, the psalmist's many enemies in Ps 3:2[1] say, "There is no salvation for him in God." In desperation the psalmist cries out,

---

61. While not using the same terms, Ps 37:27 admonishes the listener to "turn aside from evil and do good" (וַעֲשֵׂה־טוֹב). For further description of YHWH's moral values, see Pss 5:5-6[4-5]; 33:5.

62. Maloney, "A Portrait of the Righteous Person," 160. Maloney's observation applies more broadly, but I treat that below.

63. Note that זֻלּוּת is a hapax legomenon. *HALOT* 272 suggests the gloss "vileness," but the meaning is uncertain.

64. Maloney, "A Portrait of the Righteous Person," 155, likewise observes this phenomenon in the Psalter.

"save me!" (הוֹשִׁיעֵנִי) in Ps 3:8[7] (also 6:5; 7:2). McCann rightly observes that the transition to Psalm 3 dispels any notion that Psalm 1 describes a mechanistic relationship between deeds and rewards or punishment.[65]

This first section suggests that the social dialogue in Book I is really between the righteous and the wicked, and it concerns whether YHWH does indeed care about the actions and dispositions of human beings (cf. Ps 1:6).[66] If he does, then certain ethical conclusions follow. The psalmist is troubled by the brash words of the wicked person. His experience leaves him feeling as if he stands on shaky ground (esp. Ps 13:1–4). But on the question of character, the psalmist is consistent in opposition to the wicked. Hossfeld and Zenger characterize Psalms 11–14 as an image of a chaotic society, the answer to which is found in Psalm 15.[67] This leads to the following sub-collection.

Psalms 15–24

As noted above, Pierre Auffret identified a concentric structure in Psalms 15–24.[68] The following structural diagram summarizes the generic patterns in this sub-collection:

```
A Portrait of the Righteous (Psalm 15)
  B Psalm of Confidence (Psalm 16)
    C Individual Lament (Psalm 17)
      D Royal Psalm (Psalm 18)
        E Torah Psalm (Psalm 19)
      D' Royal Psalms (Psalms 20, 21)
    C' Individual Lament (Psalm 22)
  B' Psalm of Confidence (Psalm 23)
A' Portrait of the Righteous (Psalm 24)[69]
```

Auffret identifies numerous links between the various rings in this structure, but a few are very important for our study. He points out that the

---

65. McCann, "The Way of the Righteous," 141.

66. Hossfeld and Zenger suggest that the section is about proof of the saving power of YHWH in a hostile and wicked world (Hossfeld and Zenger, "Selig, wer auf die Armen achtet," 36).

67. Hossfeld and Zenger, "Wer darf hinaufziehn zum Berg JHWHs?" 176.

68. Auffret, *La sagesse a bâti sa maison*, 409–38. This is picked up in Miller, "Kingship, Torah Obedience, and Prayer." For a diachronic study of this collection, see Hossfeld and Zenger, "Wer darf hinaufziehn zum Berg JHWHs?"

69. Auffret, *La sagesse a bâti sa maison*, 409.

questions in Pss 15:1 and 24:3 encircle the limits of the collection.[70] Psalm 19 occupies an important central position, and some of its themes are echoed in Psalm 24. Both Psalms 19 and 24 refer to divine retribution and creation, establishing a link between YHWH as creator and one who intervenes for his people.[71] In addition, both psalms refer to creation and torah, so Psalm 24 serves as a fitting concluding psalm for the collection.[72] The prominence of torah in the collection is evident. The righteous person of Psalms 15 and 24 appears as an exemplar of torah piety, but that piety is in the context of YHWH's protection.[73]

Scholars have noted additional theological connections within the sub-collection. Rebecca Watson suggests that the righteous person of Psalm 15 is unmoved because of the kingship of YHWH in Psalm 24.[74] Furthermore, Psalms 15 and 24 echo the torah piety of Psalms 1 and 19. They both embody torah obedience, "whether we interpret them as entrance liturgies or not."[75] While Psalms 15 and 24 sketch the ethical life, Psalms 16 and 23 underscore the protection of YHWH for the righteous.[76] Groenewald helpfully notes some key points of contact between Psalms 15 and 16, particularly in their temple theology, or the refuge metaphor (15:1; 16:1, 11bc), and wisdom connections, or the pathway metaphor (15:2–5; 16:7, 11a).[77] Two lexical connections highlight the refuge motif. First, he notes the verb שׁכן occurs both in Pss 15:1 and 16:9.[78] In the former, the term involves the introductory question and dwelling on YHWH's holy hill, while the latter affirms that the psalmist dwells securely (בְּשָׂרִי יִשְׁכֹּן לָבֶטַח) with YHWH at his right hand. It is surely no coincidence that the root מוט is also found in Pss 15:5 and 16:8,[79] thus binding the two psalms together with the notion that YHWH is the refuge of the righteous. This confirms that the second collection of Book I (Psalms 15–24) is characterized by the confidence of

---

70. Ibid.

71. Ibid., 436.

72. Ibid., 437–38.

73. Patrick Miller notes that Psalms 1 and 2 anticipate the theme of torah in Psalm 19 and torah obedience in Psalms 15 and 24. Furthermore, the consequences for the righteous and the wicked are also a theme from Psalm 1 ("Kingship, Torah Obedience, and Prayer," 127–28).

74. Watson, *Chaos Uncreated*, 129. See also Groenewald, "Ethics of the Psalms," 427.

75. Groenewald, "Ethics of the Psalms," 425.

76. Ibid., 426.

77. Ibid., 427.

78. Ibid.

79. Ibid., 428.

Portraits of the Righteous in the Psalms

praise and thanksgiving.[80] However, the remainder of the book seems to be built around this core sub-collection to answer the question, does the righteous life lead to happiness?[81]

But first, we must recognize a few elements that demonstrate the consistency of moral vision in the section. Ironically, in this section we find the fewest verbal and conceptual parallels to the portraits of the righteous.

Character

Psalm 18 includes a concentrated exposition of the vision of moral integrity in Pss 15:2 and 24:4. This is the only psalm in Book I to mention David in the body of the Psalm, making an implicit connection between the righteous person and the king. Following a lengthy poetic description of YHWH's saving acts in verses 7–20[6–19], in verses 21[20] and 25[24] the psalmist claims that YHWH has dealt with him according to his righteousness (כְּצִדְקִי; cf. Ps 15:2) and "according to the purity of my hands" (כְּבֹר יָדַי; cf. Ps 24:4, though בַר is used there of the heart).[82] He links this righteousness to keeping the ways of YHWH, and verse 24[23] asserts the psalmist's integrity (תָּמִים; cf. Ps 15:2). The one who does righteousness is the same as the one who calls for help in Ps 18:20–21[19–20].[83]

Beyond this general moral vision are more particular issues, including speech. The righteous are the object of verbal attack. In Ps 22:7–9[6–8] the psalmist is the "scorn of mankind" (חֶרְפַּת אָדָם), whom people ridicule and mock for his trust in YHWH. The deception of the wicked is deliberately contrasted with the behavior of the righteous. The psalmist pleads innocence and truthfulness as the basis for his plea for justice (Ps 17:1, 3).

Inward orientation also matters to YHWH. Those who hate YHWH in Ps 21:9–10[8–9] face a furnace of fire (cf. Pss 15:4; 34:22[21]). In contrast to the wicked, the righteous mirror God's orientation to evil.[84] Psalm 22

---

80. Barbiero, "Le premier livret du Psautier," 475–76. The same is true of the third section, Psalms 25–34.

81. For a diachronic study of Book I, see Hossfeld and Zenger, "Wer darf hinaufziehn zum Berg JHWHs?" This study is synchronic rather than diachronic, but my interpretation of the role of the second collection would be consistent with the idea that it had editorial priority. It is difficult to be certain about any conclusions about the date of composition of individual psalms or even when they were included in the Psalter except when manuscript traditions provide evidence (for Psalm 1, see Wilson, "The Structure of the Psalter," 232–33).

82. Miller, "Kingship, Torah Obedience, and Prayer," 129.

83. Ibid., 128–29.

84. Maloney, "A Portrait of the Righteous Person," 154–55.

compares the people in verse 7[6] who despise the afflicted psalmist (בָּזוּי), to God who in verse 25[24] does not despise the afflicted one (לֹא־בָזָה).

One final ethical value concerns the character of YHWH, rather than the righteous person. In Ps 22:25[24] the testimony of thanks affirms that YHWH does not despise the עָנִי, which in this case may be best translated "afflicted" or "humble" to reflect a state of distress rather than a specific economic situation. The description of the psalmist implies captivity and the threat of the sword (vv. 19[18] and 21[20]). However, the psalmist can count his bones (v. 18[17]), so the material implications of his situation resemble economic hardship. In any case, YHWH's concern for the lowly is mirrored in the righteous person in Ps 15:5ab, who lends interest-free and does not accept bribes to condemn the innocent. However, YHWH's protection for the lowly is the point of some tension in the section.

Character's Outcome

The language about YHWH's place in this section forms part of the literary basis for identifying it as a place of refuge and delight with regard to Pss 15:1 and 24:3.[85] The holy place is the source of YHWH's help for the king (Ps 20:3[2]). The two psalms of confidence emphasize YHWH's place. In Psalm 16 YHWH himself is a "place" of joy and pleasantness (Ps 16:11). Psalm 23 ends with a confident affirmation that the psalmist will enjoy YHWH's house forever (v. 6). This leads naturally into Ps 24:3, which asks who may ascend to that holy place.[86] The section includes one important qualification about this place that is consistent with the portraits of the righteous: one must approach YHWH in righteousness (Ps 17:15).

Continuing the theme of confidence, Psalm 21:8[7] affirms that YHWH will keep the king from stumbling (בַּל־יִמּוֹט; cf. Ps 15:5). Thus the king of Psalm 21 and the righteous person of Psalm 15 enjoy the same security, in contrast to the boasting of the wicked in the previous section.

This security in Psalm 21 and the other royal Psalms (18 and 20) is guaranteed by the salvation of YHWH. Words from the root ישׁע occur frequently in the royal psalms in this section and in all of Book I.[87] Space

---

85. Although not dominant, the theme of the land familiar from Psalm 37 is found in Ps 16:3.

86. J. Gordon McConville suggests the section is unified "a sense of being, or longing to be, 'at home'" ("Who May Ascend to the Hill of the LORD?" 37).

87. Words from the root ישׁע appear in twenty-one of the thirty-nine psalms in Book I. The noun יְשׁוּעָה: Pss 3:3[2], 9[8]; 9:15[14]; 13:6[5]; 14:7; 18:51[50]; 20:6[5]; 21:2[1], 6[5]; 22:2[1]; 28:8; 35:3; 35:9; the noun יֵשַׁע: Pss 12:6[5]; 18:3[2], 36[35]; 47[46]; 20:7[6]; 24:5; 25:5; 27:1, 9; the verb יָשַׁע: Pss 3:8[7]; 6:5[4]; 7:2[1], 11[10]; 12:2[1]; 17:7; 18:4[3],

Portraits of the Righteous in the Psalms

prohibits a detailed exposition of how this theme develops more broadly, but the theme of YHWH as deliverer is at the center of the dialogue in Book I about character's outcome. The salvation of the king plays a central and explicit role in this section.

The noun יְשׁוּעָה occurs in Pss 18:51[50], 20:6[5], and 21:2[1], 6[5], all pointing to YHWH as the source of the king's salvation.[88] The noun יֵשַׁע occurs in Pss 18:3[2], 36[35], 47[46]; 20:7[6] and 24:5. Two occurrences of this word describe YHWH's provision for his king. Psalm 20:7[6] employs the term to describe YHWH's answer to his anointed "with powerful deeds of salvation of his right hand" (בִּגְבֻרוֹת יֵשַׁע יְמִינוֹ). Psalm 18:36[35] describes this provision in terms of the implements of war: "And you gave to me the shield of your salvation" (וַתִּתֶּן־לִי מָגֵן יִשְׁעֶךָ). Psalm 18:3[2] applies similar imagery to YHWH himself, comparing YHWH to the tools of warfare such as the king's shield and "the horn of my salvation" (קֶרֶן־יִשְׁעִי). In words of praise for YHWH, Ps 18:47[46] calls him "the God of my salvation" (אֱלוֹהֵי יִשְׁעִי), the same epithet applied to YHWH who grants the righteous person blessing and righteousness in Ps 24:5. Although in this section the voice of confidence dominates, this epithet is used by the voice of insecurity elsewhere (see the comments on Ps 25:2 below).

The verb ישׁע occurs in 17:7, 18:4[3], 28[27], 42[41]; 20:7[6], 10[9]; 22:22[21]. Although Psalm 17 is not explicitly royal, the language in the following psalms suggests a royal subject is appropriate. Psalm 17:7 pleads for the saving actions of YHWH on behalf of those who seek refuge in him (cf. Ps 2:12). Psalm 18:4[3] likewise calls on YHWH to save, but Ps 18:28[27] declares that YHWH delivers the humble people (עַם־עָנִי), in contrast to those with "haughty eyes" (עֵינַיִם רָמוֹת). Though the king's enemies call on YHWH, they are not delivered in Ps 18:42[41]. Psalm 20:7[6] expresses confidence that YHWH will deliver his anointed one, while verse 10[9] calls on YHWH to deliver the king when he calls. This confidence is shattered in Ps 22:2[1] as the psalmist pleads, "Why . . . are you far from saving me?" The psalmist is disoriented precisely because he feels that YHWH is slow to bring salvation. Thus the lament psalms provide the main counterbalance to the voice of confidence in this section.

28[27], 42[41]; 20:7[6], 10[9]; 22:22[21]; 28:9; 31:3, 17; 33:16; 34:7[6], 19[18]; 36:7[6]; 37:40.

88. Note the association with David in the first reference.

Ethical Ideals and Reality in Dialogic Tension in Book I

Psalms 25–34

The concentric structure of Psalms 15–24 sets it apart from the rest of the book. However, Psalm 25 is linked to Psalm 24:4 with the idiom, to "lift one's soul" (אֵלֶיךָ יְהוָה נַפְשִׁי אֶשָּׂא, v. 1),[89] apparently identifying the righteous person of Psalm 24 as the supplicant in Psalm 25.[90] Psalm 25 is then linked to the final psalm of the section, Psalm 34, at a number of levels. I note in chapter 4 that both psalms are acrostics, have an extra *pê* line, and correspond at a number of linguistic and thematic levels. In addition, Maloney notes that Ps 25:1, 13 parallel Ps 34:3[2], 23[22] with the use of the term נֶפֶשׁ, and both psalms contain sections of general praise to YHWH following personal testimony.[91] These two stand as the beginning and end of the section, with Psalm 25 forming the question about whether YHWH will hear and Psalm 34 offering the answer that he does indeed hear.[92]

As in the first section, the vision of righteous character in the third section bears remarkable similarities to the portraits of the righteous. On the other hand, the wicked bring grief to the psalmist because they break with that vision of righteous character. And again we find voices of confidence and insecurity on the question of character's outcome.

Character

The beginning of this collection demonstrates that character matters. The psalmist uses a number of words and phrases that recall the portraits of the righteous in the previous section. Psalm 25:21 regards the kind of integrity (תֹּם־וָיֹשֶׁר) envisioned in Psalm 15:2 (תָּמִים) as a safeguard for the one who asks YHWH to deliver.[93] Likewise the righteous fear YHWH and enjoy his friendship (Pss 25:12, 14; 31:20[19]; 33:18; cf. Pss 15:4; 34:8[7], 10[9], 12[11]).

The next psalm continues the theme with a more significant verbal parallel to Psalm 15:2. In Ps 26:1 the psalmist confesses that he has walked in integrity (אֲנִי בְּתֻמִּי הָלַכְתִּי), and in Ps 26:11 he makes a similar claim (cf.

---

89. So also Lescow, "Textübergreifende Exegese," 79.

90. Contra Gunkel and Begrich, Kraus does not speak of this as an individual lament but rather a prayer song (*Psalms 1–59*, 319).

91. Maloney, "A Word Fitly Spoken," 198.

92. Benun, "Evil and the Disruption of Order," 14. See also Barbiero, "Le premier livret du Psautier," 470.

93. Note that יֹשֶׁר is relatively rare in the Psalter, appearing here and in Ps 119:7. However, a related term, יָשָׁר, occurs frequently in Book I with reference to a person of integrity. See below on Ps 37:14.

41:13[12]). Both are used as a basis for a plea for help from YHWH. In Ps 26:2 the psalmist invites YHWH, "test my inner being and my heart" (צָרְפָה כִלְיוֹתַי וְלִבִּי; cf. Ps 24:4).

Psalm 26 includes a cluster of issues familiar from the portraits of the righteous.[94] The psalmist speaks of walking in YHWH's truth/fidelity (וְהִתְהַלַּכְתִּי בַּאֲמִתֶּךָ) in verse 3. In verses 4–6 the psalmist employs language that is parallel to Ps 1:1 but with terms that are more familiar from the portraits of the righteous. The psalmist makes a first-person declaration of innocence reminiscent of Deut 26:13–14 but with different ethical issues in view:

לֹא־יָשַׁבְתִּי עִם־מְתֵי־שָׁוְא	4a	I have not sat with men of deception,
וְעִם נַעֲלָמִים לֹא אָבוֹא׃	4b	And with those who are hidden I have not gone.
שָׂנֵאתִי קְהַל מְרֵעִים	5a	I hate the assembly of those who do evil,
וְעִם־רְשָׁעִים לֹא אֵשֵׁב׃	5b	And with the guilty I have not sat.
אֶרְחַץ בְּנִקָּיוֹן כַּפָּי	6a	I wash my hands in innocence,
וַאֲסֹבְבָה אֶת־מִזְבַּחֲךָ יְהוָה׃	6b	And I go around your altar, O YHWH.

This self-description touches on a handful of character concerns found in the portraits of the righteous.[95] The issue of deception in verse 4 is familiar from Pss 15:2; 24:4; 34:14[13]. Though the terms are different, doing evil in verse 5a (מְרֵעִים) is conceptually similar to the statement in Ps 15:3 about doing evil to one's neighbor (לֹא־עָשָׂה לְרֵעֵהוּ רָעָה). More significantly, the inward orientation of verse 5 toward the wicked mirrors Ps 15:4. This suggests that the refusal to join with the wicked, sinners, and scoffers in Ps 1:1 is not merely a refusal to participate in their deeds but a fundamental internal orientation. Later in the psalm verse 10 describes sinners as those whose right hand is "full of a bribe" (שֹׁחַד; cf. Ps 15:5). Psalm 26 affirms the vision of righteous character in the terms and concepts specific to Psalms 15, 24 and 34.

We find additional links to the portraits of the righteous as we continue through the collection. Both Pss 15:3 and 28:3 employ a play on words between רֵעַ, "neighbor" and רָעָה, "evil." While in the former the righteous person does no evil to his neighbor, in the latter the wicked are characterized as those who "speak peace with their friends but evil is in their hearts" (דֹּבְרֵי שָׁלוֹם עִם־רֵעֵיהֶם וְרָעָה בִּלְבָבָם). This evil intent toward the other is found also in Ps 31:14[13], where the psalmist finds his enemies plotting to take

---

94. So also Broyles, "Psalms Concerning the Liturgies of Temple Entry," 264.

95. For an argument that this ties Psalm 26 together with Psalms 24 and 25 in a ring structure, see Lescow, "Textübergreifende Exegese."

Ethical Ideals and Reality in Dialogic Tension in Book I

his life (cf. Pss 15:3; 34:15[14]; 37:37). The scorn (חֶרְפָּה) directed toward the psalmist in Ps 22:7[6] also occurs in Ps 31:12[11], but in that case the aged psalmist feels forgotten and ostracized by his neighbors. Thus the proper sense of responsibility for one's neighbor (Ps 15:3; cf. 37:21, 26) is replaced by neglect and social marginalization.

While the righteous are marked by truth-telling and keeping far from deceit (Pss 15:2; 24:4; 34:14[13]), deception partially defines the character of the wicked (Ps 31:19[18]). The wicked mask the evil intent of their hearts with false words (Ps 28:3). The psalmist speaks of deceit so often because he is the victim of it, as in Ps 27:12, where he declares he is the victim of false witnesses (עֵדֵי־שֶׁקֶר). According to Psalm 32 the righteous person is not sinless, but he is also not deceitful. The righteous person hides nothing from YHWH and thus is forgiven (Ps 32:2).

The numerous lexical connections between this third section and the portraits of the righteous confirm a consistent vision of character between them. The character traits praised in the portraits become the basis for the psalmist's plea before YHWH and even facilitate the restoration of relationship when the righteous person sins. The wicked oppress the righteous precisely by rejecting that moral vision. This raises difficulties for the psalmist because his character does not automatically lead to the life envisioned in the portraits of the righteous.

Character's Outcome

The psalmist is fairly consistent in acting on the assumption that being with YHWH is the key to life, but it is not clear that life is automatically forthcoming. With deuteronomic flair Ps 25:12–13 connects YHWH's instruction and the fear of YHWH to experiencing a good life (cf. Ps 34:13[12]) and dwelling in the land (cf. Ps 37:3, 9, 11, 22, 29). The psalmist wants to be with YHWH (26:8; 27:4).[96] The psalmist cries out to see YHWH's face (27:8), but this cry is no abstract lip-service to being in the presence of God. Instead, it is a desperate plea for help. In Ps 31:17[16] the psalmist looks for the face of YHWH to shine and bring salvation.

However, the psalmist is dismayed by YHWH's absence. Psalm 30:8[7] offers a particularly vivid "narrative" of such an experience:

וַאֲנִי אָמַרְתִּי בְשַׁלְוִי	7a	And I have said in my ease,
בַּל־אֶמּוֹט לְעוֹלָם׃	7b	"I will not totter forever."

---

96. Barbiero notes that the theme of temple characterizes the third section and links it to the previous section (Barbiero, "Le premier livret du Psautier," 471).

	8a	YHWH in your favor you made me stand as a strong mountain;
יְהוָה בִּרְצוֹנְךָ הֶעֱמַדְתָּה לְהַרְרִי עֹז		
הִסְתַּרְתָּ פָנֶיךָ הָיִיתִי נִבְהָל׃	8b	You hid your face, I was terrified.

Here again the themes of the presence of YHWH and security come together. The psalmist admits that he has taken security in YHWH for granted. When YHWH withdraws his presence, the psalmist's presumption is laid bare.

In Ps 28:2 the psalmist raises his hands to the holy place (cf. Ps 15:1; 24:3) in supplication, but he does so with a desperate plea to YHWH not to be silent or deaf to his prayer (v. 1), and he asks not to be punished with the wicked (v. 3). YHWH's help from Zion is not automatic.

Elsewhere the supplicant raises the question of YHWH's deliverance. Picking up the epithet, "God of my salvation" (אֱלֹהֵי יִשְׁעִי), familiar from Ps 24:5, Ps 25:5 declares "For you I wait all day long" (אוֹתְךָ קִוִּיתִי כָּל־הַיּוֹם). Likewise in Ps 27:9 we encounter the desperate plea of the psalmist:

אַל־תַּסְתֵּר פָּנֶיךָ מִמֶּנִּי	9a	Do not hide your face from me,
אַל־תַּט־בְּאַף עַבְדֶּךָ	9b	Do not turn away your servant in anger
עֶזְרָתִי הָיִיתָ	9c	You have been my help,
אַל־תִּטְּשֵׁנִי וְאַל־תַּעַזְבֵנִי	9d	Do not cast me off, and do not abandon me,
אֱלֹהֵי יִשְׁעִי׃	9e	O God of my salvation.

The psalmist continues to identify with his covenant God (cf. Ps 24:5), but YHWH's absence leaves him desperate.

In the third section the psalmist remains committed to the ethical ideals of the portraits of the righteous, but his experience does not entirely match up with the outcomes they envision. The beginning and ending psalms in this section illustrate well the movement from prayer to its resolution. The psalmist responds to his trouble by seeking instruction (Ps 25:4–5) and deliverance (Ps 25:2–3, 16–22). He is confident that YHWH will instruct and will deliver (Ps 25:8–10, 12–14),[97] and the answer comes in Psalm 34 with testimony of YHWH's deliverance in the first half and instruction in the second half. Still, this movement is not automatic and involves troubling delay.

---

97. Note that Mandolfo identifies these as the DV (*God in the Dock*, 54).

Psalms 35–41

The fourth section of Book I comprises Psalms 35–41. It begins with an imprecatory psalm and contains Psalm 37, the portrait of the righteous that addresses the problem of theodicy most directly. From a structural perspective, Barbiero suggests that Psalm 37 is a response to Psalm 35.[98] From a thematic perspective, once again we see remarkable consistency between the vision of righteous character in the portraits of the righteous but tension with regard to the outcome of that character.

Character

Language about character *in general* is more sparse in the fourth section. The exception involves a phrase that describes the righteous as the "upright of heart" (יִשְׁרֵי־לֵב) in Ps 36:11[10]. This phrase also occurs in Pss 7:11[10]; 11:2; 32:11. A related phrase, "the upright of way" (יִשְׁרֵי דָרֶךְ), occurs in Ps 37:14.

Instead of the general we find specific ethical description. Psalm 35 describes the wicked who devise plans to harm the righteous, which is the very thing the righteous are not to do (Pss 15:3; 34:15[14]; 37:37). In verse 4 the psalmist solicits the aid of YHWH against the enemies, who, the psalmist says, "plan my injury" (חֹשְׁבֵי רָעָתִי; cf. Ps 15:3). In verse 7 the wicked seeks to trap the psalmist "without cause" (חִנָּם; cf. Ps 37:12, 14–15, 32). The psalmist also describes betrayal by those for whom he mourned when they were sick (vv. 12–14).

Speech once again plays a prominent role in the psalmist's discourse. In Ps 35:11 the psalmist is the victim of false witnesses, and in verses 15–16 his fellows rejoice and mock when he falls. Then in verse 20 they do not speak words of peace (cf. Pss 34:15[14]; 37:37) but instead "they plan words of deceit" (דִּבְרֵי מִרְמוֹת יַחֲשֹׁבוּן), and they openly mock in verse 21 (cf. v. 26).

A number of familiar characteristics from the portraits of the righteous appear in a portrait of wicked character in Psalm 36:2–5[1–4]:

נְאֻם־פֶּשַׁע לָרָשָׁע בְּקֶרֶב לִבִּי	2a	Transgression speaks to the wicked in the midst of his heart,
אֵין־פַּחַד אֱלֹהִים לְנֶגֶד עֵינָיו׃	2b	There is no terror of God before his eyes.
כִּי־הֶחֱלִיק אֵלָיו בְּעֵינָיו	3a	For he flatters himself in his eyes,
לִמְצֹא עֲוֹנוֹ לִשְׂנֹא׃	3b	To find his guilt and to hate.

---

98. Barbiero, "Le premier livret du Psautier," 473.

Portraits of the Righteous in the Psalms

דִּבְרֵי־פִיו אָוֶן וּמִרְמָה	4a	The words of his mouth are trouble and deceit,
חָדַל לְהַשְׂכִּיל לְהֵיטִיב׃	4b	He ceases to understand and to do good.
אָוֶן יַחְשֹׁב עַל־מִשְׁכָּבוֹ	5a	Trouble he plans on his bed,
יִתְיַצֵּב עַל־דֶּרֶךְ לֹא־טוֹב	5b	He sets himself on a way that is not good,
רָע לֹא יִמְאָס׃	5c	He does not reject evil.

In contrast to the truthful internal (Ps 15:2) and external speech of the righteous (Pss 24:4; 34:14[13]), we see in Ps 36:2[1] that all sorts of trouble come from the heart of the wicked.[99] Likewise in verse 4[3] the words of the wicked are "trouble and deceit" (אָוֶן וּמִרְמָה; cf. Pss 24:4; 34:14[13]). Furthermore, in verse 5 they plan trouble (cf. 37:12, 14–15, 32) and fail to reject what is evil (cf. Ps 15:4). Not surprisingly, Broyles casts this psalm as a characterization of those who may not enter the temple.[100]

The situation is changed in Psalm 38 because the psalmist identifies his own sin as the cause of his suffering (vv. 4–6[3–5]). Still, issues of character surface in the psalmist's social relationships. His friends are distant in his suffering (v. 12[11]), but his enemies actively seek to do him harm and use deceit to snare him in verse 13[12]. They hate the psalmist without reason (שֹׂנְאַי שֶׁקֶר) and repay him evil for good in verses 20–21.

Psalm 39 focuses on the speech of the psalmist and does not deal with the enemy except to acknowledge that the presence of the enemy is a concern (v. 2[3]) and that he may have to endure the abuse of a fool (v. 9[8]). As in the previous psalm, the sin of the psalmist has caused his suffering (vv. 9[8], 12[11]). He tries to guard his way and his mouth from sin (v. 2[1]), but in his silence (v. 3[2]) he grew hot like fire (תִבְעַר־אֵשׁ, v. 4[3]), which is conceptually reminiscent of the warning in Ps 37:1, 7, 8.[101] The psalmist recognizes the risk that his own mouth poses and seeks for YHWH to address the issue. The psalmist pleads for mercy on the basis of his relationship to YHWH, that he is a sojourner with him (גֵּר אָנֹכִי עִמָּךְ, cf. Ps 15:1).

Psalms 40 and 41 close the collection and address a number of character issues. In Ps 40:9[8] the psalmist aligns himself with the righteous person of Psalm 1:2 (בְּתוֹרַת יְהוָה חֶפְצוֹ) and Ps 37:31 (cf. Ps 37:4):

לַעֲשׂוֹת־רְצוֹנְךָ אֱלֹהַי חָפָצְתִּי	9a	To do your desire, O my God, is my I delight,

---

99. In Ps 36:2[1], sin is personified and "speaks to the wicked in the midst of my/his heart." While the MT has the first person suffix, referring to the psalmist, the LXX (G) and others have the third-person suffix, referring to the wicked. Hossfeld follows the MT as the *lectio dificilior* (Hossfeld and Zenger, *Die Psalmen I*, 224–25), while Craigie (*Psalms 1–50*, 289–90) and Kraus (*Psalms 1–59*, 396–97) follow the LXX reading.

100. Broyles, "Psalms Concerning the Liturgies of Temple Entry," 273–74.

101. Though the verb there is חרה.

Ethical Ideals and Reality in Dialogic Tension in Book I

וְתוֹרָתְךָ בְּתוֹךְ מֵעָי׃ 9b And your instruction is in my inward parts.

This internalization of torah transforms the desires of the psalmist and translates into action such as declaring YHWH's צֶדֶק in the "great assembly" (בְּקָהָל רָב, v. 11[10]; cf. Ps 1:5). However, in Ps 40:15[14] the wicked take pleasure in the harm that comes to the psalmist (cf. 37:12, 14–15, 32). In Psalm 41, on his sickbed the psalmist receives a visit from his enemy who is eagerly waiting for him to die. This enemy speaks deceitfully while he is in the room and "his heart gathers trouble to him," but when he walks outside he speaks (Ps 41:7[6]; cf. Ps 15:2). He quietly plots with others to bring harm to the psalmist (Ps 41:8[7]). Psalm 41:10[9] describes the "man of peace in whom I have trusted, the one who eats my bread," as the one who betrays his sick friend by prematurely proclaiming his death (cf. Pss 34:15[14]; 37:37; Obad 7). Thus the character commitments of the psalmist are at the heart of his grief in relationship to the enemies. But what about character's outcome?

Character's Outcome

The prayer of the psalmist in Psalm 35 assumes that wickedness should have its proper end. The psalmist asks that YHWH bring shame and frustration to those who seek his harm (v. 4). Like Ps 1:4, he asks that they be like chaff before the wind (cf. Ps 37:10, 20, 35–36). In Ps 35:8 the psalmist asks YHWH to let the wicked fall into their own trap (cf. Ps 37:14–15).

But the psalmist pleads in desperation in Ps 35:17, "O Lord, how long will you see?" (אֲדֹנָי כַּמָּה תִּרְאֶה). This anticipates the motif of YHWH seeing from Ps 37:13 (see also Pss 9:14[13]; 10:11, 14; 14:2; 25:18, 19; 33:13). This motif appears later in Psalm 35. The wicked see (רָאֲתָה עֵינֵינוּ) when the psalmist falls (v. 21), and in verse 22 the psalmist calls on YHWH to answer because he has seen it too (רָאִיתָה יְהוָה). The motif also occurs in the first section of Book I. The wicked think that YHWH does not see (Ps 10:11), but the psalmist maintains that YHWH does see (Pss 10:14; 14:2). When the fourth section picks up this motif, the psalmist still believes that YHWH sees and therefore calls him to act (Ps 35:17, 22), but in Psalm 37:13 YHWH's seeing is not about present events but the future end of the wicked. YHWH sees the future, but the psalmist groans in the present. This is the source of tension for the psalmist.

Words of confidence are found in Ps 36:8–10[7–9] as the psalmist describes YHWH as a refuge and a place of abundant life. However, the psalmist worries about the reversal of this ideal of security in Ps 38:17[16], where his enemy will gloat over him when his feet slip (בְּמוֹט רַגְלִי; cf. Ps

15:5). However, in this psalm the cause of the reversal is quite clear: the psalmist has sinned, and he is bearing the consequences of his guilt (Ps 38:5[4], 19[18]).

The motif of waiting for YHWH to act that occurs in Ps 37:9 and 34 appears two more times in this section. In Ps 39:8[7] the psalmist poses the question, "Now for what do I wait? O Lord? / My hope is in you." Psalm 40 begins with a testimony of the psalmist waiting for YHWH and being rewarded with an answer (v. 2[1]).

A number of scholars have pointed out that Book I ends with two אַשְׁרֵי formulas, which provide a clue to the didactic point of the book.[102] First, the one who trusts in YHWH is happy (Ps 40:4[3]). The motif of trust is familiar from a number of psalms in Book I, in the instruction to trust in YHWH (Pss 2:12; 4:6[5]; 37:3, 5), the declaration of trust (13:6[5]; 25:2; 26:1; 28:7; 31:7[6], 15[14]; 33:21), and the affirmation that such trust in YHWH is well-placed (Pss 9:11[10]; 21:8[7]; 22:5[4], 6[5]; 32:10). Thus by the end of Book I the existential tension the psalmist feels about the delay of God's deliverance does not result in his abandoning trust but rather affirming YHWH's fidelity over the long-haul. Still, this affirmation is tempered by further pleas in Psalm 40 for YHWH to act (Ps 40:12–17[11–16]), particularly the call for YHWH not to delay (v. 17[16]).

The final אַשְׁרֵי formula in Ps 41:2[1] promises happiness to the one who considers the helpless. It follows the reference to the psalmist as among the poor and needy in Ps 40:18[17] (וַאֲנִי עָנִי וְאֶבְיוֹן), though it introduces a new term (דָּל) for the lowly and oppressed that appears only here in Book I.[103] McCann explores the development of the motif of happiness using verses with אַשְׁרֵי. He notes that the term occurs in Pss 1:1 and 41:2, thus framing Book I. While Psalm 1 is focused on relatedness to YHWH, Psalm 41 speaks of it "in terms of orientation to the needs of other people.... In effect, then, the framework of Book I portrays the happy ones as those who love both God and neighbor."[104] In addition, Barbiero notes that consideration of the poor in 41:2[1] is also linked to torah since the torah contains numerous provisions that protect the poor.[105]

---

102. Barbiero, "Le premier livret du Psautier," 455; McCann, "The Shape of Book I of the Psalter," 342.

103. Though it occurs elsewhere in the Psalter in connection with the terms previously mentioned (Pss 72:13; 82:3, 4; 113:7).

104. McCann, "The Shape of Book I of the Psalter," 344. The inclusion between Psalms 1 and 2 and 40 and 41 was previously noted by Barbiero (Barbiero, "Le premier livret du Psautier," 455).

105. Barbiero, "Le premier livret du Psautier," 451.

Ethical Ideals and Reality in Dialogic Tension in Book I

The collection ends with a statement of confidence. In Ps 41:3[2] the psalmist affirms that YHWH will keep the righteous person, preserve his life, and give him a reputation of happiness in the land (cf. Pss 34:13[12], 17[16]; 37:3, 9. 11, 22, 29, 34). He affirms that because of his integrity (בְּתֻמִּי) YHWH makes the psalmist stand before him forever (וַתַּצִּיבֵנִי לְפָנֶיךָ לְעוֹלָם; cf. Ps 15:1, 5). In contrast to the wicked who may not rise in the congregation of the righteous (Ps 1:5), the righteous may ascend to YHWH's holy place (Psalms 15, 24) and be with him forever (Pss 23:6; 41:13[12]).

In all four sections of Book I we find verbal and conceptual echoes of the character descriptions found in the portraits of the righteous. The righteous affirm the nature of good character and identify bad character as the cause of their grief. On the other hand, by their success and their haunting words, the wicked question the connection between good character and its outcome, and the psalmist is troubled by YHWH's delayed response.

IMPLICATIONS OF THE DIALOGIC ETHIC OF BOOK I

What are the implications of this complex social dialogue? It is possible to read the book as a coherent whole. In light of the above exposition, there is no reason to doubt that the psalmist and later editors and readers can hold the voice of the supplicant and the voice of the teacher together in tension, perhaps as the multifaceted consciousness of a single subject. This tension in the book reflects an integrity about the relationship between religious ideals and experience. Mandolfo and Collins correctly note that the truth is found somewhere in relating the voice of the supplicant and the DV. Although Book I may not reach the depths of dissonance found in Psalms 44 or 88, dissonance is unmistakable. Still, the psalmist does not give up hope, and his consistent ethic testifies to this.

The ethical undercurrent found in the book has not received the attention in Psalms scholarship that it deserves. Ultimately the counsel of the DV in response to the success of the wicked is to do good and to trust in YHWH. Collins suggests that when Psalm 1 is reread in light of the rest of the Psalter, its affirmation about the fates of the righteous and the wicked is "as much the first half of a question as it is a statement," thus leading to a conflict of authority and experience.[106] This conflict calls for a decision, both on the nature of the right way and on the meaning of happiness.[107] The righteous are caught in a dilemma—they can resist by the means of the wicked, but then they become the wicked, or they can maintain innocence

---

106. Collins, "Decoding the Psalms," 48–49.
107. Ibid., 50.

Portraits of the Righteous in the Psalms

and get nowhere.[108] In this way Psalm 1 anticipates the fundamental ethical decision that confronts the righteous in response to the wicked. Collins is right to cast the Psalter in terms of an ethical decision that the reader must make. We see in Book I that the righteous person does not succumb to *Realpolitik* in an attempt to achieve social or political ends at the expense of character.[109] Instead, the helpless and the powerful alike are encouraged to maintain righteous character in relationship to YHWH and others, even enemies. This suggests that Book I is a richer resource for character formation than previously appreciated.

In addition, socio-economic implications follow from the ethical vision in Book I. Contrary to the ideological readings of Brueggemann and Mandolfo, it is important to note that Book I's ethical vision concerns both the powerful and the powerless. If the DV is concerned to protect the interests of the wealthy, Psalms 15 and 37 in particular seem to contradict that interest. Elements of Book I such as the instruction in Ps 37:1, 7, and 8 are relevant to those who are helpless. They are not to be incensed by the wicked and the many desperate words of the powerless in the lament psalms. But we also find instruction by admonition and example to the powerful to have regard for the poor. The financial habits of the righteous (esp. Pss 15:4 and 37:21, 26) as well as the promise of happiness held out for those who have regard for the poor (Ps 41:2[1]) speak directly to those in positions of social power. In ancient Israel these would have been relevant for the king and anyone else with significant material means. It is commonly acknowledged that a role of the king is to protect the poor and administer justice (cf. Psalm 72). Ironically, the David of the Psalter suffers much at the hands of his enemies.[110] Creach notes that in the Psalter David is "the defender of the righteous as well as one of the righteous who suffers."[111] Therefore, in presenting a narrative of weakness and character, Book I may help the reader begin to understand the experience of the afflicted from within. If the reader is a king, then the dialogic ethic of Book I sensitizes the king to the results of abandoning torah for an ethic of power and oppression. Still, the collection resists being limited to a royal subject. As Miller notes, we must move from the center of Psalms 15–24 outward to conclude that Psalms 15 and 24 may apply to the king. The effect is to keep the relevance of these psalms open

---

108. Ibid., 51.

109. Creach rightly notes that the imprecatory psalms represent an effort not at violence but at trust in God (*Destiny of the Righteous*, 28).

110. Hossfeld and Zenger suggest on the basis of Psalm 18 that David is the type of the poor in Israel ("Wer darf hinaufziehn zum Berg JHWHs?" 176).

111. Creach, *Destiny of the Righteous*, 8.

Ethical Ideals and Reality in Dialogic Tension in Book I

both to the king and to his fellow Israelites.[112] The same is true as we consider Psalm 2 in relationship to Psalms 40 and 41, where the royal character is not explicit—it could be related to the king or any faithful person.[113]

But how do we avoid flattening the book and pursuing a monologic reading? Rather than the narrative of ideological conflict proposed by Brueggemann and Mandolfo, perhaps Book I presents something else. The voice of lament is questioning and urgent, but not hostile, pleading with God to act and secondarily forcing the reader of Book I to recognize the complexity of the relationship between character and its outcome. This is perhaps a "theological counterbalance to a rigid application of the 'retribution principle,'" which Richard Schultz argues is found in the wisdom literature.[114] If so, the larger interpretive context of Book I helps ward off extreme and simplistic notions of the connection between character and its outcome.[115] The lamenting psalmist need not despair, and the confident psalmist should not be complacent in his relationship to YHWH or think he can avoid suffering simply by doing what is right.

The dialogic ethic of Book I calls for an account of character's outcome that deals with the complexity of life. This account reveals the Psalter's value as a resource for character formation.[116] Book I's tension about character's outcome suggests two important implications for readers.

First, the psalmist embodies Alasdair MacIntyre's distinction between internal and external goods. MacIntyre defines virtue as "an acquired human quality the possession and exercise of which tends to enable us to achieve those goods that are internal to practices and the lack of which effectively prevents us from achieving any such goods."[117] This definition implies a distinction between internal and external goods. An internal good is that which is intrinsic to a given practice, while an external good is only a secondary outcome. MacIntyre uses basketball as an example of a

---

112. Miller, "Kingship, Torah Obedience, and Prayer," 131. So also Podella, "Transformationen kultischer Darstellungen," 117.

113. Barbiero, "Le premier livret du Psautier," 461.

114. Schultz, "Unity or Diversity in Wisdom Theology?" 288.

115. Mandolfo employs Bakhtin to suggest a way of bringing the tensions between the voice of the supplicant and the DV together, "Truth, in Bakhtin's terms, emerges in the midst of the tension between these two positions. That is not to say that truth lies somewhere 'between' the two positions; the truth partakes fully of both positions" ("Finding Their Voices," 44). Mandolfo's language here is instructive even if one does not resort to a narrative that involves fundamentally contradictory positions. Interestingly, Mandolfo acknowledges that the voice of the supplicant has a "tempering" effect on the DV (ibid., 49).

116. I consider this topic in the next chapter.

117. MacIntyre, *After Virtue*, 191.

practice. We may enjoy camaraderie in playing on a basketball team, which is internal to that practice, but we may secondarily become rich playing basketball in the NBA.[118] To apply this to the practices found in Book I and in particular those found in the portraits of the righteous, the practices of the covenant standing behind the Psalter involve internal and external goods. Harmonious relationship with YHWH and others is the good internal to covenant practices,[119] and righteous character enables one to dwell with YHWH on his holy mountain and enjoy שָׁלוֹם in the land, but certain external goods such as security or long life in the land are external to the practices of covenant. It does not mean that they are unimportant but that they are secondary to covenant relationship itself.[120]

How do the psalmist's ethical commitments embody this distinction? With regard to speech, the psalmist refrains from deceit. The wicked find it a convenient tool for social power, but the psalmist refuses to fall into that moral trap. Instead he maintains the kind of character that encourages love of God and neighbor. According to Ps 15:4, the righteous person remains true to his oath even when it brings injury. Such an injury may represent a roadblock to security or a prosperous life in the land.

MacIntyre notes that at times pursuing a course of virtue is at odds with the goal of attaining the external goods of a practice.[121] This is the case in the two examples cited above. The combination of the metaphors of refuge and pathway illustrate well the tension felt in the Psalter. Brown notes,

> By joining "refuge" and "pathway," the warp and woof of the Psalter's variegated tapestry, the psalmists reorient the reader on the way *toward* God, while discerning God's path *into* the fray of human existence. In the convergence of "pathways," true *communitas* is formed and refuge is found, embodied in a community of worship enabled to reflect on God's presence, to sing in praise, to pray in trust, to live with understanding, and to work for justice and righteousness. It is a community on the move toward and at the same time in communion with God.[122]

118. Ibid., 188–91.

119. Or, as Creach argues, "the righteous' greatest 'reward' is to be in God's presence" (*Destiny of the Righteous*, 5).

120. John Oswalt makes a similar point: "God's ultimate purpose for Israel is not that they should have the Promised Land, as important as that symbol is. His purpose is that they should be brought into a relationship with him whereby he could live in their midst and his holiness would not destroy them" (*Called to be Holy*, 22). Christopher Wright rightly argues that this covenant relationship was for a further purpose vis-à-vis the nations (*The Mission of God*, esp. 224–25).

121. MacIntyre, *After Virtue*, 196.

122. Brown, *Seeing the Psalms*, 53.

Ethical Ideals and Reality in Dialogic Tension in Book I

The way toward God includes a regard for community, so the pursuit of human flourishing is not anthropocentric but rather theocentric. Therefore the psalmist presses on in praying and doing what is right for relationship with YHWH and others, trusting that YHWH's faithfulness will in the end lead to the enjoyment of the good life. Thus, while not offering a formal theodicy, Book I offers a model of perseverance, of faithfulness in spite of the fact that the good life does not automatically follow from good character. Readers may learn more ethically from watching someone maintain good character in the worst of times than in enjoying ease in the best of times. A response to conflict and loss characterized by perseverance reveals much about character, which the psalmist models for readers.

However, McCann suggests a different solution to the problem involving a redefinition of "happiness":

> The conditions of life for the righteous do not consist of anything that anyone, then or now, would readily associate with happiness—pain, poverty, persecution, and poor health! To introduce the Psalter under the rubric of "happy are those...," then to follow that introduction with an impressive series of poignant prayers for help, and then to provide the closing frame for Book I that also features the concept of happiness—all this serves to suggest that the shape of human happiness according to the Psalms has nothing to do with the normal definition of happiness or blessedness (one that is even found elsewhere in the Bible) in terms of material prosperity as well as physical security and well-being. Rather, according to the shape of the self to God, constantly delighting in God's "instruction" (Ps 1:2, NRSV 'law'); and with finding "refuge in" God (Ps 2:12).[123]

McCann rightly points out that Psalms 32–34 and 40 connect happiness with trust.[124] However, in the book as a whole the psalmist never gives up hope that YHWH will bring change consistent with a normal definition of happiness. Therefore a redefinition of happiness does not solve the problem. Perhaps the distinction between internal and external goods gets us a little closer to understanding the reason for the psalmist's perseverance. However, perseverance alone does not answer the theological dissonance in Book I.

The second implication for readers provides another answer to this dissonance: Book I may reflect an eschatological move in understanding character's outcome. This eschatological move does not explicitly involve

---

123. McCann, "The Shape of Book I of the Psalter," 343.
124. Ibid., 344.

a vision of a cosmic end. Instead, the Psalter envisions YHWH's future intervention, and this provides hope for the present. This perspective may be found in a number of recent interpretations of Book I.

Tucker argues that Book I is essentially eschatological.[125] Looking at the verbs for waiting (קוה, יחל and חכה) and trust, he argues that the book commends a hopeful look toward the future, that YHWH will act on behalf of those who take refuge in him. It commends moving beyond lament to hopeful waiting for an eschatological future.[126]

Botha makes a similar argument with respect to Psalms 25 and 37. He argues that the former has numerous connections in vocabulary and concepts to the latter. One is a psalm of lament and the other is didactic, but the two share a viewpoint that he attributes to common authorship.[127] He summarizes:

> Those who *trust* in Yahweh and *wait* for him may experience *distress* and may even be *afflicted*, but since they are *humble* and *upright* in character, Yahweh will teach them his *way* so that they will not be *shamed* like the wicked, but they and/or their *descendants* will *inherit* the *Land*.[128]

The character traits shared between the two psalms include trusting in YHWH (Pss 25:2; 37:3, 5), waiting for YHWH (Pss 25:5; 21; 37: 9, 34), being humble (Pss 25:9; 37:11), and taking refuge in YHWH (Pss 25:20; 37:40).[129] Adding Psalm 34, Botha discerns a common theological viewpoint that adversity is possible but change is coming.[130] For Botha, Brueggemann's description of the eschatological reading of Psalm 37 is "completely accurate."[131]

Collins helpfully points out the building blocks of eschatology in the psalms, that is, the contrast between the way things are and the way things can be.[132] He further highlights the eschatological character of the Psalter:

> There is a question hanging over the fulfilment of God's saving initiative. Some psalms emphasize the element of non-fulfilment and frustration. Others report at least partial fulfilment.

125. Tucker, "Beyond the Lament," 121.

126. Ibid., 129–30. Although not all future-oriented language is eschatological, the essential point stands that the psalter often looks forward to a future realization of covenant promises rather than a full-fledged realization in the present.

127. Botha, "The Relationship between Psalms 25 and 37," 543–46.

128. Ibid., 547. Italics his.

129. Ibid., 556.

130. Ibid., 562.

131. Ibid., 563.

132. Collins, "Decoding the Psalms," 51.

Ethical Ideals and Reality in Dialogic Tension in Book I

Throughout the book, however, there is a recurrent orientation towards a final definitive fulfilment which is predicted, anticipated and prayed for.[133]

The tension between non-fulfillment and fulfillment (even partial) in the Psalter can become a hindrance to appropriating the psalms if the reader is not able to have a broader eschatological vision.

Many interpreters see an eschatologizing tendency in response to the fall of Jerusalem and along with it the Davidic dynasty. Mays points out that the pairing of Psalms 1 and 2 implies an eschatological assumption. The theology of Ps 1:6 is not borne out in experience—the righteous in fact suffer. Mays remarks, "nowhere in the final content of the Psalter is this faith surrendered. It is tried and questioned, but neither the way of Job nor the way of Ecclesiastes is followed. The reason is the eschatological context of the torah piety—the hope for the coming kingdom of God."[134]

Brennan suggests that the presence of Psalm 8 directs the reader to an eschatological reading. Although Psalm 8 fits with Psalms 7 and 9 because of the acclamation of the divine name (7:18; 8:2, 10; 9:3, 11), he regards it as an interpolation. "Psalm 8 can thus be interpreted as a brief outburst of jubilation, introduced at this point by the compilers of the collection as an anticipation of the distant triumph."[135] The Davidic tone set by Psalm 2 then invites a messianic and eschatological reading of the Psalter. "The Psalter comes to be seen as a magnificent dramatic struggle between the two ways—that of Yahweh, his anointed king, and the company of the just, and that of the wicked, the sinners, the evil-doers."[136]

The tension between realized and future eschatology that I highlight in Psalm 37 is part of the implications of the dialogue about character's outcome. Modern readers who deny a greater eschatological hope may find these psalms lack realism and therefore are naïve or untrustworthy. However, along with the psalmist, religious readers may find the answer to the apparent naiveté of some psalms is to see them in the context of hope in the kingship of YHWH.

---

133. Ibid., 54.

134. Mays, "The Place of the Torah-Psalms in the Psalter," 11. Likewise McCann argues the presence of royal psalms in a post-exilic collection gives "the collection an orientation to the future" ("The Psalms as Instruction," 122).

135. Brennan, "Psalms 1–8," 28.

136. Ibid., 28–29.

CONCLUSION

The dialogue in Book I is not between the voice of the supplicant and the didactic voice, though there is tension between them. Rather, the dialogue is between the psalmist and the enemy whose words and actions create theological dissonance for the psalmist. The psalmist's trust in YHWH is evident in his steadfast commitment to the ethic outlined in the portraits of the righteous. Therefore we cannot speak of a supplicant at fundamental odds with a didactic voice. Still, the statements of confidence in the outcomes of righteous character are tempered by the experience of suffering, and the delay of YHWH's help necessitates an eschatological hope undergirded by torah obedience. This dialogue wards off extreme readings of individual psalms and encourages character in response to social conflict and suffering. It may also have a didactic effect for the reader, encouraging righteous and compassionate involvement by those in positions of social power to alleviate the suffering of the righteous.

7

Conclusion and Prospects for Further Research

SUMMARY OF FINDINGS

This study has examined four portraits of righteous character as presented in Psalms 15, 24, 34, and 37. These texts have been studied as individual compositions and in their canonical context in Book I of the Psalter. The portraits envision good character in social terms.[1] They consistently affirm a life of integrity that involves seeking the good of the other, rejecting what is evil, speaking truth, and protecting the poor and helpless. In addition, these psalms present their ethical vision in relationship to a *telos* by encouraging the righteous with a theocentric vision of the good life. Character is fundamental for enjoying that good life; the social dimension of character is necessary for the maintenance of the covenant relationship with YHWH. In the Psalter's own terms, the pathway of the righteous life reaches its "destination" or outcome in relationship to YHWH.

These psalms describe this "destination" in three main ways. First, in Psalms 15 and 24 the righteous person enjoys access to YHWH's holy mountain, the temple. This connects these psalms to the rich temple and Zion theology of the Psalter, in which the concept of the good life is that

---

1. For a similar judgment about the wisdom books Proverbs, Job, and Ecclesiastes, see Brown, *Character in Crisis*, 151.

of security and blessing in the presence of YHWH. Second, in Psalms 34 and 37 the righteous person enjoys life. In Psalm 37 this life is placed in the context of the land, a motif that is remarkably rare in the Psalter.[2] Third, YHWH delivers the righteous from trouble. This theme occurs explicitly in Psalms 34 and 37 but is implied in Psalm 24.

The canonical context of the portraits of the righteous challenges the relationship between character and its outcome. Although the portraits progressively engage the problem of the suffering of the righteous, the supplicant in the lament psalms groans at the triumph of the wicked. The lament psalms highlight the complex relationship between character and its outcome, denying that the relationship is automatic or mechanistic. This creates theological dissonance, yet the psalmist becomes a model of perseverance in hope. Even in lament, the psalmist repeatedly returns to hope in YHWH's deliverance and testifies to it in his experience. Furthermore, he consistently affirms the ethic of the portraits in the face of his enemies who cause trouble by rejecting that ethic. The psalmist does not succumb to *Realpolitik* but steadfastly embodies righteous character. He does not abandon hope for the good life in the long haul. Instead, while he sometimes testifies to YHWH's deliverance in the present, he embraces the inevitable suffering of the righteous and always looks for YHWH's deliverance in the future.

THE PORTRAITS OF THE RIGHTEOUS AS A RESOURCE FOR CHARACTER FORMATION

This study must conclude by answering the second fundamental question identified in the first chapter: What resources do Book I and the portraits offer for the formation of character today? Although these psalms may serve as didactic companions while exploring the ethical dimensions of narrative, prophecy, and wisdom literature, space does not permit me to explore such possibilities.[3] Instead, I shall explore the ways in which reading the Psalter on its own may form the character of its readers.

First, we must remember that the Psalter includes diverse kinds of discourse.[4] Although Gunkel and Westermann emphasize the polar opposites of God-ward address in the Psalms (namely, praise and lament),[5]

---

2. Whybray, *The Good Life in the Old Testament*, 143.
3. Richard Briggs hints of this potential (*The Virtuous Reader*, 32).
4. I do not mean to rehearse form-critical categories here but rather kinds of discourse distinguished by the direction of their address (i.e., their implied audience).
5. Westermann, *Praise and Lament in the Psalms*, 18.

Conclusion and Prospects for Further Research

the portraits I have examined address a human audience and involve didactic discourse. The psalmist speaks to instruct implied readers directly. As Carleen Mandolfo aptly demonstrates, this didactic voice also occurs in lament psalms. However, didactic discourse is rare compared to prayer, embodied in the two extremes of lament and praise.[6] Praise and lament exist on a continuum of God-ward address, and this is the unique genius of the Psalms. As Whybray notes, the Psalms express the voice of the people to YHWH and describe their experience in ways that infuse the Psalter with a sense of actuality.[7] This God-ward address sets the Psalter apart from most other kinds of discourse in the Hebrew Bible, so the Psalter offers a unique resource for character formation. Scholars typically assume that the discourse of prayer is the only kind of discourse that needs to be discussed in relationship to the Psalms. However, this study has examined didactic discourse as a component of the Psalter. Furthermore, this study has shown that didactic discourse and the discourse of prayer exist side-by-side and deal with similar themes, sometimes using identical terms. Therefore, our account of the formative effects of the Psalter must address both.

In the history of interpretation, the discourse of prayer has been the focus of the most fruitful thinking about the use of the Psalter.[8] In the Christian tradition the classic perspective was aptly described in the fourth century by Athanasius of Alexandria in his *Letter to Marcellinus*. Athanasius identifies two distinctive features of the Psalter.

First, the Psalter offers a comprehensive and diverse vision of life in covenant relationship with God. Having described the span of Old Testament history, Athanasius remarks that the Psalter "is like a garden" incorporating the entire span of the Old Testament.[9] This perspective is mediated to the Protestant tradition through Martin Luther's comment that the Psalter is a "little Bible."[10] More recently Gerald Wilson describes the comprehensive character of the biblical psalms:

> [T]hey contain some of the earliest and yet some of the latest compositions in the OT canon, integrating as no other segment

---

6. Ibid., 11. Note that psalms of praise also address a human audience to call them to worship (e.g., Psalm 100), but they invite a God-ward address.

7. Whybray, *The Good Life in the Old Testament*, 142. J. Bardarah McCandless remarks that the psalms "enflesh the word" and are "lived theology" ("Enfleshing the Psalms," 373).

8. I shall not provide a comprehensive history of interpretation of the Psalms. See Gillingham, *Psalms through the Centuries*.

9. Athanasius, "Letter to Marcellinus," 102.

10. Luther, "Preface to the Psalter 1545 (1528)," 254. Luther claims, "In it is comprehended most beautifully and briefly everything that is in the entire Bible."

of the canon the diverse literary, historical and thematic streams that make up the Old Testament. In them royal ideology and prophetic critique, cultic theology and wisdom reflection, law and liturgy all collide and intertwine to create a complex yet piquant stew of biblical proportions. In their verses all the formative themes of promise and fulfillment, salvation and judgment, election and mission, creation and restoration, commandment and obedience coexist without embarrassment, so that in these few compositions of poetic beauty we encounter a microcosm of the OT traditions.[11]

The extent to which the Psalter represents the whole of the Hebrew Bible is open to discussion. The Psalter has its own dominant theological themes, but, as Wilson clearly states, it brings numerous themes together in creative tension. This diversity is evident from the four psalms analyzed in this study. In them we find clear links to the Torah, the prophets, and wisdom.[12] In addition to thematic connections to the rest of the Hebrew Bible, the Psalter connects with a range of human experience. Athanasius notes the Psalter's comprehensive treatment of "the emotions of the soul,"[13] a perspective famously supported by John Calvin.[14] Gerald Wilson likewise notes the diversity of human experience and emotion:

> Although we tend to run the biblical psalms through our filter of what is appropriate and inappropriate, omitting in worship those sentiments deemed less than Christian, the Psalter has no such qualms but is satisfied to let this riot of human emotions stand unexpurgated together as God's Word to us![15]

For the reader, this models a theological complexity and integrity needed today, for pastors as much as for biblical theologians. Wilson suggests the Psalter provides a paradigm for biblical theology: "Rather than a tether fastened to a mooring stake that inhibits freedom by drawing all back to a center, orthodox faith is defined at the periphery like the skin of a balloon that marks the outer boundaries of faith."[16] This paradigm involves

---

11. Wilson, "Psalms and the Psalter," 100.

12. See also Bullock, "The Shape of the Torah as Reflected in the Psalms, Book I," 1.

13. Athanasius, "Letter to Marcellinus," 108.

14. Calvin, *Commentary on the Book of Psalms*, xxxvii. See also Childs, *Old Testament Theology in a Canonical Context*, 202; McCandless, "Enfleshing the Psalms," 379–80.

15. Wilson, "Psalms and the Psalter," 101.

16. Ibid., 103.

Conclusion and Prospects for Further Research

diversity and tension.[17] To expand on Athanasius' colorful description, the garden includes roses and dandelions, mint and parsley, potatoes and mangoes. The practical implications of this apparently impossible diversity for pray-ers are significant, but they are most fully appreciated in light of what follows.

The second distinctive feature of the Psalter is that it calls for involvement. Athanasius noted that while other books in the Old Testament invite imitation of godly characters, readers of the Psalter recognize the words of the psalmist as their own words.[18] The relative absence of personal or historical indicators in the biblical psalms makes them well-suited for appropriation as the prayers of readers.[19] Gordon Wenham has recently applied this insight through the lens of speech act theory. He argues that ethical reading of the Psalter is distinct because the reader is "involved in giving very active assent to the standards of life implied in the Psalms."[20] Praying the psalms involves pray-ers in "commissive speech acts," that is, in essentially offering vows that transform their relationship to God. By appropriating the words of the Psalter as their own, readers must make an active commitment to the vision of life it propounds.[21] Wenham argues that the Psalms were meant to be memorized, and memorization makes a text part of a person's character.[22]

Involvement in the Psalter takes readers on an uncomfortable journey. In some Christian communities the genre of lament is more comfortable than the genre of praise or didactic discourse.[23] In such communities Brueggemann's prophetic call to the church to take lament more seriously has been heard.[24] Evangelical churches have been slow to heed Bruegge-

---

17. Ibid., 109.

18. Athanasius, "Letter to Marcellinus," 109. Richard Briggs rightly asserts that "almost any significant discussion of biblical texts has a *self-involving* dimension: the interpreter must interact with the subject matter of the text in ways that in turn shape or at least respond to the character of the interpreter" (Briggs, *The Virtuous Reader*, 40, italics his). However, when the Psalms are prayed as the words of the pray-er, this self-involvement reaches new depths in the soul of the pray-er.

19. Creach, *Destiny of the Righteous*, 6.

20. Wenham, "Prayer and Practice in the Psalms," 292. See also Wenham, "Reflections on *Singing the Ethos of God*," 120–24.

21. Wenham, "Prayer and Practice in the Psalms," 294. See also Wenham, *Psalms as Torah*, 57–76.

22. Wenham, *Psalms as Torah*, 53.

23. I found this to be the case in a course on the Psalms during the Fall of 2010 at McCormick Theological Seminary in Chicago. Students who were asked to write their own psalms almost invariably wrote lament psalms. See also Osherow, "Psalm 37 at Auschwitz," 60–64.

24. See especially Brueggemann, "The Costly Loss of Lament," 57–71.

mann's call and seem to prefer psalms of confidence to outright lament, though there are signs that attitudes are changing.[25] Brueggemann is largely negative about the psalms of orientation,[26] but he does not dismiss them entirely:

> In reading, singing and praying the Psalter, the most important and most interesting question is how to move from Psalm 1 to Psalm 150, from glad duty to utter delight. That move is through the rest of the Psalter. My thesis is that the way from torah obedience to self-abandoning doxology is by way of candor about suffering and gratitude about hope.[27]

The Psalter challenges theologically simplistic perspectives within the context of divine revelation. It confronts readers with their incredulity and skepticism about confident faith claims on the one hand and their reluctance to entertain doubt and disorientation on the other because readers are involved with the words they speak or pray from the Psalter. This uncomfortable journey is formative in large part because it is difficult.[28]

Reading as involvement may take on different forms for different readers. Readers who have suffered find words to express the depth of their pain that was hitherto inexpressible.[29] As participants, they are guided in sorting out the experiences and emotions of their own souls. However, readers do not always share the experience of the psalmist. In that case readers may learn by sensitization. Particularly in the experience of the suffering psalmist, the ethical implications of the enemy's behavior calls for a response from the community. Lament therefore may "mobilize an empathetic and faithful response" from the community.[30] When sensitized to the suffering of the other, the implications of the moral vision found in portraits take on a human face for readers. The "faithful response" advocated in Ps 15:5, for example, is to uphold the case of the innocent rather than taking a bribe to subvert justice.[31] That human face may also help those who have not yet experienced the psalmist's disorientation to respond with compassion to those who have. The simple act of reading a psalm may even give victims a

---

25. Recently I learned that a professor at a conservative Bible college required his students to read Brueggemann, and a conservative mission organization had a speaker who focused on lament at an annual retreat for its field workers.

26. See Nasuti, *Defining the Sacred Songs*, 176.

27. Brueggemann, "Bounded by Obedience and Praise," 71–72.

28. Briggs, *The Virtuous Reader*, 10.

29. McCandless, "Enfleshing the Psalms," 382.

30. Suderman and Grebel, "Deaf Communities."

31. So also McCandless, "Enfleshing the Psalms," 384–86.

Conclusion and Prospects for Further Research

voice to name injustice.[32] The discourse of prayer is a discourse of involvement, giving pray-ers words to understand and express their experience or provoking righteous and compassionate engagement with those who suffer. But what about didactic discourse?

Didactic discourse addresses readers directly rather than giving them words to speak to God, so its formative effects are different. Psalm 1 has drawn the attention of scholars because of its introductory position at the beginning of the Psalter. Although the torah of Ps 1:2 may not be the five books of the Psalter, the Psalter may be viewed as a book of instruction in light of other arguments. The Psalter is perhaps best understood as the fruit of reflection on Torah, but that reflection itself can be instructive. The four portraits instruct by description and admonition, as I have shown in chapters 2–5. They digest Torah and present it in the terms and images familiar from the psalmic discourse of prayer. The portraits serve as signposts on the trying ethico-theological landscape of Book I. To employ a different spatial metaphor, they offer ethical benchmarks by which to measure the behavior of the psalmist and his enemies, but they do more than that. In admonition they call readers to be righteous participants with the psalmist, and in description they show them how they can do so. They further call attention to the connection between character and its outcome to keep hope alive in the midst of a world that questions it. Michael Jinkins rightly notes that the suffering of the righteous is the "crucible of formation" as they trust in YHWH. In contrast to the Aristotelian ethic that relied on the conditions of the *polis*, the covenantal context and future hope found in Psalm 37 provides a dynamic response to ever-shifting social conditions with hope in YHWH.[33] Therefore didactic discourse serves as an important companion for the discourse of prayer, providing ethical instruction on how to respond to a variety of situations.

Finally, we must note that the poetic character of the psalms plays an important role in character formation. The terseness of poetry requires the reader to linger over the words and struggle with them. This is a double-edged sword. Persevering readers will be rewarded with greater insight just as the wise increase in wisdom (Prov 1:5; 9:9). However, readers who give up easily may perhaps be satisfied with a warm affirmation of their existing perspectives and not benefit from the formative influence of the poetry. In addition to terseness, the imagery of poetry is a factor. Form critics and historians of religion have traditionally sought to reach behind the imagery to reconstruct a historical setting. However, the poet employs imagery to

---

32. McCann, "The Hope of the Poor," 161.
33. Jinkins, "The Virtues of the Righteous in Psalm 37," 185.

create conceptual possibilities. Imagery opens new worlds of application for readers who linger over them. That is one reason why the Psalms have attained classical status in western literature. It also suggests that faithful application of the psalms may involve a measure of reinterpretation of imagery. For example, the identity of the enemy of the psalmist remains obscure, and that allows readers to apply psalms more broadly than if the identity of the enemy were restricted to a particular historical referent. Also, the imagery of YHWH as the rock, the fortress, and the refuge of the righteous may be extended to contexts quite foreign to the military context of the ANE.

PROSPECTS FOR FURTHER RESEARCH

This study has joined the growing chorus of work on the ethical reading of the Psalter, but further questions remain. In what follows I briefly explore the relationship between my thesis about Book I and the rest of the Psalter, the rest of the Bible, and the use of virtue theory in Old Testament ethics.

The Portraits of the Righteous and the Rest of the Psalter

Chief among the questions raised by my thesis is the relationship between the portraits and the rest of the Psalter. I have focused on the relationship between the portraits and Book I because they are concentrated there, but does the ethical vision found in Book I extend to the rest of the Psalter? Barbiero argues that Book I offers a theological itinerary for the whole Psalter,[34] but his analysis does not address the question of ethics. In addition, other proposals for the structure of the Psalter have emphasized change through the Psalter, whether from obedience to praise or from a focus on Davidic kingship to a focus on Torah and wisdom in light of 587 B.C.E.[35] It is clear that while Book I may anticipate many of the themes in the rest of the psalter, Books II–V do not simply recapitulate Book I. However, I shall suggest in a preliminary way some important points of continuity between the portraits and the rest of the Psalter as well as one significant point of discontinuity. Each of these calls for further study.

We find continuity in several respects. Theodicy is a consistent motif found in at least the first three books. It is widely known that Psalms 37,

---

34. Barbiero, "Le premier livret du Psautier," 480.

35. For the former, see Brueggemann, "Bounded by Obedience and Praise." For the latter, see Wilson, *The Editing of the Hebrew Psalter*; Wilson, "King, Messiah, and the Reign of God," 392.

Conclusion and Prospects for Further Research

49, and 73 address the problem of the suffering of the righteous.[36] I have considered Psalm 37 at length, so a few notes about its connection to Psalms 49 and 73 are in order. The socio-economic situation of Psalm 49 is similar to Psalm 37 in that the righteous suffer at the hands of the wicked who are more powerful (v. 6–7[5–6]). Likewise the brash but poorly placed confidence of the wicked (vv. 13–15[12–14]) reminds us of the disappearing cedar tree in Psalm 37. Psalm 49:16[15] also expresses a hope of deliverance.[37] Psalm 73 shares with Psalms 37 and 49 the concern for responding appropriately to the wicked who prosper (v. 3). In addition, several verbal and conceptual connections to other psalms in Book I supply fascinating points of continuity. Not surprisingly, the wicked are not only comfortable and wealthy (vv. 4–5), they are also violent (v. 6), and their tongues ooze with venomous speech (vv. 8–9), both of which are concerns raised repeatedly in the portraits as well as in the complaints of the supplicant in Book I. Verse 1 affirms YHWH's goodness to the pure in heart (לְבָרֵי לֵבָב), which is a verbal link to Ps 24:4 (בַר־לֵבָב). Also, verse 13 presses the central conflict of Book I, namely, whether a righteous life is lived in vain. The psalmist combines a reference to keeping his heart clean (זִכִּיתִי לְבָבִי) with washing his hands in innocence (וָאֶרְחַץ בְּנִקָּיוֹן כַּפָּי), as in Ps 24:4. In addition, the phrase, אֶרְחַץ בְּנִקָּיוֹן כַּפָּי ("I wash my hands in innocence"), occurs in Ps 26:6, which is a first-person profession of character. Therefore, at the outset of Book III the psalmist tempers the optimism of Book I about the connection between character and its outcome. The psalmist identifies the core temptation as sinful speech, which would betray the children of YHWH (v. 15). This is the heart of the concern of the psalmist in Book I. Still, pessimism does not prevail. Psalm 73:2 provides a hint of this, but the decisive moment occurs in verse 17, when the psalmist enters the temple and understands the end of the wicked. This verse links Psalm 73 conceptually to the temple theology undergirding Psalms 15 and 24, but it also employs the language of Ps 37:37–38 in speaking of the end of the wicked.[38] Furthermore, that the

---

36. See Munch, "Das Problem des Reichtums in den Psalmen 37.49.73"; Von Rad, *Wisdom in Israel*, 203–206; Waltke, "Responding to an Unethical Society"; Estes, "Poetic Artistry in the Expression of Fear in Psalm 49," 55–71.

37. Philip S. Johnston makes the interesting claim that the rescue from שְׁאוֹל in verse 16[15] refers to a separate destiny for the righteous after death. In his reading, there are differentiated destinies for the righteous and the wicked. This is consistent with the rest of the psalm. Although in verse 11[10] none can redeem their own lives, God can. The wise and the fool both die, but God redeems the life of the righteous. In contrast, the wicked who boast in their riches must leave it to others and die like cattle or sheep ("Psalm 49," 76). If this is true, then the eschatological tendency of Psalm 37 finds more full expression in Psalm 49.

38. In the Psalter the term אַחֲרִית occurs only in these two psalms and Psalms 109:13

wicked would slip in Ps 73:18 is the converse of the promise in Ps 15:5 that the righteous do not slip.[39] The swift destruction of the wicked in Ps 73:19 corresponds to the swift demise of the wicked in Ps 37:2, 10 and 35–36. The psalm ends with a confession of YHWH's incomparable worth (vv. 25–26; cf. Ps 37:4). Thus Psalms 49 and 73 not only return to the problem of the suffering of the righteous, they do so in ethical terms, wrestling with the connection between character and its outcome. But what about the broader structure of the Psalter?

Recent scholarship has emphasized that the final shape of the Psalter reflects the fall of Jerusalem in 587 B.C.E. Chief among such proposals is Gerald Wilson's contention that Book IV turns to wisdom and the kingship of YHWH in response to the failure of the Davidic monarchy.[40] Scholars have offered critique and suggestions for adjustment of Wilson's thesis. For example, Creach rightly notes that while Book II ends with a hopeful note, Book III begins and ends with serious questions about the future of David.[41] Still, as Creach notes, the future for David is not as bleak as Wilson paints it—hope of restoration is found in the royal psalms in Books IV and V (Psalms 101, 110, 132, 144).[42] The return of David in Book IV involves another portrait of righteous character, Psalm 101. It also contains a first-person portrait of righteous character. In it David professes a blameless walk (v. 2) and communion with those whose way is blameless (v. 6). The term תָּמִים is familiar from Ps 15:2, among other places. David rejects evil (vv. 3–4; cf. Pss 15:4; 24:4; 34:15[14]), punishes slander (v. 4; cf. Ps 15:3), and excludes liars from his court (v. 7; cf. Pss 15:2; 24:4; 34:14[13]). David also considers the faithful in the land in verse 6, a motif familiar from Psalm 37. The tenor in verse 8 is that of a person of power in the royal city, much like the happy one of Ps 41:1 who considers the poor.

Following another royal psalm, Psalm 110, we find twin character sketches of YHWH (Psalm 111) and the righteous person (Psalm 112). Stephen Reed notes that both of these psalms are alphabetic acrostics (cf. Psalms 34 and 37). Furthermore, some character traits such as care for the

---

and 139:9.

39. At least semantically, though the terms are different.

40. Wilson, *The Editing of the Hebrew Psalter*, 215; Wilson, "King, Messiah, and the Reign of God," 392; Wilson, "The Structure of the Psalter," 235. Cf. Robert L. Foster's argument that, based on the seam psalms, the final shape of the Psalter is meant to shape the just person. The crux of this rhetorical strategy is the problem of 587, which he suggests is a failure of the justice of God ("Led in Paths of Justice").

41. Creach, *Destiny of the Righteous*, 64, 68.

42. Ibid., 104.

Conclusion and Prospects for Further Research

poor occur in both psalms (Ps 111:5//Ps 112:5, 9).[43] Considering Psalm 112 in particular, a number of verbal echoes of Psalm 15 stand out.[44] In verse 5 the righteous person lends (חוֹנֵן וּמַלְוֶה; cf. Ps 15:5; see also Ps 37:21, 26), and in verse 6 he is never shaken (לְעוֹלָם לֹא־יִמּוֹט; cf. Ps 15:5). Furthermore, the conflict with the wicked so prevalent in Book I returns, though this time the righteous person triumphs (v. 8) while the wicked is angry and simply melts away (v. 10).

These two character sketches echo the connection between character and its outcome presented in the portraits in Book I. Psalm 112 also describes the attitude of the righteous to suffering: the righteous person trusts in YHWH (Ps 112:7), much like the psalmist of Book I. The ethic and the theology is similar.

However, there is one significant point of discontinuity to observe between Book I and much of the rest of the Psalter. The lament psalms in Book I are all individual lament psalms, which is also true of Book II, especially Psalms 51–72.[45] However, lament in the later books takes a turn toward the community. This comes to a focal point in Psalm 89, in which the community laments the loss of Davidic rule. Still, this discontinuity highlights the extent to which David is identified with the people. As Creach puts it, the destinies and David and the nation are intertwined, and in Psalm 89 this destiny hangs in the balance.[46]

In relationship to Psalm 37 I noted an individualizing tendency. The righteous individual is said to be the beneficiary of the deuteronomic covenant blessings. The events of 587 highlighted the corporate dimension of the earlier portraits of righteous. The righteousness of the king is a matter that affects the people, and the destiny of the people is tied to the destiny of the king. Although individual psalms in Book I often mask the identity of the righteous person, the editorial shape of Book I associates him with David.

I must make one final note with regard to the relationship between the ethic of Book I and the rest of the Psalter. I argue that there is a social dialogue about the connection between character and its outcome and that steadfast hope is evident in the psalmist's steadfast ethic. It remains to be seen how much this dynamic plays out in later psalms. Do the same ethical issues continue to surface outside the psalms I mention above, especially with the increasing dominance of praise in later books? With the national/

---

43. Reed, "Virtue Ethics and Psalms 111–112." See also Zenger, "Geld als Lebensmittel?" 80–81.

44. Cf. Zenger, "Geld als Lebensmittel?"

45. Westermann, *Praise and Lament in the Psalms*, 257.

46. Creach, *Destiny of the Righteous*, 61, 68.

political identity of the enemy in the communal laments,[47] how does the shift in emphasis to communal lament and communal concerns affect the ethical discourse of the Psalter? These questions remain unanswered.

The Portraits of the Righteous and the Rest of the Bible

In addition to connections within the Psalter itself, a number of questions arise about the relationship of this study to the rest of the Bible, including the New Testament.

For those engaged in biblical theology, the relationship between the Pentateuch and prophetic literature on the one hand and the wisdom literature on the other has led to wisdom being the unwanted stepchild for some, most famously for Gerhard von Rad.[48] Daniel Estes summarizes the problem, "When biblical theology is defined in terms of the events of salvation history, as has been typical in most of the prominent OT theologies, then wisdom is necessarily relegated to the margins."[49] Aside from the structural problem of favoring *Heilsgeschichte* to the exclusion of *sapientia*, scholars famously disagree about a legitimate "center" for Old Testament theology.[50] As noted above, Gerald Wilson commends the Psalter as a paradigm for biblical theology.[51] Wilson's metaphor of the balloon allows for a diversity of theological motifs within certain boundaries, but the metaphor leaves open the question whether the diversity has any internal coherence or is just a collection of diverse viewpoints.[52] This study has noted diverse intertextual connections between the portraits, including parallel passages in Isaiah and Ezekiel as well as allusions to and developments of certain texts in Deuteronomy.[53] In addition, Psalms 34 and 37 are central in the debate about wisdom psalms. As William Brown observes, the debate itself seems an intractable problem given the burden of proof required by some

---

47. Westermann, *Praise and Lament in the Psalms*, 193.

48. For a helpful summary of this conundrum, see Estes, "Wisdom and Biblical Theology," 853–58.

49. Ibid., 855.

50. For a summary of the debate, see Hasel, *Old Testament Theology*.

51. See p. 210 above.

52. To be fair, Wilson's dissertation served as the groundbreaking event in shaping a new direction for Psalms scholarship that sought to make sense of the whole Psalter from a theological perspective.

53. The prominent role of the Torah, specifically of Deuteronomy, is an area ripe for exploration. For forays into this, see Miller, "Deuteronomy and Psalms"; Bullock, "The Shape of the Torah as Reflected in the Psalms, Book I."

to demonstrate the existence of wisdom psalms.[54] However, it appears that the psalmist is able to incorporate thought that is comfortable in diverse "traditions" within a coherent, if at times troubled, collection. As the fruit of meditation on Torah, with resemblances to wisdom and prophetic literature, might the Psalter act as a crossroads of biblical theology? Estes rightly notes the thoroughly theological character of wisdom, which can be seen in the wisdom-like compositions in the Psalter. Wisdom is far from secular, has shared concerns with many other OT books, and answers basic worldview questions in similar ways.[55] The Psalter appears to be exhibit A for this reality, that OT piety involved diverse expressions of the same fundamental worldview.[56] The extent to which the Psalter is a crossroads of biblical theology remains to be explored.

This is also true with respect to the New Testament. The connection between Psalm 34 and 1 Peter has been explored by a number of scholars,[57] and the connection between the pure in heart in Ps 24:4 and Matt 5:8 has also been noted.[58] What are the implications of reading the ethico-theological dialogue in which these two psalms are situated in the Psalter for understanding these New Testament texts as well as for Christian ethics in general? My own thesis suggests that the literary and theological texts of these psalms require a reassessment of the quotations and allusions to these psalms.

The Portraits of the Righteous and Virtue Ethics

The turn to virtue in ethics presents both an opportunity and a danger. As I note in chapter 1, the revival of virtue ethics brings the character of the moral agent to center stage. This presents an opportunity to complement discussion of moral dilemmas with the substance of everyday life in community that fills the pages of the Hebrew Scriptures. The danger is that virtue ethics may not provide any more clarity for the overall context of ethics than its deontological or consequentialist forebears.

---

54. Brown, "Come, O children," 85.
55. Estes, "Wisdom and Biblical Theology," 856.
56. Bruce Waltke calls it "the same spiritual well" (*Proverbs 1–15*, 67).
57. See Eriksson, *Come, Children, Listen to Me!*; Jobes, "Got Milk?"; Hauge, "Turn Away from Evil and Do Good! Reading 1 Peter in Light of Psalm 34"; Wenham, *Psalms as Torah*, 186–89.
58. Kraus, *Theology of the Psalms*, 196; Mays, *Psalms*, 121; VanGemeren, *Psalms*, 360.

Portraits of the Righteous in the Psalms

Some accounts of virtue ethics set up an opposition between virtue and normative principles, or at least they set up a divide between the two. For example, in the Foreword to *Character Ethics and the Old Testament*, Walter Brueggemann describes the opposition between a moralistic use of law, or "universal criteria," and character ethics.[59] To do away with all moral universals may appeal to a postmodern society that is tired of moral disagreement,[60] but it may further distance readers from the ethical world of the Bible. The perspective of the editors of the same volume is more helpful. They note that character ethics is not as concerned with principles and universal norms but rather with the subtle ways Scripture shapes believers and their communities.[61]

As Alasdair MacIntyre notes, a modern appropriation of Aristotelian ethics requires a notion of *telos*.[62] MacIntyre suggests the *telos* of human beings is to be found in seeking for the good life for man, and virtues help us understand more and more the substance of that good life.[63] As a structural observation about the relationship between character and the good life, MacIntyre's account is compatible with the Old Testament ethical world. The way of the righteous involves certain communal virtues such as honesty and love of neighbor that create the conditions for blessing in communion with YHWH. However, the content of MacIntyre's "narrative order" is self-referential—the pursuit of virtue ends with the pursuit of virtue. In order to solve the problem of moral disagreement, MacIntyre has sidestepped the fundamental question of theology. Disagreement about theology lies at the heart of disagreement about morals. Failing to address theology, MacIntyre fails to adjudicate competing conceptions of a *telos*.[64]

As MacIntyre has influenced Old Testament scholars, this failure has become even more apparent. The most interesting exception to the failure to account for the *telos* of humans and human virtue is an essay by Ellen Davis. She rightly points to the basis of biblical virtues in a view of history from creation to judgment.[65] This brings us closer to a conception of the human *telos* that fits with OT ethics. However, as Brown notes in critique of Stanley Hauerwas' own argument about ethics being situated in a story, history or

---

59. Brueggemann, foreword to *Character Ethics and the Old Testament*, vii.

60. For the seminal works in pursuing a solution to the conundrum of moral disagreement in a post-Christian society, see Anscombe, "Modern Moral Philosophy," 1–19; MacIntyre, *After Virtue*.

61. Carroll R. and Lapsley, *Character Ethics and the Old Testament*, xviii.

62. MacIntyre, *After Virtue*, 202.

63. Ibid., 219.

64. Briggs, *The Virtuous Reader*, 23. See also Carroll R., *Contexts for Amos*, 82.

65. Davis, "Preserving Virtues," 200–201.

Conclusion and Prospects for Further Research

narrative is not the only genre that shapes character.[66] To focus on narrative or story involves the same danger inherent in biblical theology's focus on salvation history.

If virtue ethics is to offer any help to OT ethics, the *telos* of virtue must be articulated more fully. Norman Whybray attempts to do just that, arguing that what the Greeks call *eudaimonia* has a counterpart in Old Testament language: "The term 'the good life' is not precisely a biblical expression. ... In the Hebrew Old Testament each of the words 'good' (*ṭôb*) and 'life' (*ḥayyîm*) can convey separately a meaning not far removed from the double expression in English."[67] The Psalter presents various visions of the good life. And as I have sought to show in this study, this conception of the good life is closely tied to conceptions of righteous character. To be specific, the *telos* of the righteous life is community with the righteous and communion with YHWH. If the Psalter is a crossroads between the various "traditions" of the Old Testament, Old Testament ethics may do well to explore further the connection between theology and ethics. Such study will provide a more faithful reading of the Old Testament and provide a better foundation upon which to construct an ethic of virtue.

---

66. Brown, *Character in Crisis*, 17–18.

67. Whybray, *The Good Life in the Old Testament*, 3. See also Carroll R., "He Has Told You What Is Good," 104.

Bibliography

Alter, Robert. *The Art of Biblical Poetry*. New York: Basic, 1985.
———. *The Book of Psalms: A Translation with Commentary*. New York: Norton, 2007.
Anderson, A. A. *The Book of Psalms*. Vol. 1. NCBC. Greenwood, SC: Attic, 1972.
Anscombe, G. E. M. "Modern Moral Philosophy." *Philosophy* 33 (1958) 1–19.
Athanasius. "A Letter of Athanasius, Our Holy Father, Archbishop of Alexandria, to Marcellinus on the Interpretation of the Psalms." In *The Life of Antony and the Letter to Marcellinus*, translated by Robert C. Gregg. Classics of Western Spirituality. New York: Paulist, 1980.
Auffret, Pierre. "Essai sur la structure littéraire du Psaume 15." *VT* 31 (1981) 385–99.
———. *Hymnes d'Égypte et d'Israël: études de structures littéraires*. Fribourg: Éditions universitaires, 1981.
———. *Que seulement de tes yeux tu Regardes . . . : Etude structurelle de treize psaumes*. BZAW 330. Berlin: de Gruyter, 2003.
———. *La sagesse a bâti sa maison: Études de structures littéraires dans l'Ancien Testament et spécialement dans les Psaumes*. Fribourg, Switzerland: Editions Universitaires, 1982.
———. "YHWH, qui séjournera en ta tente? Étude structurelle du Psaume xv." *VT* 50 (2000) 143–51.
Avishur, Y. "Psalm XV—A Liturgical or Ethical Psalm?" *Dor le Dor* (1977) 124–27.
Baker, David L. *Tight Fists or Open Hands?: Wealth and Poverty in Old Testament Law*. Grand Rapids: Eerdmans, 2009.
Bakhtin, M. M. "Discourse in the Novel." In *The Dialogic Imagination: Four Essays*, translated by Caryl Emerson and Michael Holquist, 259–422. University of Texas Press Slavic Series 1. Austin, TX: University of Texas Press, 1981.
Barbiero, Gianni. "Le premier livret du Psautier (Ps 1–41): Une étude synchronique." *RSR* 77 (2003) 439-80.
Barré, Lloyd M. "Recovering the Literary Structure of Psalm 15." *VT* 34 (1984) 207–11.
Barton, John. *Ethics and the Old Testament*. 2nd ed. London: SCM, 2002.
———. *Reading the Old Testament: Method in Biblical Study*. 2nd ed. Louisville, KY: Westminster John Knox, 1996.
———. *Understanding Old Testament Ethics: Approaches and Explorations*. Louisville, KY: Westminster John Knox, 2003.
Bauer, W., et al. *A Greek-English Lexicon of the New Testament and Other Early Christian Literature*. 3rd ed. Chicago: University of Chicago Press, 2000.

Bibliography

Bauks, Michaela. "'Das Land erben' oder 'die Erde in Besitz nehmen' in Ps 36 (37 MT): ein Übersetzungsvergleich." In *Die Septuaginta—Texte, Kontexte, Lebenswelten: Internationale Fachtagung veranstaltet von Septuaginta Deutsch (LXX.D)*, edited by Martin Karrer and Wolfgang Kraus, 502-22. Wissenschaftliche Untersuchungen zum Neuen Testament 219. Tübingen: Mohr Siebeck, 2008.

Bazak, Jacob. "Structural Geometric Patterns in Biblical Poetry." *Poetics Today* 6 (1985) 475-502.

Beentjes, Pancratius C., editor. *The Book of Ben Sira in Hebrew: A Text Edition of All Extant Hebrew Manuscripts and a Synopsis of All Parallel Hebrew Ben Sira Texts*. VTSup 68. Leiden: Brill, 1997.

Begrich, Joachim. "Die priesterliche Tora." In *Gesammelte Studien zum Alten Testament*, 232-61. TB 21. Munich: Kaiser, 1964.

Bellinger, W. H. "Reading from the Beginning (Again): The Shape of Book I of the Psalter." In *Diachronic and Synchronic: Reading the Psalms in Real Time: Proceedings of the Baylor Symposium on the Book of Psalms*, edited by Joel S. Burnett et al., 114-26. Library of Hebrew Bible/Old Testament Studies 488. London: T. & T. Clark, 2007.

Benun, Ronald. "Evil and the Disruption of Order: A Structural Analysis of the Acrostics in the First Book of Psalms." *JHS* 6 (2006) 1-30.

Berlin, Adele. *The Dynamics of Biblical Parallelism*. 2nd ed. Grand Rapids: Eerdmans, 2008.

Beyerlin, Walter. *Weisheitlich-Kultische Heilsordnung: Studien zum 15. Psalm*. Biblisch-theologische Studien 9. Neukirchen-Vluyn: Neukirchener, 1985.

Birch, Bruce C., and Larry L. Rasmussen. *Bible and Ethics in the Christian Life*. Rev. ed. Minneapolis: Augsburg, 1989.

Blenkinsopp, Joseph. *Isaiah 1-39: A New Translation with Introduction and Commentary*. 1st ed. AB 19. New York: Doubleday, 2000.

Block, Daniel I. "Bearing the Name of the LORD with Honor." In *How I Love Your Torah, O LORD!: Studies in the Book of Deuteronomy*, 61-72. Eugene, OR: Cascade, 2011.

———. *The Book of Ezekiel: Chapters 1-24*. NICOT. Grand Rapids: Eerdmans, 1997.

———. "The Burden of Leadership: The Mosaic Paradigm of Kingship." In *How I Love Your Torah, O LORD!: Studies in the Book of Deuteronomy*, 118-39. Eugene, OR: Cascade, 2011.

———. *Deuteronomy*. NIVAC. Grand Rapids: Zondervan, 2012.

———. *The Gods of the Nations: Studies in Ancient Near Eastern National Theology*. Jackson, MS: Evangelical Theological Society, 1988.

———. *How I Love Your Torah, O LORD!: Studies in the Book of Deuteronomy*. Eugene, OR: Cascade, 2011.

———. "How Many is God? An Investigation into the Meaning of Deuteronomy 6:4-5." In *How I Love Your Torah, O LORD!: Studies in the Book of Deuteronomy*, 73-97. Eugene, OR: Cascade, 2011.

———. "The Joy of Worship: The Mosaic Invitation to the Presence of God (Deut 12:1-14)." In *How I Love Your Torah, O LORD!: Studies in the Book of Deuteronomy*, 98-117. Eugene, OR: Cascade, 2011.

———. "Will the Real Moses Please Rise? An Exploration into the Role and Ministry of Moses in the Book of Deuteronomy." In *The Gospel according to Moses: Literary and Theological Meditations on the Book of Deuteronomy*, 68-103. Eugene, OR: Cascade, 2012.

Bibliography

Bodine, Walter R. "Introduction: Discourse Analysis of Biblical Literature: What It Is and What It Offers." In *Discourse Analysis of Biblical Literature: What It Is and What It Offers*, edited by Walter R. Bodine, 1–18. Atlanta, GA: Scholars, 1995.

Botha, P. J. "Psalm 24: Unity in Diversity." *OTE* 7 (1994) 360–69.

———. "The Relationship between Psalms 25 and 37." *OTE* 20 (2007) 543–66.

———. "The Social Setting and Strategy of Psalm 34." *Old Testament Essays* 10 (1997) 179–97.

Botterweck, G. Johannes, and Helmer Ringgren, editors. *Theological Dictionary of the Old Testament*. Translated by John T. Willis et al. 8 vols. Grand Rapids: Eerdmans, 1974.

Brawley, Robert L., editor. *Character Ethics and the New Testament: Moral Dimensions of Scripture*. 1st ed. Louisville, KY: Westminster John Knox, 2007.

Brennan, Joseph P. "Psalms 1–8: Some Hidden Harmonies." *BTB* 10 (1980) 25–29.

Briggs, Charles A. *A Critical and Exegetical Commentary on the Book of Psalms*. Vol. 1. 2 vols. ICC. Edinburgh: T. & T. Clark, 1906.

Briggs, Richard. *The Virtuous Reader: Old Testament Narrative and Interpretive Virtue*. Grand Rapids: Baker Academic, 2010.

Brown, Francis, et al. *A Hebrew and English Lexicon of the Old Testament with an Appendix Containing the Biblical Aramaic*. Oxford: Clarendon, 1977.

Brown, Michael L. "בָּרַךְ (bārak II)." In *NIDOTTE*, edited by Willem A. VanGemeren 1:757–67. Grand Rapids: Zondervan, 1997.

Brown, William P., editor. *Character and Scripture: Moral Formation, Community, and Biblical Interpretation*. Grand Rapids: Eerdmans, 2002.

———. *Character in Crisis: A Fresh Approach to the Wisdom Literature of the Old Testament*. Grand Rapids: Eerdmans, 1996.

———. "'Come, O children . . . I will teach you the fear of the Lord' (Psalm 34:12): Comparing Psalms and Proverbs." In *Seeking Out the Wisdom of the Ancients: Essays Offered to Honor Michael V. Fox on the Occasion of His Sixty-Fifth Birthday*, edited by Ronald L. Troxel et al., 85–102. Winona Lake, IN: Eisenbrauns, 2005.

———. "The Psalms and 'I': The Dialogical Self and the Disappearing Psalmist." In *Diachronic and Synchronic: Reading the Psalms in Real Time: Proceedings of the Baylor Symposium on the Book of Psalms*, edited by Joel S. Burnett et al., 27–44. Library of Hebrew Bible/Old Testament Studies 488. London: T. & T. Clark, 2007.

———. *Seeing the Psalms: A Theology of Metaphor*. Louisville, KY: Westminster John Knox, 2002.

Broyles, Craig C. *The Conflict of Faith and Experience in the Psalms: A Form-Critical and Theological Study*. JSOTSup 52. Sheffield, UK: JSOT, 1989.

———. *Psalms*. NIBC 11. Peabody, MA: Hendrickson, 1999.

———. "Psalms concerning the Liturgies of Temple Entry." In *The Book of Psalms: Composition and Reception*, edited by Peter W. Flint and Patrick D. Miller Jr., 248–87. Leiden: Brill, 2005.

Brueggemann, Walter. "Bounded by Obedience and Praise: The Psalms as Canon." *JSOT* 50 (1991) 63–92.

———. "The Costly Loss of Lament." *JSOT* 36 (1986) 57–71.

———. Foreword to *Character Ethics and the Old Testament: Moral Dimensions of Scripture*. Edited by M. Daniel Carroll R. and Jacqueline E. Lapsley. Louisville, KY: Westminster John Knox, 2007.

———. *Isaiah 1–39*. 1st ed. Louisville, KY: Westminster/John Knox, 1998.

Bibliography

———. *Israel's Praise: Doxology against Idolatry and Ideology*. Philadelphia: Fortress, 1988.

———. "Psalm 37: Conflict of Interpretation." In *Of Prophets' Visions and the Wisdom of Sages*, edited by Heather A. McKay and David J. A. Clines, 229–56. Sheffield, UK: JSOT, 1993.

———. "Psalms and the Life of Faith: A Suggested Typology of Function." In *The Psalms and the Life of Faith*, edited by Patrick D. Miller Jr., 3–32. Minneapolis: Fortress, 1995.

———. "Psalms as Subversive Practice of Dialogue." In *Diachronic and Synchronic: Reading the Psalms in Real Time: Proceedings of the Baylor Symposium on the Book of Psalms*, edited by Joel S. Burnett et al., 3–25. Library of Hebrew Bible/Old Testament Studies 488. London: T. & T. Clark, 2007.

———. "Response to James L. Mays, 'The Question of the Context.'" In *The Shape and Shaping of the Psalter*, edited by J. Clinton McCann Jr., 29–41. JSOTSup 159. Sheffield, UK: JSOT, 1993.

———. *Theology of the Old Testament: Testimony, Dispute, Advocacy*. Minneapolis, MN: Fortress, 1997.

Brug, John F. "Biblical Acrostics and their Relationship to Other Ancient Near Eastern Acrostics." In *The Bible in the Light of Cuneiform Literature*, edited by William W. Hallo et al., 283–304. Scripture in Context 3. Lewiston, NY: Mellen, 1990.

Bullock, C. Hassell. *Encountering the Book of Psalms: A Literary and Theological Introduction*. Encountering Biblical Studies. Grand Rapids: Baker Academic, 2001.

———. "The Shape of the Torah as Reflected in the Psalms, Book I." Paper presented at the annual meeting of the Evangelical Theological Society, November 2011.

Burnett, Joel S., et al., editors. *Diachronic and Synchronic: Reading the Psalms in Real Time: Proceedings of the Baylor Symposium on the Book of Psalms*. Library of Hebrew Bible/Old Testament Studies 488. London: T. & T. Clark, 2007.

Calvin, John. *Commentary on the Book of Psalms*. Translated by James Anderson. Vol. 1. Grand Rapids: Eerdmans, 1949.

———. *Commentary on the Book of Psalms*. Translated by Henry Beveridge. Vol. 2. Grand Rapids: Baker, 1979.

Campbell, Antony F. "Form Criticism's Future." In *The Changing Face of Form Criticism for the Twenty-First Century*, edited by Marvin A. Sweeney and Ehud Ben Zvi, 15–31. Grand Rapids: Eerdmans, 2003.

Carpenter, Eugene, and Michael A. Grisanti. "רָמָה (rāmâ I)." In *NIDOTTE*, edited by Willem A. VanGemeren 3:1122–24. Grand Rapids: Zondervan, 1997.

Carroll R., M. Daniel. *Contexts for Amos: Prophetic Poetics in Latin American Perspective*. JSOTSup 132. Sheffield, UK: JSOT, 1992.

———. "'He Has Told You What Is Good': Moral Formation in Micah." In *Character Ethics and the Old Testament: Moral Dimensions of Scripture*, edited by M. Daniel Carroll R. and Jacqueline E. Lapsley, 103–18. Louisville, KY: Westminster John Knox, 2007.

———. "Seeking the Virtues among the Prophets: The Book of Amos as a Test Case." *ExAud* 17 (2001) 77–96.

Carroll R., M. Daniel, and Jacqueline E. Lapsley, editors. *Character Ethics and the Old Testament: Moral Dimensions of Scripture*. Louisville, KY: Westminster John Knox, 2007.

Ceresko, Anthony R. "The ABCs of Wisdom in Psalm XXXIV." *VT* 35 (1985) 99–104.

Cheyne, T. K. *The Book of Psalms*. London: Kegan Paul, 1888.
Childs, Brevard S. *Biblical Theology of the Old and New Testaments: Theological Reflection on the Christian Bible*. 1st ed. Minneapolis, MN: Fortress, 1993.
———. *Old Testament Theology in a Canonical Context*. Philadelphia: Fortress, 1986.
———. "Psalm Titles and Midrashic Exegesis." *JSS* 16 (1971) 137–50.
Clements, Ronald E. *Isaiah 1–39: Based on the Revised Standard Version*. NCBC. Grand Rapids: Eerdmans, 1980.
———. "Worship and Ethics: A Re-examination of Psalm 15." In *Worship and the Hebrew Bible: Essays in Honour of John T. Willis*, edited by Matt Patrick Graham et al., 78–94. Sheffield, UK: Sheffield Academic Press, 1999.
Clines, David J. A. "A World Established on Water (Psalm 24): Reader-response, Deconstruction and Bespoke Interpretation." In *The New Literary Criticism and the Hebrew Bible*, edited by J. Cheryl Exum and David J. A. Clines, 79–90. JSOTSup 143. Sheffield, UK: JSOT, 1993.
Collins, Terence. "Decoding the Psalms: A Structural Approach to the Psalter." *JSOT* 37 (1987) 41–60.
Cortese, Enzo. "Salmo 37: una interpretación en diálogo con el tercer mundo." *Estudios bíblicos* 51 (1993) 31–40.
Couroyer, B. "Idéal sapientiel en Egypte et en Israël (à propos du Psaume 34:13)." *RB* 57 (1950) 174–79.
Craigie, Peter C. *Psalms 1–50*. WBC 19. Waco, TX: Word, 1983.
Creach, Jerome F. D. *The Destiny of the Righteous in the Psalms*. St. Louis, MO: Chalice, 2008.
———. *Yahweh as Refuge and the Editing of the Hebrew Psalter*. JSOTSup 217. Sheffield, UK: Sheffield Academic Press, 1996.
———. "חָרָה (*hārâ*)." In *NIDOTTE*, edited by Willem A. VanGemeren 2:265–68. Grand Rapids: Zondervan, 1997.
Crenshaw, James L. "Gold Dust or Nuggets? A Brief Response to J. Kenneth Kuntz." *CurBR* 1 (2003) 155–58.
———. "Wisdom Psalms?" *CurBS* 8 (2000) 9–17.
Crisp, Roger. "Ethics." In *Routledge Encyclopedia of Philosophy*, edited by Edward Craig 3:435–437. London: Routledge, 1998.
Cross, Jr., Frank Moore. "The Divine Warrior in Israel's Early Cult." In *Biblical Motifs: Origins and Transformations*, edited by Alexander Altmann. Cambridge: Harvard University Press, 1966.
Crüsemann, Frank. "The Unchangeable World: The 'Crisis of Wisdom' in Koheleth." In *God of the Lowly: Socio-historical Interpretations of the Bible*, edited by Willy Schottroff and Wolfgang Stegemann, 57–77. Maryknoll, NY: Orbis, 1984.
Dahood, Mitchell J. "Note on Psalm 15:4 (14:4)." *CBQ* 16 (1954) 302.
———. *Psalms I, 1–50: Introduction, Translation, and Notes*. AB 16. Garden City, NJ: Doubleday, 1966.
Davis, Ellen F. "Preserving Virtues: Renewing the Tradition of the Sages." In *Character and Scripture: Moral Formation, Community, and Biblical Interpretation*, edited by William P. Brown, 183–201. Grand Rapids: Eerdmans, 2002.
———. *Scripture, Culture, and Agriculture: An Agrarian Reading of the Bible*. New York: Cambridge University Press, 2009.
Day, John N. "The Imprecatory Psalms and Christian Ethics." *BSac* 159 (2002) 166–86.

Bibliography

DeClaissé-Walford, Nancy L. *Reading from the Beginning: The Shaping of the Hebrew Psalter*. Macon, GA: Mercer University Press, 1997.

Delekat, Lienhard. *Asylie und Schutzorakel am Zionheiligtum: Eine Untersuchung zu den privaten Feindpsalmen mit zwei Exkursen*. Leiden: Brill, 1967.

Dijkstra, M. "A Ugaritic Pendant of the Biblical Expression 'Pure in Heart' (Ps 24:4; 73:1)." *UF* 8 (1976) 440.

Domeris, W. R. "אֶבְיוֹן (*'ebyôn*)." In *NIDOTTE*, edited by Willem A. VanGemeren 1:228–32. Grand Rapids: Zondervan, 1997.

———. "הָמָה (*hāmâ*)." In *NIDOTTE*, edited by Willem A. VanGemeren 1:1041–43. Grand Rapids: Zondervan, 1997.

Dreytza, Manfred. "כַּף (*kap*)." In *NIDOTTE*, edited by Willem A. VanGemeren 2:686–87. Grand Rapids: Zondervan, 1997.

Durant, Karen Elizabeth. "Imitation of God as a Principle for Ethics Today: A Study of Selected Psalms." D.Phil. diss., University of Birmingham, 2010.

Enns, Peter. "מִשְׁפָּט (*mišpāṭ*)." In *NIDOTTE*, edited by Willem A. VanGemeren 2:1142–44. Grand Rapids: Zondervan, 1997.

Eriksson, Lars Olov. *"Come, Children, Listen to Me!": Psalm 34 in the Hebrew Bible and in Early Christian Writings*. ConBOT 32. Stockholm: Almqvist & Wiksell, 1991.

Estes, Daniel J. "The Hermeneutics of Biblical Lyric Poetry." *BSac* 152 (1995) 413–30.

———. "Poetic Artistry in the Expression of Fear in Psalm 49." *BSac* 161 (2004) 55–71.

———. "Wisdom and Biblical Theology." In *Dictionary of the Old Testament: Wisdom, Poetry and Writings*, edited by Tremper Longman and Peter Enns, 853–58. Downers Grove, IL: InterVarsity, 2008.

Fabry, Heinz-Josef. "לֵב *lēḇ*." In *TDOT*, edited by G. Johannes Botterweck et al., translated by David E. Green, 7:399–437. Grand Rapids: Eerdmans, 1974–.

Fitzgerald, Aloysius. "The Interchange of L, N, and R in Biblical Hebrew." *JBL* 97.4 (1978) 481–88.

Foster, Robert L. "Led in Paths of Justice: Shaped by the Shaping of the Psalter." Paper presented at the annual meeting of the Society of Biblical Literature, November 2010.

Fox, Michael V. *Proverbs 1–9: A New Translation with Introduction and Commentary*. 1st ed. AB 18A. New York: Doubleday, 2000.

———. *Qohelet and His Contradictions*. JSOTSup 71. Decatur, GA: Almond, 1989.

Fredericks, D. C. "נֶפֶשׁ (*nepeš*)." In *NIDOTTE*, edited by Willem A. VanGemeren 3:133–34. Grand Rapids: Zondervan, 1997.

Freedman, D. N., et al. "נָשָׂא *nāśā*." In *TDOT*, edited by G. Johannes Botterweck et al., translated by Douglas W. Stott, 10:24–40. Grand Rapids: Eerdmans, 1974–.

Freedman, D. N. "Acrostic Poems in the Hebrew Bible: Alphabetic and Otherwise." *CBQ* 48 (1986) 408–31.

———. "Acrostics and Metrics in Hebrew Poetry." *HTR* 65 (1972) 367–92.

———, editor. *The Anchor Bible Dictionary*. 6 vols. 1st ed. New York: Doubleday, 1992.

———. "Patterns in Psalms 25 and 34." In *Priests, Prophets and Scribes*, 125–38. Sheffield, UK: JSOT, 1992.

Gaebelein, Paul W. "Psalm 34 and Other Biblical Acrostics: Evidence from the Aleppo Codex." *Maarav* 5 (1990) 127–43.

Galling, Kurt. "Der Beichtspiegel: eine gattungsgeschictliche Studie (1929)." In *Zur neueren Psalmenforschung*, edited by Peter H. A. Neumann, 168–75. Darmstadt: Wissenschaftliche Buchgesellschaft, 1976.

García de la Fuente, O. "Liturgias de entrada, normas de asilo o exhoraciones profeticas? A proposito de los Salmos 15 y 24." *Aug* 9 (1969) 266-98.

Gerstenberger, Erhard. *Psalms: Part 1: With an Introduction to Cultic Poetry*. FOTL 14. Grand Rapids: Eerdmans, 1988.

Gillingham, Susan E. "The Messiah in the Psalms: A Question of Reception History and the Psalter." In *King and Messiah in Israel and the Ancient Near East: Proceedings of the Oxford Old Testament Seminar*, edited by John Day, 209-37. Sheffield, UK: Sheffield University Press, 1998.

———. *Psalms through the Centuries*. Malden, MA: Blackwell, 2008.

Girard, Marc. *Les Psaumes: Analyse structurelle et interprétation*. Vol. 1. 3 vols. Paris: Cerf, 1984.

Goldingay, John. *Isaiah*. NIBC 13. Peabody, MA: Hendrickson, 2001.

———. *Psalms: Psalms 1-41*. Vol. 1. BCOT. Grand Rapids: Baker Academic, 2006.

Gordis, Robert. "The Social Background of Wisdom Literature." In *Poets, Prophets, and Sages: Essays in Biblical Interpretation*, 160-97. Bloomington, IN: Indiana University Press, 1971.

Grant, Jamie A. *The King as Exemplar: The Function of Deuteronomy's Kingship Law in the Shaping of the Book of Psalms*. Atlanta, GA: Society of Biblical Literature, 2004.

Groenewald, Alphonso. "Ethics of the Psalms: Psalm 16 within the Context of Psalms 15-24." *JSem* 18 (2009) 421-33.

Gross, Heinrich, and Heinz Reinelt. *Das Buch der Psalmen*. Düsseldorf: Patmos, 1978.

Gunkel, Hermann, and Joachim Begrich. *Introduction to Psalms: The Genres of the Religious Lyric of Israel (1933)*. Translated by James D. Nogalski. Macon, GA: Mercer University Press, 1998.

Gunkel, Hermann. *Die Psalmen*. 4. Aufl. Göttinger Handkommentar zum Alten Testament Bd. 2. Göttingen: Vandenhoeck & Ruprecht, 1926.

———. "Jesaia 33, eine prophetische Liturgie." *ZAW* 42 (1924) 177-208.

———. "Psalm 24: An Interpretation." *The Biblical World* 21 (1903) 366-70.

———. *The Psalms: A Form-Critical Introduction*. Translated by Thomas M. Horner. Facet Books Biblical Series 19. Philadelphia: Fortress, 1967.

Gurney, O. R., and J. J. Finkelstein, editors. *The Sultantepe Tablets*. Occasional Publications of the British Institute of Archaeology at Ankara 3. London: British Institute of Archaeology at Ankara, 1957.

Hallo, William W., and K. Lawson Younger, editors. "The Babylonian Theodicy." In *The Context of Scripture*, translated by Benjamin R. Foster, 1.154. 3 vols. Leiden: Brill, 1997.

Hamilton, Victor. "נָשָׂא (nāśā')." In *NIDOTTE*, edited by Willem A. VanGemeren 3:160-63. Grand Rapids: Zondervan, 1997.

Hamp, Vinzenz. "בָּרַר bārar." In *TDOT*, edited by G. Johannes Botterweck and Helmer Ringgren, translated by John T. Willis 2:308-312. Grand Rapids: Eerdmans, 1974-.

Harman, Allan M. "סָמַךְ (sāmak)." In *NIDOTTE*, edited by Willem A. VanGemeren 3:270-71. Grand Rapids: Zondervan, 1997.

———. "עָבַר ('ābar I)." In *NIDOTTE*, edited by Willem A. VanGemeren 3:314-16. Grand Rapids: Zondervan, 1997.

Hartley, John E. "זָמַם (zāmam)." In *NIDOTTE*, edited by Willem A. VanGemeren 1:1112-14. Grand Rapids: Zondervan, 1997.

Bibliography

Hasel, Gerhard F. *Old Testament Theology: Basic Issues in the Current Debate*. 4th ed. Grand Rapids: Eerdmans, 1991.

Hatton, Peter. "A Cautionary Tale: The Acts-Consequence 'Construct.'" *JSOT* 35 (2011) 375–84.

———. *Contradiction in the Book of Proverbs: The Deep Waters of Counsel*. Society for Old Testament Study Monographs. Burlington, VT: Ashgate, 2008.

Hauerwas, Stanley. *A Community of Character: Toward a Constructive Christian Social Ethic*. Notre Dame, IN: University of Notre Dame Press, 1981.

Hauge, Eirin Hoel. "Turn Away from Evil and Do Good! Reading 1 Peter in Light of Psalm 34." Ph.D. diss., Norwegian School of Theology, 2008.

Held, Hans-Joachim Boecker. "Hoffen auf Gott und Entschlossenheit zum Guten: Unterweisung auf dem Weg zur Gerechtigkeit in Psalm 37 und in der Bergpredigt." In *Gottes Recht als Lebensraum: FS für Hans Jochen*, edited by Peter Mommer et al., 293–302. Neukirchen-Vluyn: Neukirchener, 1993.

Hertog, C. G. den. "'Gaat tot zijn poorten in met lof': De zogenaamde 'Liturgie aan de tempelpoort' in het Oude Testament." In *Hedendaagse zoektocht naar heiligheid: Aspecten Van Heiligheid in De Bijbel En in De Joodse En Christelijke Traditie*, edited by C. J. van den Boogert and G. C. den Hertog, 17–33. Zoetermeer: Boekencentrum, 1999.

Hess, Richard S. "Questions of Reading and Writing in Ancient Israel." *BBR* 19 (2009) 1–9.

Hirsch, David H., and Nehama Aschkenasy. "Translatable Structure, Untranslatable Poem: Psalm 24." *MLS* 12.4 (1982) 21–34.

Hirsch, E. D. *Validity in Interpretation*. New Haven, CT: Yale University Press, 1967.

Holladay, William L. *A Concise Hebrew and Aramaic Lexicon of the Old Testament*. Grand Rapids: Eerdmans, 1971.

———. *The Psalms through Three Thousand Years: Prayerbook of a Cloud of Witnesses*. Minneapolis: Fortress, 1993.

Holmes, Arthur F. *Ethics: Approaching Moral Decisions*. 2nd ed. Contours of Christian Philosophy. Downers Grove, IL: InterVarsity, 2007.

Hossfeld, Frank-Lothar. "Nachlese zu neueren Studien der Einzugsliturgie von Ps 15." In *Alttestamentliche Botschaft als Wegweisung: Festschrift für Heinz Reinelt*, edited by Josef Zmijewski, 135–56. Stuttgart: Katholisches Bibelwerk, 1990.

Hossfeld, Frank-Lothar, and Erich Zenger. *Die Psalmen I: Psalm 1–50*. Neue Echter Bibel. Würzburg: Echter, 1993.

———. "'Selig, wer auf die Armen achtet' (Ps 41,2): Beobachtungen zur Gottesvolk-Theologie des ersten Davidpsalters." *JBTh* 7 (1992) 21–50.

———. "'Wer darf hinaufziehn zum Berg JHWHs?': Zur Redaktionsgeschichte und Theologie der Psalmengruppe 15–24." In *Biblische Theologie und gesellschaftlicher Wandel: für Norbert Lohfink SJ*, edited by Georg Braulik et al., 166–82. Freiburg: Herder, 1993.

Houk, Cornelius B. "Acrostic Psalms and Syllables." In *Psalms and Other Studies on the Old Testament Presented to Joseph I. Hunt*, 54–60. Nashotah, WI: Nashotah House Seminary, 1990.

Houston, Walter. "The King's Preferential Option for the Poor: Rhetoric, Ideology and Ethics in Psalm 72." *BibInt* 7 (1999) 341–67.

Howard, Jr., David M. "Editorial Activity in the Psalter: A State-of-the-Field Survey." In *The Shape and Shaping of the Psalter*, 52–70. JSOTSup 159. Sheffield, UK: JSOT, 1993.

———. "Recent Trends in Psalms Study." In *The Face of Old Testament Studies*, edited by David W. Baker and Bill T. Arnold, 329–68. Grand Rapids: Baker Academic, 1999.

———. *The Structure of Psalms 93–100*. Winona Lake, IN: Eisenbrauns, 1997.

Hunter, Alastair G. "'The Righteous Generation': The Use of DÔR in Psalms 14 and 24." In *Reflection and Refraction: Studies in Biblical Historiography in Honour of A. Graeme Auld*, edited by Robert Rezetko et al., 187–205. VTSup 113. Leiden: Brill, 2006.

Hurowitz, Victor. "Additional Elements of Alphabetical Thinking in Psalm xxxiv." *VT* 52 (2002) 326–33.

Hurvitz, Avi. "Wisdom Vocabulary in the Hebrew Psalter: A Contribution to the Study of 'Wisdom Psalms.'" *VT* 38 (1988) 41–51.

———. "צדיק = 'wise' in Biblical Hebrew and the Wisdom Connections of Ps. 37." In *Goldene Äpfel in silbernen Schalen: Collected Communications to the XIIIth Congress of the International Organization for the Study of the Old Testament, Leuven 1989*, edited by Klaus-Dietrich Schunk and Matthias Augustin, 109–12. Frankfurt: Lang, 1992.

Imes, Carmen. "Psalm 24:4 and the Decalogue: A Mutually Illuminating Relationship?" Paper presented at the annual meeting of the Evangelical Theological Society, November 2011.

James, Joshua T. "'Let The Redeemed of the Lord Say So': Israel's Storied Ethics in Their Thanksgiving Songs." Paper presented at the annual meeting of the Society of Biblical Literature, November 2010.

Janzen, Waldemar. *Old Testament Ethics: A Paradigmatic Approach*. Louisville, KY: Westminster John Knox, 1994.

Jinkins, Michael. "The Virtues of the Righteous in Psalm 37: An Exercise in Translation." In *Psalms and Practice: Worship, Virtue, and Authority*, edited by Stephen B. Reid, 164–201. Collegeville, MN: Liturgical, 2001.

Jobes, Karen H. "Got Milk? Septuagint Psalm 33 and the Interpretation of 1 Peter 2:1–3." *WTJ* 64 (2002) 1–14.

Johnston, Philip S. "Psalm 49: A Personal Eschatology." In *Eschatology in Bible and Theology*, edited by Kent E. Brower and Mark W. Elliott, 73–84. Downers Grove, IL: InterVarsity, 1997.

Kaiser, Otto. *Ideologie und Glaube: eine Gefährdung christlichen Glaubens am alttestamentlichen Beispiel aufgezeigt*. Stuttgart: Radius, 1984.

Kaiser, Walter C. *Toward Old Testament Ethics*. Grand Rapids: Zondervan, 1983.

Klein, Ralph W. *1 Samuel*. WBC 10. Waco, TX: Word, 1983.

Koch, Klaus. "Gibt es ein Vergeltungsdogma im Alten Testament?" *ZTK* 52 (1955) 1–42.

———. *The Growth of the Biblical Tradition: The Form-Critical Method*. Translated by S. M. Cuppitt. New York: Scribner, 1969.

———. "Is There a Doctrine of Retribution in the Old Testament?" In *Theodicy in the Old Testament*, edited by James L. Crenshaw, 57–87. IRT 4. Philadelphia: Fortress, 1983.

Bibliography

———. "Tempeleinlassliturgien und Dekaloge." In *Studien zur Theologie der alttestamentlichen Überlieferungen*, edited by Rolf Rendtorff and Klaus Koch, 45–60. Neukirchen: Neukirchener, 1961.

Koehler, Ludwig, and Walter Baumgartner. *The Hebrew and Aramaic Lexicon of the Old Testament*. Edited by Walter Baumgartner and Johann Jakob Stamm. Translated by M. E. J. Richardson. Electronic ed. Leiden: Brill, 1999.

Konkel, August H. "The Exaltation of the Eternal King." *Didaskalia* 1.2 (1990) 14–22.

Kraus, Hans-Joachim. *Psalms 1–59: A Continental Commentary*. Minneapolis: Fortress, 1993.

———. *Theology of the Psalms*. Translated by Keith R. Crim. Minneapolis, MN: Augsburg, 1986.

Kugel, James L. *The Idea of Biblical Poetry: Parallelism and Its History*. New Haven: Yale University Press, 1981.

Kuntz, J. Kenneth. "The Canonical Wisdom Psalms of Ancient Israel—Their Rhetorical, Thematic, and Formal Dimensions." In *Rhetorical Criticism: Essays in Honor of James Muilenburg*, 186–222. Pittsburgh: Pickwick, 1974.

———. "Reclaiming Biblical Wisdom Psalms: A Response to Crenshaw." *CurBR* 1 (2003) 145–54.

———. "Wisdom Psalms and the Shaping of the Hebrew Psalter." In *For a Later Generation: The Transformation of Tradition in Israel, Early Judaism, and Early Christianity*, edited by Randal A. Argall et al., 144–60. Harrisburg, PA: Trinity, 2000.

Lakoff, George, and Mark Johnson. *Metaphors We Live By*. Chicago: University of Chicago Press, 1980.

Lakoff, George, and Mark Turner. *More Than Cool Reason: A Field Guide to Poetic Metaphor*. Chicago: University of Chicago Press, 1989.

LeFebvre, Michael. "Torah-Meditation and the Psalms: The Invitation of Psalm 1." In *Interpreting the Psalms: Issues and Approaches*, edited by David G. Firth and Philip S. Johnston, 213–25. Downers Grove, IL: InterVarsity, 2005.

Lescow, Theodor. "Textübergreifende Exegese: Zur Lesung von Ps 24–26 auf redaktioneller Sinnebene." *ZAW* 107 (1995) 65–79.

Levenson, Jon D. "The Source of Torah: Psalm 119 and the Modes of Revelation in Second Temple Judaism." In *Ancient Israelite Religion: Essays in Honor of Frank Moore Cross*, edited by Patrick D. Miller Jr. et al., 559–74. Philadelphia: Fortress, 1987.

Levine, Herbert. *Sing unto God a New Song: A Contemporary Reading of the Psalms*. Bloomington, IN: Indiana University Press, 1995.

———. "The Dialogic Discourse of Psalms." In *Hermeneutics, the Bible and Literary Criticism*, edited by Ann Loades and Michael McLain, 145–61. Studies in Literature and Religion. London: Palgrave Macmillan, 1992.

Liebreich, Leon J. "Psalms 34 and 145 in the Light of their Key Words." *HUCA* 27 (1956) 181–92.

Lohfink, Norbert. "Die Besänftigung des Messias: Gedanken zu Psalm 37." In *"Den Armen eine Frohe Botschaft": FS für Bischof Franz Kamphaus*, edited by Josef Hainz et al., 75–87. Frankfurt am Main: Knecht, 1997.

Longman, Tremper, III. "Form Criticism, Recent Developments in Genre Theory, and the Evangelical." *WTJ* 47 (1985) 46–67.

Lunn, Nicholas P. *Word-Order Variation in Biblical Hebrew Poetry: Differentiating Pragmatics and Poetics*. Milton Keynes, UK: Paternoster, 2006.

Luther, Martin. "Preface to the Psalter 1545 (1528)." In *Word and Sacrament I*, edited by E. Theodore Bachmann, translated by Charles M. Jacobs, 253–57. LW 35. Philadelphia: Muhlenberg/ St. Louis: Concordia, 1960.

MacIntyre, Alasdair C. *After Virtue: A Study in Moral Theory*. 2nd ed. Notre Dame, IN: University of Notre Dame Press, 1984.

———. *A Short History of Ethics: A History of Moral Philosophy from the Homeric Age to the Twentieth Century*. 2nd ed. Notre Dame, IN: University of Notre Dame Press, 1998.

Maloney, Les. "Intertextual Links: Part of the Poetic Artistry within the Book I Acrostic Psalms." *ResQ* 49 (2007) 11–21.

———. "A Portrait of the Righteous Person." *ResQ* 45 (2003) 151–64.

———. "A Word Fitly Spoken: Poetic Artistry in the First Four Acrostics of the Hebrew Psalter." Ph.D. diss., Baylor University, 2005.

Manahan, Ronald E. "The Worshiper's Approach to God: An Exposition of Psalm 15." In *Authentic Worship: Hearing Scripture's Voice, Applying Its Truth*, edited by Herbert W. Bateman. Grand Rapids: Kregel, 2002.

Mandolfo, Carleen. "Dialogic Form Criticism: An Intertextual Reading of Lamentations and Psalms of Lament." In *Bakhtin and Genre Theory in Biblical Studies*, edited by Roland Boer, 69–90. Semeia Studies 63. Atlanta, GA: Society of Biblical Literature, 2007.

———. "Finding Their Voices: Sanctioned Subversion in Psalms of Lament." *HBT* 24 (2002) 27–52.

———. "A Generic Renegade: A Dialogic Reading of Job and Lament Psalms." In *Diachronic and Synchronic: Reading the Psalms in Real Time: Proceedings of the Baylor Symposium on the Book of Psalms*, edited by Joel S. Burnett et al., 45–63. Library of Hebrew Bible/Old Testament Studies 488. London: T. & T. Clark, 2007.

———. *God in the Dock: Dialogic Tension in the Psalms of Lament*. JSOTSup 357. Sheffield, UK: Sheffield Academic Press, 2002.

Martin-Achard, R. "ענה *'nh* II." In *Theologisches Handwörterbuch zum Alten Testament*, edited by Ernst Jenni and Claus Westermann 2:342–50. Stuttgart: Kohlhammer, 1973.

Matties, Gordon. *Ezekiel 18 and the Rhetoric of Moral Discourse*. SBLDS 126. Atlanta, GA: Scholars, 1990.

Mays, James L. "The David of the Psalms." *Int* 40 (1986) 143–55.

———. "The Place of the Torah-Psalms in the Psalter." *JBL* 106 (1987) 3–12.

———. *Psalms*. Interpretation. Louisville, KY: Westminster John Knox, 1994.

———. "The Question of Context in Psalm Interpretation." In *The Shape and Shaping of the Psalter*, edited by J. Clinton McCann Jr., 14–20. JSOTSup 159. Sheffield, UK: JSOT, 1993.

McCandless, J. Bardarah. "Enfleshing the Psalms." *Religious Education* 81 (1986) 372–90.

McCann, J. Clinton, Jr. "Books I–III and the Editorial Purpose of the Hebrew Psalter." In *The Shape and Shaping of the Psalter*, 93–107. JSOTSup 159. Sheffield, UK: JSOT, 1993.

Bibliography

———. "The Hope of the Poor: The Psalms in Worship and our Search for Justice." In *Touching the Altar: The Old Testament for Christian Worship*, edited by Carol M. Bechtel, 155-78. Grand Rapids: Eerdmans, 2008.

———. "The Psalms as Instruction." *Int* 46 (1992) 117-28.

———. "The Shape of Book I of the Psalter and the Shape of Human Happiness." In *The Book of Psalms: Composition and Reception*, edited by Peter W. Flint and Patrick D. Miller Jr., 340-48. Leiden: Brill, 2005.

———. "'The Way of the Righteous' in the Psalms: Character Formation and Cultural Crisis." In *Character and Scripture: Moral Formation, Community, and Biblical Interpretation*, edited by William P. Brown, 135-49. Grand Rapids: Eerdmans, 2002.

McCarter, P. Kyle. *I Samuel: A New Translation with Introduction, Notes and Commentary*. 1st ed. AB 8. Garden City, NY: Doubleday, 1980.

McConville, J. Gordon. "'Who May Ascend to the Hill of the LORD?' The Picture of the Faithful in Psalms 15-24." In *Praying by the Book: Reading the Psalms*, edited by Craig G. Bartholomew and Andrew West, 35-58. Carlisle, UK: Paternoster, 2001.

Merrill, E. H. "עָלָה ('ālâ)." In *NIDOTTE*, edited by Willem A. VanGemeren 3:402-404. Grand Rapids: Zondervan, 1997.

———. "רָגַל (rāgal)." In *NIDOTTE*, edited by Willem A. VanGemeren 3:1046-47. Grand Rapids: Zondervan, 1997.

Van der Merwe, Christo H. J., et al. *A Biblical Hebrew Reference Grammar*. Biblical Languages: Hebrew 3. Sheffield, UK: Sheffield Academic Press, 1999.

Mettinger, Tryggve N. D. *In Search of God: The Meaning and Message of the Everlasting Names*. Translated by Frederick H. Cryer. Philadelphia: Fortress, 1988.

Miller, Patrick D., Jr. "The Beginning of the Psalter." In *The Shape and Shaping of the Psalter*, edited by J. Clinton McCann Jr., 83-92. Sheffield, UK: Sheffield Academic Press, 1993.

———. "Deuteronomy and Psalms: Evoking a Biblical Conversation." *JBL* 118 (1999) 3-18.

———. *The Divine Warrior in Early Israel*. Cambridge: Harvard University Press, 1973.

———. "Kingship, Torah Obedience, and Prayer: The Theology of Psalms 15-24." In *Neue Wege der Psalmenforschung*, edited by Klaus Seybold et al., 127-42. Herders biblische Studien 1. Freiburg: Herder, 1994.

———. "The Land in the Psalms." In *The Land of Israel in Bible, History, and Theology: Studies in Honour of Ed Noort*, edited by J. van Ruiten and Jacobus Cornelis de Vos, 183-96. VTSup 124. Leiden: Brill, 2009.

———. "Poetic Ambiguity and Balance in Psalm 15." *VT* 29 (1979) 416-24.

———. *Sin and Judgment in the Prophets: A Stylistic and Theological Analysis*. Chico, CA: Scholars, 1982.

Mowinckel, Sigmund. *The Psalms in Israel's Worship*. Translated by D. R. Ap-Thomas. 2 vols. New York: Abingdon, 1962.

Muilenburg, James. "Form Criticism and Beyond." *JBL* 88 (1969) 1-18.

Munch, P. A. "Das Problem des Reichtums in den Psalmen 37.49.73." *ZAW* 55 (1937) 36-46.

Muraoka, T. *Emphatic Words and Structures in Biblical Hebrew*. Jerusalem: Magnes, 1985.

Murphy, Roland E. "A Consideration of the Classification, 'Wisdom Psalms.'" *Congress Volume Bonn 1962* (1963) 156-67.

———. *Ecclesiastes*. WBC 23A. Dallas, TX: Word, 1992.

———. "Reflections on Contextual Interpretation of the Psalms." In *The Shape and Shaping of the Psalter*, edited by J. Clinton McCann Jr., 21-28. JSOTSup 159. Sheffield, UK: JSOT, 1993.

Nasuti, Harry P. *Defining the Sacred Songs: Genre, Tradition, and the Post-Critical Interpretation of the Psalms*. JSOTSup 218. Sheffield, UK: Sheffield Academic Press, 1999.

Nel, Philip J. "שָׁלֵם (šālēm I)." In *NIDOTTE*, edited by Willem A. VanGemeren 4:130-35. Grand Rapids: Zondervan, 1997.

Neufeld, Edward E. "The Prohibitions against Loans at Interest in Ancient Hebrew Laws." *HUCA* 26 (1955) 355-412.

Neusner, Jacob, editor. *The Babylonian Talmud: A Translation and Commentary*. 22 vols. Peabody, MA: Hendrickson, 2005.

Nussbaum, Martha C. "Virtue Ethics: A Misleading Category?" *Journal of Ethics* 3 (1999) 163-201.

Olivier, J. P. J. "נָקָה (nāqâ)." In *NIDOTTE*, edited by Willem A. VanGemeren 3:152-54. Grand Rapids: Zondervan, 1997.

Olson, Dennis T. "Biblical Theology as Provisional Monologization: A Dialogue with Childs, Brueggemann, and Bakhtin." *Biblical Interpretation: A Journal of Contemporary Approaches* 6 (1998) 162-80.

Osherow, Jacqueline. "Psalm 37 at Auschwitz." In *Dead Men's Praise*, 60-64. New York: Grove, 1999.

Oswalt, John. *Called to be Holy*. Nappanee, IN: Evangel, 1999.

Otto, Eckart. "Kultus und Ethos in Jerusalemer Theologie: ein Beitrag zur theologischen Begründung der Ethik im Alten Testament." *ZAW* 98 (1986) 161-79.

———. "Myth and Hebrew Ethics in the Psalms." In *Psalms and Mythology*, edited by Dirk J. Human, 26-37. Library of Hebrew Bible/Old Testament Studies 462. London: T. & T. Clark, 2007.

———. *Theologische Ethik des Alten Testaments*. Stuttgart: Kohlhammer, 1994.

Pelikan, J., and H. T. Lehmann, editors. *Luther's Works*. 55 vols. St. Louis, MO: Concordia, 1955.

Van Pelt, M. V., and Walter C. Kaiser. "גּוּר (gûr III)." In *NIDOTTE*, edited by Willem A. VanGemeren 1:839-40. Grand Rapids: Zondervan, 1997.

———. "יָרֵא (yārē' I)." In *NIDOTTE*, edited by Willem A. VanGemeren 2:527-33. Grand Rapids: Zondervan, 1997.

———. "מוֹט (môṭ I)." In *NIDOTTE*, edited by Willem A. VanGemeren 2:865-66. Grand Rapids: Zondervan, 1997.

Perdue, Leo G. *Wisdom and Cult: A Critical Analysis of the Views of Cult in the Wisdom Literature of Israel and the Ancient Near East*. Missoula, MT: Scholars, 1977.

Podella, Thomas. "Transformationen Kultischer Darstellungen: Toraliturgien in Ps 15 und 24." *SJOT* 13 (1999) 95-130.

Poorthuis, Marcel. "King Solomon and Psalms 72 and 24 in the Debate between Jews and Christians." In *Jewish and Christian Liturgy and Worship: New Insights into its History and Interaction*, edited by Albert Gerhards, 257-78. Leiden: Brill, 2007.

Pritchard, James B., editor. *Ancient Near Eastern Texts: Relating to the Old Testament*. 3rd ed. with suppl. Princeton, NJ: Princeton University Press, 1969.

Bibliography

Von Rad, Gerhard. "'Gerechtigkeit' und 'Leben' in der Kultsprache der Psalmen." In *FS für Alfred Bertholet*, edited by Walter Baumgartner, 418–37. Tübingen: Mohr, 1950.

———. *Wisdom in Israel*. Nashville: Abingdon, 1972.

Rashi. *Rashi's Commentary on Psalms*. Edited by Mayer I. Gruber. The Brill Reference Library of Judaism 18. Leiden: Brill, 2004.

Reed, Stephen A. "Virtue Ethics and Psalms 111–112." Paper presented at the annual meeting of the Society of Biblical Literature, November 2010.

Reimer, David J. "צָדַק (ṣādaq)." In *NIDOTTE*, edited by Willem A. VanGemeren 3:744–69. Grand Rapids: Zondervan, 1997.

Rendtorff, Rolf. "The Psalms of David: David in the Psalms." In *The Book of Psalms: Composition and Reception*, edited by Peter W. Flint and Patrick D. Miller Jr., 53–64. Leiden: Brill, 2005.

Ricciardi, A. "Los pobres y la tierra segun el Salmo 37." *Revista biblica* 41 (1979) 225–37.

Richards, Kent Harold. "Bless/Blessing." In *ABD*, edited by David Noel Freedman 1:753–55. New York: Doubleday, 1992.

Ridderbos, Nic. H. *Die Psalmen: Stilistische Verfahren und Aufbau mit besonderer Berücksichtigung von Ps 1–41*. BZAW 117. Berlin: de Gruyter, 1972.

Rine, C. Rebecca. "Singing the Psalms to Profit the Soul: Psalmody and Ethical Formation in Athanasius of Alexandria." Paper presented at the annual meeting of the Society of Biblical Literature, November 2010.

Roberts, J. J. M. "The Divine King and the Human Community in Isaiah's Vision of the Future." In *The Quest for the Kingdom of God: Studies in Honor of George E. Mendenhall*, edited by H. B. Huffmon et al., 127–36. Winona Lake, IN: Eisenbrauns, 1983.

———. "The Young Lions of Psalm 34:11." In *The Bible and the Ancient Near East: Collected Essays*, 262–65. Winona Lake, IN: Eisenbrauns, 2002.

———. "Zion in the Theology of the Davidic-Solomonic Empire." In *Studies in the Period of David and Solomon and Other Essays*, edited by Tomoo Ishida, 93–108. Winona Lake, IN: Eisenbrauns, 1982.

Rodd, Cyril S. *Glimpses of a Strange Land: Studies in Old Testament Ethics*. Edinburgh: T. & T. Clark, 2001.

Ryken, Leland. *Words of Delight: A Literary Introduction to the Bible*. 2nd ed. Grand Rapids: Baker, 1992.

Ryken, Leland, et al., editors. "Grass." In *Dictionary of Biblical Imagery*, edited by Leland Ryken et al, 348–49. Downers Grove, IL: InterVarsity, 1998.

Schökel, Luis Alonso. "Contemplar y gustar (Sal 34,6.9)." *Estudios bíblicos* 57 (1999) 11–21.

———. *A Manual of Hebrew Poetics*. Subsidia Biblica 11. Rome: Editrice pontificio Istituto biblico, 1988.

Schultz, Richard L. "Unity or Diversity in Wisdom Theology? A Canonical and Covenantal Perspective." *TynBul* 48 (1997) 271–306.

Scott, R. B. Y. *The Way of Wisdom in the Old Testament*. New York: Macmillan, 1971.

Seebass, H. "נֶפֶשׁ nepeš." In *TDOT*, edited by G. Johannes Botterweck et al., translated by David E. Green 9:497–519. Grand Rapids: Eerdmans, 1974–.

Seremak, Jerzy. *Psalm 24 als Text zwischen den Texten*. Österreichische biblische Studien 26. Frankfurt am Main: Lang, 2004.

Shepherd, Jerry. "שָׁוְא (šāw')." In *NIDOTTE*, edited by Willem A. VanGemeren 4:53–55. Grand Rapids: Zondervan, 1997.
Skehan, Patrick W. "Strophic Patterns in the Book of Job." *CBQ* 23 (1961) 125–42.
———. "Structure of the Song of Moses in Deuteronomy (Deut 32:1–43)." *CBQ* 13 (1951) 153–63.
Slote, Michael. "Moral Philosophy, Problems of." In *The Oxford Companion to Philosophy*, edited by Ted Honderich, 627–31. Oxford: Oxford University Press, 2000.
Slotki, Israel Wolf. "The Text and the Ancient Form of Recital of Psalm 24 and Psalm 124." *JBL* 51 (1932) 214–26.
Smart, James D. "The Eschatological Interpretation of Psalm 24." *JBL* 52 (1933) 175–80.
Soll, William M. *Psalm 119: Matrix, Form, and Setting*. CBQMS 23. Washington, DC: Catholic Biblical Association of America, 1991.
Steingrimsson, Sigurdur Örn. *Tor der Gerechtigkeit: Eine literaturwissenschaftliche Untersuchung der sogenannten Einzugsliturgien im AT: Ps 15, 24:3–5 und Jes 33:14–16*. ATSAT 22. St. Ottilien, Germany: EOS, 1984.
Strawn, Brent A. *What is Stronger than a Lion? Leonine Image and Metaphor in the Hebrew Bible and the Ancient Near East*. OBO 212. Fribourg: Vandenhoeck & Ruprecht, 2005.
Suderman, W. Derek, and Conrad Grebel. "Deaf Communities: Considering the Ethical Cost of Losing Lament." Paper presented at the annual meeting of the Society of Biblical Literature, November 2010.
Sweeney, Marvin A., and Ehud Ben Zvi, editors. *The Changing Face of Form Criticism for the Twenty-First Century*. Grand Rapids: Eerdmans, 2003.
Terrien, Samuel L. *The Psalms: Strophic Structure and Theological Commentary*. ECC. Grand Rapids: Eerdmans, 2003.
Thiselton, Anthony C. *New Horizons in Hermeneutics*. Grand Rapids: Zondervan, 1992.
Tigay, Jeffrey H. *Deuteronomy*. JPS Torah Commentary. Philadelphia: Jewish Publication Society, 1996.
Tov, Emanuel. *Textual Criticism of the Hebrew Bible*. 2nd ed. Minneapolis: Fortress, 2001.
Treves, Marco. "Date of Psalm 24." *VT* 10 (1960) 428–34.
Tromp, Nicholas J. "Jacob in Psalm 24: Apposition, Aphaeresis or Apostrophe." In *Von Kanaan bis Kerala*, edited by W. C. Delsman, 271–82. AOAT 211. Kevelaer, Germany: Butzon & Bercker, 1982.
Tucker, W. Dennis. "Beyond the Lament: Instruction and Theology in Book 1 of the Psalter." *Proceedings, Eastern Great Lakes and Midwest Biblical Societies* 15 (1995) 121–32.
Tull, Patricia K. "Bakhtin's Confessional Self-accounting and Psalms of Lament." *Biblical Interpretation* 13 (2005) 41–55.
Vander Hart, Mark D. "Possessing the Land: As Command and Promise." *MAJT* 4 (1988) 139–55.
VanGemeren, Willem A., editor. *New International Dictionary of Old Testament Theology and Exegesis*. 5 vols. Grand Rapids: Zondervan, 1997.
———. *The Expositor's Bible Commentary: Psalms*. Edited by Tremper Longman and David E. Garland. Vol. 5. Rev. ed. Grand Rapids: Zondervan, 2006.
VanGemeren, Willem A., and Jason Stanghale. "A Critical-Realistic Reading of the Psalm Titles: Authenticity, Inspiration, and Evangelicals." In *Do Historical Matters*

Bibliography

Matter to Faith? A Critical Appraisal of Modern and Postmodern Approaches to Scripture*, edited by James K. Hoffmeier and Dennis R. Magary, 281–301. Wheaton, IL: Crossway, 2012.

Vanhoozer, Kevin J. *Is There a Meaning in This Text? The Bible, the Reader, and the Morality of Literary Knowledge*. Grand Rapids: Zondervan, 1998.

Viands, Jamie C. "The Progeny Blessing in the Old Testament with Special Attention to the Latter Prophets." Ph.D. diss., Wheaton College, 2010.

Waltke, Bruce K. *The Book of Proverbs: Chapters 1–15*. NICOT. Grand Rapids: Eerdmans, 2004.

———. "A Canonical Process Approach to the Psalms." In *Tradition and Testament: Essays in Honor of Charles Lee Feinberg*, edited by John S. Feinberg and Paul D. Feinberg, 3–18. Chicago: Moody Bible Institute, 1981.

———. "Responding to an Unethical Society: Psalm 49." *Stimulus* 1 (1993) 13–18.

Waltke, Bruce K., and Charles Yu. *An Old Testament Theology: An Exegetical, Canonical and Thematic Approach*. Grand Rapids: Zondervan, 2007.

Waltke, Bruce K., and Michael P. O'Connor. *An Introduction to Biblical Hebrew Syntax*. Winona Lake, IN: Eisenbrauns, 1990.

Walton, John H. *Ancient Near Eastern Thought and the Old Testament: Introducing the Conceptual World of the Hebrew Bible*. Grand Rapids: Baker Academic, 2006.

Wardlaw, Jr., Terrance R. "Discourse Analysis." In *Words and the Word: Explorations in Biblical Interpretation and Literary Theory*, edited by David G. Firth and Jamie A. Grant, 266–317. Downers Grove, IL: InterVarsity, 2008.

Warmuth, G. "נָקָה *nāqâ*." In *TDOT*, edited by G. Johannes Botterweck et al., translated by David E. Green 9:553–63. Grand Rapids: Eerdmans, 1974–.

Watson, Rebecca S. *Chaos Uncreated: A Reassessment of the Theme of "Chaos" in the Hebrew Bible*. BZAW 341. Berlin: de Gruyter, 2005.

Watson, Wilfred G. E. *Classical Hebrew Poetry: A Guide to Its Techniques*. JSOTSup 26. Sheffield, UK: JSOT, 1984.

Weinfeld, Moshe. *Deuteronomy and the Deuteronomic School*. Winona Lake, IN: Eisenbrauns, 1992.

———. "Instructions for Temple Visitors in the Bible and in Ancient Egypt." In *Egyptological Studies*, edited by Sarah Israelit-Groll, 224–50. ScrHier. Jerusalem: Magnes, 1982.

Weiser, Artur. *The Psalms: A Commentary*. Translated by Herbert Hartwell. Old Testament Library. London: SCM, 1962.

Wendland, Ernst R. "Genre Criticism and the Psalms." In *Biblical Hebrew and Discourse Linguistics*, edited by Robert D. Bergen, 374–414. Dallas, TX: Summer Institute of Linguistics, 1994.

Wenham, Gordon. "The Ethics of the Psalms." In *Interpreting the Psalms: Issues and Approaches*, edited by David G. Firth and Philip Johnston, 175–94. Downers Grove, IL: InterVarsity, 2005.

———. "Prayer and Practice in the Psalms." In *Psalms and Prayers*, edited by Bob Becking and Eric Peels, 279–94. OtSt 55. Boston: Brill, 2007.

———. *Psalms as Torah: Reading Biblical Song Ethically*. Studies in Theological Interpretation. Grand Rapids: Baker Academic, 2012.

———. "Reflections on *Singing the Ethos of God*." *EJT* 18 (2009) 115–24.

———. *Story as Torah: Reading Old Testament Narrative Ethically*. Grand Rapids: Baker Academic, 2004.

Bibliography

Westermann, Claus. *The Living Psalms*. Edinburgh: T. & T. Clark, 1989.

———. *Praise and Lament in the Psalms*. Translated by Keith R. Crim and Richard M. Soulen. Atlanta, GA: John Knox, 1981.

Whybray, R. N. *The Good Life in the Old Testament*. Edinburgh: T. & T. Clark, 2002.

———. *The Intellectual Tradition in the Old Testament*. Berlin: de Gruyter, 1974.

———. *Reading the Psalms as a Book*. JSOTSup 222. Sheffield, UK: Sheffield Academic Press, 1996.

Williams, Ronald J. *Hebrew Syntax: An Outline*. 2nd ed. Toronto: University of Toronto Press, 1976.

Willis, John T. "Ethics in a Cultic Setting." In *Essays in Old Testament Ethics*, edited by James L. Crenshaw and John T. Willis, 145-69. New York: Ktav, 1974.

Wilson, Gerald H. *The Editing of the Hebrew Psalter*. Chico, CA: Scholars, 1985.

———. "King, Messiah, and the Reign of God: Revisiting the Royal Psalms and the Shape of the Psalter." In *The Book of Psalms: Composition and Reception*, edited by Peter W. Flint and Patrick D. Miller Jr., 391-406. Boston: Brill, 2005.

———. *Psalms*. Vol. 1. NIVAC. Grand Rapids: Zondervan, 2002.

———. "Psalms and the Psalter: Paradigm for Biblical Theology." In *Biblical Theology: Retrospect and Prospect*, edited by Scott J. Hafemann, 100-110. Downers Grove, IL: InterVarsity, 2002.

———. "The Structure of the Psalter." In *Interpreting the Psalms: Issues and Approaches*, edited by David G. Firth and Philip S. Johnston, 229-46. Downers Grove, IL: InterVarsity, 2005.

———. "Understanding the Purposeful Arrangement of Psalms in the Psalter: Pitfalls and Promise." In *The Shape and Shaping of the Psalter*, edited by J. Clinton McCann Jr., 42–51. JSOTSup 159. Sheffield, UK: Sheffield Academic Press, 1993.

Wright, Christopher J. H. *The Mission of God: Unlocking the Bible's Grand Narrative*. Downers Grove, IL: InterVarsity, 2006.

———. *Old Testament Ethics for the People of God*. Downers Grove, IL: InterVarsity, 2004.

———. "אֶרֶץ (*'ereṣ*)." In *NIDOTTE*, edited by Willem A. VanGemeren 1:519-24. Grand Rapids: Zondervan, 1997.

———. "יָרַשׁ (*yāraš I*)." In *NIDOTTE*, edited by Willem A. VanGemeren 2:547-49. Grand Rapids: Zondervan, 1997.

Zenger, Erich. "Geld als Lebensmittel? Über die Wertung des Reichtums im Psalter (Psalmen 15.49.112)." *Gott und Geld* (2007) 73-96.

———. *A God of Vengeance? Understanding the Psalms of Divine Wrath*. Translated by Linda M. Maloney. Louisville, KY: Westminster John Knox, 1996.

Ziegler, Yael. *Promises to Keep: The Oath in Biblical Narrative*. VTSup 120. Leiden: Brill, 2008.

www.ingramcontent.com/pod-product-compliance
Lightning Source LLC
Chambersburg PA
CBHW072023240426
43667CB00044B/2261